THE DEMOCRATIC ORGANISATION

Prevailing models of organisation divide people into owners, managers, and employees, forcing especially the latter to obey, to behave, and to function well within a hierarchical and managerial pecking order. However, there is no natural law suggesting the need for such organisations, not in market economies and definitely not in modern democratic societies – and there is no justification for such types of organisation.

Arguing that most current organisations are orthodox, hierarchical, anti-democratic, oppressive, unfair, and unjust, this book presents a viable alternative, a better type of organisation – the *democratic organisation*. Diefenbach develops and provides step by step a systematic, comprehensive, thorough, and detailed general model of the democratic organisation. He describes the democratic organisation's fundamental principles, values, governance, management, structures, and processes, and the ways it functions and operates both within the organisation and towards others and the environment. Crucially, and most importantly, the democratic organisation provides the institutions and organisational context for individuals to maintain and pursue their fundamental freedoms, inalienable rights, and dignity; to manage organisations in democratic, participative, and cooperative ways; and to conduct business in considerate, balanced, and sustainable ways.

This book will be of interest to researchers, academics, practitioners, and students in the fields of management, organisation studies, strategic management, business ethics, entrepreneurship, and family business.

Dr. Thomas Diefenbach is an independent scholar, writer, researcher, professor, and consultant.

Routledge Studies in Management, Organizations and Society

This series presents innovative work grounded in new realities, addressing issues crucial to an understanding of the contemporary world. This is the world of organised societies, where boundaries between formal and informal, public and private, local and global organizations have been displaced or have vanished, along with other nineteenth century dichotomies and oppositions. Management, apart from becoming a specialized profession for a growing number of people, is an everyday activity for most members of modern societies.

Similarly, at the level of enquiry, culture and technology, and literature and economics, can no longer be conceived as isolated intellectual fields; conventional canons and established mainstreams are contested. **Management, Organizations and Society** addresses these contemporary dynamics of transformation in a manner that transcends disciplinary boundaries, with books that will appeal to researchers, students and practitioners alike.

Recent titles in this series include:

Organizational Theory and Aesthetic Philosophies
Antonio Strati

Visual and Multimodal Research in Organization and Management Studies
Markus A. Höllerer, Theo van Leeuwen, Dennis Jancsary, Renate E. Meyer, Thomas Hestbæk Andersen, and Eero Vaara

Work Orientations
Theoretical Perspectives and Empirical Findings
Edited by Bengt Furåker and Kristina Håkansson

The Institutional Theory of the Firm
Embedded Autonomy
Alexander Styhre

Culture and Change in Family Businesses
Paradoxes in Management
Saulo C. M. Ribeiro

The Democratic Organisation
Democracy and the Future of Work
Thomas Diefenbach

THE DEMOCRATIC ORGANISATION

Democracy and the Future of Work

Thomas Diefenbach

Routledge
Taylor & Francis Group

NEW YORK AND LONDON

First published 2020
by Routledge
52 Vanderbilt Avenue, New York, NY 10017

and by Routledge
2 Park Square, Milton Park, Abingdon, Oxon, OX14 4RN

Routledge is an imprint of the Taylor & Francis Group, an informa business

© 2020 Taylor & Francis

The right of Thomas Diefenbach to be identified as author of this work has been asserted by him in accordance with sections 77 and 78 of the Copyright, Designs and Patents Act 1988.

Library of Congress Cataloging-in-Publication Data
Names: Diefenbach, Thomas, 1965- author.
Title: The democratic organisation : democracy and the future of work / Thomas Diefenbach.
Description: New York, NY : Routledge, 2020. | Series: Routledge studies in management, organizations and society | Includes bibliographical references and index.
Identifiers: LCCN 2019059767 (print) | LCCN 2019059768 (ebook) | ISBN 9780367362195 (hardback) | ISBN 9780367361464 (paperback) | ISBN 9780429344671 (ebook)
Subjects: LCSH: Organizational sociology. | Organizational behavior. | Hierarchies. | Social structure.
Classification: LCC HM786 .D539 2020 (print) | LCC HM786 (ebook) | DDC 302.3/5–dc23
LC record available at https://lccn.loc.gov/2019059767
LC ebook record available at https://lccn.loc.gov/2019059768

ISBN: 978-0-367-36219-5 (hbk)
ISBN: 978-0-367-36146-4 (pbk)
ISBN: 978-0-429-34467-1 (ebk)

Typeset in Bembo
by Integra Software Services Pvt. Ltd.

CONTENTS

List of tables and figures   *viii*

Introduction   **1**
Democratic Organisations Are Novel 3
Democratic Organisations Are Necessary 3
Democratic Organisations Are Possible 5
Overview of the Book 6

1 Prevailing Organisations and Alternatives   **11**
What's Wrong with Our Organisations? 11
Viable Alternatives: Democratic Organisations 17
Interest-Oriented Democratic Organisations 19
Ownership-Oriented Democratic Organisations 24
Social and Solidarity Economy (SSE) Organisations 27
Key Criteria of Democratic Organisations 30

PART I
The Model of the Democratic Organisation   **35**

2 Libertarian Constitution   **37**
Free Will and Free Individuals 37
Self-Ownership and Inalienable Rights 39

Private Ownership and Property Rights 40
The Partnership Agreement and the Democratic Organisation 43

3 Democratic Governance   **50**
Governance: Democratic Governance 50
Democratic Institutions of Governance 52
Legitimate Authoritative Sources 57
Democratic Governing 59
'Good Governance' 64
Democratic Governance of the Democratic Organisation 66

4 Democratic Management   **69**
Hierarchy and/or Heterarchy: Democratic Management 69
Self-Management 72
Representative Management 77
Participative Management 80
The Elements of Democratic Management 85

5 Equalising Empowerment   **88**
From Equal Rights to Equal Power and the Idea of Equalising
   Empowerment 88
Meaning(s) and a Three-Dimensional Concept of Empowerment and
   Disempowerment 90
The Formal, Psychological, and Social Disempowerment of the Many 94
Empowering the Disempowered Many 97
The Formal, Psychological, and Social Empowerment of the Few 103
Disempowering the Empowered Few 108
How Equalising Empowerment Works 122

6 Considerate Conduct of Business   **131**
Conduct of Business: Considerate Conduct of Business 131
People: Social Orientation and Social Behaviour 132
Planet: Pro-environmental Behaviour 139
Profit: Economic and Other Performance 146

7 General Model of the Democratic Organisation   **154**
The General Model of the Democratic Organisation 154
Democratic Organisations Are Better, Do Better, and Perform Better 164

PART II
Attractiveness, Legitimacy, and Vulnerabilities of Democratic Organisations
169

8 The Case for Democratic Organisations
171
(Alleged) Disadvantages and Weaknesses of Democratic Organisations 171
Why People Start or Join Democratic Organisations 182
Strengths and Advantages of the Democratic Organisation 187

9 Legitimate and Illegitimate Organisations
192
Freedom of Contract and the Legitimacy of Organisations 192
The Legitimacy of Various Types of Organisations 194
Different Types of Organisation – and What to Do about Them 203

10 The Iron Threat(s) of Disproportional Empowerment
207
The Phenomenon of Disproportional Empowerment 207
Social Processes and Dynamics Detrimental to the Democratic Organisation 209
A Sequence of Disproportional Empowerment 211
Consequentialist and Non-consequentialist Arguments against Disproportional Empowerment 216
People's Part in the Emergence of Disproportional Empowerment 222
People Who Consciously Strive for Power and Empowerment: 'Anti-social Perpetrators' 223
People Who Cause Disproportional Empowerment Accidentally: 'Unreflective Doers' 228
People Who Let Disproportional Empowerment Happen: 'The Disengaged' 231
Preventing the Threat(s) of Disproportional Empowerment 237

Final Remarks
242

Bibliography   *244*
Index   *269*

TABLES AND FIGURES

Tables

1.1	Types of democratic organisation	18
2.1	The libertarian constitution of the democratic organisation	46
3.1	Rules of transparency and transparent decision-making within democratic organisations	62
3.2	Three levels and elements of 'good governance'	65
4.1	Levels of participation in self-management and representative management	81
5.1	Empowering the disempowered within democratic organisations: from disempowerment to empowerment	123
5.2	Disempowering the empowered within democratic organisations: from empowerment to disempowerment	124
8.1	Strengths and advantages of the democratic organisation	188
9.1	Levels of legitimacy of organisations	203
10.1	A sequence of disproportional empowerment	215

Figure

7.1	General model of the democratic organisation	155

INTRODUCTION

To date, almost all of the organisations we have worked for have been fairly orthodox, hierarchical, anti-democratic, oppressive, unfair, and unjust. They have divided people into owners and workers, managers and employees, forcing especially the latter group in each of these two pairs to obey, to behave, and to function well within a managerial pecking order.

However, there is no natural law that suggests the existence (or need) for such organisations – not in market economies and definitely not in modern democratic societies. People in principle are free to decide what kind of organisation they want to establish or to work for. And, of course, there *are* alternatives to the orthodox organisation – for example, cooperatives, partnerships, associations, worker- or employee-owned firms, collectivist organisations, utopian communities, participative organisations, democratic corporations, social enterprises, civil society organisations, heterarchies, network-like organisations, and commons-based peer production.

All these types of organisation, as different and diverse as they may be, have some features in common that differentiate them fundamentally from the orthodox organisation. These features, when identified properly and put together coherently, establish not only an *alternative* but also a *better* type of organisation. Although there have been some interesting and excellent descriptions of individual alternative organisations, as well as empirical success stories and partial models, so far there has been no comprehensive development of a complete and detailed conceptual model of such an alternative type of organisation and all its key features.

This book attempts to develop such a conceptual model – that is, a systematic, comprehensive, thorough, and detailed *general model of the democratic organisation*.[1] Particularly, it presents and describes the democratic organisation's fundamental principles and values, governance and management, and structures and processes, as well as the way(s) it functions and operates both within the organisation and towards others and the environment. Furthermore, it shows how the people of the democratic organisation – its owners and members – reason, act, and behave within and on the basis of the organisation's institutions.

The democratic organisation is a social system of *free* people and *democratic* institutions – both mutually reinforcing and necessitating each other. Every formal social system that claims to enable and protect the freedom of individuals *must* be based on, and function according to, *democratic* principles and standards that provide *all* members of the social system (1) with the same fundamental rights, responsibilities, and opportunities (2) to govern the social system and themselves either directly or through representatives accountable to everyone, (3) to organise and to manage all work and issues individually or collectively in collaborative and democratic ways, (4) to be equally empowered, and (5) to conduct business in considerate and decent ways. Accordingly, the democratic organisation's main features are as follows:

1. A *libertarian constitution* that appreciates and protects all members' inalienable rights of self-ownership as well as private ownership and corresponding equal rights, responsibilities, and legal entitlements;
2. *Democratic governance* (based on legitimate authority, separation of powers, subsidiarity, transparency, accountability, and 'good governance') that allows all members of the organisation to participate in democratic decision-making and to decide the policies and direction of the organisation ('shared governance');
3. *Democratic management* (self-management, representative management, and participative management) that enables all members of the organisation to manage their work and the conditions of their work themselves, and to manage organisational affairs and the organisation either individually or collectively;
4. *Equalising empowerment*, i.e. all members of the organisation are formally, psychologically, and socially empowered to participate equally in decision-making, to pursue legitimate individual and collective interests, and to further their personal development;
5. *Considerate conduct of business*, i.e. the democratic organisation and its members conduct their activities (including providing goods and services) both within the organisation and towards others and the environment in ways that are moderate, balanced, decent, ethical, fair, and just, and that are consistent with a social orientation, pro-environmental behaviour, and sustainable economic performance.

The democratic organisation is a systematic and comprehensive concept that is (a) novel, (b) necessary, and (c) possible.

Democratic Organisations Are Novel

The idea of an alternative (e.g. cooperative, participative, collective, and demo-cratic) organisation is definitely *not* new. On the contrary, since the early 19th century, *associations*, *cooperatives*, and *(professional) partnerships* have become fairly established forms of organisation in many industries (Tocqueville 1835–1840/2003, Hirst 1994, Fung 2003, Barley & Kunda 2006, Empson & Chapman 2006, Adler et al. 2008, Restakis 2010, Von Nordenflycht 2010, International Co-operative Alliance 2013, Webb & Cheney 2014). In the second half of the 19th century, the notions of *worker-managed companies*, *employee-owned companies*, and even *worker-managed economies* became attractive (Bowles et al. 1993). And the 1970s and 1980s saw the emergence of some of the most radical forms of alternative organisation, such as *participatory democracy*, *participative organisations*, the *self-managed firm*, and the *collectivist organisation* (Pateman 1970, Dahl 1971, Roths-child-Whitt 1976, 1979, Jones & Svejnar 1982, Rothschild-Whitt & Lindenfeld 1982, Hodgson 1984, Rothschild & Whitt 1986), followed by some more moder-ate models of *economic democracy* in the 1990s (Dahl 1985, Bachrach & Botwinick 1992, Ellerman 1992, Arnold 1994, Hirst 1994, Archer 1995). Since the 2000s a whole range of long-established alternative organisations – such as self-help groups, exchange networks, community-based organisations, social and political movements, not-for-profit or non-profit organisations, non-governmental organ-isations, social enterprises, micro-financed businesses, and fairtrade organisations – have been subsumed under the term *Social and Solidarity Economy* (Vakil 1997, Defourny & Delvetere 1999, Fournier 2002, United Nations 2003, Teegen et al. 2004, Willetts 2006, Allard & Matthaei 2008, Solidarity Economic Working Group for USSF 2007 2008, Kerlin & Gagnaire 2009, Nyssens 2009, Kelly 2012, Haque 2013, Lans 2013, Lewis 2014, Wallimann 2014, Ould Ahmed 2015, Utting 2015, Vilchez 2017, North & Cato 2018).

Each of these forms of organisation is successful and compelling in its own right. With its purposes, principles, design, and functioning, the democratic organisation can be seen in the tradition of these alternative and progressive concepts of organisations. But the model of the democratic organisation does not only refer to or utilise ideas from these concepts. The democratic organisation is a *representation* of the most fundamental principles and features of these alternative types of organ-isation. It resembles and represents the key features of these alternative organisations in a single systematically and deductively developed, comprehensive, consistent, thorough, and detailed *general model*. Such a general model has never been attempted before. In this sense, the democratic organisation is a *novelty*.

Democratic Organisations Are Necessary

The arguments for the democratic organisation also show that it is *necessary* – not just as an exotic option for alternative idealists in niche markets but as *the* standard model for private and public organisations in any industry, market, or social economy. In order to explain why we should – even *need* to – replace the archaic, hierarchical, and oppressive types of orthodox organisation, I first want to give a personal account of my own experiences in organisations.

For the best (or worst) part of the past 36 years, I have been working full time or part time for orthodox organisations in the private and public sectors. Altogether, I have worked for around 27 different organisations in various countries on four continents – always as a little cog in a big machine, like most of us. Throughout these years, I very rarely have come across decent organisational structures, processes, management, work environments, or organisational cultures. The strategies, mission and vision statements, management policies, and processes of the organisations I have worked for have largely been ludicrous. Many were plastered with inept and mediocre managers and wannabe leaders with distorted personalities. Dysfunctional supervisors mostly micro-managed and belittled their subordinates (and were quite effective in doing so), and a sometimes toxic organisational culture filled the corridors, hearts, and minds of all of us little people, keeping us in check but also turning us into psychopaths on a treadmill trying to survive each day (mostly by self-censoring and behaving obediently). My work, the way it was organised, and fulfilling what I was told to do altogether required only a small proportion of my actual competencies, professional knowledge, and expertise. I was only allowed to decide around 10% of what I did and how I did it; the other 90% was decided by said inept, micro-managing managers or supervisors – or, worse, administrators, who usually had little if any knowledge of the actual work I did.

I don't think that my personal experience or reactions are unique; on the contrary, during all those years I saw countless colleagues suffering under the work regimes of orthodox organisations (just as I saw many spineless careerists and opportunists, incompetent managers, professionals, and administrators thriving and surviving under those conditions). And in both my theoretical and my empirical research, I came across many empirical case studies and examples that painted the same picture of orthodox organisations as severely distorted, hierarchical and oppressive, managerial, and miserable social systems. In such places, the insufficiencies, organisational misbehaviour, maltreatment, and injustices are not just individual incidents but *inherent, systemic* features of a *fundamentally* flawed and *highly* dysfunctional system. It is not just that there are a few bad apples among managers and orthodox organisations – the very institutions are rotten to the core.

It might well be that orthodox, hierarchical, and oppressive organisations are the prevailing type of organisation and constitute the un-normal normality of organised work. But people deserve better. If we are serious about the idea that individuals ought to be free and be treated decently, and ought to live and work under conditions and within institutions that appreciate their fundamental and inalienable rights, and if we are serious about the universal principles and values of freedom, democracy, equality, and justice, and the idea that each and every social system (e.g. organisations and nation-states) must adhere to those principles, then we *must* replace the prevailing orthodox, hierarchical, anti-democratic, oppressive, unfair, and unjust standard type of organisation with the democratic organisation.

Organisations and other social systems *can*, and *must*, be designed and maintained as fully fledged *democratic* systems that enable and protect the equal, fundamental human, civil, and democratic rights of all their members. The democratic organisation is the *only* type of organisation that provides and guarantees freedom, democracy, equality, and justice for *all* its members. It is the *only* type of organisation that has the institutions and organisational context to enable individuals to maintain and pursue their fundamental freedoms and inalienable rights. And it is the *only* type of organisation that at the same time is consistent with the fundamental principles and values of a fully fledged democratic and modern society, acknowledges the requirements of the natural environment, and is capable of achieving multi-dimensional socio-economic outcomes in a balanced and sustainable manner. We need such organisations.

Democratic Organisations Are Possible

It is relatively easy to criticise things. The real challenge is to come up with something better, to develop a positive alternative that is *possible* and *feasible*, i.e. a *realistic* alternative that is not only better per se but also convinces real people that it makes sense and can be done.

Back in 2009, I concluded in my book *Management and the Dominance of Managers* with the following assertion:

> The idea that change is possible and necessary is completed by the demonstration of *positive alternatives*. We need to provide existing positive examples or develop new concepts of true alternatives to managerial organisation and the dominance of managers. Probably the most important, and definitely the most difficult, part of any critical enterprise, is to provide an *elaborated and realistic* positive alternative to the status quo. (Diefenbach 2009a, p. 236)

I repeated (or reminded myself of) these ideas in the conclusion to my book *Hierarchy and Organisation* when I argued that:

> We need to further develop our understanding of *all* necessary preconditions for truly hierarchy-free types of organisation and societies – i.e. the right values that guide individual attitudes, behaviour, and social actions *and* the right and necessary institutions to put into place; which types of institution can guarantee the achievement and maintenance of truly democratic and non-hierarchical social systems and the containment of power and control without becoming themselves a bedrock of uncontrolled and oppressive power and control? This is the core question of any attempt

to free the individual as well as to create free organisations and free societies. (Diefenbach 2013a, p. 237)

Hierarchy and Organisation was 'merely' a critical book (like *Management and the Dominance of Managers* before), but already at that time I had the feeling that I needed to answer the 'So what?' question: if orthodox, hierarchical, and managerial organisations are – allegedly – so inefficient, unsustainable, oppressive, unfair, and unjust, what is the alternative? Is there a *viable* alternative at all? Therefore, since 2012 I have been searching for, and working quite intensively on, such a viable alternative type of organisation (and also an alternative type of economy and society – but this will be the subject of my next book). The current book – or, more accurately, the *general model of the democratic organisation* that is developed in this book – is the answer to the 'So what?' question. The democratic organisation is the viable alternative to orthodox organisations.

Crucially, then, the democratic organisation is *possible*. For every principle and feature that I put forward in this book as key elements of the democratic organisation, I provide various empirical examples showing that it can work, and *how* it can work. Every proposition is based on sound theoretical arguments. There is a wealth of references and empirical evidence showing that such organisations are, indeed, possible – anytime and anywhere in the world. The democratic organisation is not just wishful thinking but a realistic concept. It is possible to establish, to maintain, and to protect democratic organisations – theoretically as well as practically. We *must* do it – not only because we *can*, but because it is worthwhile and the right thing to do. People deserve it. In this sense, the democratic organisation is not only a *model* but also an *agenda* or guide for those who attempt to implement it.

Overview of the Book

The book is organised into 10 chapters. Chapter 1 stands alone and provides a scholarly introduction to the problem by briefly assessing the whole range of prevailing and alternative types of organisation. Part I then comprises Chapters 2–7 and develops the general model of the democratic organisation step by step. Each of Chapters 2–6 focuses on one of the key features of the democratic organisation (i.e. libertarian constitution, democratic governance, democratic management, equalising empowerment, and considerate conduct of business). Chapter 7 then presents the whole *general model of the democratic organisation*. It is possible to read Chapter 7 first, especially if the reader would like to get an immediate idea of what the democratic organisation is all about. Part II, comprising Chapters 8–10, then provides some discussion of key aspects and specific fundamental problems of the democratic organisation and its foundations. In more detail, Chapters 1–10 address the following areas.

Chapter 1 takes stock of the range of existing organisations. It investigates what is wrong with our organisations (in particular the most common types of organisations) and examines how they are ill-designed in their principles, purposes, structures, and processes and how they are dysfunctional for people. On the basis of this analysis, the chapter makes the case for alternative organisations. It looks at various viable alternatives – interest-oriented democratic organisations (such as associations, cooperatives, or partnerships), ownership-oriented democratic organisations, and the whole range of Social and Solidarity Economy organisations. The chapter identifies what all these existing alternative organisations have in common and outlines the key criteria of democratic organisations.

Part I (Chapters 2–7) then develops the general model of the *democratic organisation*, which is *fundamentally* different from all orthodox, hierarchical, managerial, and oppressive organisations as we know them. Chapters 2–6 describe the main elements of the model, i.e. the *libertarian constitution* of the democratic organisation, its *democratic governance* and *democratic management*, the principles of *equalising empowerment*, and the democratic organisation's *considerate conduct of business*.

Chapter 2 briefly states and explains the key principles and values – *libertarian* values – the democratic organisation is based on: individual freedom, self-ownership and individuals' inalienable rights, individual and collective private ownership (of everyone), and a partnership agreement that appreciates and guarantees all these rights for everyone who owns, works for, or is a member of the democratic organisation.

Chapter 3 then outlines the democratic organisation's *governance*, i.e. the formal institutions that define how it is governed and how it functions. The chapter makes the case for *democratic* governance – an organisational democracy comprising some of the key institutions necessary for a fully fledged democracy. It explains how the organisational institutions of democratic governance and management (boards, councils, committees, and assemblies) are designed and function according to democratic standards, i.e. according to the very same principles they are created to realise and protect ('good governance'). In particular, it describes in some detail how democratic organisations are governed on the basis of the fundamental principles of separation of powers (checks and balances), subsidiarity, democratic decision-making, transparency, and accountability. Members of the democratic organisation govern the organisation and organisational affairs democratically and collectively, i.e. decisions are made by all members of the organisation or its relevant parts (*direct* or *participative democracy*), or by elected representatives and office-holders (*representative democracy*).

Chapter 4 is about *democratic management*, or how an organisation can be managed democratically. This chapter develops a concept of democratic management that consists of three intertwined parts: *self-management, representative management*, and *participative management*. This is management of the people, by the people, for the people. Chapter 4 argues that in the democratic organisation the main focus is on self-management; *all* members of the organisation, both as individuals and as groups of people, are entitled, encouraged, and enabled to organise and manage their own work, work-related issues, and administrative affairs as much and as far as possible. Managerial functions that are not covered by self-management are delegated to representatives who are elected democratically, and controlled and held accountable by those whom they represent (representative management). Finally, participative management makes sure that all members of the democratic organisation have equal rights and opportunities to participate in formal decision-making processes at all levels of the organisation.

Whereas the first three chapters of Part I are primarily about the *institutions* of the democratic organisation, Chapter 5 focuses particularly on *people* – especially people's social relationships, and particularly the social processes and dynamics that arise in an organisation with regard to its governance and management. In this area the concept of *empowerment* is relevant, as it can help in the analysis of the people side of an organisation. According to this concept, empowerment can be differentiated into three types: (a) *formal empowerment* (formal roles and positions with elevated status, and responsibilities and prerogatives within the official structures and processes of an institutionalised social system), (b) *psychological empowerment* (a state of mind or feeling of being powerful or being empowered to be in control, or the feeling of having self-efficacy or an internal locus of control), and (c) *social empowerment* (reasonably established positions and status, a sense of self-worth, positive images of self and others, and the resources and opportunities to pursue one's interests within an interactive social context). Following this categorisation, Chapter 5 elaborates on the fundamental idea that all members of the democratic organisation should be formally, psychologically, and socially *equally empowered* to govern and manage the organisation and to participate in decision-making (*equalising empowerment*). The chapter provides various measures that can be taken to equalise empowerment, i.e. it outlines ways to empower disempowered people and to disempower (overtly) empowered people formally, psychologically, and socially until both have (approximately) equal power.

Chapter 6 analyses how the democratic organisation conducts business. It develops the notion of *considerate conduct of business* as a guiding principle for how organisations should do business and act. The principle is operationalised via the widely known 'triple bottom line' concept, in which individual and institutional actors' behaviour is assessed and judged along three dimensions – social, environmental, and economic ('people, planet, profit'). Chapter 6 demonstrates that democratic organisations have a strong (pro) *social orientation* and accordingly demonstrate social, or even prosocial, behaviour (i.e. compared to orthodox organisations they show more mutually beneficial cooperation and reciprocal behaviour, a stronger community orientation, and more decent, honest, fair, just, responsible, and ethical behaviour). They also have a *pro-environmental orientation* and behaviour (i.e. they appreciate, and are more concerned about, the (local) environment; they have explicitly pro-environment goals and purposes in their business model; and they use and offer more environmentally friendly technologies, products, and services). Finally, this chapter shows that democratic organisations' economic orientation and performance are also more compelling; democratic organisations usually operate in sustainable ways, achieve higher and better organisational performance, and are profitable and economically successful.

At the end of Part I, Chapter 7 outlines the general model of the democratic organisation and assesses it in its entirety. The democratic organisation's main features – a libertarian constitution, democratic governance, democratic management, equalising empowerment, and considerate conduct of business – are highlighted and analysed. The chapter concludes by demonstrating why and how democratic organisations are better, do better, and perform better.

Whereas Part I develops the model of the democratic organisation, Part II provides some discussion. Every model or theory raises questions about (some of) the explicit or implicit assumptions on which it is built, as well as its design, functioning, or implications. This is equally the case for the democratic organisation – especially since this model is fairly different from the usual types of organisation we work for and challenges this orthodoxy and our understanding of what an organisation is or how it should be. Part II focuses on some of the major challenges for the democratic organisation, in particular with regard to its legitimacy, vulnerabilities, and attractiveness.

Part II starts with Chapter 8, which makes the case for the democratic organisation. It looks carefully at claims relating to (alleged) disadvantages and weaknesses of the democratic organisation and potential reasons why there are not more democratic organisations, in particular the (un)attractiveness of organisations (for certain people), organisations' (mis)fit with an institutional context, (in)sufficient financial resources, lack of qualified personnel and competencies, (in)efficient internal processes (of decision-making), and (in)sufficient external performance and outcomes. Chapter 8 also interrogates various reasons why people start or join democratic organisations, covering the purposes and conduct of business, organisational and interpersonal aspects, and psychological, intrapersonal, and attitudinal aspects. Finally, Chapter 8 comprehensively summarises the strengths and advantages of the democratic organisation.

Concerning the constitution and foundation of the democratic organisation (see Chapter 2), one of the main assumptions the model is built on is the fundamental claim that the formal, legal, and social relationships between the people who constitute and run the organisation (its owners and members) must be based on an agreement (*partnership agreement*) that establishes and guarantees their equal rights. This means that the *employment contract* – which provides owners/employers and employees with *different* bundles of rights and responsibilities – is neither suitable nor appropriate for the democratic organisation. In fact, it is neither suitable nor appropriate as the legal basis and framework for *any* kind of organised work or social relationship. Chapter 9 therefore discusses and demonstrates the questionable nature and illegitimacy of the standard employment contract, its formal design, and its substance. The chapter argues not only that the employment contract is impossible from a logical point of view (because of the inalienability of people's minds and free will) but also that the employment contract goes against people's fundamental freedoms: that it is anti-democratic, enables systematic inequality and exploitation, and is unjust *in principle*. The only possible conclusion is that, because of its fundamental flaws, the employment contract should be rendered not only illegitimate but also illegal.

With its libertarian constitution, and its principles, structures, and processes of democratic governance and democratic management, the democratic organisation represents (or claims) a kind of ideal standard – how organisations should be. Hence, Chapter 9 interrogates what kinds of (existing) organisation meet, or do *not* meet, the democratic standards put forward with the model of the democratic organisation. Various types of organisation are analysed (radical, profit-maximising, orthodox, alternative, and democratic types of organisation) with regard to whether or not they meet democratic standards – and what can be done with them if they don't.

Finally, Chapter 10 focuses on the vulnerabilities of the democratic organisation, especially on challenges that come from within and might threaten its very existence. The chapter comprehensively and systematically analyses possible causes of *disproportional empowerment* (i.e. the empowerment of the few and disempowerment of the many). To do this, it develops the concept of disproportional empowerment, which shows how the actions or inactions of concrete people are behind and trigger such abstract processes. It shows how disproportional empowerment emerges as a pattern or sequence and why it must be thwarted (some consequentialist and non-consequentialist arguments against disproportional empowerment are provided). People's part in the emergence of disproportional empowerment is analysed with regard to three types of people and their behaviours that cause it: they may strive consciously for power and empowerment (*anti-social perpetrators*), cause disproportional empowerment accidentally (*unreflective doers*), or let it simply happen (*the disengaged*). The chapter provides a range of measures that can prevent disproportional empowerment from becoming a serious threat to the democratic organisation.

Note

1 I introduced the term 'democratic organisation' in 2009 in my book *Management and the Dominance of Managers* (Diefenbach 2009a) as follows: 'Throughout the whole period of capitalism, there have been alternatives and there are many examples of successful alternative businesses out there. For example, types of organisations such as the "*democratic organisation*" (e.g. partnerships, co-operatives, employee-owned companies) take the idea of empowerment and workplace democracy very seriously. They comprise ideas like worker participation in strategic and operational decision-making, autonomous work groups, profit-sharing, co-partnership, and shared ownership ... Democratic organisations provide convincing solutions to the problems of managerial dominance, excesses in hierarchical decision-making processes, and the prevalence of managerial ideology and rhetoric. They also resist the exploitation, conditioning, and de-motivation of employees. Democratic organisations are *a real as well as realistic alternative to managerial organisations*' (p. 237, italics in original).

1

PREVAILING ORGANISATIONS AND ALTERNATIVES

What's Wrong with Our Organisations?

An *organisation* can be understood as a formal or informal entity that structures the relationships and activities of members or elements of a system. Obviously, organisations can come in very different types and forms. However, around the world, one particular type of organisation has become the legal and ideological standard model and prevailing type of organisation, having been propagated extensively by conservative rulers, politicians and businesspeople, economists, and management and organisation theorists, such as Taylor (1911/1967), Coase (1937), Fayol (1949), Drucker (1954), Chandler (1962), and Friedman (1962/ 1982). It is the 'hierarchical organisation', 'bureaucratic organisation', 'managerial organisation', 'corporation' (or 'company'), or 'firm' – i.e. a legally or formally established entity that provides people with fundamentally different, mostly opposing, legal, formal, organisational, and managerial rights and responsibilities that correspond with various types of formal position (such as owners, managers, and employees or staff). I call this the *orthodox organisation*. Because of its ideological, rhetorical, and historical prevalence, people understand organisations mostly as orthodox organisations and (can) hardly imagine other types or conceive that other types are possible or even *necessary*. The orthodox organisation is the un-normal normality of organised social and economic activities. Yet, it is one of the worst social systems created by humans and has done much more harm than good throughout the centuries of its existence and operation. With its distinct features, it represents *everything that is wrong with our organisations*.

The System of the Orthodox Organisation[1]

First, the orthodox organisation is *hierarchical* (Jaques 1990). In other words, positions – and people! – are put into a vertical order of superiority and inferiority, and domination and subordination. People have different rights and responsibilities, different levels of influence and power, and different privileges and prerogatives within the organisation according to their legally defined and protected statuses and positions as owner, manager or employee, superior or subordinate, leader or follower, and master or servant. The hierarchy is comprehensive, systematic, and thorough. It underpins all policies, structures, processes, performance measurement, and control systems of the organisation. Hierarchical order is based on and functions according to the principle of command and control, where one person tells another person what to do, when to do it, how to do it, and even why to do it, and also controls, 'motivates', and punishes that person (altogether, this is called 'management', 'supervision', or 'leadership'). The hierarchical organisation deprives the vast majority of its members of freedom (or freedoms) as well as fundamental human and civil rights; it neither protects them from the arbitrary power of superiors (negative freedom) nor provides them with the rights to and opportunities for sovereignty, self-determination, and personal development (positive freedom) (Malleson 2014, p. 33). Instead, hierarchy puts people into a dynamic, thoroughly structured, managed, and controlled social order of superiority and inferiority, and dominance and obedience. It stands for giving and receiving orders (nowadays called 'instructions', 'advice', 'guidance', 'help', 'support', or even 'having a conversation'), controlling and being controlled, telling and being told, guiding and being guided, and leading and being led. Hierarchy reduces free and intelligent people to cognitive and emotional toddlers.

Evidently, hierarchy means the systematic introduction, establishment, maintenance, and ideological justification of *inequality* between individuals or groups of people (Laumann et al. 1971, Mousnier 1973, Abercrombie et al. 1980, p. 130, Pollitt 1990, p. 6, Sidanius & Pratto 1999, Levy et al. 2001, p. 10, Sidanius et al. 2004, Diefenbach 2009a, p. 126). It is the fundamental idea and key characteristic of hierarchy that privileges and prerogatives are allocated *unequally* among the members of a social system, and moreover this inequality is *systematic*: the higher, the more; the lower, the less. Hierarchical order is an elaborate social stratification system of artificially created and enhanced differences between people who should have equal rights and equal opportunities.[2] The orthodox organisation is *deliberately* designed to provide only *some* people with rights and resources, material goods and power, and advantages and opportunities to pursue *their* interests and to achieve *their* goals (owners and senior managers of the orthodox organisation) – while systematically excluding others from those chances (lower managers, employees, and/or lower-level members of the orthodox organisation). In this sense, the orthodox organisation is mainly a tool for gaining and securing privileges and advantages for *certain* individuals and groups of people while thoroughly excluding others – *many* others. (Via exclusive ownership rights and employment contracts) it creates a comprehensive micro-cosmos of unequal social positions and relations that systematically privileges the interests and viewpoints of some individuals and groups while silencing and marginalising others (Levy et al. 2001, p. 2). In this sense, the orthodox organisation resembles and replicates nothing more than an unequal, stratified, and hierarchically differentiated society – the ideology of social differentiation between 'the rulers' and 'the people', or between the 'haves' and 'have nots'. It is *institutionalised discrimination* (Sidanius et al. 2004, p. 847) – a despicable class society in miniature.

The systematic privileging of the few comes, and can only happen, at the expense of the many others. The latter are systematically disadvantaged in almost every respect organisational life has to offer (legal rights and entitlements; responsibilities; participation in decision-making and management; income, such as salaries and profit; status and recognition; and efficacy and self-esteem). They are systematically *exploited*. 'Exploitation' can be defined as 'a relationship in which unearned income results from certain kinds of unequal exchange' (Gouldner 1960, p. 165) – and the orthodox organisation is a social system of institutionalised unequal and exploitative exchange par excellence. For instance, (most) employees or members of orthodox organisations are remunerated well below what their value-adding contribution justifies, i.e. they do not get a fair share of the value-added and profit their work has created and are, hence, not compensated appropriately (e.g. Miller 1990, p. 175, Van Parijs 1995, p. 147, Carson 2008, p. 381). The orthodox organisation is the formal, legal, and organisational vehicle for the egoistic pursuit of individual and group interests at the expense of others by utilising and exploiting them. For individual superiors and for small dominating minorities and power elites, the orthodox organisation is the best and most suitable form of social system for extracting labour, goods, and services from a majority (Burnham 1941, p. 123, Scott 1990, p. 21, Beetham 1991, p. 58, Stoddart 2007, p. 196). It is *specifically* designed and maintained for social dominance and exploitation.

Finally, the orthodox organisation is thoroughly *un*-democratic, even *anti*-democratic (Miller 1990, p. 7, Dahl 1998, p. 182). All decisions within the organisation are made not democratically by its members, but single-handedly by individual owners, senior managers, or other superiors, or by an unelected and non-representative panel (e.g. board, project, or work group). Only *they* have the prerogative and exclusive right to make decisions. And, crucially, they are neither controlled nor held accountable by those for whom they make their decisions (Malleson 2014, p. 27).[3] Decisions made by owners or managers cannot be debated or challenged but are simply passed down along hierarchical lines as orders or instructions. *All* governance, management, and decision-making processes follow this principle. There is no bottom-up, only top-down control – *comprehensive, systematic, multi-dimensional, and thorough top-down control* of all subordinates that amounts to surveillance and oppression. Subordinates have no right of free speech or freedom of assembly (Carnoy & Shearer 1980, p. 246). Subordinates' only right, even obligation, is to follow and execute the orders made by their superiors, to comply, and to behave. 'Most employees are subject to managers they did not elect and to rules in which they had little or no say. They are subordinates, a role manifestly at odds with the ideal of the democratic citizen' (Mayer 2001, p. 221). There is no (right to) self-governance or collective governance; no representative or participative management; no subsidiarity, autonomy, or (full) participation (Fournier 2002, p. 204, Wright 2010, p. 50). As the old adage goes, democracy stops at the factory gate (or, nowadays, the firewall of the company's servers). The orthodox organisation is *alien to the ideas of democracy and democratic society*; it is autocratic or oligarchic *in principle* and anti-democratic both *de jure* and *de facto*. The orthodox organisation is fundamentally flawed; most of its members are not as free as they could or even should be, its governance and management are anti-democratic, and people are put into unequal, hierarchical, and oppressive relationships, structures, and processes and are treated unfairly and unjustly. It is a social system of no democracy in principle (Dahl 1985, p. 55, Sauser 2009, p. 157, Schweickart 2011, p. 152, Doran 2013, pp. 85–86). It is simply not good and unacceptable.

The People of the Orthodox Organisation[4]

Clearly, a social system that is systematically and in principle hierarchical, antilibertarian, unequal, exploitative, and anti-democratic – like the orthodox organisation – is not good for people. Or, to be more precise, it is *very* good in *some* respects for *some* people (owners, senior managers, and supervisors, who can pursue their individual and group interests; enjoy privileged and exclusive rights, responsibilities, and preferential treatments; and dominate and enrich themselves by using and exploiting others) and it is bad for *many* (lower managers, employees, and other subordinates, who are stripped of their basic civil rights and freedoms; managed, controlled, and punished like servants; and used and exploited like things). The orthodox organisation *harms* people – *considerably*.

Despite managers' and leaders' public image (which can even amount to an ideology and mystification) as skilful and competent practitioners (e.g. Thompson 1961, Burns 1978, Bass et al. 1987, Masi & Cooke 2000, Aronson 2001, Gill 2003, Siebens 2005, Ilies et al. 2006, Van Vugt 2006, Kark & Van Dijk 2007), the reality is quite different; 'flawed leaders are everywhere' (Kellerman 2005, p. 3). Especially in orthodox organisations, one can easily find superiors and managers with distorted personalities, 'damaged' organisational actors, and organisational psychopaths.

Organisational psychopaths are opportunists and careerists who have learned to adapt to the paradoxical and pathetic workings of orthodox organisations in ways that are beneficial for their personal advancement but disastrous for their moral and emotional health. They are administrators, bureaucrats, technocrats, and managerialists who show quite some mastery in navigating organisational rules and policies and utilising them to their advantage. They are very skilful in political manoeuvring and in delivering senseless management talk, preferably via non-interactive media such as mission and vision statements, strategic plans, or memos. Personally, they are colourless, dull, unimaginative, anti-social, anti-intellectual, mean, self-serving, and manipulative. They lack both empathy and social and emotional intelligence; they treat others in rather functionalistic and disrespectful ways; and they overall show low levels of moral development and decency (Bassman & London 1993, Ashforth 1994, Rayburn & Rayburn 1996, Vredenburgh & Brender 1998, Vickers & Kouzmin 2001, Diamond & Allcorn 2004, Vardi & Weitz 2004, Boddy 2006).

Comparatively high numbers of organisational psychopaths can be found in larger hierarchical organisations because these institutions provide the right conditions and incentives (managerial positions, structures and processes, resources, influence and power, and time and career opportunities) for people to show and utilise the traits, skills, and tactics of an organisational psychopath to their advantage (Boddy 2006, pp. 1462, 1466). Moreover, they are found at higher rates among people with managerial responsibilities and other people higher up the hierarchical ladder, because organisational psychopaths are disproportionately skilful and successful in pursuing organisational, managerial, and political careers and in gaining management and leadership positions (Kellerman 2005, p. 4). It is difficult to say whether it is people with already distorted personalities who are attracted to orthodox organisations and become managers and superiors (*selection* or *self-selection*) *or* whether it is the hierarchical structures and processes that turn people into damaged superiors (*socialisation*). It probably is both (self-)selection *and* socialisation processes that over time turn many managers into a rather underwhelming collection of mediocre organisational psychopaths.

Beside *damaged superiors* there are also *damaged subordinates* in the orthodox organisation.[5] The *ideology of subordinates* is largely about subordinates' fit into the prevailing hierarchical structures and processes, their compliance and obedience, and their smooth functioning within the institution (Scott 1990, p. 58, Ashforth 1994, p. 759, Courpasson & Dany 2003, p. 1232). 'Good' reasons are provided for why subordinates are lower down the hierarchical order, why they deserve to be there, why this is the way it should be, and why this should not change (Jost & Hunyady 2005, p. 260). As a consequence, subordinates usually do not only function well because they *have to* but because they *want to* since this is what constitutes 'the good subordinate'.

Hierarchical social order is largely about the systematic degradation and infantilisation of subordinates (Jacques 1996, p. 81, Diamond & Allcorn 2004, p. 26). Most subordinates are expected and made to show 'patterns of behaviour that dehumanize, depersonalize, and infantilize' (Diamond & Allcorn 2004, p. 26). They have deeply internalised feelings of inferiority, are authoritarian, show the appropriate levels of obedience and 'learned helplessness', and place high value on conformity and order (Bassman & London 1993, p. 22, Ashforth 1994, p. 759, Van Vugt 2006, p. 361).

Although most subordinates experience their lower, limited, and patronised status as constraining and often humiliating, and would escape if they could (Beetham 1991, p. 3), they nonetheless try their best to function and to fit and carry on. The question is why do subordinates contribute to, even actively support, the very system that oppresses and disadvantages them? One possible explanation for people's willingness to function smoothly within oppressive structures is that it corresponds with humans' psychological need for order, security, structure, closure, and uncertainty avoidance – and hierarchical social orders like the orthodox organisation cater for those needs (Tajfel & Turner 1979, Ashforth & Mael 1989, Sidanius & Pratto 1999, Sidanius et al. 2004, Elstak & Van Riel 2005, Jost & Hunyady 2005, Musson & Duberley 2007). Such needs are created and nurtured artificially via threats and reassurances embedded in dominant ideology, via rewards and punishments, and via endless processes of socialisation, if not to say indoctrination and conditioning, of people during their time within primary, secondary, and tertiary educational institutions. To a great extent, employees are already subordinates *before* they join a (new) orthodox organisation. As in the case of superiors, it is a combination of (self-)selection and socialisation that makes (certain) people fit into the all-comprising hierarchical order of the orthodox organisation.

The Need for an Alternative

The orthodox organisation has some specific features that make it a distinct type of organisation – and an extremely bad one:

- *Hierarchy*: Hierarchical order places people into a comprehensive, thoroughly structured, and all-inclusive vertical order of domination and subordination. It turns them into superiors and subordinates, and the former rule the latter on the principle of command and control.
- *Inequality*: Rights and responsibilities, power, resources, and opportunities are allocated unequally among the members of the organisation. In this way, only a few are systematically privileged (owners and senior managers) and the many are systematically discriminated against and marginalised (lower managers and employees).
- *Exploitation*: The few pursue their individual and group interests at the expense of, and by utilising and exploiting, (many) others – largely by denying them their basic civil and legal rights and freedoms, by extracting and appropriating all value-added and profit from the organisation, and by denying others their fair share.
- *Anti-democratic governance*: The whole enterprise is organised, managed, and maintained in thoroughly undemocratic, even anti-democratic ways. Decisions are made by unelected, non-representative, and uncontrolled owners or

managers and are passed down to subordinates as orders or instructions that cannot be debated or challenged.

- *Damaged superiors*: Most superiors are organisational psychopaths who are primarily interested in, and capable of coping with, the dysfunctional workings of the orthodox organisation in ways that are beneficial for their personal advancement. However, they show low levels of moral development and are either not willing to or not capable of engaging with others in decent and respectful ways.
- *Damaged subordinates*: Most subordinates are largely made to fit happily and willingly into the prevailing hierarchical order, are expected to comply with their supervisors' instructions, and must show the required signs of inferiority, obedience, and learned helplessness.

Of course, the orthodox organisation also has some strengths and provides advantages (for certain people) and, once in place, is quite a robust and lasting institution. It would not have become the prevailing form of organisation if it were a mere rhetorical and unrealistic device, or a completely dreadful place (although in some respect it *is*!). However, it is equally clear that, given its main features as outlined in the preceding list, the orthodox organisation is an abysmal institution and simply unacceptable. No organisation should be constituted, designed, managed, and maintained in ways that go against the fundamental and inalienable human and civil rights of people or against the fundamental values and principles of free and fully fledged democratic societies (e.g. freedom, democracy, equality, and justice). And no people should be exposed to such a system. Too many organisations we work for are hierarchical, oppressive, anti-libertarian, and anti-democratic to an extent that puts them in direct opposition to the fundamental values we appreciate and actually need for work and a life of dignity. *Something is rotten in our private and public organisations* – and we need to fix it. The orthodox organisation is *not* – or should not be – the norm; it is an anomaly within a free and democratic society and it is an insult to free and intelligent people. It needs to be replaced. Our organisations must be different – *fundamentally* different.

Viable Alternatives: Democratic Organisations

There have already arisen various ideas for types of organisation that are *fundamentally* different from the orthodox, hierarchical, profit-oriented organisation (e.g. Parker et al. 2014). In fact, there is a whole range of viable alternative types of organisation that put people (and their equal rights, needs, and concerns) first and that are (potentially) democratic in their governance and management, that are non-hierarchical and participative in their organisational structures and processes, and that use multi-dimensional objectives in the pursuit and conduct of their business.[6] Together, they might be called *democratic organisations*.

Democratic organisations share characteristic features (see the section 'Key Criteria of Democratic Organisations', especially p. 31) but they also vary depending on the purpose(s) for which they were established and are maintained. For example, some democratic organisations are established by people who want to pursue certain (political, social, or economic) interests together with other like-minded people (associations, cooperatives, and partnerships). Other democratic organisations are established in order to enable people to own and manage their work, as well as the organisational, material, and immaterial means of their work, individually and collectively (e.g. worker-managed companies, employee-owned companies, and collectivist organisations). And then there are democratic organisations that are established to first and foremost tackle social, environmental, or economic problems (i.e. Social and Solidarity Economy (SSE) organisations). Table 1.1 provides an overview of some of the most prominent types of democratic organisation.[7]

TABLE 1.1 Types of democratic organisation

Interest-Oriented Democratic Organisations

- Associations (Tocqueville 1835–1840/2003, Hirst 1994, Fung 2003)
- Cooperatives (Restakis 2010, International Co-operative Alliance 2013)
- Partnerships (Barley & Kunda 2006, Empson & Chapman 2006, Adler et al. 2008, von Nordenflycht 2010)

Ownership-Oriented Democratic Organisations

- Worker-managed companies, employee-owned companies, the worker-managed economy (Bowles et al. 1993)
- Participatory democracy, participatory and self-managed firms (Pateman 1970, Jones & Svejnar 1982, Hodgson 1984, Bachrach & Botwinick 1992)
- Collectivist organisations, democratic workplaces (Rothschild-Whitt 1976, 1979, Rothschild-Whitt & Lindenfeld 1982, Rothschild & Whitt 1986)
- Shared governance (Srivastva & Cooperrider 1986)
- Democratic corporations, circular organisations (Ackoff 1994)
- Self-determination (Romme 1999)

Social and Solidarity Economy Organisations

- Self-help groups, exchange networks, neighbourhood organisations, community projects, community development trusts, community-based organisations, volunteer groups, activist groups, social and political movements, private voluntary organisations, cooperatives, credit unions, associations, foundations, charities, not-for-profit or nonprofit organisations, non-governmental organisations, social enterprises, ethical businesses, micro-financed businesses, worker-managed enterprises, fairtrade organisations (Vakil 1997, Defourny & Delvetere 1999, Fournier 2002, United Nations 2003, Teegen et al. 2004, Willetts 2006, Allard & Matthaei 2008, Solidarity Economic Working Group for USSF 2007 2008, Kerlin & Gagnaire 2009, Nyssens 2009, Kelly 2012, Haque 2013, Lans 2013, Lewis 2014, Wallimann 2014, Ould Ahmed 2015, Utting 2015, Vilchez 2017, North & Cato 2018)

These alternatives are not just theoretical concepts but real, productive, and highly successful types of organisation that have proven their viability for decades, if not centuries. In the following sections, some of the key features of these types of democratic organisation will be highlighted briefly in order to provide some understanding of what democratic organisations are, and what they are about. The presentation shows the broad range and variety – the sheer breadth and depth – of valid alternatives to the orthodox organisation.

Interest-Oriented Democratic Organisations

First, there are democratic organisations that are set up and maintained by people for the purpose of pursuing their particular social, political, economic, and/or professional interests jointly with like-minded others in collective and collaborative ways. These democratic organisations reflect and represent the interests of their members in their design, their governance, and how they work. Such organisations therefore could be called 'interest-oriented democratic organisations.' The main examples are associations, cooperatives, and partnerships. Each will be briefly described in turn.

Associations

As early as the late 18th and early 19th centuries – i.e. well before (early) capitalism propelled the orthodox organisation to its unprecedented rise and dominance – a type of organisation emerged that provided free and equal people with the opportunity to organise and pursue their common interests – the *association*. Because of this historical relevance, this section allows some scholars from around that time to provide first-hand accounts.

On his extensive travels across parts of the U.S. in 1831, the French political scientist Alexis de Tocqueville (1805–1859) realised the advantages associations provide for individuals as well as communities and society as a whole. He concluded:

> The most natural freedom open to man after that of acting on his own is that of joining forces with his fellows and acting in common. The right of association appears to me, by nature, almost as inalienable as individual liberty. (Tocqueville 1835/1840/2003, pp. 224–225)

In his *Principles of Political Economy* (1848), the great British philosopher and political economist John Stuart Mill (1806–1873) highlighted the important role associations (would) play in organising economic activities in an equal manner and in achieving and maintaining equality of, and among, free people:

The form of association, however, which if mankind continue to improve, must be expected in the end to predominate, is not that which can exist between a capitalist as chief, and workpeople without a voice in the management, but the association of the labourers themselves on terms of equality, collectively owning the capital with which they carry on their operations, and working under managers elected and removable by themselves. (quoted in Erdal 2011, p. 147)

At roughly the same time, the French philosopher and politician Pierre-Joseph Proudhon (1809–1865) also argued for an economic system based on associations:

In cases in which production requires great division of labor, and a considerable collective force, it is necessary to form an ASSOCIATION among the workers in this industry. ... Every industry, operation or enterprise, which by its nature requires the employment of a large number of workmen of different specialties, is destined to become a society or a company of workers. (Proudhon 1851/2012, p. 49)

Two decades later, the Swiss–French political anarchist and philosopher James Guillaume (1844–1916) argued in his *Ideas on Social Organization* (1876) in a similar vein:

Every workshop, every factory will therefore represent a workers' association which will remain at liberty to administer itself howsoever it may see fit, as long as the rights of the individual are safeguarded and the principle of equality and justice put into practice. (quoted in Guérin 1980/2005, p. 252)

Just from these few original quotes one can get a good idea of the libertarian, democratic, and egalitarian spirit that shapes and suffuses the association as an organisational form and that, thereby, makes it fundamentally different from the feudalistic and capitalist orthodox organisation.

An association is an organisation of *equals*, i.e. it is voluntarily established, jointly owned, and collectively and democratically managed and maintained by free and equal people in order to pursue their common goals and interests (Proudhon 1851/2012, pp. 49, 54–56, Hirst 1994, p. 44, Berger & Neuhaus 2000, p. 171). All members have equal rights and responsibilities, in particular equal property and employment rights and equal formal status. In other words, an association is without either hierarchy or superior–subordinate relationships. Many associations work at a local level. They are examples of small local self-organising groups and are part of (the voluntary self-governance of) communes and communities so that decisions are made democratically by those who will be affected by them (Fournier 2002, pp. 202–209, Reedy 2002, p. 181).

Clearly, associations are good for people; they protect people's individual human and civil rights; enhance freedom, democracy, equality, and justice;[8] and develop people's social and political attitudes, civic skills, and democratic norms, values, and behaviours. As Fung (2003, p. 520) states, 'such virtues include attention to the public good, habits of cooperation, toleration, respect for others, respect for the rule of law, willingness to participate in public life, self-confidence, and efficacy'. Tocqueville (1835–1840/2003) called associations 'schools of democracy' since they teach their members how to organise themselves, pursue common goods and interests, debate, make decisions collectively, and uphold the common institutions of government and governance. In this sense, the association provides a prototype of the democratic organisation – as well as the organisational and governmental foundations of a free and democratic society.[9]

Cooperatives

A second type of democratic organisation fairly similar to the association – and of equal historical relevance and standing – is the *cooperative*.[10] Like associations, cooperatives are organisations established and maintained voluntarily by individuals on the basis of equal rights and responsibilities, participation, and democratic decision-making (e.g. Hoover 2008, p. 240, Doran 2013, pp. 87–88). In contrast to associations (which have primarily social or political purposes), cooperatives primarily have commercial, economic, and financial purposes (e.g. farming, housing, utility supply, consumer, or banking cooperatives; credit unions; and mutual insurance companies) – although in pursuing those purposes they also serve social purposes.

According to the International Cooperative Alliance (2013, p. 8), cooperatives are based on seven principles (see also CICOPA 2004, p. 3, Iuviene et al. 2010, p. 6, Macdonald 2013, p. 4):

1. *Voluntary and open membership*: People are free to join and to leave.
2. *Democratic member control*: Control is enacted through democratic processes on the basis of one member, one vote.
3. *Members' economic participation*: Members contribute capital and control its use and investments collectively.
4. *Autonomy and independence*: Especially in economic and financial matters, the cooperative operates independently of banks and external investors.
5. *Education of members*: The cooperative continually provides education, training, and information for its members.
6. *Cooperation between cooperatives*: Cooperatives do business and cooperate largely with other cooperatives, individuals, and alternative types of organisation.
7. *Concern for community*: Cooperatives are locally embedded and contribute to local social and economic developments.

Probably the best known (and most widely researched) cooperative is Mondragón. The Mondragón cooperative (formally known as the Mondragón Corporation) was founded in 1956 and has grown into a federation of about 250 worker cooperatives in the Basque Country with around 75,000 employees ('Mondragon Corporation' 2019; for a good description of Mondragón see Azevedo & Gitahy 2013). Agirre et al. (2014) provide an excellent description of Mondragón's governance model:

> [The Mondragón cooperative] is founded on a firm commitment to solidarity and uses democratic governance methods, fosters participation (involvement of people in the management, profits and ownership of their companies) developing a shared project which unites social, business and personal progress and fosters training and innovation through the development of human and technological skills. Democratic governance is considered key to greater organizational effectiveness ... and is imperative for achieving higher levels of innovation and performance. ... Organizational democracy applies to substantial democratic structures, where employees have the possibility of exercising influence over critical decision-making concerning tactical and strategic issues in the organization. This means that employee participation in decision-making is mandatory and is institutionalized in direct and indirect forms (general assembly, employee representation on the board, safety committees, etc.). Additionally, employees often hold shares in their organization's equity capital. ... The conception of democracy in Mondragon includes aspects derived from the 'power to the people' idea, whereby organizational democracy is conceived as 'one worker, one vote, regardless of the share of capital owned'. (p. 389)

The 'labour-owned, labour-managed' cooperative, where workers hire capital and manage the enterprise collectively as its legal owners, is a commercially efficient and effective way of doing business and a valid alternative to the capitalist company (Meade 1993, p. 85, Arnold 1994, p. 49, International Co-operative Alliance 2013, p. 2, Novkovic & Webb 2014, p. 285).

Like associations, cooperatives represent and nurture the principles and values of freedom, democracy, equality, and justice. In line with their primarily commercial and economic purposes, they also propagate and support self-help, social responsibility, and solidarity (International Co-operative Alliance 2013). 'Co-operatives develop individual participation, can build personal self-confidence and resilience, and create social capital. Cooperative institutions create long-term security; they are long-lasting, sustainable and successful' (International Co-operative Alliance 2013, p. 2). Cooperatives in general are *very* good at doing business – *and* they are very good for people (Crowe 2013, p. 76, Ellwood 2013, p. 34, Murray 2013, p. 26).

Partnerships

A third type of alternative organisation, the *partnership* or *professional service firm (PSF)*, can be considered alongside associations and cooperatives, although its democratic credentials are not as clear cut as those of the other two, especially in regard to the crucial aspects of equality and democratic governance. Like a cooperative, a partnership is an enterprise that is managed and controlled jointly by those who own it (in this case, partners) for the pursuit of their common professional *and* economic interests. Partnerships are established by practitioners of the same or very similar professions. Examples include law firms, management consultancies, accounting consultancies, marketing firms, medical centres, private hospitals, architectural firms, and engineering consultancies (Barley & Kunda 2006, p. 51, Von Nordenflycht 2010, pp. 166, 391).

Partnerships' main characteristics are that they provide and apply professionals' specialist knowledge as customised solutions to clients' problems (Empson et al. 2015, pp. 4–8) and that they organise, manage, and govern those professional and business activities collectively.[11] The core ideas of a partnership are that the partners are equals, the partners have equal (legal, formal, and managerial) rights and responsibilities, power and authority are widely distributed among the partners, and decisions are made collegially, democratically, and consensually (Brock 2006, p. 160, Malhotra et al. 2006, p. 174, Von Nordenflycht 2007, pp. 430–431, Harlacher & Reihlen 2014, p. 143).

The professional partnership model would be an ideal or perfect partnership (seen from the perspective of the *democratic* organisation) if *all* who worked for the partnership were partners and all the partners were equals. However, the conceptual and empirical reality of many partnerships – or professions – is quite distinct from the perfect partnership. Most partnerships are thoroughly hierarchical and oligarchic. Their organisational structure is based on the so-called Cravath model (Gand 2010, Leblebici & Sherer 2015, p. 196), which differentiates between senior partners, junior partners, and non-partners and places them in a hierarchical relationship according to principles based on formal and chronological seniority. The superiority of (senior) partners is based on a professional's (certified) expertise and years spent in the firm. Only senior partners have the right and privilege to govern, manage, and make crucial decisions. Moreover, only some of the people who work for a partnership are partners. Partner status, or *owner* status, is confined to an exclusive circle of professionals within the firm (Empson & Chapman 2006, p. 142).

Such 'governance by senior partners only' is not only an example of the classical hierarchical division of labour but also fairly oligarchic and elitist (Suddaby & Muzio 2015, pp. 27–28, 33). In addition, partnerships have become increasingly *managerial* – i.e. some professionals create and fill management positions and make decisions about running the business single-handedly. For example, Leblebici and Sherer (2015, p. 189) raised the following criticism: 'Consider governance in a fairly typical larger Professional Service Firm (PSF). While the firm was once governed like a partnership in which partners all had a say in firm matters, it now behaves more like a corporation in the way that it carries on business.' And, just like in a corporation, higher status members (senior partners) extract rents from other professionals and staff lower down in the division of labour (Barley & Kunda 2006, p. 51, Suddaby & Muzio 2015, p. 33).

Thus, differentiated and nuanced judgement is required when it comes to assessing whether a given partnership constitutes a democratic organisation. A *perfect* partnership (in which *all* members are partners with equal rights and responsibilities) is based on democratic principles, has democratic governance and management structures and processes in place, and, thus, could be considered a democratic organisation. In contrast, a *hybrid* or *imperfect* partnership (in which only *some* members are partners with various degrees of rights and status) has an exclusive hierarchical order and is only good for *some* (mainly senior) partners, but not for many others (e.g. junior partners and ordinary staff). In this respect it is nothing but an ordinary orthodox organisation.[12]

Ownership-Oriented Democratic Organisations

Interest-oriented democratic organisations – such as associations, cooperatives, or partnerships – represent appropriate and viable organisational options for people to collectively and collaboratively pursue their social, political, and/or economic (commercial and financial) interests in legal, legitimate, decent, democratic, fair, and just ways. However, the brief description and discussion of (imperfect or hybrid) partnerships and PSFs earlier in this chapter showed the importance of *equal rights* – that *all* people working for a democratic organisation must have *equal* rights. In a socio-economic context, and also especially concerning organisations, in which there is coordination of joint socio-economic activities, *ownership rights* – or *property rights* – are crucial; they entitle as well as enable people to make decisions (in regard to the things they own, i.e. their 'property'), to act (e.g. to use the things they own as they deem right), and to bear the consequences of their decisions and actions (e.g. to earn an income and to enjoy the fruits of their labour) (Honoré 1961, Arnold 1994, p. 44, Christman 1994, p. 227, Ingram 1994, p. 30, Learmount & Roberts 2006, p. 146, Mack 2010).[13] Therefore, *all* members of an organisation *must* have *individual and joint legal ownership of the organisation*. They must own the organisation, *especially* if they work for it.[14]

This fundamental notion or principle lays the foundation for *ownership-oriented democratic organisations*. Traditionally, such organisations are called 'worker-owned companies', 'worker-managed companies', 'workers' self-management', 'employee-owned companies', or 'self-managing organisations' in order to indicate that there is no differentiation between 'capital' and 'labour' or between 'managers' and 'employees' in such organisations; everyone who works for the organisation owns, manages, and controls it (e.g. Bowles et al. 1993, Lee & Edmondson 2017).[15]

With her *collectivist organisation*, the widely recognised American sociologist Joyce Rothschild (also known as Rothschild-Whitt) provided one of the best and most comprehensively developed concepts of the democratic–collectivist organisation, self-management, and the democratic workplace (Rothschild-Whitt 1976, 1979, Rothschild-Whitt & Lindenfeld 1982, Rothschild & Whitt 1986). The main idea of the collectivist organisation is that it is an organisation without hierarchy; *all* members of the collectivist organisation have the right to full and equal participation, to debate and decide organisational affairs collectively and democratically (Rothschild-Whitt 1979, p. 512). Rothschild-Whitt and Lindenfeld (1982, p. 6) explained the idea in detail:

> Democratic workplaces are united in their attempt to break down the division between management and labor, planners and workers, so that all who do the work of the organization have an equal voice in its management and a fair share of the fruits of their labor. What they are seeking to alter, then, is nothing short of the structure of power in organizations. The aim is not the simple *transference* of power from one official to another; it is the *abolition* of the pyramid *in toto*. It is an attempt to accomplish organizational tasks cooperatively and democratically, without recourse to hierarchal authority structures or the stratification systems that accompany them.

The concept of the collectivist organisation comprises various principles that are consistent with and mutually reinforce each other (Rothschild-Whitt & Lindenfeld 1982, pp. 6–7):

1. Full worker participation in decision-making exists at all levels of the organization. Enterprises are controlled by those who work in them. In small organizations, decisions are generally made by the entire collective in frequent meetings. Larger organizations have some kind of management positions, but managers are elected on the basis of one person, one vote and can be recalled by the members; the workforce as a whole retains ultimate authority.

2. All who work in an organization share in its net income and decide democratically how income and surplus should be distributed. The tendency is toward equality ...

3. The means of production (land, buildings, machinery) are socially owned and kept in trust as community assets. They may be owned either directly by a firm's workers, or by a trust controlled by them, or leased from community organizations or government.

4. The main purpose of each firm is not the maximization of profit, but the maximization of community well-being. This includes fair income for those who work in the enterprise and workers' control of their own work. ... Community well-being also includes providing goods or services that are socially useful, of high quality, and ecologically sound ...

5. Profit, or surplus after paying overhead and wages, belongs to all who worked to create it. It may be shared in the form of bonuses,

or, it may be used for social and community purposes such as education, health clinics, or day-care centers. A vital use of the surplus is for reinvestment within the firm or in other worker-managed enterprises to create new jobs ...

6. In democratically managed enterprises, labor hires capital. As long as capital is scarce there may have to be interest paid for its use, but suppliers of capital (e.g., banks) do not exercise control over the enterprise and usually do not share the profits.

Some years later, Romme (1999) developed the concept of *self-determination*, which elaborates further how ownership-oriented or collectivist democratic organisations function. According to Romme (1999, p. 804), self-determination means the capacity of people to act autonomously either as individuals or as a group. They establish a formal organisation – and thus their formal relationship, rights, and responsibilities – on the basis of shared ownership and a partnership contract, i.e. as equals who share authority between themselves. Correspondingly, the organisational structures and processes are heterarchical, i.e. cooperation is based on equivalence, mutual adjustment, horizontal communication, and collective self-regulation.

Kokkinidis (2012, p. 244) provided some telling evidence that worker-owned companies and collectivist democratic organisations actually work:

> Therefore, the case of the Argentinean ERTs [*empresas recuperadas por sus trabalhadores* – 'worker-recovered enterprises'], albeit small, is interesting because their egalitarian and self-management practices, with their emphasis on horizontality and direct democracy, constitute a social experiment of organizing work differently. These experiments nicely illustrate the workers' capacity to take control of their working lives and that coordination of collective action within an organisation, but also within a network of organisations, is possible without representatives and hierarchical forms of governance. They also address in creative ways the well-known 'iron law' of Michels according to which there is a natural tendency in the most democratic of organisations towards hierarchism; and they do so by giving emphasis on horizontality and participatory democracy which undermines any member's attempt to centralise power at the expense of the group.

As both the theoretical concepts of and the empirical evidence for ownership-oriented democratic organisations show, the important thing is that all governance, management, and control rights as well as *de facto control* are with 'the workers', i.e. with *everyone* who works for or is a member of the democratic organisation. In this sense, governance, management, and control in the democratic organisation are based on universal ownership and property rights and resemble those of a *participatory democracy* (Pateman 1970, Jones & Svejnar

1982, Hodgson 1984, Bachrach & Botwinick 1992). According to Bachrach and Botwinick (1992, p. 2), 'in the workplace, participatory democracy is a political system in which all members of a firm, together with representatives of the community, participate equally in setting agendas and determining policy decisions for the firm'.

Participatory democracy means *full* participation (according to Arnstein's 1969 'ladder of participation'[16]); all members of the organisation not only are informed and consulted but also have equal formal rights and opportunities to participate actively in joint decision-making and execute complete control over the organisation, organisational affairs, and those who fulfil functional roles and positions that might involve making decisions. When this is the case, a democratic organisation is fully functioning and delivering on its promises.

Social and Solidarity Economy (SSE) Organisations

Besides democratic organisations that are primarily set up and maintained to serve their members' individual and common interests or to provide equal rights of ownership, property rights, and corresponding responsibilities for all who work for them, there are also types of democratic organisation that are first and foremost oriented towards achieving specific social, political, societal, socio-economic, and/or environmental purposes – and *then* (also) catering for their members' interests or addressing ownership rights. They offer, and actively aim for, economic and social paradigms and ways of doing business that represent real alternatives to capitalist market economies and orthodox organisations. These alternatives can be subsumed under the term *Social and Solidarity Economy* (SSE).[17] North and Cato (2018, pp. 6–7) provide one of the best descriptions of the main rationale(s) of an SSE:

> We conceptualise the social and solidarity economy as that sector between the public and private sectors that consists of grassroots-generated economic initiatives through which goods and services are produced by organisations that have social and environmental aims, and are guided by objectives and practices of cooperation, solidarity, ethics and democratic self-management. The SSE sector aims to replace fundamentally unjust or unequal social, economic and power relations with democratically run institutions providing sustainable livelihoods, in order to bring about democratically run, economically just, socially inclusive and environmentally sustainable futures.

The following three definitions are provided to give a better idea of the main notions and rationales that are usually ascribed to this (new) type of economy:

- 'The social economy is that part of the economy ... that organises economic functions primarily according to principles of democratic co-operation and reciprocity … guaranteeing a high level of equality and distribution, and organising redistribution when needed … in order to satisfy human basic needs, in a sustainable way' (Moulaert & Nussbaumer 2005, p. 2079).

- 'Solidarity economy initiatives can … be loosely defined as practices and institutions on all levels and in all sectors of the economy that embody certain values and priorities: cooperation, sustainability, equality, democracy, justice, diversity, and local control' (Allard & Matthaei 2008, p. 6).
- '[The] SSE is fundamentally about reasserting social control or "social power" … over the economy by giving primacy to social and often environmental objectives above profits, emphasising the place of ethics in economic activity and rethinking economic practice in terms of democratic self-management and active citizenship' (Utting 2015, p. 2).

As Table 1.1 showed, the SSE comprises a whole range of democratically run local and regional enterprises of various types and legal forms, in particular self-help groups, exchange networks, neighbourhood organisations, community projects, community development trusts, community-based organisations, volunteer groups, activist groups, social and political movements, private voluntary organisations, cooperatives, credit unions, associations, foundations, charities, not-for-profit or non-profit organisations, non-governmental organisations (NGOs), social enterprises, ethical businesses, micro-financed businesses, worker-managed enterprises, and fairtrade organisations (Vakil 1997, p. 2060, Allard & Matthaei 2008, p. 1, Kelly 2012, pp. 141–142, Haque 2013, pp. 332–333, Lans 2013, p. 164, Lewis 2014, p. 26, Wallimann 2014, p. 51, Ould Ahmed 2015, p. 428, Utting 2015, p. 1, Vilchez 2017, p. 257, North & Cato 2018, p. 7). It is important to note that the SSE spans *all sectors* of economic activity, i.e. for-profit as well as non-profit and voluntary activities (Allard & Matthaei 2008, p. 6, Lewis & Swinney 2008, p. 35, Lans 2013, pp. 166–167, Laville 2015, pp. 48–49, Utting 2015, p. 1).

SSE groups, movements, organisations, and networks exist in any society, but especially in free and fully fledged democratic societies (together with interest- and ownership-oriented democratic organisations, they constitute not only a portion of the economy but also a large part of 'civil society'). As diverse as SSE organisations obviously are, they have some things in common.

The SSE demonstrates that organisations, businesses, and the economy *can* – and *should* – be built on and function according to different principles. As the term 'Social and Solidarity Economy' indicates, SSE organisations first and foremost pursue *social* goals in their orientation and activities. This is, they address and aim at reducing social problems and needs, and they serve and benefit individuals, groups of people, and/or (their) community by providing private or public goods and/or services to people and/or entities that need them. In doing so, they create social value, i.e. enhance individual and collective social and socio-economic wealth, welfare, and well-being – and may bring about social, economic, and even political change. As Eliasoph (2011, p. 222) explained: 'Many of these organizations have a mission to "build community," increase participation, promote diversity, and strengthen civic engagement – to bring governance "closer to the people" and "the people closer to each other."'

The second principle and objective is *solidarity*. Very often, this term is mentioned without further specification or explanation. However, by going through some of the SSE literature,[18] one can gain an understanding of what the idea or concept of 'solidarity' might represent and can operationalise it. Solidarity of SSE organisations with their stakeholders mainly means that (1) social and economic relationships are based on, and aim for, cooperation, mutual benefits and reciprocity, and the fair distribution and allocation of all costs and revenues (instead of competition, opportunism, and egoistic rent-seeking); (2) partnerships and cooperation are long term; (3) there is joint decision-making, transparency, and knowledge-sharing among all participants; and (4) there is a focus on capacity-building and local development. Solidarity is especially demonstrated with (a) other SSE organisations (value-based solidarity); (b) oppressed, disadvantaged, and exploited people, groups of people, or even countries (anti-oppression solidarity); and (c) people, organisations, and movements that strive for social, economic, environmental, and political development and change (vision-based solidarity) (Solidarity Economic Working Group for USSF 2007 2008, p. 392).

True to their purposes, SSE organisations demonstrate social values and solidarity largely towards *others* (and almost all of the SSE literature, self-descriptions, and discussions are about this aspect). However, in order to be fully consistent with their goal of providing a fundamentally different alternative to capitalist or neo-liberal modes of economic activity and orthodox organisations, SSE organisations must also apply these social values and the notion of solidarity to *themselves*, i.e. to their organisational design, structures, and processes; how they function and operate internally; how their members are treated and treat each other; and how they manage and collaborate. SSE organisations should be structured, operate, and function in line with the social goals they pursue and the principle of solidarity they practise towards others (Defourny & Delveterre 1999, p. 16, Moulaert & Nussbaumer 2005, p. 2079, Allard & Matthaei 2008, p. 6, Lans 2013, pp. 166–167, Utting 2015, p. 2). That is, SSE organisations are (or should be):

- jointly owned and controlled by all their members (and other relevant stakeholders);
- governed and managed collectively in participatory and democratic ways;
- focused on treating, enabling, and empowering all their members equally; and
- focused on upholding and following (in their internal practices and external activities) the principles and values of individual and collective responsibility, freedom, democracy, equality, justice, and sustainability.

If they meet these principles, then SSE organisations are, or come close to, fairly typical fully fledged democratic organisations. Nonetheless, many SSE organisations are *not* owned by their members, are *not* participatory and egalitarian but instead hierarchical with autocratic or oligarchic decision-making structures and processes (e.g. radical activist groups, conservative or even extremist groups and communities, larger NGOs, organisations of faith, trade unions, the professions, centralised associations, and autocratic family businesses or social enterprises) (e.g. Hutter & O'Mahony 2004, p. 3, Lewis 2014, pp. 23–25). Despite pursuing very honourable goals, demonstrating social values and solidarity towards others, and doing many good deeds, such SSE organisations resemble more orthodox, or even radical or totalitarian, organisations with all their faults and weaknesses. *Doing* good (or *claiming* to do good) does not mean that someone *is* good. SSE organisations *can* be democratic organisations – but only if they live up to their principles in their external *and* internal orientations and operations.

Key Criteria of Democratic Organisations

In the sections above, various types of democratic organisation were described in detail:

- *interest-oriented democratic organisations* (i.e. associations, cooperatives, and partnerships);
- *ownership-oriented democratic organisations* (i.e. worker-managed companies, employee-owned companies, self-managing organisations, collectivist organisations, and participatory democracy); and
- *SSE organisations* (e.g. self-help groups, exchange networks, neighbourhood organisations, community projects, community development trusts, community-based organisations, volunteer groups, activist groups, social and political movements, private voluntary organisations, cooperatives, credit unions, associations, foundations, charities, not-for-profit or non-profit organisations, NGOs, social enterprises, ethical businesses, micro-financed businesses, worker-managed enterprises, and fairtrade organisations).

Democratic organisations can pursue multiple purposes, serve several interests of their founders and members, have quite diverse organisational structures and processes (of governance and management) in place, and differ in what kinds of activities they conduct in what way(s). Nevertheless, (in their ideal-typical manifestation) *all* democratic organisations have various things in common, or key criteria that define them as democratic organisations, in particular (Vanek 1971, pp. 1, 8–9, Rothschild-Whitt 1979, p. 512, Jones & Svejnar 1982, Rosen 1984, pp. 313–316, Bachrach & Botwinick 1992, p. 2, Bowles et al. 1993, p. 129, Ulrich 1993, pp. 412–442, Archer 1995, pp. 31–32, Poole 1996, Melman 2001, p. 272, Caspary 2004, pp. 239–240, Kelly 2012, pp. 141–142, Diefenbach 2019, p. 553):

1. *Individual and collective ownership*: Members own the organisation, have ownership status, and have corresponding equal rights, responsibilities, and legal entitlements (e.g. rights of information, participation in decision-making, management and control of the organisation, and profit-sharing).

2. *Democratic governance and decision-making*: All members have equal formal rights as well as actual opportunities to participate in strategic and operational decision-making (either directly or via democratically elected representatives), and to decide the policies and direction of the organisation ('shared governance' or 'workplace democracy').

3. *Non-hierarchical modes of organisation and management*: There is no hierarchy in the sense of top-down 'order and control' and there are no superior–subordinate relationships; instead there are heterarchical relationships between formal positions and people. Managers are democratically elected and controlled representatives, and management is provided individually or collectively in the form of transparent, interactive, and collective processes and shared activities ('self-management', 'participative management', and 'full participation').

4. *Empowerment*: All members of the organisation are equally empowered, i.e. they have the same formal rights and opportunities to decide their work and the conditions of their work, to pursue their individual and collective interests, and to personal development.

5. *Multiple purposes and considerate conduct of business*: The democratic organisation provides goods and services, and conducts its activities, in ways that are consistent with a social orientation, pro-environmental behaviour, and sustainable economic performance ('people, planet, profit').

Following these criteria, the democratic organisation can be defined as *a non-hierarchical organisation that pursues and serves multi-dimensional (social, political, legal, economic, and/or environmental) purposes in considerate, balanced, and sustainable ways and that is owned, managed, and controlled individually, collectively, and democratically by all of its members, who have equal rights, and are equally empowered, to participate fully in the governance and management of the organisation, organisational affairs, and activities.*

As shown earlier (see Table 1.1, p. 18), there already exist many types of organisation (whether as theoretical concepts or real enterprises) that are *potentially* democratic organisations because of the principles they are built on, the purposes they pursue, their design, and how they function and conduct business accordingly. Most people are simply not aware that there is – and has been for more than two centuries – such a scope of alternative organisations that have many ideas and features in common and that come close to what could be called the 'standard model' of the democratic organisation. Hence, in order to show how a fully fledged democratic organisation could, or even should, look like, Part I (Chapters 2–7) now systematically develops a general model of the democratic organisation.

Notes

1 This sub-section is based on criticism and arguments that I developed in my book *Hierarchy and Organisation: Toward a General Theory of Hierarchical Social Systems* (Diefenbach 2013a), in particular sub-section 2.2.2 ('The System of Hierarchy') in Chapter 2 ('The Longevity of Hierarchy') and Section 3.2 ('The Core Structure of All Hierarchical Social Relationships') in Chapter 3 ('A General Theory of Hierarchical Social Systems'). It also draws upon Chapter 8 of my book *Management and the Dominance of Managers* (Diefenbach 2009a).

2 In a similar vein, Bachrach and Baratz (1970, pp. 43–44) described orthodox management as 'a set of predominant values, beliefs, rituals, and institutional procedures ("rules of the game") that operate systematically and consistently to the benefit of certain persons and groups at the expense of others. Those who benefit are placed in a preferred position to defend and promote their vested interests. More often than not, the "status quo defenders" are a minority or elite group within the population in question.'

3 Schweickart (2011, p. 48) rightly pointed out that 'it is a striking anomaly of modern capitalist societies that ordinary people are deemed competent enough to select their political leaders – but not their bosses. Contemporary capitalism celebrates democracy, yet denies us our democratic rights at precisely the point where they might be utilized most immediately and concretely.'

4 This sub-section to some extent is based on sub-section 2.3.3 ('The People of Hierarchy') in Chapter 2 ('The Longevity of Hierarchy') in my book *Hierarchy and Organisation: Toward a General Theory of Hierarchical Social Systems* (Diefenbach 2013a).

5 It should be mentioned that the roles of 'superior' and 'subordinate' are not understood here as fixed and static but represent *relational* constructs. This is, many members of orthodox organisations (or hierarchical social orders in general) are not only *either* superior *or* subordinate but can also be formal or informal *superiors* in certain situations (in regard to certain people) and *subordinates* in other situations (concerning other people).

6 Throughout this book I use the terms 'conduct of business' or 'way(s) of doing business' for the way(s) organisations act and operate as an entity. Crucially, conduct of business does *not* just mean buying and selling goods or services or profit-maximising competitive behaviour in a narrow sense, but more generally *the way(s) an individual or collective actor (organisation) acts and operates while pursuing its purpose(s)*.

7 In Table 1.1, the differentiation of democratic organisations into three different types (interest oriented, ownership oriented, and Social Solidarity Economy) is *not* meant as a taxonomy or even a typology (i.e. a complete and consistent classification of democratic organisations into mutually exclusive types). Instead, it is intended as a heuristic device to indicate that democratic organisations can have different prime orientations or purposes while they also have many features in common with other types of democratic organisation. For example, associations, cooperatives, and worker-managed companies are also Social and Solidarity Economy organisations.

8 According to Fung (2003, p. 515), 'associations enhance democracy in at least six ways: through the intrinsic value of associative life, fostering civic virtues and teaching political skills, offering resistance to power and checking government, improving the quality and equality of representation, facilitating public deliberation, and creating opportunities for citizens and groups to participate directly in governance'.

9 'Associationalism' (or 'associative democracy') is one of the most compelling forms and concepts of political and economic self-governance and participative governance of economic and social affairs at local and societal levels (see Hirst 1994, Cohen & Rogers 1995, Fung 2003). But the focus here is only on associations as a particular type of organisation.

10 For a brief overview of the history of (the idea of) cooperatives see Restakis (2010, pp. 27–54) or Mills (2013). For a good description (of the main characteristics or advantages) of cooperatives see Gregory (2013), Harrison (2013), International Co-operative Alliance (2013), or Webb and Cheney (2014). For data and numbers about cooperatives see International Co-operative Alliance (2010), Restakis (2010, p. 3), Altmann (2014, p. 177), Birchall (2014, p. 5), Webb and Novkovic (2014, p. 3), or Millstone (2015, pp. 88–90).

11 As Malhotra et al. (2006, p. 174) note, '[the] partnership as a governance form embodies three beliefs: the fusion of ownership and control; a form of representative democracy for purposes of strategic and operational decision-making; and the non-separation of professional and managerial tasks'.

12 Also associations and cooperatives – and indeed *any* type of democratic organisation – can be, or become, quite hierarchical and oligarchic, and can turn into fairly orthodox organisations (the problem of 'oligarchisation', which will be discussed at quite some length in Chapter 10: 'The Iron Threat(s) of Disproportional Empowerment'). However, whereas associations and cooperatives may become hierarchies or oligarchies *accidentally*, partnerships can be hierarchical, oligarchic, and elitist *by design*.

13 The importance of private ownership and property rights will be discussed in some more detail in the section 'Private Ownership and Property Rights' in Chapter 2 ('Libertarian Constitution').

14 As Fournier (2002, p. 203) rightly pointed out: 'Self-governance requires free access to, and control over, the means of production, and therefore the elimination of the division between owners of capital (be it land, tools, or raw material) and labour.'

15 For example, Hunnius (1971) described how workers' self-management worked in the former Yugoslav economy, and Kokkinidis (2012) analysed South American (particularly Argentinean) 'worker-recovered enterprises' (*empresas recuperadas por sus trabalhadores*, or ERTs).

16 See the section 'Participative Management' in Chapter 4 ('Democratic Management') for a more detailed discussion of the concept of participation.

17 Alternative terms are 'solidarity economy' (e.g. Allard & Matthaei 2008, Allard et al. 2008), 'social economy' (e.g. Defourny & Develtere 1999, Smith & Teasdale 2012, Lans 2013, Krishna 2014, Wallimann 2014, Utting 2015), and, especially in Latin America, *economía popular y solidaria* (popular and solidarity economy, or PSE) (Vilchez 2017, p. 253). For definitions of these terms see Vilchez (2017, pp. 254–256). Then there are various terms for more individual concepts within SSE, such as 'generative economy' (Kelly 2012) or 'LowGrow model' (Victor 2014, pp. 104–112). Finally, there are alternative economic models in the global justice movement (Park 2013), such as 'eco-capitalist globalisation model', 'alternative regionalism of solidarity economy model', 'nation-state centric localisation model', 'de-growth subsistence economy model', 'eco-socialist model' and 'anarcho-communist model'.

18 Salamon and Anheier (1998, p. 216), Neamtan (2005, n.p.), Lewis and Swinney (2008, p. 31), Smith and Teasdale (2012, p. 156), Lans (2013, p. 168), Ould Ahmed (2015, p. 428), Reed (2015, pp. 105–106), Saguier and Brent (2017, p. 264).

PART I
The Model of the Democratic Organisation

2

LIBERTARIAN CONSTITUTION

Free Will and Free Individuals

Social systems, such as organisations, are established and function on the basis of, and represent, (explicit and/or implicit) *contractual* and *social* relations between individuals (Jensen & Meckling 1976). When individuals *agree* to engage and cooperate with others via various forms of mutually binding agreement, the underlying – and necessary! – assumption is that individuals are, and must be, *free* – free to form, to formulate, and to realise their will, and to enter, maintain, and exit the kinds of agreements and relations they have chosen.[1] Individuals' *own free will* – as well as their ability to show and practise their free will – is *essential*.[2] Agreements and socio-legal relationships (such as social interactions, economic transactions, involvement with organisations, and other forms of cooperation) are voluntary and based on mutual consent if, and only if, individuals (are able to) express and exercise *their* free will (Friedman 1962/1982, pp. 13–14, 22–23, Vanberg 2004, p. 6, Peel 2011, p. 448) – and only then are such agreements *legitimate*.[3] Therefore, if a social system (such as the democratic organisation) is to be legitimate, it *must* be constituted, based on, and maintained according to the free will of its founders and members – *all* its founders and members.

Moreover, individual freedom means that individuals do not only *have* a free will but also *are* free! – free from external restraint (negative freedom) and free and able to act upon their own will (positive freedom). The Russian British social philosopher Isaiah Berlin portrayed the notion of (positive) freedom and an existentialist understanding of the free individual very well in his *Two Concepts of Liberty* (quoted in Carter et al. 2007, p. 44):

> The 'positive' sense of the word 'liberty' derives from the wish on the part of the individual to be his own master. I wish my life and decisions to depend on myself, not on external forces of whatever kind. I wish to be the instrument of my own, not of other men's, acts of ill. I wish to be a subject, not an object; to be loved by reasons, by conscious purposes, which are my own, not by causes which affect me, as it were, from outside. I wish to be somebody, not nobody; a doer – deciding, not being decided for, self-directed and not acted upon external nature or by other men as if I were a thing, or an animal, or a slave incapable of playing a human role, that is, of conceiving goals and policies of my own and realising them.

Both the idea of a free will and the free individual are rather complex constructs comprising various dimensions of individuals and their particular context. These dimensions include (1) the existential (being, self-mastery, physical health, and capabilities), (2) the psychological (mental health, feelings, personality traits, and personal and social identity), (3) the cognitive (knowledge, intellect, and competences), (4) the moral (values and moral development), (5) the legal (constitution, laws, rules and regulations, and rights), (6) the political (political system, parties, political programmes and policies, and public affairs), (7) the social (institutions, norms, civil society, and the media), and (8) the economic (infrastructure, resources, business, and the economy).

All of these dimensions, conditions, and aspects are relevant and play some role in the freedom (or lack of freedom) of individuals. In regard to (entering, maintaining, or exiting) binding agreements and the establishment of organisations, it is especially individuals' specific rights and responsibilities that define their freedom.

People's immediate rights and responsibilities are specified and reflected in a social system's *constitutional foundations*. The constitutional foundations of an organisation are the first principles, conceptual ideas, and concrete terms of how the organisation is designed and functions. They often come in the form of a written legal agreement or contract, but there can also be 'implicit' elements (such as underlying (shared) worldviews, values, or propositions of the contracting parties). It is worth considering an organisation's constitutional foundations because the way it is fundamentally conceptualised influences to a great extent its purpose(s), its actual governance and management, how people (its members) relate to each other, and how the organisation as a whole functions internally and operates within its environment.

This chapter is about the constitutional foundations of the *democratic* organisation. It specifically focuses on individuals' fundamental right of *self-ownership* and the inalienable rights associated with it as well as the idea of *private ownership* and property rights. Together, self-ownership and private ownership suggest a particular form of contract (the *partnership agreement*) and a particular type of organisation (the *democratic organisation*) where all members are owners with equal rights and responsibilities.

Self-Ownership and Inalienable Rights

The rights and responsibilities of free individuals are encapsulated in the fundamental idea of *self-ownership*. The idea of self-ownership is one of the cornerstones of libertarian thinking and goes back to John Locke's (1632–1704) famous proviso put forward 1689 in his *Second Treatise* (Locke 1689/1998, p. 123).[4] It begins: 'Every man has a property in his own person. This nobody has any right to but himself.' 'To own oneself' is one of the fundamental ideas of the concept of the free individual, a principle shared by proponents of left-libertarianism (e.g. Gerald Allan Cohen, Michael Otsuka, Hillel Steiner, Peter Vallentyne, and Phillippe Van Parjies) *as well as* right-libertarianism (e.g. Milton Friedman, Friedrich Hayek, and Robert Nozick).[5] Self-ownership clarifies that it is the individual that is the owner of themselves – and no one else! Being free means that *everyone is their own master only* (Pateman 1970, p. 26).

Self-ownership means that individuals have certain fundamental *rights* in themselves simply because they are humans, or individuals.[6] According to such an understanding, the individual, first and foremost, owns themselves, i.e. they basically own all that biologically belongs to the individual and what constitutes human beings as individuals or persons. This is, the individual owns their body and mind. 'Body' means all the tangible parts of a human being, whereas 'mind' means the whole range of intangible essentials that define humans, or their being and existence as humans: an individual's personality and individuality as well as the mental (cognitive, psychological, emotional, and intellectual) competencies and ability to feel, think, make decisions, behave, act purposely, and bear responsibility for their actions or inactions.

Concerning every single aspect of their mind, heart, and soul, the individual has sole rights (of self-ownership). Crucially, these rights are *inalienable*, i.e. they are rights that cannot be transferred even if one wanted to (Ellerman 1992). Inalienable rights cannot be taken away from an individual because they are *essential* criteria that define and constitute the individual. People *cannot* give away or sell their mind, heart, or soul (only metaphorically or in fiction can they lose their heart or sell their soul). Hence, self-ownership is justified by an existential, non-consequentialist argument; humans have natural/inalienable rights in themselves (i.e. their heart, mind, soul, competencies, and capabilities) because this is what constitutes them as humans. People cannot transfer or be without those rights in themselves because otherwise they would cease to exist as humans – as individuals. That they can neither transfer those rights to someone else nor leave them 'at the front door' when they join and enter an organisation means that every institution and organisation that respects individuals as individuals *must* acknowledge their inalienable rights of and to self-ownership – and the institutions or organisations must be designed and maintained accordingly.

Private Ownership and Property Rights

Evidently, the individual owns itself (and is not owned or rented by anyone else) and has natural and inalienable rights to itself. But how about *things* (whether tangible or material things, or intangible things such as property rights, legal titles, or an organisation as a legal entity) – the *right of ownership* of things? Traditionally, libertarians especially, such as classical philosophers of the Enlightenment including Locke and the French philosopher Jean-Jacques Rousseau (1712–1778), established and justified the right of ownership ('private property') as a natural right (Mack 2010). The right of ownership – beside life and liberty (which could be seen as the right of self-ownership) – was seen as one of the fundamental rights that cannot be surrendered in the social contract (e.g. Boaz 1998, Reno 2009, Kekes 2010). In his *Discourse on the Origin of Inequality* (1755), Rousseau (cited in Kramnick 1995, p. 424) stated apodictically that 'to be possible for each to have something' was the first rule of justice. And the libertarian and socialist political economist Thomas Hodgskin (1787–1869) made an important distinction between 'natural' and 'artificial' property rights whereby the former is defined as:

> the right of individuals, to have and to own, for their own separate and selfish use and enjoyment, the produce of their own industry, with power freely to dispose of the whole of that in the manner most agreeable to themselves, as essential to the welfare and even to the continued existence of society. (cited in Carson 2008, p. 412)

However, ownership of *things* (private ownership) is *not* a natural (i.e. inalienable) right of individuals like the ownership of *oneself* (self-ownership). Tangible or intangible identifiable things *can* be transferred and people *can* live and work without *owing* things (e.g. in a collectivist society, organisation, or group without private ownership, when they work for others as employees or they rent or lease property). Members of a social system can agree upon and decide whether private ownership of things and property rights exists as a legal fiction – but they cannot decide whether self-ownership and the related inalienable rights of individuals in themselves exist and matter. The inalienable rights of individuals *always* exist and matter, even in situations or contexts where they are ignored. Nevertheless, there are at least two arguments for seeing private ownership of things as a fundamental right of free individuals: a consequentialist one and a non-consequentialist one.

The consequentialist argument draws attention to the fact that private ownership of things (and the possession of the related property rights; see the list on p. 42) obviously makes a *big* difference for people if and when ownership matters – for their social status; their self-image and the image others hold of them; their identity and dignity; their material, psychological, and social well-being; their motivation and performance; and their opportunities and personal development. Concerning *all* of these aspects, individuals *with* private ownership in general fare considerably and decisively better than individuals *without* ownership. People who own the things they need for their daily life and who own the means for their work (be it physical tools, materials, machinery, land, property, capital, legal titles, or entities such as organisations) are in a much better position than people who do not have or do not own those means. Private ownership makes a *fundamental, existential* difference for people.

It should be noted that the statement that private ownership of things (and possession of the related property rights) is good for people is conditional, i.e. the statement is only valid in regard to situations or social systems where private ownership matters. This means that individuals, or groups of people, can either individually or collectively decide that no property rights whatsoever (shall) play a role. For example, there are religious, spiritual or political concepts suggesting that it actually is better for people *not* to have private ownership of things, i.e. to live without, or minimal, material possessions ("worldly goods" or "worldly possessions") in order to find inner peace, harmony, enlightenment and freedom, or to establish a "better" society. In this sense, people do *not have to* own things if they don't want to – and this might be good for those people and they (may) find what they were searching for *because* of abstaining from (almost) all material things and possessions (the crucial condition in such cases, though, is that *all* individuals involved have decided *freely* and *consciously* that ownership (rights) do not exist and do not matter and that *all* individuals involved also follow and practise this maxim).

In a similar vein, the right of private ownership of things does not mean or suggest that people have to have (more and more) things. In this sense, making the case for private ownership and property as *rights* of people (and making the case that these rights make people more free when ownership matters) does not mean making the case for *consumerism*, i.e. the idea – or marketing ideology – that people can find happiness, develop themselves, and become free (only) by buying and possessing certain products or services, especially by buying and owning more and more stuff (that they do not need).

Thus, the statement that private ownership of things (and related property rights) is good for people is meant only as a qualified statement about a fundamental right or entitlement in regard to situations where individuals engage in economic, social, or private activities where they (have to) use tangible or intangible things *and* where private ownership and property rights (explicitly or implicitly) *matter*, i.e. where private ownership and property rights are not excluded (by voluntary consent of everyone involved).

Besides this consequentialist argument for private ownership of things (its factual advantages and what it means for people), there is also a non-consequentialist argument. Private ownership implies a whole range of rights – *property rights*. Property rights based on private ownership are some of the most comprehensive, robust, and strongest rights one can find in private law (particularly in contract law, property law, business law, and succession law). They comprise (Honoré 1961, Arnold 1994, p. 44, Christman 1994, p. 227, Ingram 1994, p. 30, Learmount & Roberts 2006, p. 146):[7]

1. the right to possess a thing, i.e. the right to exclusive physical control and non-interference;
2. the right to use the thing owned for personal purposes and enjoyment;
3. the right to manage the thing owned, i.e. the right to decide who can use the thing and for which purpose(s);
4. the right to any income from the thing owned when it is used;
5. the right to the capital value of the thing;
6. the right to security, i.e. immunity from expropriation or use without permission by others;
7. the right and power to transfer the thing to others by sale, as a gift, or as a bequest;
8. the absence of any term (i.e. temporal limitation) on the possession of any of these rights, liberties, etc.;
9. a prohibition on harmful use, i.e. a duty to refrain from using the thing in a way that harms others or violates the rights of others;
10. liability to execution, i.e. liability to judgement debt, insolvency, and/or taxation; and
11. residuary character, i.e. when the thing is held by others, the right to the residue, which means the return of all rights when the others' term is up or they forfeit it for any reason.

Only private ownership provides these rights. These property rights establish, guarantee, and protect the interests of free individuals in regard to material and immaterial things as well as in regard to others (persons or institutional actors). For example, Arnold (1994, p. 44) observed that 'it is primarily through these incidents of ownership that private individuals control the means of production to further their private interests'.

In a situation or context where ownership and property rights matter, individuals *must* own (individually or collectively) what they use in order to conduct their life and work, since without such rights (the full range of property rights) individuals are not entitled to make decisions about those things and, thus, they are not (entirely) free and sovereign. In this sense it can be stated that in a situation or context where ownership matters, property rights make individuals free. Hence, when it comes to conducting one's life or work (i.e.

conducting private, social, or economic activities for which things are used), it is paramount for individuals to be in possession of the relevant property rights for those things (i.e. to own those things). Therefore, besides *self*-ownership, there must also be *private* ownership of things. Or, to put it slightly differently: for free individuals, *self*-ownership constitutes *private* ownership. Self-ownership *of* everyone constitutes private ownership *for* everyone.

Furthermore, this suggests that the formal and legal relationships of individuals in and with a formal entity (e.g. an organisation or nation-state) must be consistent with their right of self-ownership and the inalienable rights stemming from it as well as their right of ownership and property rights. In a social system, such as an organisation, individuals must have a legal status that provides these ownership and property rights. Therefore, *all* founders and members of an organisation that appreciates individuals' freedom and inalienable rights of self-ownership must have *legal ownership of the organisation*.[8] They must own the organisation and its assets, *especially* when they work for it.

The Partnership Agreement and the Democratic Organisation

So far it has been established that free individuals have inalienable rights stemming from their *self-ownership* (i.e. their right to their cognitive, psychological, emotional, and intellectual competencies and ability to feel, think, make decisions, behave, act purposely, and bear responsibility for their actions or inactions) *and* they (ought to) have property rights stemming from the concept of *private ownership* (i.e. the right to possess, use, manage, or transfer things they own, and the right to the income from, capital value of, and residue of the things they own).

This raises the question of what kind of formal or contractual agreement free individuals can – or must – reach when they want to organise themselves or their activities in a formal social system (such as a social relationship, continuous economic exchange, cooperative, organisation, private institution, or nation-state) so that the agreement is in line with, and simultaneously accommodates, their rights of self-ownership and private ownership. Such an agreement must meet the following criteria:

1. *All* individuals involved in establishing the formally agreed organisation and who become its members *must* have *equal* legal and formal status and *must* have *equal* rights and responsibilities.
2. In order to have *equal* rights and responsibilities, *all* founders and members of the organisation *must* be its (individual and collective) *owners* since otherwise they could not have and enjoy the same whole range of inalienable rights of self-ownership and private ownership.
3. So that all owners of the organisation can make full use of and enact their rights and responsibilities, they also need to manage and work for it. Hence,

each member of the organisation is simultaneously owner, manager, and employee.

4. Since all members of the organisation make use of their rights simultaneously, they own, manage, and control the organisation they work for *together*, i.e. individually *and* collectively. In this sense, they are *all* (legal, formal, and organisational) *partners*.

The legal and contractual form that best meets these criteria is a *partnership agreement*.[9] The basic notion of a partnership agreement is that everyone who works individually or jointly with others in a formalised way individually and collectively owns, manages, and controls the properties, activities, and results of this enterprise and has the same rights and responsibilities. A partnership agreement specifies at least the following aspects (NI Direct 2015):

- monetary and non-monetary contributions to the partnership;
- shares and distribution of profits (and losses), deposits, and withdrawals;
- the partners' rights, responsibilities, authorities, management duties, means of participation in the governance and management of the enterprise, and role in collective decision-making;
- labour rights, such as regular remuneration, a minimum wage, contributions to national social insurance, working hours, rest breaks, health and safety standards, paid annual leave, pension entitlements, labour protection rights (in particular the right not to be unfairly dismissed or discriminated against unlawfully), legal redundancy pay, statutory sick pay, and maternity, paternity, and adoption leave and pay;
- entrance and exit of partners; and
- dispute resolution.

There is quite some leeway around the design of these issues and the specific terms of a partnership agreement, but the *fundamental* notion is clear: it is about *free* people cooperating and engaging with others via a binding partnership agreement on the basis of self-ownership and private ownership (and the inalienable rights and property rights related to these), and these people have *equal* legal and formal status, rights, and responsibilities as partners. Only in such a partnership agreement of equal and joint individual and collective rights and responsibilities can individuals' inalienable rights of self-ownership and private ownership be appreciated and preserved.

Such a partnership agreement also acknowledges and confirms that partners working for the common enterprise have – besides their status as owners and managers – employment status (and therefore enjoy all the associated labour rights) in the sense that their work is fully integrated into the business (Weir 2003, pp. 450–451, Turner 2013, pp. 83–95, NI Direct 2015, Employment Rights Act 1996 2019). But they are *not* regarded as employees in the sense of working for someone else, being told what to do and directed by another person, and being subject to detailed control by that person; partners work *with* others, not *for* others! Thus, such a partnership agreement relating to formally organised cooperation between free individuals overcomes the division between owners of capital and labour and between employer and employees (Fournier 2002, p. 203), and guarantees all members their equal and inalienable rights and responsibilities.

This *collaboration of equals* established by a partnership agreement is *democracy* realised and practised in the economic and social sphere. *Demos kratos* – power or government of the people, by the people, for the people – is the logical foundation and continuation of the idea of free individuals cooperating with each other voluntarily in formal and institutionalised ways on the basis of and via a partnership agreement (or social contract). It is the *only* form of agreement (as well as of government and governance) that accommodates free individuals and their inalienable rights. In this sense, the great political theorist Robert Dahl (1985, pp. 56–57) concluded that 'the process of government should as far as possible meet democratic criteria, because people involved in this kind of association possess a *right*, an inalienable right to govern themselves by the democratic process'. It is the inalienable right of people – stemming from their status as free individuals and their self-ownership – to govern and rule themselves collectively and democratically (Cohen 1998, p. 185, Bevir 2006, p. 430, Canovan 2008, p. 353, Wright 2010, p. 180).

The idea of free people working together on the basis of a legitimate agreement such as a partnership agreement suggests, and even necessitates, a certain type of organisation: a jointly owned and controlled enterprise (Ellerman 1992, Schweickart 1993, p. 289, Howard 2003, p. 175) – in short, a *democratic* organisation. The *democratic organisation* is the legal, formal, and organisational institutionalisation and realisation of regular joint work and cooperation of free individuals based on the principles of self-ownership, private ownership, and a legally binding agreement (partnership agreement) that appreciates and protects the inalienable equal rights and responsibilities of all members of the organisation. Any organisation formally established and maintained by free individuals *must* be a democratic organisation since this is the *only* type of organisation that appreciates, enables, guarantees, accommodates, protects, and promotes the status, inalienable rights, and responsibilities of free individuals.

Together, the notions and concepts of (1) free individuals and self-ownership (and people's inalienable rights related to it), (2) private ownership (and property rights related to it), and (3) a partnership agreement providing all parties with the equal legal and formal status of partners and equal rights and responsibilities are the libertarian constitution of the democratic organisation. The whole argument about the constitutional foundations of the democratic organisation can be summarised as shown in Table 2.1.

TABLE 2.1 The libertarian constitution of the democratic organisation

---

Self-Ownership and Inalienable Rights

1. Social systems, such as organisations, are established and function on the basis of, and represent, (explicit and/or implicit) *contractual and social relations* between individuals.
2. The creation and maintenance of legitimate contractual and social relations necessitate *free will*. Only if individuals (are able to) express and exercise *their own free will* are binding agreements, social relationships, and other interactions (such as economic transactions or cooperation) voluntary and legitimate.
3. The individual is the owner of themselves (*self-ownership*) – and no one else! Everyone owns themselves, i.e. the whole range of essentials of their own personal existence: their personality and individuality; their mind, body, and soul; and the mental (cognitive, psychological, and emotional) and bodily competencies and ability to feel, think, make decisions, behave, act purposely, and bear responsibility for their actions or inactions.
4. The rights covered by one's self-ownership (i.e. one's personality and individuality; mind, body, and soul; and competencies and capabilities) are *inalienable* rights and *cannot* be transferred.
5. Every institution and organisation that respects individuals as individuals must explicitly acknowledge their inalienable right of and to self-ownership.

Private Ownership and Property Rights

6. Free individuals must own (individually or collectively) what they need and use to conduct their work and lives (*private ownership*).
7. The legal or formal relationship of an individual to a legal entity (such as an organisation or nation-state) must be consistent with their right of self-ownership and the inalienable rights stemming from it as well as private ownership and the property rights related to it.
8. In order to accommodate the notions of free individuals' self-ownership and private ownership, *all* individuals involved in the establishment of a formally agreed social system (such as a social relationship, economic exchange, cooperative organisation, private institution, or nation-state) *must* be of *equal* legal and formal status and must have *equal* rights and responsibilities.
9. *All* founders and members of an organisation that appreciates individuals' inalienable rights of self-ownership must have *legal ownership* of the organisation and the whole range of property rights, i.e. they must be its (individual and collective) owners.

The Partnership Agreement and the Democratic Organisation

10. Everyone who works individually or jointly with others in a formalised way individually and collectively owns, manages, and controls the properties, activities, and results of this joint enterprise.
11. People who own, manage, and control an enterprise together are *partners*.
12. The most appropriate legal form to constitute the collaboration of free individuals in an organisation is the *partnership agreement*.

(*Continued*)

TABLE 2.1 (Cont).

13. The democratic organisation is the legal, formal, and organisational institutionalisation and realisation of regular joint work and cooperation of free individuals based on the principles of self-ownership, private ownership, and a legally binding agreement (partnership agreement) that specifies the inalienable equal rights and responsibilities of all members of the organisation.

14. Any organisation formally established and run by free individuals *must* be a democratic organisation since this is the *only* type of organisation that enables, guarantees, accommodates, protects, and promotes the status, inalienable rights, and responsibilities of free individuals.

With such constitutional foundations, the democratic organisation provides the broadest possible range of equal rights for *all* its members. Later on in this book it will become clear that this libertarian notion is crucial for the design and functioning of the democratic organisation, its members, and their status, relationships, and behaviour; in a social system, a libertarian constitution suggests *democratic* governance and *democratic* management, equal rights and equal (social and political) power, and empowerment of all members of the social system as well as a particular considerate conduct of business *by necessity*.

Although the libertarian constitution is a particular approach to constituting the democratic organisation, it nonetheless is based on relatively general principles and assumptions that are of *universal* value and relevance (e.g. the notions of individual freedom(s) and free individuals, private property, equal rights and responsibilities, and democracy and democratic arrangements). It is therefore relatively open to, and compatible with, any approach, theory, or model of social system that explicitly or implicitly promotes, or at least tolerates, these universal principles.

It should also be clear that the model or notion of the democratic organisation is not confined to one particular form or type of organisation. As indicated in Chapter 1, many types of organisation can be established, organised, managed, and maintained as democratic organisations, for example cooperatives, professional partnerships, associations, worker-managed enterprises, employee-owned companies, community-based enterprises and community-based organisations, social enterprises, not-for-profit or non-profit organisations, non-governmental organisations, formally established networks of self-employed freelancers or contract workers – or any other type of organisation that is compatible with, and adheres to, the principles and the spirit of the democratic organisation.[10] The following chapters show how the democratic organisation can be designed, maintained, and function so that it stays true to its principles and idea(l)s.

Notes

1 Although I generally refer to 'individuals' who enter into binding agreements, it would be more accurate to say 'legally entitled individuals with full mental capacity', since in all cultures and societies there are some exceptions and limitations to the status and free will of individuals. For example, minors; cognitively, psychologically, or emotionally severely immature or limited people; temporarily intoxicated, distressed, or otherwise incapacitated people; and people with diminished capacity because of underlying medical conditions or severe illness often are limited in their legal status and in making (legally binding) decisions, i.e. in expressing their free will. But the argument developed here is about individuals in a very general sense and it therefore is not necessary to make further differentiations within the text.

2 The notion of individual free will is well established and protected as a philosophical, moral, and legal fiction by various philosophical concepts and the notion of human rights, as well as by constitutions, the law, and institutions of (fully fledged) democratic societies. The idea of people having – or that they ought to have! – free will has been deeply embedded in philosophical and legal theorising throughout the ages. It can be traced back to ancient Greek and Roman philosophers (e.g. Socrates and Seneca), leading thinkers of the Enlightenment (e.g. John Locke, Voltaire, Jean-Jacques Rousseau, and Immanuel Kant), early socialists (e.g. Pierre-Joseph Proudhon), classical economists (e.g. Adam Smith and John Stuart Mill), and neo-liberal economists (e.g. Milton Friedman).

3 This is also evidenced by the fact that contracts usually are deemed to be not only illegitimate but also null and void or even illegal when the free will of one or both parties was missing or severely hampered when the contract was signed – e.g. because of deception, duress, undue influence, coercion, or lack of explicit or implicit consent.

4 It can be traced back even further, at least to the English Leveller (freedom fighter) Richard Overton (d. 1664). In two pamphlets published in 1646 and 1647, Overton put forward the idea of 'self-propriety', i.e. that every individual owns themselves and has certain inalienable rights (Mill 1859/1998, pp. 121–122 and Watner 1980, pp. 410–411, who provide some key quotes from those pamphlets). Nonetheless, usually Locke's proviso is considered the starting point and point of reference for libertarian reasoning.

5 Though the two strands differ considerably in how strongly self-ownership should be understood and how it relates to other principles such as equality, fairness, and (distributive) justice (Fried 2004, p. 67, Arneson 2010, pp. 171, 182–183, Russell 2010, p. 138).

6 The term 'ownership' should not be understood as a mere legal or economic term but in a much broader sense. For instance, Otsuka (2003, p. 15, footnote 14) suggested that if 'property in persons' or 'self-ownership' sound too 'commercial', these terms can be replaced with 'rights'.

7 This categorisation of property rights is based on the article 'Ownership' by the British lawyer and jurist A. M. Honoré (1961). According to Fried (2004, p. 72), the first modern categorisation of property rights can be traced back even further to the works of the American jurist Wesley Hohfeld, who differentiated various types of property rights in two articles in 1913 and 1917: 'Some Fundamental Legal Conceptions as Applied in Judicial Reasoning' (1913) and 'Fundamental Legal Conceptions as Applied in Judicial Reasoning' (1917).

8 For example, Empson and Chapman (2006, p. 144) argued in the same vein: 'A property rights perspective emphasises that when key income-generating assets are proprietary to individuals, they should share jointly in the ownership of the firm and participate directly in decision-making ... This decision-making authority

should extend far beyond the basic control of operational issues to include fundamental strategic issues.'

9 It is (very) important to note that proposing a partnership agreement as the contractual
basis for the democratic organisation does not mean that only (the legal entity of)
partnerships are deemed as a suitable type of democratic organisation. A partnership
agreement as described or referred to here is meant only in its most general meaning
and as an exemplary form of contract that is capable to provide the contractual basis for
a whole range of different types of democratic organisations as listed in Table 1.1 on
p. 18.

10 Chapter 9 ('Legitimate and Illegitimate Organisations') comprehensively and systematically discusses which types of organisation are illegal, illegitimate, tolerable,
consistent, and inconsistent with the fundamental principles and values of freedom
and democracy.

3
DEMOCRATIC GOVERNANCE

Governance: Democratic Governance

Having looked first at the constitutional foundations of the democratic organisation (its libertarian constitution), the focus can now shift towards its design: the structures and processes of its functioning.

Every system functions according to *rules* to some degree.[1] To some extent, rules constitute, shape, enable, and regulate the system, its functioning, and the behaviour of its members. In a social system, these rules can emerge unintended via routine behaviour and the daily actions and interactions of the members of the system. They can also be created and crafted deliberately by (some) members and/or formally drafted and institutionalised via formal institutions and procedures. This whole framework of rules and relevant institutions and their workings can be subsumed under the term *governance*.

Because of its functions, governance is of fundamental importance to a social system – especially when it is a formally established and institutionalised social system like an organisation.[2] There have been times when scholars have written about and practitioners have attempted to implement organisations, networks, economies, or whole societies and nation-states with as few (explicit) rules or governance as possible (Rothschild & Whitt 1986, Marshall 1993, Fenton 2002, Chartier & Johnson 2012). Such a notion might make sense and might work to some extent – for instance, in order to avoid or counterbalance overtly bureaucratic systems and/or to provide members of the system with the necessary space to make use of their freedom and creative potential. There definitely can be 'too much' and/or 'bad' governance (e.g. bureaucracy or totalitarian regimes).

Nonetheless, no social system can do without governance; if there were no or little formal or explicit principles and regulations, then there surely would be informal or implicit ones – and probably worse than formal ones (e.g. the proverbial 'law of the jungle'). It therefore is paramount for every formal social system that its governance (including its institutions and workings) are designed and maintained as explicitly and as considerately as possible.

Based on various definitions (Boyte 2005, p. 536, Bevir 2013, Jessop 2013, Levi-Faur 2014, pp. 8–9, Schneider 2014, p. 130, and Weiss 2000, p. 797, the last of whom who provided a whole collection of definitions from multiple international agencies), governance might be defined as follows: *governance* means that *institutions* or *actors* (e.g. government, governmental agencies, public regulators, assemblies, councils, associations, civil society organisations, citizens, audit firms, owners, boards, or committees) *govern* (i.e. steer, regulate, and control) particular entities (i.e. an entire social system, parts of it, or phenomena within it) on the basis of and according to *authoritative sources* (i.e. a set of formal principles, norms, laws, policies, rules, regulations, guidelines, codes of conduct, procedures, and administrative practices along with a constitution) whereby the *conduct of governance* may be seen, assessed, and judged against the criteria of 'good governance'.

The various elements of this definition – the key elements of governance (i.e. institutions of governance, authoritative sources, governing, and 'good governance') – will be addressed and discussed in turn in the following sections with regard to the governance of the democratic organisation.

Governance is about *governing particular entities*. These entities can be a whole social system (e.g. a group of people, a community, an organisation, a network, markets, industry, an economy, a society, a nation-state, a region, or multinational or global entities), parts of a social system, certain members of a social system, or certain phenomena or issues (e.g. legal, political, social, economic, environmental, or technical issues, common affairs, or collective goods). To govern means to set and to observe rules and standards; to steer or regulate the entity, phenomenon, or issue; to provide guidance; to shape, supervise, and control preferences, choices, and behaviour of members of the entity; and to provide feedback, incentives, awards, sanctions, and punishment. These activities are done systematically and regularly. Because of its systematic and regular workings, governance results in (or at least contributes considerably to) the emergence and continuation of legal, political, administrative, and social order.

Any particular governance framework must fit the social system it governs (and is part of) in order to be, and to be perceived as, legitimate and effective. If a social system is a democracy then it needs *democratic* governance *by necessity*. This means that the democratic organisation *must* also have *democratic* governance in place, i.e. a comprehensive and robust set of formal institutions and practices that define and outline how the organisation as a whole as well as in its parts is designed, maintained, and functions according to democratic principles.

This chapter therefore looks at *democratic governance* – how it is designed and how it functions for organisations. First, the organisational institutions of governance are described – the *democratic institutions of governance* an organisation needs to have in order to be democratic. The discussion especially focuses on two features or principles: separation of powers and 'checks and balances', and subsidiarity. The following sections then identify *legitimate authoritative sources* on which any governance must be built, and how *democratic governing* (democratic decision-making based on transparency and accountability) can happen. Next, the notion of 'good governance' is introduced and it is argued that (only) democratic governance is 'good governance'. The concluding section of this chapter then provides an overview and summary of the complete concept and virtuous circle of democratic governance. It is shown how all these elements and principles of governance together lay the foundations for *democratic governance*, and how democratic governance can be designed for, and conducted in, the democratic organisation.

Democratic Institutions of Governance

Organisational Institutions of Governance

Governance is provided by certain *institutions* or *actors*. These institutions or actors can be public authorities (e.g. government, governmental agencies, public regulators, or national, regional or local assemblies), private organisations (e.g. associations, civil society organisations, or audit firms), individual actors (e.g. citizens), or institutions within organisations (e.g. boards, committees, councils, or assemblies). Institutions of governance must fit the system(s) they will govern, i.e. they must be based on, and function according to, the very same principles they are designed to realise and to protect. *Democratic* social systems necessitate *democratic* institutions of governance. Accordingly, a *democratic* organisation's institutions of governance *must* be themselves *democratic* institutions – i.e. their structures, their composition, and the way(s) they work and function must be democratic.

(Larger) democratic organisations have organisational institutions of governance such as boards, committees, councils, or assemblies.[3] In order for these governing bodies to be democratic, they must fulfil the following formal conditions (Ostergaard & Halsey 1965, p. 26, Srivastva & Cooperrider 1986, pp. 707–708, Weisskopf 1993, pp. 6–7, Ackoff 1994, p. 118, Bowman & Stone 2004, p. 275, Upchurch et al. 2014, p. 49):

- They must be democratically established and controlled by all members of the democratic organisation on the basis of legitimate authoritative sources.
- All members of these organisational institutions of democratic governance must be elected by the members of the democratic organisation.

- Diverse membership in these organisational institutions should be achieved via *democratic competition* (also called 'competitive democracy'), i.e. different candidates or groups should openly compete to be elected or appointed to the formal positions.
- Elections or appointments to these institutions must be free, transparent, competitive, democratic, regular, and frequent.
- There must be institutional safeguards in place to directly limit the power, responsibilities, and authority of offices and office-holders, such as regular turnovers in office, role rotation, limitations to the length and number of terms in office, and limitations on the number of board and committee memberships a person can hold.
- In the organisational institutions of democratic governance, it must be possible for any issue to be addressed, discussed, deliberated, and decided upon according to democratic rules, standards, and procedures.

Measures such as the ones listed above are necessary in order to make and to keep organisational institutions of governance as democratic as possible. The organisational institutions of governance of the democratic organisation are fairly similar to some of the institutions of governance of a *fully fledged* and *fully functioning* democratic state.[4] As democratic institutions, these governing bodies add another truly democratic element to the democratic organisation (Lipset 1952/2010).

And they work. Actually, they work pretty well – also and especially within and for organisations:

- In his classic investigation of the U.S.-based International Typographical Union, Lipset (1952/2010, pp. 9–14) identified several internal structures that prevented and counterbalanced tendencies of oligarchisation: there was significant membership participation and referenda were often held (p. 10); there were permanent, vigilant, and active opposition groups; there were frequent secret elections of senior officials and administrators; and there were regular and frequent turnovers in office.
- Ostergaard and Halsey (1965, p. 26) found political (management and membership) committees and an elected representative assembly to be useful institutions for 'stimulating membership participation and increasing the effectiveness of democratic control'.
- In regard to the widely known (and researched) Mondragón cooperative (actually, a network of hundreds of cooperatives mainly in northern Spain), Bowman and Stone (2004, p. 275) found that 'democracy is central and turns on membership. Ultimate control of production, income spread, and board seats [are decided by] the yearly general assembly. It elects the board of directors (*consejo rectoral*) which appoints management. The assembly elects a watchdog council (*consejo de vigilancia*) to monitor management and a social council (*consejo social*).'

- While analysing the institutions of economic democracy, Malleson (2013, p. 99) found that:

> The co-ops that are the most successful at maintaining vibrant egalitarian democratic practices are ones that are successful at building three things: a structure of parliamentarian democracy, a structure of participatory democracy, and a culture of participation. The co-ops that are the most successful at maintaining overarching parliamentarian structures of democracy (general assemblies operating on the basis of one person, one vote; transparency; availability of information; and so on) are the ones that develop mechanisms for maintaining healthy democratic competition in order to prevent the same clique from winning election after election. As in political democracy, workplace democracy works best with active internal opposition (a 'loyal opposition') so that dissatisfied people can form different groups and organize different platforms to ensure new ideas are heard and new leaders enter into management.

Hence, not only are there good theoretical and conceptual reasons and arguments but there is also compelling empirical evidence for having *democratic* institutions of governance in the democratic organisation, in *any* organisation.

Nevertheless, it is not only important that each and every institution of governance is democratic for and by itself but also that the various institutions of governance relate to each other in *democratic, heterarchical* ways. How this can be achieved in the democratic organisation is shown in the next two sub-sections, which focus on two tried-and-tested concepts: *separation of powers*, which provides horizontal balance and control between institutions, and *subsidiarity*, which provides vertical balance and control.

Separation of Powers and 'Checks and Balances'

To institutionalise governance (actually, *any* institutionalisation) is to institutionalise *power* (Lukes 1974) – the power to make decisions that are relevant to others; formulate principles, norms, and values; create laws, rules, regulations, policies, and sanctions; enforce the law and control compliance; and praise and punish. However, a single institution of governance holding all of these powers would be an uncontrolled monopoly on power, a totalitarian regime – which, obviously, would be incompatible with the notion of the democratic organisation (or any democratic system). The solution is various institutions of governance responsible only for certain parts of governance and, thus, *separation of powers*.

Separation of powers (*trias politica*) is an idea from political theory about keeping the three branches of a nation-state (legislative, executive, and judicial) separate and independent of each other so as to ensure good governance (Sud & VanSandt 2011, p. 136). The political economist Vincent Ostrom argued in his *The Political Theory of a Compound Republic* (1971/1987) that the concept of separation of powers is a *necessary* element of any system of democratic governance and self-governance. Fairtlough (2005, pp. 28–29) drew attention to the fact that the separation of powers is a type of heterarchy – i.e. a relation between elements of a system where none is dominant (like the children's game of rock, paper scissors). In this sense, separation of powers is a very efficient instrument that can limit (the use of) power as well as reduce the possibility of abuse of power (Ostrom 1971/1987, p. 85, Epstein 1987/1998, pp. 44–47, Fairtlough 2005, p. 67, Sauser 2009, p. 157, Sud & VanSandt 2011, p. 136, Lynn 2014, p. 26).

What works for the nation-state also works for organisations; organisations' institutions of governance should also be designed and function *heterarchically*, i.e. according to the principle of separation of powers. The fundamental idea is that no single unit (e.g. board of directors) or position (e.g. 'the owner' or CEO) in the organisation should ever have, or gain, a monopoly on power, influence, or decision-making.[5] Instead, to apply the principle of separation of powers to (democratic) organisations would mean having *multiple* boards (of directors and other representatives) or committees that are responsible for different areas of governance. For example, one board (the executive) manages the organisation and its daily affairs, and runs the business; another board (the judiciary) oversees and controls the organisation and the executive; and a third board (the legislative) is responsible for drafting authoritative sources such as the constitutional partnership agreement, policies, rules, and regulations. All of these – and other boards, (general) assemblies, and committees –need to be fully functioning on a permanent and regular basis, provided with the necessary resources and far-reaching powers according to the democratic organisation's constitution, and held accountable by all members of the organisation (the owners) on a regular basis. Having multiple (well-designed and well-functioning) institutions of governance in the organisation that focus on different areas and functions of governance contributes considerably to the democratic foundations of the organisation.

The various democratic institutions of governance are not only designed and maintained in order to function efficiently and effectively on their own but also, and crucially, to *check and balance* each other. In his *The Spirit of Laws*, the French philosopher Montesquieu (1689–1755) (1748, quoted in Carter et al. 2007, p. 94) pinned down the main rationale of *checks and balances*: 'So that one cannot abuse power, power must check power.' And Dahl (1985, p. 8) explicitly (and quite rightly) stated that 'a necessary condition for liberty is the existence of strong barriers to the exercise of power'. Checks and balances constitute a particularly strong institutional principle that contributes to restricting power by enabling and encouraging institutions of governance to mutually control and limit each other (Casella & Frey 1992, p. 641). All advanced and fully fledged democracies without exception are built and rely strongly on checks and balances between, but also within, the three branches of government. In the case of the democratic organisation, this would mean that all organisational institutions of governance are constitutionally authorised – even obliged and factually enabled – to control (check, balance, hold accountable, and sanction) other organisational institutions.

Altogether, within any formalised democratic social system, such as the democratic organisation, *powers must be separated (separation of powers) and mutually control each other (checks and balances)* so that: (1) no formal position of authority or organisational institution has a monopoly on power; (2) no power is concentrated in the hands of individuals (autocracy), groups of people (oligarchy), or particular units; and (3) sufficient institutional safeguards are in place to limit the power and authority of those in office and with power.

Subsidiarity

Separation of powers and checks and balances confine power *horizontally*. But there is also a principle and concept that balances power *vertically* – the principle of *subsidiarity*. This principle suggests that any task or function that *can* be performed at a lower level *should* be performed at the lowest possible level (Dahl 1970, p. 102, Eberly 2000, pp. 24–25, Wolff 2005, pp. 133–134). For example, Hirst (1994, p. 32) explained the concept of subsidiarity in regard to the state:

> First, [it is important] that each level of authority or administration performs only such functions as are absolutely necessary to it, and that its powers of jurisdiction not exceed those functions. Central state institutions would exist solely for certain particular purposes and would have no general power of legislation over or intervention in, the affairs of 'lesser' authorities. Those lesser territorial or functional bodies would not exist by its *fiat* alone and would enjoy autonomy in performing their own specific functions.

Subsidiarity means that matters are governed and administered, that issues are addressed and solved (or attempts are made to solve them), where things happen and matter, or where the causes and consequences are relevant (i.e. in a local context or at operational levels in an organisation). This means that people 'on the ground' are entitled and empowered to make decisions and are responsible for taking action where they are, i.e. in their neighbourhood or in the workplace. In this sense, practising subsidiarity helps 'to make democratic governance locally more relevant, accountable and transparent, as well as more effective and efficient' (Nauclér 2005, p. 98).

The principle of subsidiarity can also be applied to organisations – *particularly* to organisations. It means that organisational institutions of governance should be located not (only) 'at the top' but also throughout and across the organisation; that they should be as open, inclusive, and participative as possible; and that formal decision-making should take place (also) at the lowest possible levels. Clearly, within an organisational context, the idea of *subsidiarity* is the direct opposite of the *chain of command* ('line management') principle, which claims that power (and key responsibilities and functions such as making decisions) should be allocated at the highest possible level, at the top, and communicated downwards. *Chain of command* is consistent with hierarchy, autocracy, oligarchy, and an authoritarian, top-down approach to leadership, decision-making, management, and control. In contrast, *subsidiarity* is consistent with heterarchy, democracy, and a participative, bottom-up approach to leadership, decision-making, management, and control. In this sense, subsidiarity is consistent not only with the fundamental idea of the democratic organisation but also with the ideas of free individuals, participation, and empowerment.

In sum, separation of powers is the means of horizontal checks and balances on power, whereas subsidiarity is the means of vertical checks and balances. For the democratic organisation, this means that its institutions of governance are all made as powerful as possible in order to conduct their constitutional tasks and responsibilities effectively, but at the same time their powers *are systematically limited by other institutions of governance and conferred to lower levels* so that they cannot overstep their legitimate authority or gain too much (or even absolute) power.

Legitimate Authoritative Sources

Governance – *any* governance – is based on *authoritative sources*. Authoritative sources can consist of formal principles, norms and values, a constitution, laws, rules and regulations, policies and procedures, guidelines, codes of conduct, or administrative practices. Such authoritative sources provide guidance and advice on how a system and its key parts should be designed, be maintained, and function; what is more and less preferable (or even 'good' and 'bad'); how issues will be handled; and how people should behave and act – what they should and should not do. Because of their fundamental importance and character, authoritative sources provide necessary and comprehensive guidelines for the design and workings of institutions of governance as well as the behaviour of people.

Usually, authoritative sources are explicit, carefully crafted, institutionalised, and protected. They are meant to last for some time (even when altered) and to be as comprehensive, detailed, and specific as possible. Nonetheless, even in the case of a very clear formulation, they often can be interpreted, construed, and applied in various quite different ways and their meaning(s) and way(s) of being applied and implemented can be contested.

Like any other formally institutionalised social system, the democratic organisation is based on various authoritative sources. For example, the democratic organisation is constituted and maintained on the basis of a formal, legally binding *partnership agreement* that itself is based on certain business, labour, and contract laws and regulations. A democratic organisation (of some size and age) might also have mission and vision statements, strategic and operational plans, policies, codes of conduct, principles of responsible management, and sustainable business, ethics, and compliance statements. Further authoritative sources may outline more specifically the various tasks, functions, rights, and responsibilities of governing bodies, units, and committees; specify formal positions; allocate power and resources; and specify decision-making mechanisms, responsibilities, and accountability within the democratic organisation.

All these authoritative sources bear meaning and relevance for the members of the organisation (as well as external stakeholders) and its governance – even if people do not know about them in detail or care about them. As official documents, they state and clarify what is relevant and not relevant, important and not important, expected and not expected, allowed and not allowed. They are used and referred to in order to establish and shape reality, and they imply how reality must be seen and approached.

Because of their fundamental meaning and great relevance to the social system, its governance, and its members, authoritative sources must be *legitimate*. In order to be legitimate, they must fit the spirit, nature, institutions, and people of the social system they are made and are relevant for, in particular in terms of (1) the principles, norms and values, rules and regulations, policies, guidelines, and advice they put forward (*internal consistency*); (2) the way(s) these are produced (or adapted from somewhere) (*emergence*); and (3) the way(s) they are applied (*application*).

Hence, in order to correspond with the fundamental ideas of a *democratic* social system and, thus, to be legitimate, the authoritative sources of the democratic organisation must:

1. *Reflect and champion the values of (individual) freedom, democracy, equality and justice (internal consistency)*: For example, in their partnership agreement, the owners must agree on and adhere to their inalienable rights to self-ownership and private property, their civil and human rights, principles of democratic governance, and principles of equality and justice that provide all partners or members of the democratic organisation with the same rights, responsibilities, treatment, and opportunities.

2. *Have been produced, deliberated, and decided upon democratically, in transparent and participative ways (emergence)*: For instance, a strategy, or strategic plan, is usually one of the most fundamental authoritative sources of an organisation; it has organisation-wide relevance for everyone and makes an impact at strategic and operational levels. In a democratic organisation, all members of the organisation must be involved in developing the strategy, must have opportunities to participate throughout the whole process of strategy development (i.e. during strategy analysis, formulation, and implementation), and must also be involved in finally deciding the strategy (either directly or via a general assembly or functional committees).

3. *Be implemented and applied in democratic, participative, fair, and just ways (application)*: For example, organisational policies must be implemented and applied to everyone in open, transparent, equal, and just ways. Since all members of the democratic organisation have the same legal status as equal partners, they also have equal rights to participate in profit-sharing (and responsibilities to bear losses). Certainly, organisations can choose from various profit-sharing schemes that differ in how they calculate individuals' (monetary and non-monetary) contributions and how they distribute profits (among those individuals). However, whatever scheme is decided by the partners, it must be applied to *all* partners in the same way.

Democratic Governing

By applying legitimate authoritative sources to issues and people, democratic institutions of governance *govern* the social system (or parts of it) and public affairs just as they were set up to do. What kind of governance these (institutional) actors provide depends largely on their own nature, design, and functioning – the reasons and purposes for which they were set up; their structures (e.g. autocratic, oligarchic, democratic, hierarchical, or heterarchical); the institutions' and actors' (actual or perceived) duties, rights, responsibilities, and relationships; and the processes and mechanisms of agenda-setting, policy-making, decision-making (decentralised or centralised, individually or collectively, or formally or informally), control, and compliance – as well as the people who serve in these institutions of governance and the members of the social system.

Again, the mode of governing must fit the social system and its institutions of governance. In the case of a *democratic* social system and *democratic* institutions, this governance must be *democratic*. The following sub-sections elaborate on what democratic governing means and what it should look like. They particularly focus on democratic decision-making, transparency, and accountability as key elements and characteristics of democratic governing.

Democratic Decision-Making

A key part of governing an organisation is making decisions about its fundamental principles, design, structures, processes, and workings. Crucially, the question is *who makes what kinds of decisions and in what way(s)*?

From a legal point of view, it is relatively clear who should make the decisions in democratic organisations. As owners of the democratic organisation, *all* members have a *legal right* ('property right'[6]) to participate fully in decision-making (Vanek 1971, pp. 8–9, Rothschild-Whitt 1979, p. 512, Bachrach & Botwinick 1992, p. 106, Bowles et al. 1993, p. 129, Archer 1995, pp. 31–32, Caspary 2004, pp. 239–240).[7] Moreover, in a democratic social system, *everyone* is *equally* entitled to be involved in decision-making systematically and regularly simply because of the general idea of democracy (Dahl 1979/2006, p. 109, called this 'the criterion of political equality'). This understanding of participation in democratic decision-making as a *political* right is the cornerstone of *participatory democracy* (Rothschild & Whitt 1986, p. 2). Hence, in the democratic organisation – and *only* in the democratic organisation – legal rights (property rights) and political rights (political equality) converge; *all* members of the democratic organisation are entitled to be involved in all types of decision.

From a governance perspective, the way(s) decisions are made is important because decision-making processes must fit the type of social system. Obviously, in an autocracy decisions are made by a single person in an authoritarian style, in an oligarchy decisions are made by a few people 'behind closed doors', and in a democracy decisions are made 'by all' either via direct participation or via representatives. Whereas decision-making processes within the democratic organisation can vary based on the type of decision to be made and other factors, these organisations nonetheless share the basic notion of being as democratic, open, inclusive, fair, and transparent as possible. In probably the best academic paper ever written on democratic, participative, or egalitarian organisations, Srivastva and Cooperrider (1986, p. 697) explained the central idea and nature of democratic or collective decision-making within organisations:

> Amplifying the theme of inclusion, the consensus ideal premises that: (1) organizational decisions, plans, or rules become morally binding to the extent that they emerge from a process where all relevant stakeholders have access to full, active, and mutual involvement in their determination, (2) the ultimate basis of authority does not rest with any one individual (or set of individuals) based on ownership, formal position, or expertise; rather, it is based on the dynamic consent of the group, and (3) there is not authority that can unilaterally command obedience nor any tradition that can demand conformity without seeking to elicit

voluntary agreement on the basis of dialogue, persuasion, or negotiation, i.e., use of logic, facts, or appeal to values.

Sargent (2008, p. 270) gives a good example of how decisions can be made democratically within the daily reality of organisations, based on her own experience as an activist who worked for a cooperative publisher:

> We were also able to be 'efficient' by making adjustments in our voting procedure. We mainly used one person/one vote, majority rules, with attention to a strong minority. This system worked extremely well. We didn't want trying [sic] to achieve consensus to hold up producing books; we also wanted to know what kinds of disagreements there were in the group. Utilizing a strong minority was a good check on decisions, as well. If a few people felt strongly enough to hold up a decision and argue their case, then perhaps we were making a hasty decision. As it turned out, the strong minority reversed many decisions and promoted some of the best discussions.

One might say that all decisions that are about constitutional, strategic, or operational issues (and not purely about functional tasks conducted by individuals) should be made democratically and in accordance with democratic standards, i.e. by all members of the organisation or by its relevant parts (direct or participative democracy), by elected or appointed representatives, or by office-holders who are controlled, are held accountable, and can be removed from office by democratic means (representative democracy).

Transparency

It is crucial to assess the quality and conduct of governance. Democratic governance, especially, is inherently based on and linked to comprehensive and far-reaching *transparency* (Grimond 1971, p. 93, Romme 1999, p. 811, Caspary 2004, p. 240, Bevir 2006, p. 434, Greenwood 2007, pp. 356–357, Tolbert & Hiatt 2009, Breindl 2010, p. 45, Erdal 2011, pp. 180–182). Within an organisational context, transparency means that all members of the organisation have free and equal access to, and are automatically provided with, all relevant non-confidential information about the formal organisational policies, rules, and regulations of governance; the general procedures for making decisions; and specific information relevant to the particular decision-making they are involved in. Table 3.1 shows what transparency means and how transparency can be realised in regard to the democratic governance of organisations.

TABLE 3.1 Rules of transparency and transparent decision-making within democratic organisations

---

- All members of the organisation have the right to free and equal access to all non-confidential data and information.
- The organisational policies, rules, and regulations of governance, in particular for making decisions, are explicit and publicly available, adhere to democratic standards, and can be contested and changed within the framework of democratic standards.
- Formal knowledge about how decisions are made, as well as administrative expertise and procedural know-how, is made available to all members of the organisation.
- It is clear who is involved in the decision-making in which functions and based on which criteria.
- All members involved in a particular decision-making process or event (e.g. a meeting) are automatically informed about the topic and agenda, issues to be discussed and decided, and procedural aspects well before the event takes place.
- Relevant information is made available to all people involved in the decision-making well before the issue is debated and decisions are to be made.
- Formal decision-making events are open to every member of the organisation (either as a participant or as an observer).
- The actual process of decision-making takes place in democratic, fair, and transparent ways, and decision-making happens openly and according to the formal rules and good practices of democratic debate and decision-making.
- Minutes are taken during decision-making processes, and these are kept and made accessible to everyone.
- All members of the organisation are automatically informed about constitutional and strategic decisions that have been, or are to be, made.

Accountability

Transparency enables accountability (and accountability necessitates transparency). Accountability is not only highly relevant as an *ex post* measure to hold actors responsible for their actions or inactions but also as an *ex ante* measure to influence actors (trying) to meet prescribed standards and to act as expected. Based on various definitions in the literature (Chisolm 1995, p. 141, Scott 2000, p. 39, Ebrahim 2003, pp. 813–814, Keohane 2003/2006, p. 701, Morlino 2004, pp. 17–18, Bovens 2006, p. 9, Brown 2006, p. 210, Esmark 2008, p. 276, Schillemans 2008, pp. 176–177, Considine & Afzal 2013, p. 372), accountability may be defined as follows:

> *Accountability* is the obligation of an individual, group, or institution to give account (i.e. to report, provide information, answer for, explain, justify, and assume responsibility) for their actions (i.e. decisions, activities, behaviour, conduct, and performance) to certain other individual(s), group(s), or institution(s) that have the right, duty, and ability to hold

them accountable and to impose possible consequences (sanctions, rewards, or punishment) on the former for what they have done assessed against predefined criteria (standards, expected behaviour, or outcomes).

'Who is accountable to whom about what?' is the question at the centre of accountability. 'Who is accountable to whom' indicates that (at least) two actors (individuals, groups of people, or institutional actors) are in a particular relationship with each other where one is being held accountable and the other is holding accountable. Accountability may be required of an individual, group, or institution at a *higher* level ('upwards accountability', e.g. subordinate to superior, employee to manager), at *the same* level ('horizontal accountability', e.g. individual to peers, organisation to stakeholders), or at a *lower* level ('downwards accountability', e.g. delegate to electorate) (Scott 2000, p. 42, Morlino 2004, pp. 17–18, Schillemans 2008, pp. 175–176).

Traditionally (i.e. in classical hierarchical superior–subordinate relationships, centralised nation-states, and stratified societies), accountability has largely occurred *upwards*: a lower actor must give account to a higher or more powerful actor and is controlled and sanctioned by that actor. In a democratic system it is exactly the opposite: accountability occurs *downwards*, i.e. the higher or more powerful actor must give account to the lower actor (and is controlled and sanctioned by that actor). Hence, in the democratic organisation, and in *any* social system that is based on the principles and values of democracy, accountability reflects democratic principles and values. For example, Malleson (2014, p. 41) pointed out that large cooperatives 'still have order-givers and order-takers. But those who give orders are now fundamentally accountable to those who take them. This is what makes a co-op a democracy and not a hierarchy.' It is a spirit of *democratic accountability* (Bowles & Gintis 1993, p. 82) that provides all members of a social system with equal opportunities to control conduct of office and decision-making.

For the democratic organisation, this actually means *multi-dimensional accountability* with at the same time horizontal, top-down, *and* bottom-up accountability (Keohane 2003/2006, p. 701). Horizontal accountability is performed and achieved via checks and balances between organisational institutions of governance on the basis of separation of powers; top-down accountability via democratically elected or appointed boards, committees, and office-holders, which hold accountable those units and members of the organisation for whom they are responsible; and bottom-up accountability via all members of the organisation holding accountable their elected and appointed office-holders.

Such a *system of multi-dimensional accountability* means that every institution and office-holder (1) can be called upon at any time by anyone to explain and to justify the conduct of their office, in particular about decisions made (or not made) and consequences caused; (2) has to assume responsibility for their actions or inactions; and (3) may face positive or negative consequences for their actions or inactions.

'Good Governance'

Besides its formal design, one of the most important questions about governance is how it is done, i.e. how institutions of governance *actually* govern on the basis of legitimate authoritative sources. To some extent this is about the technical functioning of governance, i.e. whether institutional actors are sufficiently enabled, competent, and willing to provide efficient and effective governance. But how governance is conducted is even more of a *qualitative* issue; it requires assessment and judgement of how *well* governance is functioning and happening in what ways. It is about how *good* governance is – and *for whom*.

People expect, or at least hope for, 'good' governance. 'Good governance' has even become an established term and concept used by international and national institutions of governance, auditing, and economic and social development; governing bodies such as the United Nations, the World Bank, and the International Monetary Fund; and other public and private organisations. The concept of 'good governance' not only tries to describe and analyse how well institutions of governance actually govern but also attempts to identify the causes of 'good governance' – the underlying (necessary) aspects that enable and even produce 'good governance'.

The concept of 'good governance' is relatively broad and multi-dimensional, comprising mainly political, socio-philosophical, ethical, and social parameters. The aspects identified and included in a particular concept of 'good governance' vary with its purpose, the area where it is applied, and the convictions and worldviews of those who use such concepts. But if one focuses on the most widely mentioned concepts (e.g. Bovaird & Löffler 2009, p. 10, United Nations Economic and Social Commission for Asia and the Pacific 2009, Kneuer 2012, pp. 879–880) it is possible to identify the key elements and even various levels of 'good governance' as shown in Table 3.2.

The basic governance functions (*formal administration*) are provided by *any* type of institution or political system, i.e. by autocratic, oligarchic, or democratic states and by hierarchical or heterarchical organisations. Even the most totalitarian, autocratic, or oligarchic regimes (which often claim to be 'democracies') provide all of the basic functions of governance, potentially in somewhat comprehensive, robust, and intensive forms (which is one of the factors that makes them oppressive police or surveillance states). Some even might call this 'good governance' (usually the proponents of such regimes). In such instances, however, the 'good' of 'good governance' should not be understood as a value judgement implying 'quality' but rather as a marker *only* indicating that governance is formally consistent with the logic of the system it governs (e.g. an authoritarian regime has authoritarian and draconian laws, very strong and powerful governmental institutions, a fully functioning administration and administrative apparatus, comprehensive accountability, control and surveillance, and comprehensive use of the 'rule of law').

TABLE 3.2 Three levels and elements of 'good governance'

Level	Elements
3: Promotion of universal values, human rights, and civil rights (*civil society*)	• Universal protection and promotion of all human and civil rights • *Substantive* 'rule of law' • No corruption • Ethos that cherishes the fundamental values of freedom, democracy, equality, and justice • Freedom of expression (voice), free and independent media, and public debates and deliberation • Freedom of association (voluntary and independent interest groups, civil society organisations, and political parties)
2: Fully fledged and fully functioning democratic political system (*democracy*)	• Legitimate authoritative sources • Democratic institutions of governance • Separation of powers, or 'checks and balances'; strong and independent legislative; strong and independent judiciary (non-discriminatory laws and impartial judicial processes); regulated executive • Subsidiarity (decentralisation with devolution of resources and decision-making to lower levels) • Political system (multiple independent political parties; regular, free, and fair elections; and elected office-holders) • Democratic decision-making (inclusiveness and full participation); transparency; and upward, downward, and horizontal accountability
1: Basic functions of government and governing (*formal administration*)	• Strong and stable governmental institutions (government and governmental agencies) • Functional administration (efficiency, effectiveness, productivity, performance, and sustainability) • *Formal* 'rule of law' • Upward accountability and top-down control

Clearly, in their governance, authoritarian regimes and hierarchical organisations will not – and *cannot!* – go beyond the basic functions of government, governance, and formal administration (level 1). A fully functioning political system and democracy (level 2) and the promotion of civil society (level 3) via governance is – and *can* be – provided *only* by fully fledged democratic nation-states, institutions, or organisations – and only *this* is real 'good governance'. In this case, governance is not only *formally* consistent with the social system in question (a democratic society, nation-state, institution, or organisation) but also *substantively* consistent; 'good governance' is good (i.e. 'good' as a value judgement) because it enables and provides democracy and civil society. It is democratic governance in democratic ways. 'Good governance' needs democracy – and governance *must* be democratic in order to be good and legitimate.

In the case of the democratic organisation, 'good governance' means that democratic institutions of governance (i.e. organisational institutions of governance based on the principles of separation of powers or 'checks and balances', and subsidiarity) govern the organisation democratically (i.e. via democratic decision-making, transparency, and accountability) on the basis of legitimate authoritative sources that appreciate and protect the fundamental human, civil, and legal rights of all members of the democratic organisation. That is, 'good governance' of the democratic organisations comprises and works on all three levels[8] – and only with comprehensively developed and successfully implemented 'good governance' is a democratic organisation indeed a *democratic* organisation.

Democratic Governance of the Democratic Organisation

As the investigation in this chapter has revealed, it is possible to have full, comprehensive democratic governance in and of organisations – to have organisations that are governed democratically. The key elements in the democratic governance of organisations are:

1. *Democratic institutions of governance*: The democratic organisation's institutions of governance (e.g. boards, committees, councils, or assemblies) are *democratic* institutions. They are designed and maintained according to democratic principles and standards, and their structures and composition (i.e. the way(s) they operate and function) are democratic. In order to avoid an undemocratic concentration of power, sufficient institutional safeguards are in place (e.g. separation of powers, the principle of subsidiarity, and democratic control of office and office-holders) to limit the power and authority of those in office or with power.

2. *Legitimate authoritative sources*: Democratic institutions of governance are based on, and function according to, legitimate authoritative sources (e.g. business and contract laws, legal rules and regulations, a partnership agreement, mission and vision statements, a strategy and operational plans, and codes of conduct) that are adopted, drafted, developed, and modified democratically, in transparent and participative ways. The sources' content and implications reflect the ideas and values of 'good governance' and the democratic organisation.

3. *Democratic governing*: All members of the democratic organisation govern the organisation and its affairs collectively, either directly or via democratically elected representatives (direct, representative, or participative democracy). All office-holders have to report to those whom they represent, and they are controlled, are held accountable, and can be removed from office

by democratic means (accountability). All decisions that are about constitutional, strategic, or operational issues are made democratically. Members have free and equal access to all relevant, non-confidential information about the democratic organisation's policies and organisational affairs (transparency).

4. *'Good governance'*: For the democratic organisation, 'good governance' has several aspects. (a) The organisational institutions of governance and the basic functions of government and governing are designed, work, and are provided on the basis of the rule of law and according to democratic standards (level 1 – formal administration). (b) All organisational institutions of governance (boards, councils, committees, and/or assemblies) and positions of power are based on and confined by legitimate authoritative sources; contained and controlled via separation of powers (*trias politica*), 'checks and balances', and the principle of subsidiarity; have members who are elected, controlled, and held accountable by those they represent; and employ decision-making processes that are democratic and transparent (level 2 – democracy). c) All owners' and members' inalienable human, legal, and civil rights are equally protected and promoted, and there is substantive rule of law, freedom of expression, and freedom of association within the democratic organisation (level 3 – civil society).

Notes

1 The term 'rules' is not meant here literally but as a general placeholder for a whole range of regulators that shape and direct systems, people, and their behaviour (see the discussion of 'legitimate authoritative sources' on pp. 57–59).
2 When organisations are under discussion, the term 'corporate governance' is often used (e.g. Turnbull 1997, Jegers 2009). Although this term theoretically can be applied to *any* formal organisation, whether public or private, for-profit or not-for-profit, it usually is only applied to corporations in very narrow, orthodox, and instrumental terms (i.e. mostly focusing on external and internal control institutions and mechanisms, due diligence, management ethics, and codes of conduct). Therefore, instead of 'corporate governance' I use the more general and broader term 'governance' (and later 'democratic governance'), as described and defined here and throughout the book.
3 In smaller democratic organisations, governance is usually less formalised. For example, instead of formal and formalised governance bodies, such an organisation might only have casual, formal, or informal (group) meetings where issues of governance are discussed. Nonetheless, such meetings should adhere to the principles of democratic governance and decision-making.
4 Although there are, of course, also differences. With respect to institutions of governance the biggest differences between the democratic state and the democratic organisation are that there are no political parties, public administration or independent media within the latter.
5 This idea, obviously, is exactly the opposite to what is found in any kind of orthodox, hierarchical organisation, where eventually all power is concentrated at the top in a single position and/or in a collective body.

6 It should be reiterated that property rights entitle owners to make decisions *only* in regard to *property* (i.e. material or immaterial assets or 'things') and *not* in regard to *people*. As the discussion about individuals' free will on pp. 37–39 revealed, making decisions about people is only possible in a discursive way and with their consent (see also Chapter 4: 'Democratic Management'), i.e. by acknowledging self-ownership and people's inalienable rights related to it. Only in the democratic organisation do property rights and self-ownership rights coincide.

7 Though the actual decision-making can be delegated to representatives who are held accountable by the members, the electorate. This topic will be addressed in the section on 'Representative Management', pp. 77-80.

8 A few elements of 'good governance' are not relevant or applicable to organisations or the internal governance of democratic organisations (e.g. a strong and independent judiciary, fully fledged and fully functioning political system or political parties, and free and independent media). But, besides those exceptions, 'good governance' of democratic organisations comprises all the other elements.

4

DEMOCRATIC MANAGEMENT

Hierarchy and/or Heterarchy: Democratic Management

Things must be managed – which means that there must also be management in the democratic organisation. Whereas governance provides the general framework for designing and maintaining an organisation, management provides the specific concepts, functions, and actions to run the organisation on a daily basis. Concerning governance, it is clear that only *democratic* governance corresponds with the fundamental ideas and principles of the democratic organisation. The same is true of management: only *democratic* management fits the democratic organisation. Management in the democratic organisation *must* be democratic since otherwise it would go against the organisation's fundamental principles.

This chapter is about the establishment, design, and functioning of *democratic management*. Democratic management is fundamentally different from any prevailing management orthodoxy, in particular from the traditional hierarchical, exclusive, top-down type of management (and managers!) that has been the dominant managerial concept and ideology since the late 19th century.[1] The crucial question, of course, is what exactly is *democratic management* – and how does it work?

In general, management means 'handling' things and people and comprises key functions such as planning, organising, leading, and controlling. In this sense, management is a *relationship* between people and things; *who plans, organises, leads, and controls what and whom?* (For a social system with some or many members) possible solutions are that (1) one person manages and everyone else is managed (autocracy), (2) a few people manage and many are managed (oligarchy), or (3) all manage and no one is managed (democracy). The first two solutions result in forms of *hierarchy*, whereas the last results in *heterarchy*.

As argued in Chapter 1, hierarchy can be understood as a comprehensive, thoroughly established social system of vertically arranged social positions of superiors and subordinates in which the former have the exclusive right and means to give orders to, control, and sanction the latter, who have the duty to carry out the orders and to obey.[2] Clearly, the democratic organisation could not function with such a formal chain of command and vertical social relationships, i.e. with hierarchy. Within the democratic organisation, formal social relationships cannot be hierarchical for *legal* reasons (all members have equal rights and responsibilities due to their owner status, the partnership agreement, self-ownership, and the impossibility of transferring inalienable rights) and *governance* reasons (the principles and mechanisms of democratic governance – in particular separation of powers, checks and balances, subsidiarity, and democratic decision-making – suggest equal rights to participate in running the organisation).

For these reasons, there cannot be hierarchical superior–subordinate relationships or autocratic management in the democratic organisation. There can only be such organisational structures, processes, and types of management that are consistent with the concepts, rights, and responsibilities of collective private ownership and democratic governance. In this sense, the organisational structure of the democratic organisation (including as the framework for management) is to be described and understood better as a *heterarchy*. A heterarchy is a system where all the elements are unranked. A heterarchical social system consists of horizontally arranged social positions. In the case of a formalised social system such as an organisation, this means that all the elements (i.e. all formal positions and all members via their roles, functions, and positions) ideally have equal power and authority to influence the system and common issues and affairs within the system (Girard & Stark 2002 called this 'distributed authority' or 'relations of lateral accountability').

The concept of heterarchy fits quite well with the democratic organisation and has valuable implications for conceptualising democratic management. Joyce Rothschild (also known as Rothschild-Whitt), one of the leading (if not *the* leading) organisation studies scholars of collectivist organisations since the late 1970s, captured the notion of the heterarchical democratic organisation and management perfectly (Rothschild-Whitt & Lindenfeld 1982, p. 6):

> Democratic workplaces are united in their attempt to break down the division between management and labor, planners and workers, so that all who do the work of the organization have an equal voice in its management and a fair share of the fruits of their labor. What they are seeking to alter, then, is nothing short of the structure of power in organizations. The aim is not the simple *transference* of power from one official to another; it is the *abolition* of the pyramid *in toto*. It is an attempt to accomplish organizational tasks cooperatively and democratically,

without recourse to hierarchal authority structures or the stratification systems that accompany them.

Making the case for heterarchy and against hierarchy in fundamental terms is the right thing to do – for *any* social system and, therefore, also for the democratic organisation. It is an argument for structural relationships between positions and social relationships between people that are equal, non-authoritarian, legitimate, and democratic.[3]

It should be clear that attempting to have the democratic organisation based, and functioning, on heterarchical social relationships between people does not mean a 'structureless' organisation or anarchy. Within the democratic organisation there are still various necessary 'hierarchies'. In any formally established social system there is, and must be, a *legal* hierarchy between (its) authoritative sources. For instance, the (external) constitution as well as corporate, contract, and labour law are superior to the partnership agreement and predefine to quite some extent what exactly can be agreed in it. In turn, the terms agreed in the partnership agreement provide some guidelines for the organisation's vision and policies, operational plans must be in sync with the organisation-wide policies and strategy, and so on. The hierarchy of authoritative sources creates and guarantees formal and procedural consistency and legitimacy.

Moreover, there is also an *institutional* hierarchy between the various organisational institutions of governance. For example, decisions made by the board of executives or by the general assembly are of higher relevance than decisions made by a shop-floor workers' committee or project team, and institutions in the headquarters are of more functional relevance than local institutions. Institutional hierarchy provides the administrative consistency that any diversified, multi-layered social system requires. The case against hierarchical order, therefore, is not a case against *all* hierarchical orders of and within a formalised social system, but against *social* hierarchy, i.e. against *institutionalised unequal social relationships*, *social dominance* and *stratification*, and therefore orthodox, hierarchical management.

For the democratic organisation, the issue of 'hierarchy vs. heterarchy' is about avoiding management producing power differentials and social inequality and avoiding power being systematically and exclusively allocated to positions that are not controlled and held accountable by democratic means.[4] Hence, the question, or task, is not how to get rid of management but how to organise management (the bundles of managerial functions or management tasks) so that it is compatible with the democratic organisation.

From legal, constitutional, and conceptual perspectives, the democratic organisation is very clear about the allocation and conduct of management functions; there is no stylised or factual distinction or separation between owners and managers (separation between ownership and control) or between managers and workers (separation between management and work) (Zeitlin 1974, pp. 1074–1075, Rothschild-Whitt & Lindenfeld 1982, p. 6, Bowman & Stone 2004, p. 275). *Every* member of the democratic organisation is simultaneously an owner, a manager, and an employee or worker in legal as well as in practical terms. Therefore, there is no separation or distinction between people with and without managerial responsibilities. *Every* member of the democratic organisation has all the rights and responsibilities, and can conduct all the tasks and functions, that are related or directly linked to the legal status of owners. Every member is an owner-manager. *All* members of the democratic organisation have equal rights and responsibilities to conduct the whole range of management functions and to make decisions (Ackoff 1994, p. 117). Management in the democratic organisation is 'management of the people, by the people, for the people' – *all* people.

That *all* members of the democratic organisation are legally and constitutionally entitled and required to conduct *all* management functions and responsibilities provides an important and necessary clarification. The question, though, is how *exactly* management functions should be allocated and conducted, and by whom, in the spirit of *democratic* management and consistently with the notion of the democratic organisation. The following sections develop the concept of democratic management by focusing on its three main elements:

- *self-management* (by individuals, by self-managing groups of people, or via collective authority structures);
- *representative management* (via democratic organisational institutions and democratic managers); and
- *participative management* (participation in decision-making of all via *full* participation).

Self-Management

In regard to the allocation of management functions in the democratic organisation, the *principle of subsidiarity*, introduced in Chapter 3 in the context of democratic governance (see pp. 56–57), is helpful in developing the notion and concept of self-management. In Chapter 3, subsidiarity was defined as 'any task or function that *can* be performed at a lower level *should* be performed at the lowest possible level'. In this sense, the principle of subsidiarity is understood against the backcloth of, and in regard to, *hierarchical* systems. The principle, however, can also be seen with regard to and applied to *heterarchical* systems in the sense of moving from smaller to larger elements of a social system until the whole system is reached. In the case of the democratic organisation, this would mean (1) individuals, (2) (work or project) groups, (3) networks, and (4) the whole organisation. Self-management at each of those levels looks as follows.

Individuals

In the elaboration of the principle of subsidiarity in Chapter 3, I argued (italic added):

> Subsidiarity means that matters are governed and administered, that issues are addressed and solved (or attempts are made to solve them), *where things happen and matter,* or where the causes and consequences are relevant (i.e. in a local context or at operational levels in an organisation). This means that people 'on the ground' are entitled and empowered to make decisions and are responsible for taking action where they are, i.e. in their neighbourhood or in the workplace.

Understood in this way, self-management means that it is, or should be, the individuals themselves that first and foremost manage their work and make decisions about their work as far as possible (i.e. as long as it does not impact on others' work). *Those who do the work should manage it and make decisions about it* – or, to put it slightly differently, *decisions should be made by those who implement the decisions* (Rothschild-Whitt & Lindenfeld 1982, p. 1, Melman 2001, p. 272). In this sense, in respect to their own work, individual members of the democratic organisation provide (all) management functions. No one tells an individual what to do, when to do it, how to do it, or why to do certain tasks. Others might give the individual information about their work but it is the individual – and *only* the individual – who makes the decisions.

(Work or Project) Groups

Obviously, self-management puts each and every individual first – but this, of course, does not mean that the individual members of an organisation manage their work in an isolated manner. More often than not, tasks are related to other members' work and need to be coordinated or even carried out in collaboration with others. Several individual members of the organisation might work together as a team, project group, or organisational unit permanently or temporarily. In the case of collaborative or overlapping work, individuals (should) conduct all management functions in joint and cooperative ways. In the democratic organisation, self-management is done in and by *self-managing groups.* Such groups are fairly independent in how they self-organise and self-manage themselves and the work they do (Ward 1971, p. 290). According to Sauser (2009, p. 160), 'self-managing teams operate with participative decision-making, shared tasks, and the responsibility for many of the managerial tasks performed by supervisors in more traditional settings'. It is self-evident that all individuals engaged or involved in any form of such collective self-management must do so freely, must debate and deliberate, and must find means of self-management and collective decision-making that are consistent with democratic principles and standards.

Networks

Several individuals and groups of people are then connected via *networks*, i.e. in organisational structures and processes where no single element dominates all others (i.e. hierarchy) but all elements are of the same or similar status (i.e. heterarchy). The main idea is that a network consists of autonomous, 'self-directed units based on decentralization, participation, and coordination' (Castells 1996 cited in Ekbia & Kling 2005, p. 163). Hales (2002, p. 54) gave a good description of idea of the network within organisations:

> The internal network organization is conceived as a loose federation of informally constituted, self-managing, often temporary, work units or teams within which there is a fluid division of labour and which are coordinated through an internal market, rather than rules, and horizontal negotiation and collaboration, rather than hierarchy ... Instead of a hierarchy of vertical reporting relationships there is a 'soft network' ... of informal lateral communications, information sharing and temporary collaboration based on reciprocity and trust.

According to Miles and Snow (1995 cited in Ekbia & Kling 2005, p. 163), the management of the network is viewed as 'a shared responsibility among colleagues, not as a superior–subordinate relationship'.

The Whole Organisation

Besides individuals, groups of people (teams and projects), and networks conducting management functions independently and in their own right and by their own methods (though in compliance with democratic principles and standards), self-management can also be achieved with the help of *self-managing institutions*. For example, when Srivastva and Cooperrider (1986, p. 689) investigated the physician group practice of the Cleveland Clinic (a private, nonprofit tertiary care centre located in northeastern Ohio), they found that:

> A dynamic self-regulating system of cooperative governance has been established whereby the traditional distinction between management and labor has effectively been eliminated. Those who do the specialized work of the organization also control all aspects of the organization – medical

and administrative – through a collective authority structure encompassing decision-making at the operational, tactical, and strategic levels.

A 'collective authority structure' can be any kind of democratic institution that is self-organised, managed, and used by all members of the relevant unit (or even the whole organisation), i.e. where all members directly participate in, and contribute to, that management institution. For instance, a general assembly or formalised virtual processes of deliberation and decision-making represent such self-managing institutions. Such institutions are quite developed and robust forms of self-management.[5]

Subsidiarity in Self-Management

All in all, when the principle of subsidiarity is applied to the notion of self-management, it becomes clear that in a democratic organisation 'those who do the work' also carry out all management functions at all levels, i.e.:

1. each and every individual member of the democratic organisation manages their work (and themselves) as comprehensively and as far as possible;
2. self-managing groups of people (teams, projects, or organisational units) manage their work and themselves as well as the cooperation and decision-making processes among their members as much as possible according to democratic rules and standards;
3. individuals and groups of people manage their cooperation with other individuals and groups of people in and via network-like structures and processes; and
4. via collective structures of authority – such as general assemblies or (online) forums – all members of the democratic organisation manage the organisation and organisational affairs in democratic ways.

Thus, in a more complex democratic organisation, the management functions of planning, organising, leading, and controlling are provided by self-managing individuals, groups of people, networks, and organisation-wide institutions – in *that* order. It is probably this particular arrangement in which various actors execute management tasks and responsibilities individually and collectively according to the principle of subsidiarity that makes self-management so comprehensive and significant. Some organisation scholars even talk about 'self-managing organisations'. For example, as Lee and Edmondson (2017, p. 39) explain:

> We define self-managing organizations (SMOs) as those that *radically decentralize authority in a formal and systematic way throughout the organization.* What distinguishes self-managing organizations from managerial hierarchies and from efforts to make managerial hierarchies incrementally less

hierarchical is that SMOs eliminate the hierarchical reporting relationship between manager and subordinate that serves as the core building block of the managerial hierarchy and constitutes its key mechanism of control. In self-managing organizations, all employees hold well-defined decision rights that cannot be superseded by someone simply because s/he is the 'boss.'[6]

Although it has been mentioned several times, it should be reiterated that self-management in democratic organisations is *democratic* self-management, i.e. all management functions are provided, and management decisions are made, by individuals, groups, networks, or institutions according to democratic principles and standards. The following two empirical examples give an idea of how (and that) democratic self-management can work.

Paul Burrows, one of the co-founders of the Mondragon Bookstore & Coffee House collective, a non-hierarchical workers' cooperative that existed in Winnipeg from 1996 to 2014, described how self-management worked there (Burrows 2008, p. 280):

> In terms of decision making, one of the goals of Mondragon is to create a work environment in which each worker-member can carry out their tasks without managerial supervision, and each is taught the necessary skills to make any day-to-day business decisions that might be required. Part of the reason behind this is to avoid a workplace characterized by unequal knowledge and divisions of labor, in which a single individual is considered indispensable, or might argue for special privileges on the basis of some monopoly on information or skills. In positive terms, this has to do with creating a workplace that empowers its members, fosters solidarity, and puts democracy and equality into practice. ... Ultimately, the basic goal of the workplace with respect to decision making is to give each worker a good deal of latitude for self-management of their own work circumstances, but within the constraint of meeting collectively agreed upon priorities, tasks, and policies that affect the group as a whole. The idea is to develop a system that balances individual and collective needs in a way that is both fair and efficient.

Dafermos (2012, pp. 8–9) provided a good empirical example of how democratic self-management can work at the individual and micro level when he analysed FreeBSD (where 'BSD' stands for Berkeley Software Distribution), an open-source software community of a volunteer core team, several hundred developers ('committers'), and thousands of contributors:

> If authority is defined as a relationship in which an actor obeys a specific command issued by another ... then FreeBSD is essentially

an organisation without authority. There is no such thing as giving or following orders in FreeBSD. The administrative organ of the project – the core team – cannot tell committers what to do. When a decision needs to be made, it is made collectively by consensus. If, in the Weberian tradition, we take the basis of authority as the decisive organisational feature, then the mode of organisation of FreeBSD is collectivist, based on direct-democratic procedures of decision making. Seen from the perspective of the division of labour in the project, FreeBSD is decentralised and anti-hierarchical: tasks are self-selected by committers as their needs and interests best dictate. The resulting division of labour is spontaneous in the sense that it emerges from the choices of the committers rather than from a central designer. Their rejection of supervisory hierarchy is analogous to the autonomy from managerial control other professionals enjoy on account of being expected to exercise judgment and discretion in their daily work, but there is a fundamental difference: while professionals working in organisations, even in the most 'adhocratic' ones, are invariably subject to some measure of hierarchical control …, hackers have totally ousted hierarchical authority from their organisational frame. Committers work without supervision, shouldering themselves the ultimate responsibility that the modifications they make to the codebase have been adequately tested and do not clash with the work of other committers. … In FreeBSD those who work also manage.

Representative Management

Work, work-related issues, the context of work, and even organisational issues and affairs can and *should* be managed first by individuals themselves. However, as an organisation grows in size, it becomes increasingly difficult and ultimately impossible for the organisation, its organisational affairs, or its managerial issues to be managed by every member via self-management or direct democratic management because of time restraints, complexity, or efficiency issues (Dahl 1970, pp. 67–68, Rothschild-Whitt 1979, p. 512, Bowles et al. 1993, p. 139, Cheney 1995, p. 174, Davis 2001, p. 29, Wright 2010, p. 155). Thus, in larger democratic organisations there is some division of labour, differentiation, and specialisation, including concerning management functions. Organisational institutions and individual positions are formally established and allocated with the task of providing management functions and managing organisational affairs that go beyond individuals' or groups of people's wills or capacities to self-manage.

Such organisational institutions can be special organisational units (e.g. boards, committees, assemblies, or councils[7]) or individual formal positions where managerial tasks and management functions are clustered. Both organisational institutions and individual positions represent formal (part-time or full-time) management positions and create the formal (part-time or full-time) roles of 'managers' – but then alarm bells (should) ring!

Formal organisational institutions and management positions *as such* are not a problem even for the democratic organisation – but they are a problem, a *serious* problem, if they are drawn up and function like traditional, orthodox ones, i.e. hierarchical and with line management authority equipped. Formal management positions are greatly worrying when they are provided with bundles of those orthodox management tasks and responsibilities that create social dominance, inequality, and hierarchy – i.e. management tasks that provide a person with power over others, such as having explicit line management authority in the sense of giving orders; supervising, controlling, and sanctioning others; making decisions that are about others or relevant to others; and/or providing leadership or guidance.[8] This is one of the fundamental problems of orthodox organisations (or hierarchical social systems in general) – and a fundamental threat to, and challenge for, any democratic organisation: formal positions may be provided with orthodox management tasks, managerial 'rights', and managerial responsibilities (if not to say privileges and prerogatives) that put these formal roles and positions – and the role-holders! – in an *unequal* or *hierarchical social relationship* with others, and create and establish superior–subordinate relationships, social dominance and subordination, exploitation, and infantilisation.

It is fairly obvious that such a traditional, hierarchical, and authoritarian understanding of management, management positions, and managers would be inconsistent – and incompatible – with both the spirit and the letter of the democratic organisation (or any social system that caters for free individuals). Organisations do not need this kind of formal position, which accumulates social power and resources – and they do not need this kind of office-holder or manager (Watson 2006, p. 170). Hence, in the democratic organisation, formal management positions – whether in organisational institutions or as individual roles and positions – are *fundamentally* different. The way management is provided as a specialist function by formal management positions in the democratic organisation I call *representative management* (and the people in these formal management positions could be called *representatives* and not 'managers' – although because of convention I suppose that the established term 'manager' will continue to prevail and I, therefore, will also use the term 'managers').

Representative management means that although there are formal positions of management and office-holders we can call 'managers' for convenience, there are no 'managers' in the sense of 'bosses', or 'superiors' (Nielsen 1985, pp. 67–68, Macdonald 2013, p. 6) – if one understands 'manager' in the traditional way as someone who has line authority, i.e. gives orders to, controls, and sanctions subordinates. Instead, representative management in the democratic organisation means in particular (Bowles et al. 1993, p. 139, Weisskopf 1993, pp. 9–10, Arnold 1994, p. 206; and especially Morrell & Hartley 2006, pp. 484–485; Malleson 2014, p. 41):

- *Election or appointment of representatives*: All representatives (managers) serving in any kind of management position are elected or appointed democratically by those whom they represent. Managers may be elected or appointed either directly by the relevant members of the organisation (or a relevant part of it) or indirectly by members of an organisational institution (e.g. a council or general assembly). Elections and appointments of representatives must be free, fair, competitive, and transparent on the basis of one person, one vote.
- *Conduct of office*: All democratically elected or appointed representatives (are obliged to) execute the will of those whom they represent and carry out their responsibilities within clearly defined boundaries. There is no people-oriented authority ascribed to any managerial role, i.e. no manager is formally entitled and empowered to give orders, to control, or to punish anyone, and no manager can 'tell' another person what to do, when to do it, how to do it, or why to do something – *anything*. Managers can ask, suggest, or encourage people to do certain things, but they do not have the power to force people.[9] Moreover, representative managers do not *give* but *receive* instructions. They have no line management responsibilities but 'service responsibilities' in the sense that they (should) follow the instructions they were given truthfully and to the best of their abilities. As representatives it is their main responsibility, even obligation, to conduct their office according to the will of the people, the organisational institutions of governance, and the relevant authoritative sources.
- *Control of representatives*: All democratically elected or appointed representatives are controlled, held accountable, reconfirmed, or replaced by those whom they represent (the electorate) and/or by institutions formally provided with the task of overseeing the conduct of office of representatives. Every manager is accountable to every member of the organisation on a democratic basis. Any delegation of power or authority (from an electorate to its representative(s)) is accompanied by an equivalent accountability, i.e. the electorate (or the institution appointed to act on its behalf) has the right to oversee the representative and their conduct of office, to receive any relevant information from the representative, to steer and regulate the representative's conduct of office, and to sanction the representative as appropriate and in accordance with the stipulated laws, rules, and regulations.

The institutions and positions of representative management are *democratic* institutions and positions, i.e. they are constituted, based on, operated, staffed, and managed according to democratic principles and standards. Together, the guidelines for election or appointment, conduct of office, and control of representatives and managers make sure that representative management is as democratic as possible. This means that management positions (and managers) that are consistent with the idea of representative management are *legitimate* – they have *legitimate authority* (Raz 1986/2009, pp. 21–105). According to Beetham (1991, p. 3), 'where power is acquired and exercised according to justifiable rules, and with evidence of consent, we call it rightful or legitimate'. In this sense, it might be stated apodictically that authority is *only* legitimate when it is (1) is based on the consent of free people, i.e. is democratically elected or appointed; (2) operates on the basis of, and within a constitutional and legal framework of, explicit and justifiable rules and a clear mandate; and (3) is accountable to, controlled, and sanctioned by those who are subjected to it.[10] These criteria are crucial for representative management (and managers or representatives); *then* – and *only* then – is management *legitimate* (Archer 1995, p. 35, Leach 2005, p. 326).

Participative Management

The fundamental notion of democratic organisations – that individuals, i.e. *all* members of the organisation, have equal rights and the responsibility to make all the decisions – raises the question of how exactly individuals can get involved in the collective self-management or representative management of their own work, organisational affairs, and the organisation as a whole.

Such an involvement of people can be achieved via *participation* or *participative management*. Participation is one of the key mechanisms for managing and running social systems collectively and democratically (Pateman 1970, Dahl 1971, Mulder 1971, Dachler & Wilpert 1978, Mansbridge 1980, Rothschild-Whitt & Lindenfeld 1982, Srivastva & Cooperrider 1986, Held 1987, Bachrach & Botwinick 1992, Dahl 1998, Heller et al. 1998, Strauss 1998, Heeks 1999, Stohl & Cheney 2001, Cheney 2002). In the democratic organisation – or *any* democratic system – participation *as such* is justified by the very idea of democracy or democratic systems: governance 'of the people, by the people, for the people'. However, it is important to realise that people's involvement or participation can be of varying scopes and intensities. Participation can be imagined as a continuum with various levels ranging from very weak (number 1 in the following list) to very strong (number 6) (Arnstein 1969, Heller et al. 1977, p. 572, Rothschild-Whitt & Lindenfeld 1982, p. 4, Pretty 1995, Strauss 1998, pp. 18–20, Atzeni & Ghigliani 2007, p. 10, Cornwall 2008):

1. No or minimal information;
2. Information only;
3. Opportunity to be heard, to provide an opinion, and to vote;
4. Consultation and advice is taken into consideration;
5. Joint decision-making and codetermination;
6. Complete control.

For any fully fledged democratic system, participation must be as comprehensive and far-reaching as possible for *all* members on the basis of equal and democratic principles (Fromm 1956/1971, p. 323, Pateman 1970, p. 24, Vanek 1971, pp. 8–9, Dachler & Wilpert 1978, p. 12, Rothschild-Whitt 1979, p. 512, Bachrach & Botwinick 1992, p. 2, Bowles et al. 1993, p. 129, Archer 1995, pp. 31–32, Melman 2001, p. 272, Caspary 2004, pp. 239–240).[11] In regard to the democratic organisation, participation means that *all* members of the organisation have equal (legal and political) rights and actual opportunities to participate regularly in the governance and management of the organisation and organisational affairs. More specifically (and perhaps more relevant for individuals), participation means that individuals are involved in the conduct of management functions (i.e. planning, organising, leading, and controlling) and in formal decision-making processes at all levels of the organisation (constitutional, strategic, and operational) that are relevant to them. Participation guarantees that governance and management are *democratic* governance and *democratic* management.

The questions then are how participation and participative management look in the democratic organisation in regard to self-management and representative management, and how these three types of democratic management relate to each other. Table 4.1 provides a systematic overview.

TABLE 4.1 Levels of participation in self-management and representative management

Type of Management	Mode	Level of Participation of the Individual
Representative management	*Representative institutions*: Within (larger) democratic organisations there are institutions of democratic governance and representative management, such as boards, councils, or committees. They are designed and maintained, and operate and function according to the principles and standards of representative democracy. These institutions are transparent, open, and accountable to every member of the organisation. Any issue can be addressed, deliberated upon, and decided there following democratic rules, standards, and procedures.	Level 3: opportunity to be heard, to provide an opinion, and to vote
	Managers: Formal management positions do not come with any line authority. Individual office-holders ('representatives' or 'managers') are elected or appointed democratically, controlled, held accountable, and removable from	Level 5: joint decision-making and codetermination

(*Continued*)

TABLE 4.1 (Cont).

Type of Management	Mode	Level of Participation of the Individual
	office by those whom they represent. Managers are obliged to conduct their office democratically and to carry out their responsibilities and conduct their management functions jointly and in close cooperation with those whom they represent.	
Self-management	*Self-managing institutions*: Self-managing individuals and groups can create temporary or permanent self-managing institutions (e.g. assemblies) that function according to democratic rules, standards, and procedures. All members of the democratic organisation are members of these institutions and have equal rights to participate in and contribute to them and to the debates and decision-making processes happening there.	Level 3: opportunity to be heard, to provide an opinion, and to vote
	Networks: Individuals and groups can engage and collaborate with others in and via network-like structures and processes, i.e. networks. These networks are self-organised and self-managed, and are maintained and function via the participation and contributions of their members. Decisions are made, and things are done, via decentralised cooperation happening across the evolving network.	Level 4: consultation and advice is taken into consideration
	Groups: Individuals routinely participate in permanent or temporary self-managing groups (also called teams or organisational units). Self-managing groups are organised and function according to democratic principles and standards. Collective formal decision-making within these groups is open, transparent, inclusive, and deliberative, and decisions are reached either by majority or by consensus. Within the democratic organisation they reflect the notion of direct democracy the most.	Level 5: joint decision-making and codetermination

(*Continued*)

TABLE 4.1 (Cont).

Type of Management	Mode	Level of Participation of the Individual
	Individuals: Participation starts with the individual – with each and every single member of the social system. Via self-managing their individual work, organisational issues related to their work as well as themselves, individuals participate in and contribute to the ongoing operation and functioning of the democratic organisation.	Level 6: complete control

As explained in regard to governance, formal decision-making within the democratic organisation happens according to democratic standards and the principle of subsidiarity. Participative management follows the same rationales. Within the democratic organisation, participation or participative management starts with individual and collective self-management and stretches all the way up to organisation-wide representative management:

- Each and every individual member of the democratic organisation has complete control over their area of work and responsibilities. This level of autonomy reflects or resembles the idea(l) of full participation, i.e. that in the democratic organisation individuals are in complete control of their work (level 6 of participation).
- Also in their immediate work collaborations – whether this is in self-managing groups, teams, or organisational units or with representative managers – individual members of the democratic organisation score very high in participation (level 5). This is mainly because the fundamental modus operandi of self-managing groups or representative managers is collaboration and joint decision-making on the basis of democratic rules and standards, i.e. enabling individuals to participate profoundly.
- Where wider, more indirect forms of collaboration between individuals and groups of people (such as in and via networks) are concerned, the scope of individuals' participation resembles level 4, i.e. members of the network communicate, negotiate with, and consult each other and take others' advice into consideration.
- Finally, individuals reach the lowest level of participation (level 3) in regard to their engagement with self-managed or representative (organisation-wide) institutions of democratic governance and management. Participation here is fairly formalised and less direct. It mostly consists of receiving and providing

information, attending (open) debates and deliberations, voicing opinions (opportunities to be heard), and voting on issues.

There obviously is a decline in the level of participation from individual and collective self-management to organisation-wide institutions of representative management; with respect to the governance and management of their work and immediate work context, members of the democratic organisation are in full control, provide all management functions, and decide things either individually or jointly with others. This type and intensity of participation exemplifies direct democracy. Individuals' participation in organisation-wide institutions is then more about scrutinising information, voicing opinions, voting, and holding representatives accountable. These activities and individuals' involvement resemble participation in a (fully fledged and fully functioning) representative democracy.

Of course, participation, especially how decisions are made, also depends on the people involved (see Chapter 5) as well as organisational 'technicalities'. For example, size matters; whether all members of an organisation or an organisational unit can actually participate in making decisions directly is subject to the total number of members and opportunities for debate. Larger numbers of people (and space or time constraints) usually lead to participation and decision-making procedures that draw more on representative than direct governance and management.

These issues also depend on the type of decision that needs to be made. Decisions can be about operational, strategic, or constitutional issues. Operational issues concern daily business and management issues; strategic issues concern the purpose(s), business model, direction, and ways of doing business of the whole organisation (or large parts of it); and constitutional issues are largely of a legal, statutory, or regulatory nature. Operational decisions take place at the individual level, within groups, within teams, or within organisational units in the workplace largely via direct participation and joint decision-making. Strategic decisions may be delegated to democratically elected or appointed boards or committees, and this process may be accompanied by open, organisation-wide discussions and decisions (in a general assembly). Decisions on constitutional matters will be highly formalised, organisation wide, preceded and accompanied by public discussions and debates, and probably include some sort of formal voting.

However, whatever the (actual or alleged) 'technicalities' relevant to a particular decision-making process and people's participation, it should be clear that *participative management* as a whole is a *fundamentally* different management concept from any other; managing and governing democratic organisations on the basis of, and in the spirit of, participative management mainly means *expanding* participation in decision-making across all issues and levels (constitutional, strategic, and operational) and making decision-making procedures as inclusive, transparent, and democratic as is possible and feasible. It means making decisions the democratic way. And it works.[12]

The Elements of Democratic Management

Democratic management is a comprehensive and detailed concept that comprises self-management, representative management, and participative management:

1. *Self-management*: It is the fundamental idea of *self-management* that work and work-related issues are managed (i.e. planned, organised, led, and controlled) by the people and that people also manage themselves. Accordingly, all members of the democratic organisation have a fairly broad scope and opportunities to make decisions and to organise and manage their own work, the conditions of their work, and organisational affairs by themselves individually and/or via self-managing groups, networks, and institutions that are organised and function according to democratic principles and standards.

2. *Representative management*: In larger democratic organisations there are formally established organisational institutions of governance and management (boards, committees, councils, or assemblies) as well as individual management positions with the task of managing organisational affairs and/or delivering management functions that go beyond individuals' or groups of people's wills and capacities to self-manage. Institutions and positions of representative management are *democratic* institutions and positions, i.e. they are constituted, are based on, operate, are staffed, and are managed according to democratic principles. This means in particular:

   • *Election or appointment of representatives*: All representatives serving in any kind of management position are elected or appointed democratically, and elections and appointments of representatives are free, fair, transparent, democratic, and competitive.

   • *Conduct of office*: All democratically elected or appointed representatives (are obliged to) execute the will of those whom they represent and carry out their responsibilities within clearly defined boundaries. Additionally, they have no line management responsibilities but instead have 'service responsibilities'.

   • *Control of representatives*: All democratically elected or appointed representatives are supervised, controlled, held accountable, reconfirmed, or replaced by those whom they represent (the electorate) and/or by institutions formally provided with the task of overseeing the conduct of office of representatives.

3. *Participative management*: *All* individual members of the (democratic) organisation have equal rights and opportunities to participate in and collaborate with self-managing groups and organisational institutions of representative management, in particular with regard to the management of the organisation and organisational affairs, formal decision-making processes

at all levels of the organisation (constitutional, strategic, and operational), and decisions that are either relevant to the whole organisation or affect members directly.

Conceptualised in such a way, democratic management is an end in itself worth striving for. But it is also a means, and provides the means, to make organisations better places – *much* better places. Democratic management offers the main rationales, concepts, formal structures, and processes for organising and managing not only work and organisational affairs but also social positions and social actions in non-hierarchical, equal, inclusive, and participative ways. And it puts people in charge – each and every single individual member of the democratic organisation. In this sense it contributes to the democratisation of work and workplaces, organisations and society. Only *democratic management* is the right and appropriate management concept for the democratic organisation – actually, for *any* social system that appreciates individuals.

Notes

1 For further information about, and a thorough critical analysis of, orthodox management and managers, see my book *Management and the Dominance of Managers'* (Diefenbach 2009a), in which I developed a multi-dimensional theory relating to the social dominance of managers within an institutional context.

2 My book *Hierarchy and Organisation: Toward a General Theory of Hierarchical Social Systems* (Diefenbach 2013a) contains a comprehensive and systematic analysis and critique of the concept, ideology, and many dangers and downsides of (formal and informal) hierarchy.

3 In regard to hierarchy, the focus here is only on *formal* structures. Hierarchy, of course, is a much more complex and multi-dimensional phenomenon – and a danger to the democratic organisation. Chapter 10 ('The Iron Threat(s) of Disproportional Empowerment') provides a broad discussion and analysis of intended or unintended processes within the democratic organisation that threaten its principles, its ideas, and even its very existence.

4 'To positions that are not controlled and held accountable by democratic means' is added as a qualifier to make clear that orthodox, autocratic management positions (i.e. the 'classic' line manager) are not compatible with a democratic organisation (or with any formalised democratic system). Later in this chapter (see pp. 77–80) it will be argued that the democratic organisation *can* have formal management positions – but these positions come with no line authority and the office-holders, even if they are called 'managers', are *representatives* who are elected, controlled, and held accountable by those they represent and those whose will they execute.

5 Otherwise such democratic institutions need to be seen more as part of 'representative management', which will be addressed in the next sub-section.

6 They added (Lee & Edmondson 2017, p. 46): 'Self-managing organization is an apt label to capture radical approaches to less-hierarchical organizing for two reasons. First, by eliminating the hierarchical reporting relationship between manager and subordinate, individuals and groups must "manage" themselves. Second, the term appropriately emphasizes that radically decentralized organizations necessarily operate (accomplish work) through an ongoing dynamic process rather than by building a static operating structure … removing the hierarchical reporting relationships between managers and subordinates.'

7 These are the same organisational institutions that are responsible for the democratic governance of the organisation (see 'Organisational Institutions of Governance' in Chapter 3). Especially when it is about constitutional or strategic issues governance and management overlap considerably.

8 As a brief side remark for clarification: none of these are 'rights'. The fundamental management functions (planning, organising, leading, and controlling) and managerial responsibilities (e.g. making decisions or even making sure that others conduct their tasks as expected) do *not* include the 'right' to give orders, to control, or to sanction others. In the democratic organisation there are no such 'rights'. Actually, in no free and democratic organisation or social system are there such 'rights' or 'responsibilities'. *Between free individuals there cannot be orders, only consent.* The 'right' to give orders cannot be deduced from ownership rights (they only cover rights in regard to material and immaterial assets, or 'things') or from any other legitimate authoritative source of private law. Neither do organisational responsibilities establish any right to give orders, to control, or to sanction others. The *only* legitimate way to establish a 'right to give orders' (and to control and to sanction others) is via *public* law and regulations, i.e. where legitimate institutions or actors of authority ('authorities') are provided with such legal rights and entitled to use them for, and within the range of, their official duties.

9 Srivastva and Cooperrider (1986, p. 707) argued that 'while hierarchy remains, it is not hierarchy in the sense of chain-of-command. Instead, it is best depicted as a "chain-of-consent"'. Lee and Edmondson (2017, p. 46) described this notion as follows: 'The core element of self-managing organizations is radical decentralization of the authority typically granted to managers. We define radical decentralization as the elimination of the reporting relationship between manager and subordinate. In radically shifting authority to non-managerial roles, individuals in self-managing organizations no longer report to a manager who has broad and diffuse authority to allocate work, direct execution of tasks, monitor performance, sanction or fire employees, and determine promotions or raises. Indeed, the notion of "reporting to" someone who has "authority over" you becomes anathema in a self-managing organization.'

10 In a similar vein, Morrell and Hartley (2006, pp. 484–485) described political leaders' authority as legitimate if the political leaders (1) are democratically elected (2) representatives (3) who are vulnerable to deselection and (4) operate within as well as influence a constitutional and legal framework, (5) with authority that is based on a mandate whereby (6) membership of the electorate is set out in law. Morrell and Hartley's concept provides a pretty good idea of how the roles and positions of managers can be understood in the concept of representative management if they are to have legitimate authority. Malleson (2014, p. 41) summarised this idea as follows: 'Ideally, a co-op structure means that all people in positions of power and authority are elected, revocable, and accountable to the rank and file. Authority no longer derives from shareholding and property rights, but, ultimately, from the consent of the workers themselves.'

11 Also known as 'participative governance', 'shared governance', 'equal opportunity of political influence', or 'effective participation'; see classic works on participative democratic organisations such as Pateman (1970), Dahl (1971), Mulder (1971), Dachler and Wilpert (1978), Mansbridge (1980), Rothschild-Whitt and Lindenfeld (1982), Srivastva and Cooperrider (1986), and Bachrach and Botwinick (1992).

12 For instance, Mulder (1971, p. 31) concluded: 'It has been considered desirable to reduce differences in power between different levels in society, in organizations, and in groups; and participation in decision making by the less powerful members has been assumed to be one of the best means to this end.'

5

EQUALISING EMPOWERMENT[1]

From Equal Rights to Equal Power and the Idea of Equalising Empowerment

A libertarian constitution, democratic governance, and democratic management provide the principles, mechanisms, organisational structures, and processes for the democratic organisation to *formally* be a fully fledged democratic system. Together, they represent the *institutions* of the democratic organisation. However, *social* systems, like organisations, comprise institutions *and* people. In this sense, it is – of course – not only (formal) *institutions* (i.e. principles, rules and regulations, structures, and processes) but also *people* (i.e. their interests and perceptions, attitudes and behaviour, and actions and inactions) that make and shape a social system and cause it to work – and with people come psychological and social dimensions, and socio-psychological complexities and dynamics for the social system.

The question is how a social system's institutions (of governance and management) and its people (their existence and behaviour) are, or can be, related in ways that are consistent with the system's fundamental principles and values.

One of the fundamental principles of the democratic organisation – like any democratic system – is that people have *equal rights*, especially equal rights to decide on the design and functioning of the system to which they belong. People's equal right(s) to govern and to manage this system and its operations can be understood as *political equality* (Held 1987, p. 34). Dahl (1970, p. 12) made this point succinctly when he said that 'no authority can be democratic unless it is based on some principle of political equality'. And Held (1987, p. 78) argued in his *radical model of developmental democracy* that 'citizens must enjoy political and economic equality in order that nobody can be master of another and all can enjoy equal freedom and dependence in the process of collective development'.

Equal rights and political equality mean that people (must) have *equal power* (Mansbridge 1977, p. 321). Democratic organisations are built on, and for, the idea of equal rights and equal power, to provide all their members with the greatest possible freedom, equal power, and the means to govern and manage the democratic organisation and organisational affairs according to *their* interests and as *they* deem right, to pursue *their* interests, and to act and behave as *they* deem right and as is right in a democratic context – in one word: to make them equally powerful. Democratic organisations' formal structures and processes of democratic governance and management are designed and made to *empower* people – to empower them *equally*. The overall idea is that disempowered people should be empowered and empowered people should be *dis*-empowered formally, psychologically, and socially until both have equal power. I call this the principle of *equalising empowerment*.[2]

Equalising empowerment is about achieving and guaranteeing the *political equality* of every member of the social system concerning governance, management, and decision-making. Equalising empowerment is about individuals having equal power to influence the system they belong to and common issues and affairs within the system. In this sense, the idea of empowerment of all members of the democratic organisation *does* have an egalitarian component – but *only* in the sense of equal(ising) power (and equal opportunities to participate in decision-making) in the governance and management of the democratic organisation. The democratic organisation is *not* an attempt to equalise everyone and everything and to establish an egalitarian society. And it is *not* about equalising people. This would not only be unrealistic but would also go against the democratic organisation's own fundamental principle of protecting individuals' freedoms, autonomy, and integrity and, as a consequence, tolerating individual and social differences.

Despite all efforts to equalise empowerment there will, of course, still be differences and inequalities in the democratic organisation – as even the most progressive proponents of participatory or collectivist organisations (e.g. Kanter 1972, Rothschild-Whitt 1976, 1979, Mansbridge 1977, 1980, Rothschild & Whitt 1986) and researchers of egalitarian (hunter-gatherer) societies (e.g. Boehm 1993, Wiessner 2002) have noticed. There still (and always) will be *individual differences* in personality, talents, skills, competencies, knowledge, motivation, and/or commitment, and *social differences* in positions, status, social relationships, interaction (communication, cooperation, competition, and participation), and/or influence.

Such differences, some of which may even turn into systemic inequalities, will occur and remain even in the most democratic organisations. That people are different; do more or less than others; have different roles, positions, tasks, and responsibilities; and do things differently is normal for any social system. Moreover, in the sense of non-totalitarian, open, and democratic social systems that appreciate people's individual rights and freedoms, it *should* be like that;

freedom and democracy inherently entail differences and diversity. The demo-cratic organisation does not do anything about *those* differences (on the contrary, it protects, upholds, and nurtures those values). If it did, it would actually be acting against its own principles and values.

The principle of equalising empowerment suggests empowering the disem-powered many and disempowering the empowered few until the two are equally empowered only in respect to the conduct of governance and management func-tions. The following sections show how this can be achieved. A three-dimensional concept of empowerment and disempowerment is introduced that identifies the formal, psychological, and social dimensions of empowerment. The next four sections then focus on an analysis of people's formal, psychological, and social empowerment – or disempowerment – and on measures to formally, psychologic-ally, and socially *empower the disempowered many* and *disempower the empowered few*. The chapter closes with a discussion of how equalising empowerment works.

Meaning(s) and a Three-Dimensional Concept of Empowerment and Disempowerment

In management and organisation studies, the idea of *empowerment* has been around since the 1970s (Bachrach & Botwinick 1992, Perkins & Zimmerman 1995, Gandz & Bird 1996, Seibert et al. 2004, Greasley et al. 2005, Maynard et al. 2012, Pratto 2016). Since then, rhetoric about empowerment has been rife in orthodox, hierarchical organisations. However, the most far-reaching efforts towards empowerment have been tried in participative organisations, e.g. cooperatives (Jones & Svejnar 1982, Rosen 1984, Cheney 1995, Poole 1996), utopian communities (Kanter 1972), collectivist organisations (Rothschild-Whitt 1979), and hybrid organisations and networks (Stohl & Cheney 2001, Hales 2002, Ekbia & Kling 2005).

(Within an organisational context) *empowerment* can be defined technically as 'delegation of authority to the lowest level in an organization where a competent decision can be made' (Seibert et al. 2004, p. 332) so that the members of the organisation have 'the authority to make and implement their own decisions' (Greasley et al. 2005, p. 355).[3] Empowerment means that 'decisions are made by those who implement them' (Collier & Esteban 1999, p. 177). In its most general understanding, 'empowerment' might be defined as *people having or getting the power, freedom, skills, resources, capabilities, and opportunities to manage themselves and the affairs that are relevant to them, and to reason, decide, and do what they deem right.*

How far empowerment *actually* empowers people depends on how the con-cept is understood and realised. At one end of the spectrum there are mere instrumental, if not cynical, concepts of empowerment that are mainly meant to give employees or other subordinates the *feeling* of being empowered – while authority, managerial responsibilities, and control remain with superiors or power elites. At the other end of the spectrum there are fundamental concepts of egalitarian–democratic organisations and communities that give people *actual* ownership and control and ideally enable them to rule themselves (Rosen 1984, p. 312, Wilkinson 1998, Greasley et al. 2005, p. 355, Rothschild 2009, p. 596, Maynard et al. 2012). For the democratic organisation, obviously, only the highest level of empowerment is appropriate (just as only the highest level of participation is appropriate – i.e. *full* participation and *complete* control – as argued in Chapter 4 in the context of participative management).

Empowerment taken seriously brings many advantages for organisations and their members alike (Kanter 1971, p. 66, Vanek 1971, p. 17, Ackoff 1994, p. 111, Collier & Esteban 1999, p. 177, Bowman & Stone 2004, p. 280, Greasley et al. 2005, p. 358, Heywood et al. 2005, pp. 557, 559, Carson 2008, pp. 522, 524, O'Neill 2009, p. 384, Erdal 2011, pp. 19, 189, Maynard et al. 2012, pp. 1247–1249, Fernandez & Moldogaziev 2013, Altmann 2014, p. 182):

- *Formal and organisational advantages*: Organisational members have more power and actual control over their work and working lives, higher levels of responsibility, and more accountability since decisions are made by those who implement them. Work and workplaces are more attractive, there are lower rates of absenteeism and turnover, and there are higher levels of job performance and overall performance.
- *Psychological and attitudinal advantages*: Organisational members have a greater sense of personal control over their tasks and environment, greater motivation and engagement, higher (job) satisfaction, greater commitment to the organisation, more organisational loyalty, a greater sense of dignity and personal worth, more self-respect, and a higher quality of work life.
- *Social advantages*: Organisational members are more willing to share (their) skills and knowledge. There is more trust, sociability, collegiality, cooperation, and reciprocity between members of the organisation and a higher likelihood of members engaging in organisational citizenship behaviour.

Obviously, whether one is able to do what one wants and deems to be right depends on various factors or dimensions. Originally, empowerment focused on the roles and positions, related responsibilities, and conditions of the immediate work context (Maynard et al. 2012, p. 1234), such as work design and job characteristics. It also added organisational settings (e.g. policies, structures, and processes) and managerial aspects (e.g. access to resources, planning, decision-making, leading, organising, and controlling). All of these factors might be summarised as the formal dimension of empowerment and herein will be called *formal empowerment*.

Later a second dimension became increasingly relevant: *psychological empowerment*, which is mainly about people's subjective perceptions, cognition, self-efficacy, and the feeling of being empowered (Christman 1994, Zimmerman 1995, Seibert et al. 2004, Greasley et al. 2005, Maynard et al.

2012, Chen et al. 2014, Miguel et al. 2015, van Dop et al. 2016, Yu et al. 2018). This second dimension has become increasingly dominant, especially in its orthodox, 'business-oriented' or 'management-oriented' version. This concept of psychological empowerment is rather instrumental in the sense that it first focuses on the (alleged) *needs* of the organisation (and/or its owners or managers) and then on how employees *need* to be 'empowered' so that they can conduct their tasks more efficiently and effectively (for the sake of the organisation). The main (unspoken but all-determining) criterion is performativity. Aspects such as 'motivation', 'organisational commitment', 'personal development', and the 'psychological contract' are largely seen in terms of their usefulness in increasing employees' performance. The currently prevailing concept of psychological empowerment is fairly limited and largely instrumental in its scope, interpretation, and application. In contrast, the version or concept of psychological empowerment developed and applied here focuses on the individual and its personality and attitudes, needs and wants.

The formal and psychological dimensions of empowerment are indeed highly relevant. What has been completely missing so far in any concept of empowerment in management and organisation studies is the social or interpersonal dimension, i.e. *social empowerment* (what an individual is and can do among others). This is particularly surprising since organisations are one of the most common and most differentiated types of *social* system. Therefore, this chapter proposes a *three-dimensional concept of empowerment* that comprises (1) formal empowerment, (2) psychological empowerment, and (3) social empowerment:

1. *Formal empowerment* can be understood as providing people with formal roles and positions within the official structures and processes of an institutionalised social system and the official responsibilities and entitlements, rights and duties, privileges and prerogatives, signs and symbols (of power and status), and (access to) resources and opportunities that come with such formal arrangements to act, make decisions, manage, and control (others).
2. *Psychological empowerment* might be described as a cognitive state of mind or feeling of being powerful or being empowered, particularly having reasonable personal confidence in one's own abilities (efficacy and self-esteem), perceived personal control of what happens to oneself and in one's own life (locus of control), and the cognitive and emotional capabilities to achieve personal goals (goal attainment).
3. *Social empowerment* can be defined as people having reasonably established positions, status, worth, self-images, and images of how they are perceived by others (social identity); adequate and sufficient resources, opportunities, social skills, and competencies to pursue their legitimate interests and to achieve their goals within a social context; the ability to initiate, maintain, and manage social relationships, interpersonal communication, cooperation, and conflict sovereignly; and the ability to behave accordingly, i.e. to demonstrate the whole range of confident and competent behaviour of a free and independent individual within a social context.

Reasoning about empowerment along the lines of this three-dimensional framework reveals another important point: there is not only empowerment but also *dis*-empowerment – a crucial aspect that has not been addressed so far in the entire empowerment literature. 'Disempowerment' may be defined as *any reduction in people's capabilities (a) to conduct their lives (i.e. to reason, feel, decide, act, and interact) in ways that can be reasonably thought of as appropriate for human beings in a particular socio-cultural context and (b) to be equal members of a given social system (i.e. formally, psychologically, or socially they are not as empowered as other members of that social system).*

Like empowerment, disempowerment can happen in all three dimensions:

1. *Formal disempowerment* can be understood as people having 'lower', less powerful, or less influential formal positions; having no or few (managerial) responsibilities; having less access to information and resources; not being involved in formal decision-making; and regularly carrying out tasks that are portrayed or seen as inferior. In a word, people who are formally disempowered are *subordinates*.
2. *Psychological disempowerment* can be described as people showing low levels of self-esteem, a lack of confidence and self-respect, high levels of power distance, and/or any other psychological traits of the *obedient personality*.
3. *Social disempowerment* can be defined as people being marginalised; having their social identities despised or stigmatised; lacking (access to) resources and opportunities; being excluded from important and meaningful processes of sense-making, debate, and decision-making; and/or being disadvantaged in any other way concerning social resources or their participation in social life.

People can be empowered – or disempowered – by anonymous institutions (formal empowerment), by themselves (psychological empowerment), or among or via others (social empowerment). Often those people who become empowered or empower themselves possess more of the following characteristics: (a) they are more keen to and capable of acquiring formal roles and positions of power and influence and the privileges and opportunities that come with such formal arrangements (*formal empowerment*), (b) they have personal confidence in their abilities and (perceived) personal control of what happens in their lives (*psychological empowerment*), and/or (c) they have a diligently developed social identity; initiate, maintain, and manage social relationships, interpersonal communication, cooperation, and conflict sovereignly; and demonstrate the corresponding behaviour of a free individual (*social empowerment*). In contrast, those people who become *dis*-empowered or who *dis*-empower themselves have *less* of these characteristics.

Each of the three dimensions of empowerment and disempowerment can be seen (theoretically) as independent of the others. In practice, though, there usually is quite some correlation between the various dimensions of (dis) empowerment. For instance, people who are formally empowered often also feel themselves to be and see themselves a more powerful – and disempower others. There is also a considerable body of empirical evidence that formally empowered employees often show higher levels of psychological empowerment (Greasley et al. 2005, p. 358, Maynard et al. 2012, p. 1243, Francescato & Aber 2015). They then use their privileged and powerful positions and higher self-esteem to gain social dominance, i.e. to empower themselves socially – often against and at the expense of others. In turn, their social empowerment helps them to become even more formally empowered (e.g. by being provided with greater formal responsibilities, being promoted to a higher position, or being formally appointed to committees or other special roles or positions) – whereas others become formally, psychologically, and socially even more disempowered. The empowerment of the few and disempowerment of the many are often intertwined, and they influence and mutually reinforce each other considerably. Empowered members of an organisation can exert their formal, psychological, and social power and influence increasingly in multiple ways whereas disempowered members cannot – which further reinforces and enlarges the existing and emerging patterns of formal, psychological, and social empowerment and disempowerment. Over time, these pattern and processes become persistent and manifest themselves more and more clearly.

The following sections analyse how the empowerment of the few and the disempowerment of the many happen in democratic organisations – and what can be done about it, i.e. how *equalising empowerment* (empowering the disempowered and disempowering the empowered formally, psychologically, and socially until both have equal power) can be achieved. In order to keep the analysis relatively simple, the various forms of empowerment and disempowerment will be looked at individually.

The Formal, Psychological, and Social Disempowerment of the Many

One part of the solution to equalising empowerment is to empower those who are disempowered. But before it is possible to think about how members of (democratic) organisations can be formally, psychologically, or socially empowered, it is necessary to look at the causes, i.e. whether, how, and why they may be *dis*-empowered (within the democratic organisation).

Formal Disempowerment

Orthodox, hierarchical organisations disempower most of their members *systematically* and *routinely* by depriving them of their fundamental, inalienable rights and placing them in lower positions within the hierarchical order (Diefenbach, 2013a). People who are formally disempowered in such ways are *subordinates*.

From a constitutional and conceptual perspective there is no such formal disempowerment in democratic organisations: all members have equal rights and status (via their status as owners and partners), there is no formal hierarchy (and, therefore, no 'lower' positions), and there are no formal superior–subordinate relationships between people (because of the absence of formal line management). Furthermore, democratic governance and democratic management make sure that every member of the democratic organisation gets the same rights and sufficient opportunities to participate in the governance and management of the organisation and organisational affairs.

However, within *all* types of organisation, i.e. even in democratic organisations, people still can be *formally* disempowered in various ways (e.g. Nelson 2001, Ekbia & Kling 2005, Guimerà et al. 2006, Oberg & Walgenbach 2008, Rank 2008, Crowley 2012): by having less official access to information and resources, being less involved in formal or managerial decision-making, or having lesser (managerial) responsibilities to manage and control key activities (than people in formal institutions of governance or in positions of representative management). Because of their formal roles and positions, some members of staff are less powerful and less influential. In that sense they are formally disempowered – though it must be stressed that members of the democratic organisation are not formally disempowered *in principle* (like most members of orthodox organisations) but *technically*.

Nevertheless, any formal disempowerment is a serious and worrying issue because it disadvantages members of a social system systematically and comprehensively. For example, Young (2008, pp. 80–81) explained some of its consequences:

> People differently positioned in structural processes often have unequal opportunities for self-development and access to resources, to make decisions about both the conditions of their own action and that of others, or to be treated with respect or deference. These structural inequalities do not determine that every member of a less-privileged group suffers deprivation or domination. They do, however, make most members of structurally-disadvantaged groups more vulnerable to harm than others. They also put constraints on the ability of group members to achieve well-being. It is these vulnerabilities and limitations that define structural injustice more than the amount of goods or power individuals may have at a particular time.

Psychological Disempowerment

Members of organisations can also be psychologically disempowered – and most actually are. In orthodox, hierarchical organisations subordinates regularly show deeply entrenched feelings of inferiority, low levels of work-related self-esteem, lack of confidence and self-respect, and high scores on power distance.

In other words, they have internalised the identity of the 'good' subordinate. Hierarchical social order is mostly about the systematic degradation and infant-ilisation of people (Jacques 1996, p. 81, Diamond & Allcorn 2004, p. 26). In orthodox organisations and other hierarchical systems, subordinates are expected and made to show 'patterns of behaviour that dehumanize, deperson-alize, and infantilize' (Diamond & Allcorn 2004, p. 26). According to Ashforth (1994, p. 759), 'bureaucratically-oriented individuals tend to be somewhat insecure, suspicious, authoritarian, dogmatic, and lower in ability, and tend to place a higher value on conformity and order'.

Counterintuitively, in democratic organisations most members can *also* be expected to be 'good' subordinates and to show the personality traits and behaviour of the *obedient personality*. It is certainly the case that the notions of self-management, participation, and non-hierarchical structures and processes require, if not to say necessitate, psychologically strong, empowered members. However, for example, self-managing groups and units may put immense pressure on members to be 'team players', i.e. to have the mentality and to demonstrate the willingness and ability to 'fit', 'contribute', and 'perform' (read: 'behave') as expected (by the team leader and/or other powerful team members). In some respects they regulate, if not reduce and weaken, members' psychological strength (Alvesson & Willmott 2002). 'The team' – or any simi-lar collectivist ideology of 'we', 'family', or 'them and us' used as a rhetorical device by powerful actors – can be an all-encompassing metaphor, the ideological as well as actual regime that reduces most of its members to well-functioning and replaceable parts of a greater whole and disempowers them psychologically as well as practically. In her empirical research, Akella (2003, p. 54) found 'that learning organisations are, in reality, practising hegemonic regimes under the pretence of employee democracy and empowerment'. Because of such identity regulation from outside (and a corresponding exter-nally initiated and supported internalisation of dominant values and beliefs), the locus of control can be taken away from members. Little wonder then that many 'team' members' efficacy, self-esteem, and perceived personal control can be relatively low and minimal.

Social Disempowerment

Finally, social disempowerment is a profound and serious issue in any social system. Members can be socially disempowered by (1) low status, stigmatisation, marginalisation, or social exclusion; (2) having insufficient resources or being socially disadvantaged in any other way concerned with pursuing their legitimate interests; (3) not being able to initiate, maintain, and manage social relationships, interpersonal communication, cooperation, and conflict sovereignly; and/or (4) behaving accordingly, i.e. demonstrating the whole range of obedient behaviours of the 'good' subordinate.

As is the case for formal and psychological disempowerment, social disempowerment of the many is a constituting and systemic element of the orthodox, hierarchical organisation – but it can also emerge in the democratic organisation. In fact, democratic organisations can be even *more* socially controlling and disempowering than orthodox types of organisation (Barker 1993, Jacques 1996, Jermier 1998, Courpasson 2000, Akella 2003, Kärreman & Alvesson 2004, Varman & Chakrabarti 2004, Courpasson & Clegg 2006, Ackroyd & Muzio, 2007, Crowley 2012). This is because non-hierarchical social systems usually have less (or at least less prescriptive and regulative) formal policies, rules, and regulations that define and clarify people's official social status and behaviour. Moreover, the formal structures and processes (of governance and management) of non-hierarchical social systems are in many respects less rigid and bureaucratic but more enabling and empowering than those of hierarchical social systems. Individuals, therefore, are (required to be) more socially active and interactive. Greater social activity and engagement can be 'good' (in the sense of social embeddedness, belongingness, support, encouragement, and cooperation) or 'bad' (in the sense of social pressure, aggression, discouragement, and competition). Especially because of the latter, democratic organisations can be rather challenging places for some or even many people. For whatever reasons and in whatever ways, people may not feel comfortable or be able to cope with rather unstructured social processes – they may not feel (or be) 'strong' enough to navigate, act within, and cope with the social dynamics of a participative system. As a consequence, they may increasingly be excluded – or exclude themselves – from processes of sense-making, debate, and decision-making; from participating in organisational and social life; and from taking or creating opportunities for their personal development within a social context.

Instead of engaging openly and sovereignly with others, they may be more willing and keen to pre-emptively adapt and follow silently (others and/or written and unwritten rules). Like subordinates in orthodox organisations, they demonstrate 'a willingness to comply with authority, a preference for impersonal and formal relationships with others on the job, a desire for strict adherence to rules and procedures, and a need to identify with the organization and conform to norms' (Ashforth 1994, p. 759). Hence, even members of democratic organisations may conform (voluntarily and willingly) to (assumed) expectations, follow 'rituals of subordination' (Scott 1990, pp. 2, 66), and show the appropriate levels of 'learned helplessness' (Bassman & London 1993, p. 22, Van Vugt 2006, p. 361) – i.e. behave in socially disempowered and self-disempowering ways. Additionally, members of participative, empowering, and democratic organisations can be socially rather *dis*empowered – and can demonstrate rather (self-)disempowering behaviour.

Empowering the Disempowered Many

Overall, if one believes in the fundamental idea(s) of the democratic organisation one might be quite concerned and disappointed about the possible existence or emergence of formal, psychological, or social disempowerment of its members. Nevertheless, the democratic organisation *does* have the means to pre-emptively prevent this from happening and to combat the disempowerment of the many. The following three sub-sections discuss measures for the formal, psychological, and social empowerment of the disempowered many in turn.

Formal Empowerment

Formally, all members of the democratic organisation are already quite empowered by its official structures and processes of *democratic governance* (democratic institutions of governance, legitimate authoritative sources, democratic governing, and 'good governance') and *democratic management* (self-management, representative management, and participative management). The concepts of *self-management* and *subsidiarity* especially empower members of the democratic organisation *considerably*. Together, these two concepts make sure that – unlike in orthodox organisations – especially members without formal management positions *can*, and actually *do*, conduct management functions and carry out managerial responsibilities as much as possible. Formal office-holders' managerial responsibilities are then as minimal and as residual as possible. In that way, formal disempowerment of members without formal management roles is kept relatively contained in the democratic organisation.

Nonetheless, because of the existence of specialised institutions of governance (boards, committees, and councils) and formal management positions within the democratic organisation, those who are *not* office-holders of such formal positions *are* formally disempowered; they (naturally) have less access to information and resources, have fewer (managerial) responsibilities, and are less involved in formal decision-making compared to people in management positions. (Even) the democratic organisation creates or opens up this formal power differential. The question is how this power gap can be closed by formal means, or at least minimised. There are several tools readily available in the democratic organisation:

- Having access to, and being provided with, all the information relevant to their work and the management of the entity they belong to empowers non-office-holders and is crucial to enable them to participate in decision-making. A very thorough application of the principle of *transparency* (see p. 61 in Chapter 3) significantly helps to counter the information imbalance. According to this principle (as defined in Chapter 3), all members of the organisation have free and equal access to, and are automatically provided with, all relevant non-confidential information about the formal organisational policies, rules, and regulations of governance; the general procedures for making decisions; and specific information relevant to the particular decision-making they are involved in. In this sense, every office-holder and manager is *bound to* provide non-office-holders with relevant information. Making information relevant to the execution of management functions routinely available to all members is not discretionary but *compulsory*.

- Transparency provides the basis for holding managers and office-holders *accountable* – another principle of democratic governance that was outlined in Chapter 3 (see p. 62). According to this principle and concept, it is not an option but an *obligation* of office-holders to account for their decisions and actions (or non-decisions and inactions) at *any time* to *anyone* who has a legitimate interest. Accountability is a very powerful tool for those who have the right and means to assess, judge, sanction, and alter an office-holder's conduct of office.
- Transparency and accountability provide some necessary groundwork for the concept of *legitimate authority* – embodied in the democratic organisation via the concept of *representative management* (see pp. 77–80). According to this concept, all managers are *representatives* (and *not* supervisors) that are (a) elected or appointed democratically, (b) obliged to execute the will of those whom they represent, and (c) supervised, controlled, held accountable, reconfirmed, or replaced by those whom they represent (and/or by institutions formally provided with the task of overseeing the conduct of office of representatives). Specified in that way, the notion of legitimate authority not only limits the ability of any kind of superior–subordinate relationship to emerge but also turns the tables in favour of non-office-holders; *they* are the formally empowered ones.
- In addition, according to the principles of *participative management* (see pp. 80–84), members of the democratic organisation have equal rights and opportunities to participate in formal decision-making processes at all levels of the organisation and to collaborate with organisational institutions of representative management, including individual management positions. And participation means *full* participation – which severely blurs the lines between formal positions of management and non-management positions and between office-holders and non-office-holders.

Altogether, it may be argued that formally empowering (actually or potentially) disempowered members of the democratic organisation is not so much about inventing new measures but about applying existing ones thoroughly: the notions and concepts of transparency, accountability, legitimate authority, and participation are each rather sharp tools. Together, especially seen against the wider background of democratic governance and democratic management, they formally empower disempowered member of the democratic organisation more than sufficiently.

Psychological Empowerment

Psychological empowerment focuses on individuals *as such* – their feelings and perceptions of being empowered, their mindsets, and their personal identities

(Seibert et al. 2004, pp. 332, 335, Greasley et al. 2005, p. 356, Maynard et al. 2012, pp. 1234–1235, Chen et al. 2014, Yu et al., 2018). There are various understandings concerning which areas psychological empowerment covers. According to Zimmerman (1995), psychological empowerment comprises three dimensions: intrapersonal, interactional, and behavioural. In contrast, here only the *intra*personal dimension is meant as psychological empowerment, whereas the other two dimensions are subsumed under social empowerment (which will be discussed in the next sub-section). Focusing on the intrapersonal dimension, Conger and Kanungo (1988, p. 474) define psychological empowerment as 'a process of enhancing feelings of self-efficacy among organizational members'. Menon (quoted in Greasley et al., 2005, p. 357) described psychological empowerment as 'a cognitive state of perceived control, perceived competence and goal internalisation'. And according to Miguel et al. (2015, p. 901), psychological empowerment addresses 'how people think about themselves and includes monitoring and self-perceived effectiveness for controlling motivation, skills, and perception domains or beliefs about their own skills'. Altogether, psychological empowerment might be defined as personal confidence in one's own abilities (self-esteem), perceived personal control of what happens in one's life (locus of control), and the cognitive and emotional ability to achieve personal goals (goal attainment).

Legitimate social systems – be they groups, organisations, or even nation-states – are not completely responsible for the state of mind of their members (only totalitarian regimes think that they have this responsibility). However, social systems, of course, represent some of the contextual factors that influence people's feelings and perceptions (about themselves, others, and the wider environment). In this sense, there *are* ways that disempowered members of the democratic organisation can be empowered, or empower themselves, psychologically. As argued in Chapter 4, democratic management is particularly based on the notion that people manage their own work, work-related issues, and organisational affairs first and foremost by themselves (according to the concept of *self-management* and the principle of *subsidiarity*). *There is nothing more (psychologically) empowering than actually doing things, making decisions, being in charge of something, and being responsible for something.* And, in democratic organisations, if people cannot conduct all management functions by themselves then they at least all have equal (legal and political) rights and actual opportunities to participate regularly in all governance and management functions (i.e. planning, organising, leading, and controlling) and in all formal decision-making processes at all levels of the organisation (constitutional, strategic, and operational) that are relevant to them (according to the concept of *participative management* and the principle of *full participation*). Together, the concepts of self-management and participative management and the principles of subsidiarity and full participation provide individual members with broad and far-reaching rights, opportunities, and responsibilities in regard to the management of their work and themselves.

In so doing, they (may) increase individual members' self-esteem, sense of having an internal locus of control, and sense of goal attainment considerably and help them to feel psychologically empowered.

With the focus on the individual it should be clear that self-management and participative management are not reduced to instrumental concepts that primarily aim at enabling people to fit better into existing social systems and to function smoothly within – and for! – predefined organisational regimes, purposes, structures, and processes. True psychological empowerment means that people are seen as, put first as, and develop into *autonomous individuals*, and that they (can) feel free to reason, decide, and act as *they* deem right, necessary, and appropriate. The focus is on *individuals'* self-management and participative management; although the democratic organisation is a collective enterprise, it is *not* 'the collective' but *individual* members that are operating and cooperating (and who are, thus, responsible for all performance and success). The fundamental notions of the free individual and self-ownership as well as individuals' actual status as owners provide strong rationales to stave off the oppressive elements of collectivist regimes. Individuals who are self-managing their work and participating in the management of organisational affairs have every reason to think independently without interference from external authorities (*independent intellect*); to be able and confident to formulate their own will and manage themselves and social affairs accordingly (*self-mastery*); and to feel confident about themselves and their personality traits *as individuals* with a developed personal identity *and* social orientation (i.e. with developed emotional, social, and cultural intelligence and prosocial behaviour).

Social Empowerment

As explained on p. 92, social empowerment can be understood as empowerment of people within and by an interactive social context. It refers to how well their positions, status, and worth are established among others (social identity); how much and how well they can pursue their interests relative to others (interests); what they are able to do and to achieve in social situations (social skills and competencies); and whether they behave accordingly.

How much people are socially empowered primarily depends on how they see themselves among others and how they are seen by others – i.e. their *social identity* (e.g. Tajfel & Turner 1979, Ashforth & Mael 1989, Musson & Duberley 2007). Tajfel (1978, p. 63) argued that social identity can be understood as that part of an individual's self-concept 'which derives from his knowledge of his membership of a social group (or groups) together with the value and emotional significance attached to that membership'. According to Hogg et al. (1995, p. 257), 'the perception that one is enacting a role satisfactorily should enhance feelings of self-esteem, whereas perceptions of poor role performance may engender doubts about one's self-worth, and may even produce symptoms of psychological distress'.

With its fundamental principles and values of individual freedom, democracy, equality and justice, self-ownership, and equal rights and responsibilities, the democratic organisation provides a values framework with which members can positively identify and around which they can develop a sound social identity (provided that these values are acknowledged and practised by all members of the organisation in their regular daily activities, communication, and cooperation). Moreover, social empowerment means what one can actually *do* within a social context – i.e. whether one can realise one's interests. Social empowerment means the ability to pursue one's interests within a social context; the ability to have an influence and an impact on others, within a range of possibilities from merely being accepted to making others behave in certain ways; and even the ability to have one's values institutionalised and/or internalised by others (these three abilities equate to Lukes' 1974 three dimensions of power). To pursue one's interests in a social context makes one powerful if one is able to voice one's interests, take action, and achieve goals.

Therefore, it is crucial that members of the democratic organisation see sufficient opportunities in the processes of democratic governance and democratic management to pursue their interests. This can mainly be achieved by comprehensively institutionalised participation – *full* participation in all governance and management functions as well as in all relevant formal decision-making processes (as explained on pp. 80–81): participation in the self-management of individuals' work; in temporary or permanent self-managing groups, networks, or institutions; in the conduct of management functions; and in organisational institutions of democratic governance and representative management (e.g. boards, councils, committees, and/or assemblies).

This, finally, hints at the importance of having the *social skills and competencies* that are relevant and necessary within a (particular) social context for maintaining one's position, pursuing one's interests, and participating in the governance and management of common affairs. Having appropriate social skills and competencies means that one can successfully navigate social situations. It means that one has, or can acquire, the knowledge and the cognitive, emotional, social, and cultural intelligence and capabilities necessary to make sense of, critically reflect on, and cope with social phenomena; to initiate, maintain, and manage social relationships sovereignly; to communicate and interact effectively with others; and to behave and act within a specific social context as is required, as one deems right, and/or as one feels comfortable as a free individual.

Obviously, people have various levels of such social skills and competencies (to some extent related to their personalities and personal backgrounds) – and members of the democratic organisation are no different. Because of its fundamental ideas of self-management, participative management, cooperation, and participation, the democratic organisation provides manifold opportunities to acquire, to practice, and to improve one's social skills and competencies, and to develop and to empower oneself socially, mainly via 'learning by doing'. But these opportunities are at the same time challenges, and perhaps significant challenges for some members. The democratic organisation, therefore, must also provide comprehensive training and ongoing support for members' personal and skills development. In some respects this is probably even more the case than in orthodox organisations, because even in fully developed democratic societies not many people have been socialised, educated, and provided with the skills and competencies necessary for self-management and participative management.

The Formal, Psychological, and Social Empowerment of the Few

Like in any other organisation, in the democratic organisation there is the possibility that some people will be formally, psychologically, or socially 'overtly' empowered – that they will become much more empowered than 'the rest'. The formal, psychological, and/or social empowerment of the few is problematic and illegitimate when it happens at the expense of others, threatens others' fundamental and inalienable (human and civil) rights, or otherwise impacts negatively on their legitimate interests, equal opportunities, life chances, or personal development. Thus, in any social system that claims and aspires to protect and to enable the individual – *all* individuals – or that claims and aspires to be democratic, to be based on, and to promote equal rights and equal opportunities, *disproportionately* and *illegitimately* empowered members need to be disempowered (until they are as equally empowered as others).

Before it is possible to look at how illegitimate (inappropriate, unfair, and unjust) empowerment of the few can be reduced, nullified, or even completely avoided, it is necessary to understand how some members of a social system (here, a democratic organisation) can be formally, psychologically, and/or socially overtly empowered.

Formal Empowerment

Most democratic organisations (especially larger ones) have various institutions of governance and individual management positions. These formal positions, despite being designed, maintained, and controlled fairly tightly by the principles of democratic governance and representative management, can formally empower office-holders in at least three different ways.

First, formal management positions empower their holders by providing privileged and exclusive access to relevant and crucial information, tangible and intangible resources, and decision-making processes (while at the same time excluding other members of the organisation – non-office-holders – from this kind of access and potential usage). It is even meant to be the case that with the creation of specialised management positions, office-holders gain specific management knowledge and competencies (which they then must use to execute the tasks and management functions for which they are responsible).

Hence, even in participative and empowering, relatively non-hierarchical democratic organisations, some members can be formally more empowered than others because of their formal positions and responsibilities.

For example, when Jane Mansbridge (1980, p. 210) researched participatory workplaces in a U.S. crisis centre (with the pseudonym 'Helpline') in the early 1970s, she found that:

> Helpline's staff believed in equal salaries, equal respect, and equal power. But Helpline's division of labor precluded an equal distribution of power. Fund raising, representing one's service group ..., or acting as coordinator, vice coordinator, or treasurer provided individuals with resources that gave them greater than average power over the direction of the organization.

Burrows (2008, p. 283) described very clearly how the problem constitutes itself within organisations:

> If some people have jobs that are empowering, and others that are exclusively deadening or menial, the former will *necessarily* dominate all conceptualization of policy options, all proposals for structural change, all discussion at meetings, and all decisions which affect the business and workers as a whole. The latter will listen, and perhaps debate proposals made by others, and even vote if such is required – but the very nature of their work package will limit their knowledge and skills, and thus their ability to participate effectively as equal partners in the workplace.

Even in democratic organisations formal management positions might be created that formally empower office-holders considerably.

The second way that office-holders can be formally empowered relates to democratic organisations' democratic and participative nature, which leads to a tendency in these organisations to create and establish more and more formal institutions of governance and management, such as boards, councils, committees, and assemblies. These formal bodies create many formal positions and functions that are, theoretically, available to all members. Nevertheless, often it is only a minority that actively seeks appointment to such formal positions and responsibilities. For whatever reason, some members volunteer for more formal positions than others. This not only empowers those individuals formally but also overall creates a rather unhealthy constellation of governance and management.

The *accumulation of formal positions and functions* is a serious issue. Although 'legal' (if the relevant authoritative sources do not have any limitations in regard to holding offices), the accumulation of formal positions and functions – and the formal empowerment of 'grey eminencies' that goes hand in hand with it – is definitely a problem for democratic organisations since it provides a few individuals with largely uncontrolled power (it actually creates an oligarchy). Moreover, it goes against the idea of separation of powers and 'checks and balances' (office-holders can be members of the very same committees that provide legislation for the executive positions they hold or that are supposed to check their conduct of office). A (severe) unequal allocation of formal positions and functions decidedly goes against the spirit of *democratic* self-governance and self-management.

The final way that office-holders can be formally empowered relates to *illegitimate* empowerment (by others or themselves), which results from their carrying out their role like orthodox management, i.e. claiming line management responsibilities and demonstrating an autocratic or authoritarian management style. Managers may do this not because they are formally compelled, entitled, or encouraged to do so (as in a hierarchical organisation) but because of their *personality*, *attitudes*, and *personal management style*. In the context of the social empowerment of the empowered few, there are 'aggrandisers', 'petty tyrants', and 'careerists', who are exactly the type of people who commonly demonstrate such autocratic and authoritarian management styles. Alternatively, the people who act in this way may just think they should behave like a 'boss' in their formal role and management position and micro-manage everything and everyone.

Although this is not a full abuse of power (like corruption or other illegal activities while in office), it establishes a (personal) management style and regime that are in stark contrast to the ideas of representative management and cooperative collaboration. Such a managerialistic, micro-managing, or even autocratic management style can be quite patronising, annoying, and stressful, especially for those who have to work with such a managerialistic manager. Moreover, it represents a serious problem for the democratic organisation because it changes an originally acceptable formal management position and conduct of office into formal management practices that are fundamentally inconsistent and at odds with the principles of democratic management. It is not an exaggeration to say that *managerialism*, i.e. the implementation and application of orthodox management and performance measurement concepts in non-hierarchical social systems, represents a serious threat to the very nature and existence of these systems.[4]

Overall, formal empowerment of the few can happen in the democratic organisation largely by individuals gaining and holding legitimate management positions, in particular via:

- accumulation of specific (management) knowledge and competences via formal management positions;
- accumulation of formal positions, roles, and functions, such as membership of formal institutions of governance and management;
- conducting office like orthodox management, i.e. claiming line management responsibilities and demonstrating a micro-managing, autocratic, or authoritarian management style.

Psychological Empowerment

Work – understood not as (mere) 'salaried, dependent work' but in a very general sense as any kind of human cognitive and/or physical transformative or creative activity – can be psychologically empowering (e.g. by providing satisfaction, increased confidence in one's abilities, control, and achievements). Work within an organisational context can be even more empowering (because of the additional structural and procedural means, resources, and opportunities an organisation provides, which can make work a lever for one's own confidence, competencies, and capabilities). And work for a democratic organisation can be extremely empowering (because its governance and management structures and processes primarily provide for, and require, *self*-management and *self-managing* individuals).

There is nothing wrong with being, or trying to be, psychologically empowered. On the contrary, as argued earlier, psychological empowerment – i.e. having reasonable personal confidence in one's own abilities (self-esteem and self-efficacy), perceiving that one has personal control of what happens to oneself and in one's life (locus of control), and having the cognitive and emotional ability to achieve personal goals (goal attainment) – is a characteristic and necessary condition of the 'sane' person (a concept developed by Fromm 1956/1971). Psychological empowerment, though, can be a rather unhealthy phenomenon in both absolute and relative terms. In *absolute terms*, this is the case when confidence turns into hubris, personal control into obsessive control (or even obsessive-compulsive personality disorder), and goal orientation into fixation. In *relative terms*, this is the case when one's own psychological empowerment is largely seen, pursued, and achieved relative to others, i.e. a relational construct where one's psychological empowerment happens at the expense of others – where it depends on and leads to the formal, psychological, and social disempowerment of others. Such psychological empowerment is not only based on an inflated self-image but also about seeing oneself as 'superior' *relative to others*; *being* 'superior' suggests being superior *to others* and being *a* superior to others. In this sense, this kind of psychological empowerment means that some people regard themselves not only *as* superiors and 'leaders' (e.g. Coutu 2005) but also as *superior to others* – and these others are perceived not only as subordinates and followers but also as *inferior*.

Individuals who think in this way largely follow stereotypical scripts of orthodox leadership theories or ideologies, such as *trait leadership theory* (Carlyle 1841/1888, Conger & Kanungo 1988), that claim that powerful people (such as leaders) have personality traits, cognitive abilities, skills, and competencies that (only) *some* people have.[5] Clearly, there can be only a few of such superiors or leaders (ideally, only one), and there can be, and *must* be, many subordinates or followers (ideally, masses). This is where and why this kind of psychological empowerment of the few is troublesome for everyone involved and not legitimate; it is largely based on and achieved by aggrandising some in rather questionable and unhealthy ways and by belittling many others – again, in rather questionable and unhealthy ways.

Social Empowerment

On p. 92, social empowerment was defined as people having reasonably established positions, status, worth, self-images, and images of how they are perceived by others (social identity); adequate and sufficient resources, opportunities, social skills, and competencies to pursue their legitimate interests and to achieve their goals within a social context; the ability to initiate, maintain, and manage social relationships, interpersonal communication, cooperation, and conflict sovereignly; and the ability to behave accordingly, i.e. to demonstrate the whole range of confident and competent behaviour of a free and independent individual within a social context.

As in the case of psychological empowerment, there is nothing wrong with members of a social system striving for social empowerment – as long as an individual's social empowerment does not come at the expense of others. This is where, and why, the social empowerment of the few becomes problematic. For example, in his research on egalitarian tribes, Wiessner (2002, p. 233) pointed out that *aggrandisers* – 'who alter egalitarian institutions to suit their own ends through debt, coercion, or marginalization' and vie for elevated social status, prestige, and wealth – are the key reason for the emergence of inequality (p. 234). 'Ambitious' people, such as aggrandisers, often empower themselves socially in rather questionable ways that may be summarised as *organisational misbehaviour* (Bassman & London 1993, Rayburn & Rayburn 1996, Vredenburgh & Bender 1998, Vickers & Kouzmin 2001, Zapf & Gross 2001, Bryant & Cox 2003, Vandekerckhove & Commers 2003). Ashforth (1994, pp. 756–757) provided a good description of some of these countless little acts of empowered people's daily inappropriate behaviour, in this case autocratic managers:

> Recurring elements appear to include: close supervision, distrust and suspicion, cold and impersonal interactions, severe and public criticism of others' character and behaviour, condescending and patronizing behaviour, emotional outbursts, coercion, and boastful behaviour; they suggest an individual who emphasizes authority and status differences, is rigid and inflexible, makes arbitrary decisions, takes credit for the efforts of others and blames them for mistakes, fails to consult with others or keep them informed, discourages informal interaction among subordinates, obstructs their development, and deters initiative and dissent. Pervasive themes in these descriptions are a tendency to overcontrol others and to treat them in an arbitrary, uncaring, and punitive manner.

People showing, and empowering themselves via, such organisational misbehaviour might be called 'petty tyrants' (Ashforth 1994), 'Machiavellians' (Rayburn & Rayburn 1996), 'egotistic leaders' (Aronson 2001), or simply 'modern careerists' (Vickers & Kouzmin 2001). But, however they are called, they share the common feature that their main concerns and deliberate actions are primarily geared towards personal gain (under an official rhetoric of serving the greater good and masked by demonstrating the etiquette of collegiality) and belittling others. They 'care about their own personal power and status, often depending on conspiracies and excuses, and resorting to distortion of truth and manipulation of followers to their own ends' (Aronson 2001, p. 253). As argued by Knights and O'Leary (2006, p. 126), their conduct of office and managerial responsibilities constitute 'a failure of ethical leadership that derives from the pre-occupation with the self that drives individuals to seek wealth, fame and success regardless of moral considerations'.

Social empowerment of the few, especially when it is primarily about the pursuit of personal interests against and at the expense of others, is deeply problematic from a principle-based and practical standpoint for those who are directly or indirectly exposed to such behaviour as well as for any democratic social system. It is illegitimate, socially unacceptable, immoral, and sometimes even illegal – and it can happen in democratic organisations.

Disempowering the Empowered Few

The formal, psychological, and social empowerment of the few constitutes serious and systemic problems for the democratic organisation as well as for most of its members. Together, these forms of empowerment seriously threaten the very idea and even the existence of the democratic organisation. If they happen widely and regularly, they change the democratic organisation into a hierarchical autocracy or oligarchy, i.e. turn it into an orthodox organisation. The illegitimate and disproportional empowerment of the few, therefore, must not only be addressed thoroughly and specifically but also tackled with measures that are consistent with the democratic organisation's principles and values.

Formal Disempowerment

Formal management positions, even without line authority, empower office-holders considerably, mostly by providing them with privileged access to relevant and crucial information, resources, and decision-making processes. Therefore, it is crucial to *directly limit the authority of offices and office-holders*. As discussed in the context of the formal empowerment of the disempowered (see pp. 98–99), the concepts of democratic governing (in particular *transparency* and *accountability*) and representative and participative management are particularly responsible for providing such necessary measures.

(Compulsory) transparency makes sure that managers do not have exclusive access to or possession of information and cannot use information as a strategic or tactical tool. Moreover, they have legitimate authority only as representatives and are obliged to carry out their role according to the will of those whom they represent. They are controlled and held accountable by those people and/or by formal institutions of governance. As Erdal (2011, p. 164) argued:

> The fact that the directors are accountable to the employees does change things. When you know that you can be sacked by the people you are leading, your attitude will be different. ... You will tend to be keen to make sure that your decisions are well understood, and that you have listened to the opinions of the people you are leading. You will also tend to pay attention to the reasonable desires and needs of the employee-owners.

Moreover, (compulsory) transparency means that all of the managerial responsibilities and management functions that office-holders execute are open to full participation, i.e. all members of the relevant unit are entitled to be involved in decision-making. When O'Mahony and Ferraro (2007, p. 1089) researched the emergence of governance in an open-source community (Debian), they discovered that the governance system was particularly designed to limit the authority (of leaders) through democratic means:

> We found that Debian members were only interested in supporting a positional basis of authority if this role was also limited in ways that facilitated democratic control by the rest of the community. We found that positional authority, once created, was limited in four ways that preserved democratic rule. First, the Debian constitution requires those with positional power to defer to the wishes of the collective by making 'decisions which are consistent with the consensus of the opinions of the developers.' Second, a Debian project leader is subject to the same rules as any member; he or she is not entitled to special privileges. ... A third limit on positional power is the failsafe measure of recall by the collective via general resolution. Any member has the right to propose a general resolution that can counter a leader's actions. ... The fourth way that democratic rule constrains positional authority is through a countervailing source of authority. For example, projectwide decision-making power is split between the project leader and a technical committee empowered to 'decide any technical matter where developers' jurisdictions overlap'.

Concerning the accumulation of formal positions and functions, organisations can easily limit terms of office (e.g. to two or four years; Hernandez 2006, p. 116) and limit the number of memberships of boards or committees a person can hold. Moreover, they can make sure that everyone has not only equal *rights* but also equal *opportunities* to hold office and that membership is diverse (Dahl 1985, pp. 21–22, Bachrach & Botwinick 1992, p. 71, Jaumier 2016, p. 7).

However, even if all possible formal policies and means of regulation of democratic governance and democratic management are in place to confine and limit formal management positions and office-holders as far as possible, there is still the possibility that office-holders will formally empower themselves disproportionately. This is the case when office is conducted like orthodox management. For instance, even if managers do not have any formal line authority or supervisory responsibilities (in the spirit of democratic management), managerialistic managers can still (try to) micro-manage others and demonstrate a rather autocratic or authoritarian management style.

Formal measures to counter such personal management styles are possible but limited. There can be company policies, rules, and regulations clarifying and outlining that only democratic or participative management styles are acceptable and that managerialistic, micro-managing, or even autocratic or authoritarian management styles are not acceptable and will not be tolerated. Such policies can influence how office-holders conduct their roles and management functions and can serve as a reference for those who might be exposed to managerial misconduct. These *formal* means of handling personal management styles can be effective, but *social* means (see the sub-section 'Social Disempowerment' on pp. 111–112) are probably even more so in countering such behavioural and relational issues.

Psychological Disempowerment

On p. 106 it was argued that the psychological empowerment of the few can be a rather unhealthy phenomenon in absolute terms, both for *those who are empowered* (e.g. hubris; obsessive control and fixation; mixed score in openness to experience; high conscientiousness, extraversion, and neuroticism; but low agreeableness) and in relative terms for *others* (who may experience bullying, patronising treatment, and belittlement from the empowered person). It tends to be rather *extreme, unbalanced* types of people who are overtly empowered psychologically or who seek to empower themselves psychologically at the expense of others – organisational psychopaths.

Hence, the idea emerges of psychologically disempowering the empowered few by encouraging them to develop a more balanced, more moderate, and less ambitious personality and a strong prosocial orientation – or similar psychological traits and orientations. However, notions such as 'balance' and 'moderation' may not be suitable means to counter the disproportional psychological empowerment of the few. There is a practical argument and a principle-based argument.

The practical argument is that such suggestions – even if well meant – are probably rather unrealistic. Moderate, let alone decent or even ethical, psychological traits and orientations simply do not fit with the majority of (overly) ambitious people, aggrandisers, careerists, autocratic leaders, and other organisational psychopaths. Most people with strong egocentric and anti-social personality traits (high scores in conscientiousness, extraversion, and neuroticism, and a low score in agreeableness) are neither willing to nor capable of showing more decent personality traits or social behaviour.[6] Their imbalanced personality traits and non-social, if not to say anti-social, orientation is 'their personality', 'what drives them', 'what works for them', and 'what is good for them' (from their perspective) – so why should they change?[7] Countless managers have gone through 'leadership training courses', 'communication workshops', and 'participative management seminars' to no or little avail.[8]

The principle-based argument concerns the notion of free individuals and people's right to self-ownership. As argued in the context of the discussion of the libertarian constitution of the democratic organisation (see Chapter 2), in a democratic system that acknowledges, guarantees, and supports people's rights and status as free individuals and their inalienable rights in themselves, attempts to change people directly are illegitimate. People's minds, personality traits, personal identity, and even character and typical attitudes (altogether their 'personality') form the inseparable part of the individual that falls under self-ownership and are, therefore, sacrosanct and protected by individuals' inalienable rights in and to themselves (and are further protected by human and civil rights). Hence, within a democratic system – actually, within *any* social system – measures to empower or disempower, or otherwise *directly* shape or change, people personally or psychologically find their limits when it comes to the personality and individual inalienable rights of the system's members.[9]

Measures intended to shape, alter, or steer people's personalities are only legitimate as long as they respect these boundaries. This means that with respect to people's personalities and anything else that is covered and protected by individuals' inalienable rights of self-ownership (and/or human or civil rights) there can only be *indirect* measures, i.e. measures targeted at the conditions, context, or situation people live within, and providing options and incentives (rewards and/or punishment) so that people are still free to choose and to make decisions.

Social Disempowerment

Finally, it shall be inquired how the empowered few can be socially *disempowered*. As already explained, a minority of members of a social system can be *socially* empowered by (1) having high(er) status, or exclusive possession of and/or access to crucial tangible or intangible resources; (2) being disproportionately advantaged and capable of pursuing their personal or group interests against and at the expense of others and the whole; and/or (3) showing corresponding domineering and manipulative attitudes and (mis)behaviour.

These are some of the typical characteristics of social dominance (Sidanius & Pratto 1999) and power elites (Mills 1956). Each of them goes against the fundamental principles of the democratic organisation and indeed any other decent social system. Together, they seriously threaten the very idea and functioning of the democratic organisation. Wiessner (2002, p. 235), therefore, rightly demanded that 'egalitarian norms and relations must be constantly enforced against aggrandizers and free riders'. However, it is probably fair to assume that most of the socially empowered few are neither willing to nor capable of undoing their own social dominance, their privileged status, and their social power. The initiative to achieve equal social relations between empowered and disempowered, or between leaders and followers, therefore must come from those who are not socially empowered (Srivastva and Cooperrider 1986 called this the 'egalitarian spirit' or 'egalitarian ideal', whereas Boehm 1993, pp. 228–233, called it 'egalitarian behaviour'). Or, as the founder of the Mondragón cooperative, José María Arizmendiarrieta, once said (quoted in Erdal 2011, p. 196): 'Our beloved democracy can degenerate into a dictatorship through the abuse of power by those at the top – but also through the failure of those at the bottom to use the power they have.' In this sense, it is now time to look at what 'those at the bottom' (the disempowered many) can do – or even *must* do – to socially disempower 'those at the top' (the empowered few) in order to achieve equal social relations. The remainder of this sub-section looks at various ways in which the empowered few can be socially disempowered, in particular by:

- challenging privileging knowledge and privileging positions;
- exercising social control, especially upward control;
- carrying out social actions to confine leaders and to contain the social dominance of leaders and other aggrandisers;
- promoting an organisational culture of equal(ising) power.

Challenging Privileging Knowledge and Privileging Positions

Based on the discussion so far, it seems clear that probably all societies will sooner or later have well-defined and well-protected areas where 'special' knowledge and skills reside (e.g. sacred sites or temples, monasteries, secret societies, professions, universities, consultancies, bureaucracies, and administrations) – and also 'special' people who are the ones, *the only ones*, allowed to and (allegedly) capable of accessing, understanding, and using this special knowledge (e.g. priests, monks, social elites, professionals, academics, managers and leaders, bureaucrats, and administrators). It is relatively obvious that such protected and monopolised knowledge, along with its exclusive access and usage, creates privileged positions and, as a consequence, rather large power differentials and unequal social relationships.

Rothschild and Whitt (1986, p. 60) therefore called for a '"demystification" of specialized knowledge', i.e. 'efforts to simplify, explicate, and make available to the membership at large formerly exclusive knowledge' (Rothschild & Whitt, 1986, p. 106). As they further explained (p. 114):

In its essence, demystification is the opposite of specialization and professionalization. Where experts and professionals seek licenses to hoard or at least get paid for their knowledge, collectivists would give it away. Central to their purpose is the breakdown of the division of labor and pretense of expertise. In effect, demystification reinforces egalitarian, democratic control over the organization.

Rothschild and Whitt might have gone a bit too far in the spirit of the 1970s and early 1980s when they suggested breaking down specialisation, division of labour, professionalisation, and expert knowledge as such. But they definitely had a point when they criticised all of the (potential) social dominance and inequalities that are related to, and might stem from, exclusive knowledge and privileges, specialisation, and professionalisation. In this sense, it is not professional or special knowledge per se that is problematic but professional or special knowledge that is, or is portrayed and used as, *privileging* (differentiating, dividing) knowledge. *Privileging knowledge* is data, information, knowledge, skills, or capabilities that create social inequalities and power differentials when used and applied in certain ways, and that provide the possessor of that knowledge with the ability to enlarge their status, to dominate others, and to rule, (mis)lead, and exploit them. Privileging knowledge is not professional knowledge and technical expertise per se but their exclusive and controlled accessibility, calculated application, and selective usage in a social context (i.e. in a social relationship, or a social situation of interaction, communication, cooperation, or competition) that empowers some and disempowers others. In this sense, it is not about counteracting professional knowledge *as such* (or its operational use and application) but about demystifying and combatting its privileging, calculated presentation, use, and application at the interface between the professional and the non-professional, and making sure that it does not create a power differential.

Mystification of knowledge, unfortunately, is exactly what is currently seen with the prevailing 'management knowledge'. It appears that the modern understanding of management was particularly invented to create, elevate, and protect a new power elite, the 'managers'. Only *they*, so it is claimed, have the knowledge, skills, and abilities to manage (the corporation and people) 'professionally' (Burnham 1941, Drucker 1954, Petit 1961, Rosen 1984, Willmott 1984, Deem & Brehony 2005, Diefenbach 2009a).

This portrait could not be further from the truth. Actually, *all* people with full capacity manage, are capable of managing, and are managers (Grey 1999). According to Willmott (1984, p. 350), '"management", in the sense of reflexive social action, is intrinsic to human agency'. Every adult manages their daily work, life, tasks, and activities across the whole range of management functions (planning, organising, leading, and controlling) in knowledgeable, competent, multi-dimensional, and complex ways (Grey 1999, p. 564). The management of modern life requires handling countless pieces of information, making hundreds of decisions every day, and using skills and competencies from various professions, including, of course, business and management. Every street vendor conducts the same range of management functions as any celebrated billionaire entrepreneur or CEO of a multinational corporation – and the former often face much more challenging business environments, take relatively more risks, work much harder, and deserve their hard-earned income much more than the latter.

So, even if there are 'managers' or other specialists in the democratic organisation (i.e. people who are officially elected or appointed office-holders of management positions) and even if these people are 'learned' managers with special qualifications, professional knowledge, and expertise, the management functions they execute are *not* 'special' – and also their status as managers has nothing (or should not have anything) 'special' about it. Managers merely do what almost everyone else also does – or is potentially capable of doing. Mystification of management, management knowledge, or managers has no place in organisations or society.

It is a similar case with the notion of 'leaders' and 'leadership'. As outlined on p. 106, trait leadership theory (and similar ideologies, such as charismatic leadership) claims that leaders are 'special' because they have the necessary personality traits, abilities, skills, and competencies to be leaders and that only *some* people have or can truly acquire these attributes. And only *they* can provide the leadership necessary for everyone else. This orthodox, if not to say archaic, idea and ideology of leadership and leaders can – and must! – be challenged in principle. Kerr and Jermier (1978) argued that 'professionals', 'knowledge workers', and competent people in general do not need leaders *at all* to do their jobs. Such people know why and how to do their jobs, what is necessary to do their work, what guides and motivates them, and how to guide and motivate themselves respectively. I agree with Kerr and Jermier – but I would even go one step further and say that *no one* needs a leader to do their work, be a part of society, or live their life. We are all grown-ups.

Rejecting the archaic notion of 'the leader' or leaders still leaves room for members of a social system to provide leadership. But this requires an understanding of leadership that is fundamentally different from any trait leadership theory or other orthodox leadership ideology. One such approach to a more enlightened and democratic understanding of leadership is *distributed leadership*, i.e. leadership understood as a shared activity of co-creating social meaning, values, and orientations provided by all members of a social system alternately or collectively that is open to contestation, change, and reinterpretation (Grint 2010, pp. 89–90, Sutherland et al. 2014, p. 764). For example, in their investigation of four anarchistic political activist groups and organisations, Sutherland et al. (2014) found that direct or participatory democracy, combined with efforts to distribute leadership knowledge and skills more equally among all members of an organisation, provides a relatively good basis for having all members contribute to the provision of leadership and, in doing so, avoids the emergence of leaders. As they explained (p. 769):

To combat the emergence of leaders, each organization made efforts to construct a participative democratic environment. Generally, democracy and participation were *the* key principles underpinning these organizations, and representative democracy was rejected in favour of a more radical/direct approach. This was something that the organizations strove towards in their blueprints for social change, and sought to realize in their here-and-now organizational practices. ... In each organization, decision-making was the main activity in which participative democracy was sought.

They continued (p. 771):

Experienced individuals were therefore allowed, and often encouraged, to offer their thoughts on certain situations, but efforts were made to ensure that they did not become permanent 'leaders'. Rather, it was preferred for the leadership of the group to develop organically due to *shared* expertise and skills instead of being determined by *individuals'* cultural capital or styles and behaviours. ... After everyone felt they had the relevant information, an open discussion was held, where no members were considered to be more or less knowledgeable, and meaning-making became something that the group collectively engaged in. Instead of allowing more experienced members to become leaders and take on responsibilities individually, efforts were made to ensure that knowledge and skills were distributed amongst a variety of leadership actors.

It is quite obvious that distributed leadership not only is consistent and highly compatible with democratic governance and democratic management but also helps considerably to prevent leaders or privileging knowledge emerging. In a truly democratic system there is simply no place for protected and monopolised knowledge or positions (such as orthodox management and autocratic managers or trait leadership ideology and privileged leaders) – or for power differentials artificially created via specialised knowledge or positions.

Exercising Social Control, Especially Upward Control

Challenging existing protected and monopolised knowledge or positions, and preventing the emergence of new 'special' knowledge and positions, requires that people keep an eye on those areas where knowledge is created and processed – and on the people who access and use such knowledge (for whatever purposes or ends). The main idea is to make sure that those in charge do not aggrandise themselves. One possible way of doing this is by *social control* (Chekroun 2008, pp. 2142–2143).

Generally speaking, social control means putting social and/or informal pressure on members of a social system to abide by its prevailing norms and values. Social control comprises (1) observing people existing and acting in the social realm (their appearance, feelings, reasoning, communication, attitudes, and behaviour), (2) judging their existence and acting on the basis of and against prevailing social norms and values, and (3) approval or disapproval of their being and acting followed by (4) direct or indirect reactions and sanctions (rewards or punishment) appropriate to the judgement by members of the social system.

Social control can be done *informally*, i.e. by members of a social system without formal authority (e.g. family, friends, peers, neighbours, passers-by, colleagues, and the like), or *formally*, i.e. by members of a social system or institutions with formal authority ('the authorities', institutions of the legal system, the government, or the state). In the context under discussion in this chapter, it is mostly about informal social control, i.e. social control provided by members of the democratic organisation without formal functions or positions of authority.

Social control can take place in the form of *downward* control (superiors controlling subordinates), *upward* control (less empowered control the powerful), or *horizontal* control (mutual monitoring and peer pressure) (Ostergaard & Halsey, 1965, pp. 70–71, Hernandez 2006, p. 115, O'Mahony & Ferraro 2007, p. 1089, Erdal 2011, p. 51, Leach 2013, pp. 37–38, Jaumier 2016, Langmead 2016). When it is about socially disempowering the empowered few, upward control is of particular relevance.[10] As Ostergaard and Halsey (1965, pp. 70–71) noted: 'The crucial test is the extent of the influence wielded by the members [of the cooperative] over those who exercise authority and this cannot be measured merely in terms of participation figures.' According to Hernandez (2006, p. 115): 'The rank-and-file's ability to maintain control over their elected officials is a reflection of workplace democracy.' Some examples may provide a better understanding of how social control can work in a democratic organisation:

- Hernandez (2006, pp. 115, 118) describes how upward control happened in a Mexican cooperative (Pascual):

The threat of concentration of power is expressed in three different ways at Pascual. First, there are factors pushing for the development of charismatic and professional leadership. Second, individuals attempt to gain control and power within the cooperative. Third, corrupt behavior of people in supervisory and administrative positions threatens workers' ability to maintain control. Workers counterbalance these oligarchic forces and sustain control by challenging authoritarian and abusive representatives and recalling them from office, demanding consistent contact with the rank-and-file, and keeping a watchful eye on all the activities performed by the elected leaders. ... Pascual workers' efficacy, the constant watch over representatives and the existence of a law defending their exercise of collective power and democracy have sustained workers' control over their elected officials.

- When O'Mahony and Ferraro (2007, p. 1089) researched the emergence of governance in an open-source community, they realised that the governance system was particularly designed to limit the authority of leaders through democratic means and social control, such as: (1) people with positional power and other office-holders were required to make sure that their decisions were consistent with the consensus of opinion of others involved, (2) project leaders were subject to the same rules as other members and were not entitled to any special privileges, (3) any member had the right to propose a general resolution that could counter a leader's actions, and (4) decision-making powers were split between project leaders and a technical committee.
- In a French cooperative sheet-metal factory, Jaumier (2016) found continual efforts to 'prevent chiefs from being chiefs'. In particular, he understood (p. 1) that:

> Three types of day-to-day practices appear to be central for members of the co-operative in circumventing the coalescence of power in the hands of their chiefs: a relentlessly voiced refusal of the divide between chiefs and lay members; a permanent requirement for accountability, and endless overt critique towards chiefs; and the use of schoolboy humour.

As the examples indicate, in democratic organisations social control especially means upward control of the empowered few in public by all members of the democratic organisation. It means making sure that neither the holders of elevated formal positions nor overtly active or ambitious individuals aggrandise themselves; gain illegitimate power, dominance, and influence over others; or become or turn themselves into formal or informal leaders – and if they do so, they are 'pulled back to earth'. The next sub-section will show how exactly this can be done and achieved.

Carrying Out Social Actions to Confine Leaders (and Other Aggrandisers)

To a large extent, social control means *taking action* – especially *social* actions. The key thing is that people, i.e. disempowered members, actually *do* things. Social actions can be understood as people's voluntary activities in the public sphere that have a political or pedagogical intent or dimension. They are activities that are pursued deliberately in regard to particular issues or people in order to achieve some change relating to the issue in question or the currently prevailing status quo. Ober (2003, pp. 19–20) gave a good and telling historical example of the spirit and idea of social action against the powerful:

> In his speech *Against Meidias*, written in 346 BCE, a half-century after the trial of Socrates, Demosthenes presents a detailed brief for why the

laws must remain authoritative if the dignity of ordinary citizens is to be protected from attacks by powerful, wealthy, clever men. Demosthenes assumes that powerful men will always desire to demonstrate their power by harming the weak, and he does not consider the possibility that they would be restrained by any internal concern for abstract justice. Nor are the laws themselves, mere inscribed letters, capable of guaranteeing compliance. Rather, the appropriate insurance of legal authority is the collective action of the citizenry: the legal judgment and its consequences. Vigorous public punishment of outrageous behavior will serve to intimidate the powerful and will force them into compliance with the will of the many. In Demosthenes' argument, it is thus the mass of citizens, acting as jurors on the initiative of a voluntary prosecutor, that is the collective agent that ensures the authority of law. It is only when the people are unwilling to use their collective power to restrain the powerful that the law will lose its authority.

This spirit of social actions carried out in the public sphere can be also applied to and seen in organisations, especially democratic organisations. To provide some empirical examples and insights:

- Lipset (1952/2010, p. 17), presenting the first findings and analysis of his famous case on 'the internal politics of the International Typographical Union' (Lipset et al., 1956), showed that 'the rank and file' can indeed 'keep very much on the alert'; they stayed suspicious of their officials and rejected outright some of their proposals to change policies (e.g. when officials wanted to increase their own salaries or their mandate, or extend their term in office).
- When Rothschild and Whitt (1986, p. 105) investigated a collectivist medical clinic, they found that:

  Angry conflicts between the doctors and the paramedical staff erupted frequently. Members were confounded by the paradox of doctors who endorsed egalitarian principles in concept, but who seemed in practice to usurp decision-making power. In response, members charged the doctors with being guilty of 'elitism,' 'authoritarianism,' and 'professionalism.'

- In his participatory ethnographic research into how democracy and equality were practically achieved in a French cooperative sheet-metal factory, Jaumier (2016) found that workers regularly criticised members of the executive board, mainly as one of several means to limit the board's power and to show its members that they should not go beyond their mandate. As he explained (pp. 16–17, 20):

What mattered to them [the members of the cooperative] was first and foremost the act of criticizing [the executive board], independently of its content. While one could conclude from this that criticising is, for Scopix members, an end in itself, such a conclusion would in fact be inaccurate: rather, it is one of various means that co-operators use to limit chiefs' power. Indeed, the continuous flow of criticism and of requests for accountability that targets the board members keeps them alert not to go beyond their mandate. ... At Scopix, criticism again does not always take issue with real facts. What matters most is simply that the flow of speech or critique be sustained, thus indefinitely reaffirming the infinite nature of chiefs' debt. Within Scopix, this state of affairs may be tough to experience. While the current foreman is mentally resilient and has the advantage of knowing the tricks that he himself long performed as a shop-floor worker, his two immediate predecessors left the company, the first due to burn-out and the second to being systematically played and cheated by workers.

As these empirical examples show, social actions can take place in various forms, such as critical public opinion and voicing concerns, discontent, open criticism and ridicule, holding people in power accountable, disobedience, symbolic or concrete actions (political activism), and limitation, reduction, or even termination of people's elevated roles and positions.

The main, and crucial, difference between social and formal (or even legal) actions is that the latter *must* conform with authority and be consistent with existing (formal) rules and regulations whereas the former *can*, but does not *have to*, comply with the prevailing authorities and regulations. In fact, social actions are *meant to challenge* authority (even legitimate authority). This explains why the notion of social action usually does not exist in the blueprint of autocratic or oligarchic social systems, such as dictatorships or hierarchical, orthodox organisations. In such regimes, social actions are excluded from the range of allowed activities, even formally and/or legally forbidden, seen with suspicion, and actively combatted by those in power and their followers. In contrast, the principles, regulations, and workings of democratic social systems not only allow social actions but even *encourage* and *require* social actions (Boehm 1993, p. 230, Cheney 1995, p. 186).

Social actions fill the gap that democratic governance and democratic management cannot fill with their strongly formalised concepts and approaches. In return, democratic systems offer favourable conditions in which members *can*, and *do*, express their opinions and show autonomous, non-obedient, and even challenging behaviour. In the democratic organisation, the existence of elaborate democratic institutions, egalitarian management, and leadership styles, and an assertive social or organisational culture, can and should considerably shape members' mindsets, attitudes, and behaviour towards a 'democratic mentality', including initiating or participating in social actions. In this sense, social actions at the same time disempower the empowered and empower the disempowered. They contain the power and social dominance of leaders and the powerful, and turn those people into (relatively) 'powerless chiefs' – they help to 'prevent chiefs from being chiefs' (Clastres quoted in Jaumier 2016, p. 10). Additionally, social actions empower the disempowered by providing them with yet another tool (or range of tools) with which to state *their* opinions unreservedly; to question and challenge prevailing orthodoxies, inequalities, and injustices; and strive for change.

Promoting an Organisational Culture of Equal(ising) Power

Together, a continual demystification of privileging knowledge and privileging positions, social control (especially upward control), and social actions lead to an *organisational culture of equal(ising) power* (Osterman 2006, p. 628, called it a 'culture of contestation'). For example:

- In a precursor to his investigation of 'the internal politics of the International Typographical Union' (Lipset et al., 1956), Lipset (1952/2010, p. 14) found a deeply embedded 'concern of the members to keep control over their officers'. He noted that 'a certain suspicion of or at least lack of complete enthusiasm for officials exists even among the supporters of a given administration' and that the 'members are critical of the motives of union "politicians"' (p. 17).
- In his analysis of decision-making processes, power, and control in Mexican cooperatives, Hernandez (2006, p. 128) identified a similar culture of contestation:

  Forces pushing for democracy include scepticism toward, and willingness to challenge, authority; readiness to recall representatives; expectations that the representatives maintain contact with rank-and-file, honesty and effectiveness; expectation to participate fully in board and committee meetings; and a participatory culture (belief in workers' right to self-determination and commitment to defend this right) developed through the labor struggle.

- While researching a network of institutionalised civil society organisations in the U.S. (Southwest Industrial Areas Foundation), Osterman (2006, p. 639) found that:

  Despite the presence of an oligarchical group of organizers, the heightened sense of agency of the members, combined with the culture of contestation, has enabled members to maintain a strong sense of energy (i.e., avoid becalming) and enabled the Southwest Industrial Areas Foundation to avoid goal displacement.

He concluded (p. 636) that:

> The idea that a culture of assertiveness or contestation is healthy for the
> organization is reminiscent of Coser's (1956) claim that conflict can be
> functional for organizations because it helps subgroups define their own
> interests, creates a balance of power between groups, and by providing
> an outlet for differences, prevents exit behavior.

One can imagine that it takes a lot to create and maintain an open and
vibrant culture of contestation and equal(ising) power. The formal structures and
processes of democratic governance and democratic management (e.g. formal
institutions of deliberation and decision-making, representative management, and
full participation) only provide the – necessary – framework or basis. The organisational culture of equal(ising) power itself must come from the members of the
organisation – in particular, obviously, from its disempowered members.

This, first and foremost, requires psychologically empowered, confident, and
caring members: individuals who have a strong, comprehensively developed
personal identity and who dare to voice their opinions and speak their mind.
And they must have a relatively strong social orientation, i.e. they must care
that the social aspects and dimensions are consistent with the principles and
values of the democratic organisation. Osterman (2006, p. 643) called this 'a
strong sense of agency and a skepticism of authority'. If this is the case, then
individual members will contest and challenge those who seemingly do not
comply with, act, or behave according to democratic ideals.

This contestation has to happen in the open (and, obviously, also according
to the principles and values of the democratic organisation) so that other members can see it and join in.[11] In contrast to orthodox organisations, the democratic organisation actually provides some public spaces and encourages members
to address issues openly (via democratic institutions of governance such as
boards, committees, and assemblies; democratic decision-making at all levels and
across levels; transparency; and full participation in all management affairs). But it
takes quite some effort, encouragement, and perhaps even training and direct
support to reach the point where not just a few individual members voice their
concerns publicly (at this point they may still be perceived or portrayed as 'devi-
ants' and 'troublemakers') but the majority of the members regard open deliberation and contestation as normal and practise it routinely. Most people are
simply not used to it, as most societies and organisations (even fully developed
and functioning democratic societies and organisations) simply do not socialise
and educate their members to become citizens.

Public debate, deliberation, and discussion; criticism of organisational affairs and
conduct of office; and an overall culture of contestation are values in themselves.
Moreover, they are of great functional value since they evidently strengthen the
democratic side of the democratic organisation and help to address and solve issues

in more comprehensive, nuanced, and inclusive ways. An organisational culture of equal(ising) power can help considerably to level disproportional social empowerment. If a social system has a fully developed culture of contestation it is highly likely that not only 'technical' or 'operational' issues will be addressed in the open but also, and perhaps predominantly, issues of democratic governance and democratic management, the conduct of office of powerful office-holders, and issues of (unequal) power, inequality, and injustice will be addressed in this way. It tends to be the case that, by addressing those issues openly, the status, power, and influence of the powerful are reduced (because of the very fact that they have to engage in those discussions and their actual power may be confined as an outcome). At the same time, the status, power, and influence of the disempowered are increased. Over time, a well-functioning culture of equal(ising) power serves to disempower people who were previously empowered (at least in public) and to empower many of the more disempowered members.

In summary, probably the most promising way to disempower the empowered is to disempower them *socially*, i.e. that *others* disempower them socially. Challenging privileging knowledge and privileging positions through demystification, social control (especially upward control), social actions (in particular to contain the social dominance of leaders and other aggrandisers), and an organisational culture of equal(ising) power can remove the power distance between (aspiring) leaders and (possible) followers considerably. Social disempowerment also has the advantage that it does not aim directly at people's personalities and does not attempt to change them (it leaves them as they are) and instead aims 'only' at (changing) people's public and interpersonal behaviour. This can work – especially when one understands how aggrandisers and other (organisational) psychopaths reason and act. Most of them do so mainly, if not exclusively, at pre-conventional levels of moral development (Kohlberg 1976), i.e. they reason, operate, and behave with a very narrow egocentric perspective oriented towards dominance and obedience, rewards and punishment, and opportunistic social exchange. At the same time, they are very conscious – and concerned – about their social status and public image. This means that public opinion, social control, and social actions serve as rewards and punishment and can steer the behaviour of the empowered few without the need to change their (unchangeable) personalities. They can remain who they are. All they have to do is to change some of their most obvious behaviour. And since their reasoning and behaviour are mostly opportunistic, they are unlikely to have a problem with doing so. In a democratic system, power-hungry careerists will do (almost) anything *not* to appear like power-hungry careerists. This is where and why public social disempowerment has a chance to work.[12]

How Equalising Empowerment Works

The preceding sections provided a detailed analysis of the scope of formal, psychological, and social empowerment of the few and disempowerment of the many in democratic organisations – and what can, or even should, be done to empower the disempowered and to disempower the empowered until both have equal power (according to the principle of *equalising empowerment*). Empowerment is about empowering the powerless *and* disempowering the powerful formally, psychologically, and socially until all members of a social system are sufficiently and equally empowered and able to do their work and conduct their lives in ways appropriate for free individuals. Tables 5.1 and 5.2 offer brief summaries of the issues and measures relating to empowering the disempowered and disempowering the empowered.

TABLE 5.1 Empowering the disempowered within democratic organisations: from disempowerment to empowerment

Formal disempowerment	Formal empowerment
Members can be formally disempowered by not being allowed to hold formal management positions and therefore having less access to relevant and crucial information, tangible and intangible resources, and decision-making processes.	Non-office-holders can be formally empowered via a very strict and thorough application of the principles of democratic governance (*subsidiarity*, *transparency*, and *accountability*) as well as the concepts of democratic management (*self-management* and *(full) participation* or *participative management*). By applying these principles and concepts, non-office-holders can participate in decision-making processes at all levels and in regard to all issues on equal terms with office-holders.
Psychological disempowerment	Psychological empowerment
Members' efficacy, self-esteem, and perceived personal control can be relatively low and minimal because of identity regulation, 'team' rhetoric, or other collectivist and oppressive regimes.	Self-management and participative management especially provide individual members with broad and far-reaching opportunities and responsibilities concerning the management of their work and, therefore, (may) increase individual members' self-esteem, locus of control, and goal attainment considerably. The fundamental notions of the free individual and self-ownership as well as individuals' actual status as owners provide strong rationales to keep away the oppressive elements of collectivist regimes.
Social disempowerment	Social empowerment
Members can be socially disempowered by: (1) low status, stigmatisation,	Members can enhance their social identity via positively identifying with the

(*Continued*)

TABLE 5.1 (Cont.)

marginalisation, or social exclusion; (2) having insufficient resources or being socially disadvantaged in any other way in regard to pursuing their interests; (3) not being able to initiate, maintain, or manage social relationships, interpersonal communication, cooperation, or conflict sovereignly; and (4) behaving accordingly (i.e. demonstrating the whole range of obedient behaviour of the 'good' subordinate).

fundamental values and principles of the democratic organisation, pursue their interests via full participation in the processes of democratic governance and democratic management, and develop their social skills and competencies and demonstrate the relevant behaviour of a free and empowered individual via engaging in social relationships.

TABLE 5.2 Disempowering the empowered within democratic organisations: from empowerment to disempowerment

Formal empowerment	Formal disempowerment
Office-holders can be formally empowered by holding formal management positions (and therefore having access to relevant and crucial information, tangible and intangible resources, and decision-making processes), accumulating formal positions and functions, and/or carrying out their role in an orthodox management style (i.e. in an autocratic or authoritarian management style usurping line management responsibilities).	Formal disempowerment of office-holders can be achieved through direct limitations of their formal responsibilities and authority via formal principles and regulations of democratic governance (especially via the principles of transparency, accountability, and legitimate authority); democratic management (via full participation); limitation of the number of memberships, formal positions, and functions, and the length of terms in office. Office-holders may also be influenced in how they carry out their roles and management functions by company policies, rules, and regulations clarifying that only democratic and participative management styles are acceptable and that any managerialistic, micro-managing, or even autocratic or authoritarian management styles are not acceptable and will not be tolerated.
Psychological empowerment	Psychological disempowerment
(Overly) ambitious individuals can be psychologically empowered in absolute terms (e.g. hubris; obsessive control and fixation; mixed score in openness to experience; and high conscientiousness, extraversion, and neuroticism but low agreeableness) as well as in relative terms	It may be imagined that psychologically overtly empowered people can be helped to become more moderate and balanced and to develop a social, or even prosocial, orientation. But such a notion is either *unrealistic in practical terms* (most organisational psychopaths are neither

TABLE 5.2 (Cont.)

(e.g. personal empowerment of the individual through seeing themselves as a superior or leader while at the same time belittling subordinates and followers).	willing to nor capable of showing more decent personality traits or social behaviour) or *illegitimate in principle* (in a democratic system that acknowledges, guarantees, and supports people's rights and status as free individuals and their inalienable rights in themselves, it is not permitted to attempt to change people directly).
Social empowerment	Social disempowerment
Social empowerment of the few is primarily about the pursuit of personal interests and personal gain against and at the expense of others, and about demonstrating organisational misbehaviour in order to belittle, dominate, manipulate, and bully others.	The socially empowered can be disempowered by (1) *challenging exclusive knowledge and privileging positions* by demystification (e.g. via the idea that everyone is able to manage or to lead and/or contribute to distributed leadership); (2) *social control*, especially upward control (in particular making sure that (self-)empowered members do not aggrandize themselves, gain illegitimate power, or become leaders); (3) *social actions* to confine leaders (in particular to contain the social dominance of leaders and other aggrandizers by criticising and challenging them openly); and overall (4) an organisational culture of contestation and of equal(ising) power.

Whether it is the formal, psychological, or social disempowerment of the many or the formal, psychological, or social empowerment of the few, both constitute serious problems and challenges for the democratic organisation. The causes of both are fairly similar and can be found in the same areas, namely:

- One of the main factors contributing to the *formal* empowerment of the few and the formal disempowerment of the many is privileged formal roles, positions, and responsibilities and related access to (or exclusion from) relevant and crucial information, tangible and intangible resources, and decision-making processes. The empowered few have these positions and this access (and the institutionalised means to make use of them), whereas the disempowered many do not.
- Some of the main causes of the *psychological* empowerment of the few and the psychological disempowerment of the many are possession vs. lack of efficacy, self-esteem, and (perceived) locus of control. On average, the empowered few score high whereas the disempowered many score low on these items.

- Causes of the *social* empowerment of the few and the social disempowerment of the many can be found in social status; having sufficient resources and opportunities to pursue one's interests; and being able to initiate, maintain, and manage social relationships, interpersonal communication, cooperation, and conflict sovereignly and behaving accordingly. The empowered few are socially advantaged and more privileged, competent, and capable, whereas the disempowered many are socially disadvantaged, marginalised, less competent, and less capable concerning those aspects.

The reasons why and ways in which the many are disempowered and the few are empowered are fairly similar to each other. Possible remedies for these problems can also be the same for both problems, but they can vary too:

- *Formal* empowerment of the many and formal disempowerment of the few can be achieved by largely the same means, i.e. by designing formal roles, positions, and responsibilities as democratically as possible and by providing or limiting access to information, resources, and decision-making via strict application of the principles of *transparency*, *accountability*, *representative management*, and *full participation*. When taken seriously and applied in earnest, each of these principles is a very powerful tool that can be used to limit office-holders' formal power and to increase non-office-holders' formal power until both are (*almost*) on equal grounds when it comes to information, resources, and decision-making.[13]
- Measures concerning the *psychological* empowerment of the many and the psychological disempowerment of the few differ considerably. In respect of the former it is mainly self-management (and the principle of *subsidiarity*) and participative management (and the principle of *full participation*) that provide individual members with broad and far-reaching opportunities and responsibilities concerning the management of their own work and, thus, (may) increase *individual* members' self-esteem, sense of having an internal locus of control, and sense of goal attainment considerably. However, the exact opposites of these measures (i.e. taking away such opportunities from the empowered few) would *not* work in regard to disempowering them because their psychological empowerment mainly stems from *inherent* personality traits and not from externally provided opportunities.
- Concerning the *social* empowerment of the many and the social disempowerment of the few, the possible measures are also very different. As for their social empowerment, disempowered members can or should take positive measures mainly *by themselves*, for example positively identifying with and living the fundamental values and principles of the democratic organisation, fully participating in the democratic governance of the organisation, and engaging in social relationships (although it must be admitted that such social behaviour may be challenging for certain people, and even learning by doing,

training, and skills development may not provide complete and sufficient support). In contrast, the social disempowerment of the few can only be done *by others* – it is up to the people to demystify privileging knowledge and positions, exercise social control (especially upward control), and carry out social actions to confine leaders and other aggrandisers.

In summary, democratic organisations have a very broad range of robust means and mechanisms that (can) empower the disempowered many and (can) disempower the empowered few. There may be more measures, but the ones put forward here at least provide a good understanding of what democratic organisations *can* do – and, as the examples and empirical evidence have shown, what can be achieved if people are serious about protecting social systems against usurpation by a few. The keys to achieving this are institutions *and* people.

The democratic organisation's institutions of governance and management are designed to *confine and control power.* There are checks and balances horizontally between different organisational institutions (*separation of powers*) and vertically decision-making is located at the lowest possible levels (*principle of subsidiarity*). There is full *transparency* in regard to every formal role and position; governance processes; policies, rules, and regulations; managerial decision-making; and the conduct of business – i.e. members of the organisation have free and equal access to all relevant non-confidential information (or the right to ask for such information) and can use this information to provide checks and balances. All office-holders, especially those in formal management positions, are *representatives*, elected or appointed democratically, and are obliged to execute the will of those whom they represent. They have no line management responsibilities, and their formal responsibilities and authority of office are limited by the principles and regulations of democratic governance, representative management, and legitimate authority. They are controlled regularly, held accountable, and removable from office by democratic means (*accountability*). The number of formal positions or memberships any individual can hold is limited, as is the length of any term in office. Fully fledged democratic systems like the democratic organisation have multiple overlapping and mutually controlling institutions that keep power – and power-oriented actors – at bay.

At the same time, the democratic organisation's institutions of governance and management are designed to *empower and enable individuals* – especially those who are *not* empowered – to manage themselves, organisational affairs, and the organisation as a whole collectively and, in doing so, to avoid the democratic organisation descending into oligarchy. Following the principles of self-ownership and subsidiarity, in the democratic organisation *self-management* comes first; *all* members of the democratic organisation are entitled, encouraged, and enabled to organise and manage (individually or collectively) their own work, work-related issues, and organisational affairs, and to conduct *all* management functions (planning, organising, leading, and controlling) relevant to their work as *they* deem appropriate and necessary. Members may decide to delegate functions to formal positions of representative management but keep control over those functions. Moreover, participative management links self-management and representative management, i.e. at all levels of the democratic organisation there is *full participation*. Participative management means that *all* members of the democratic organisation have equal rights and opportunities to participate in all formal decision-making processes. All decisions – whether about constitutional, strategic, or operational issues – are made democratically, i.e. either by all members of the organisation or by its relevant parts (via self-management or by direct or participative democracy) or by elected representatives or office-holders (via representative management and representative democracy). Altogether, the institutions of self-management, representative management, and participative management entitle and empower all members of the democratic organisation to manage and control the organisation, organisational affairs, and conduct of office.

With their confining and enabling features, the democratic organisation's institutions of governance and management are *instrumental* for the *people* – how they govern and manage the organisation and their work as well as how they govern, manage, control, and empower or disempower themselves and others. Crucially, the institutions are not abstract entities of only theoretical worth and use but are thoroughly embedded in the fabric of the democratic organisation and part and parcel of members' daily work and experiences. All members of the democratic organisation are *routinely* enabled and confined by its institutions to conduct their work, to participate in the governance and management of the organisation and organisational affairs, and to be empowered as much as is appropriate and necessary. There is no 'big secret' to why the democratic organisation functions and why its members can maintain it. *People maintain, protect, and perpetuate the democratic organisation not because of exceptional idealism but because in their daily work they act on the basis of, act within, and utilise comprehensive and robust democratic institutions that reflect, protect, and support their interests.* That's it.

Notes

1 In this chapter I draw upon and use material from some of my previous works, in particular Diefenbach (2013a, 2016, 2019) and Diefenbach and Sillince (2011).
2 The opposite of *equalising empowerment* is *disproportional empowerment*, i.e. where only a few members of a social system are (formally, psychologically, or socially) empowered whereas the many are disempowered. Disproportional empowerment is a typical characteristic of social dominance and hierarchical social systems, but it can also occur in democracies and democratic system and can damage them considerably. The issue(s) of disproportional empowerment are addressed comprehensively in Chapter 10 ('The Iron Threat(s) of Disproportional Empowerment'). Chapter 10 provides a very thorough analysis of, and possible explanations for, *why* and *how* disproportional empowerment, social dominance, autocracy, and oligarchy can emerge and happen in (democratic) organisations, i.e. the *reasons* for and *causes* of disproportional empowerment as well as what can be done about them.

3 Note that empowerment resembles the idea of subsidiarity, which was explored and utilised in Chapters 3 and 4 concerning democratic governance and democratic management.

4 For a description and analysis of managerialism (and its devastating consequences) see my paper 'New Public Management in Public Sector Organisations: The Dark Sides of Managerialistic "Enlightenment"' (Diefenbach 2009b).

5 Or can acquire. In practical terms, trait leadership ideology usually is accompanied by a *generic leadership theory* that assures overtly ambitious people that the abilities, skills, competencies, and even personality traits necessary for being or becoming a leader can be acquired via socialisation, education, training, and personal development.

6 Actually, it is rather difficult for *everyone* to alter (some of) their personality traits, attitudes, or behaviour – just think about all those (broken) New Year's resolutions.

7 This statement is perhaps a tad too pessimistic. Probably every person who is not a complete psychopath or sociopath in a clinical sense (or otherwise severely mentally ill or morally so distorted that they have a chronic medical disease or condition) is *potentially* capable of developing a social orientation and demonstrating prosocial behaviour (although it may be difficult for them to achieve; see previous note). But in the case of egotistic power-players and careerists it would take quite some professional intervention, social support, and pressure at a scale and over an extended period of time that is usually not provided in an organisational context.

8 One supervisor I came across had multiple framed leadership seminar certificates on the wall behind the massive office desk with two computer-screens and two workstations. And she called herself 'a people person'. This supervisor was one of the worst micro-managing, bullying, and inept managers I encountered in my 36 years of working in hierarchical organisations – and I saw quite a lot of mediocre managers, organisational psychopaths, and useless wannabee leaders.

9 This is another fundamental difference between democratic or libertarian and nondemocratic or totalitarian systems (such as autocracies, oligarchies, or hierarchical organisations); the latter do not respect this boundary and try to model people directly so that they fit either to certain ideal types or into stereotypical roles that are consistent with the system.

10 The term 'upward control' would be most fitting in a formally organised hierarchical or stratified social system to describe subordinates' or people's control of their superiors or rulers. Although the democratic organisation is not hierarchical or stratified, I use the term 'upward control' in order to indicate that members of the organisation (ought to) control those with power – especially the empowered few, who may have established an informal hierarchy or even represent an informal ruling elite.

11 On a personal note: I was regularly surprised by the positive feedback I received from some of the disempowered members of the organisations I worked for when I publicly addressed or criticised managerial malpractices or other issues that were perceived to be 'the elephant in the room'. Even a few individual managers admitted that 'something has to be done' – and, *very* occasionally, something *was* done. However, admittedly, most (disempowered as well as empowered) members stayed silent and in all of the orthodox organisations I worked for I never saw an 'organisational culture of equal(ising) power' emerging. This was rather disappointing. Actually, my personal experience suggests exactly the opposite; it seems that in academic institutions there is a disproportionally high percentage of cognitively, emotionally, socially, and especially morally severely limited and distorted, mean, and useless cowards, psychopaths, inept managers, and dysfunctional leaders – especially among academics who also carry out management functions – and the higher those positions are the worse it is. But it is probably the case that some politicians, lawyers, doctors, engineers, or civil servants would say the same about their professions or the organisations for which they work.

12 Admittedly, since the careerists do not really change, they will continue to demonstrate various types of organisational misbehaviour in order to dominate, manipulate, exploit, and bully others. Measures of social disempowerment need to be accompanied by rather straightforward measures of formal disempowerment (e.g. comprehensive and robust laws, rules and regulations against anti-social behaviour, principles of ethical management, anti-harassment policies, fair and supportive complaint procedures, HR and legal support for all members of the democratic organisation, and so on) in order to be effective.

13 'Almost' because one of the fundamental principal–agent or moral hazard problems, *information asymmetry* (and, as a consequence, a power differential and possible abuse of the information advantage), can never be solved completely. However, the conditions in the democratic organisation (equal rights and status of all members as owners, no formal superior–subordinate relationships, and no line management authority but instead democratic management, transparency, accountability, and full participation) are fundamentally better than in orthodox organisations, which serves to keep principal–agent and moral hazard problems at a minimum and manageable.

6

CONSIDERATE CONDUCT OF BUSINESS

Conduct of Business: *Considerate* Conduct of Business

The first four chapters of Part I were about the democratic organisation's design and internal workings, i.e. its libertarian constitution, democratic governance, democratic management, and people's empowerment or disempowerment. It is now time to examine how the democratic organisation as an entity acts and performs, i.e. how it conducts its business. *Conduct of business* can be understood as the way(s) an individual or organisation acts and performs (internally as well as among and towards others and the environment) while pursuing its purpose(s).

In this sense, this chapter focuses on the democratic organisation's purposes, orientations, actions, behaviour, interactions, and performance(s) as an entity in its environment(s) and among others.[1] The basic proposition is that democratic organisations pursue very different purposes, behave and act *fundamentally* differently, and perform differently (much *better*!) compared to orthodox, hierarchical, and profit-maximising organisations because they *are* different and better.

These differences can perhaps best be encapsulated in the idea that democratic organisations conduct business *considerately*. *Considerate conduct of business* means that an organisation – within its purposes, strategies, policies, governance, management, structures, processes, and control and performance measurement systems – takes explicitly and equally into account the legitimate interests, problems, and needs of individuals, groups of people, other organisations, institutions, society in general, and the natural environment; the intended and unintended outcomes and consequences of its activities, actions, and inactions; and acts accordingly in balanced and sustainable ways that avoid or minimise negative, and create or increase positive, impacts on others, the wider system, and/or the natural environment.

Considerate conduct of business means doing the things one does *decently*. Although democratic organisations can be established for very different purposes, can be designed and maintained very differently, and may conduct their business in different ways, they all have the intention to conduct their business decently. How – and why! – *exactly* they do and achieve this will be interrogated and demonstrated in this chapter along three dimensions: social, environmental, and economic, i.e. 'people, planet, profit' (the widely known 'triple bottom line' concept). It will be shown that democratic organisations' considerate conduct of business is a reflection of their fundamental principles and the *institutions* on which they are built; *people*'s (i.e. their members') beliefs, values, and behaviour; and the link(s) and dynamic interplay between institutions and people that is so typical of democratic organisations – and only of this type of organisation.

People: Social Orientation and Social Behaviour

(Pro)social Orientation and Behaviour

In their purposes, goals, values, behaviour, and actions, individual and collective actors (i.e. individuals, groups of people, organisations, and institutions) can show a *social* or even *pro*-social orientation and behaviour – or a lack of social orientation and even *a*-social or *anti*-social behaviour. A *social orientation* means that an actor takes others' existence and genuine interests explicitly into account in their reasoning and acting in non-instrumental and cooperative ways. A *prosocial orientation* (also called, comprising, or implying 'prosocial personality', 'prosocial motivation', and 'prosocial behaviour'; Van Lange 2000, Grant & Berg 2010) means that an actor *actively* tries to improve others' existence or the conditions of their existence. A prosocial orientation implies a concern for others and their welfare, and being helpful to other persons, but not at the expense of one's self-interest (Deutsch 1986, p. 16, Grant & Berg 2010, p. 5).[2] It means a 'desire to have a positive impact on other people or social collectives' (Grant & Berg 2010, p. 1). A prosocial orientation shapes not only people's minds but also their actual behaviour and social interactions. People with a prosocial orientation show predominantly social or even prosocial behaviour, in particular more cooperation (enhancement of joint outcomes), generosity (enhancement of others' outcomes), and equality (enhancement of equality in outcomes) (Van Lange 2000).

Radical, utility-, or profit-maximising actors (such as the 'homo economicus' or the capitalist firm or corporation) do not have a social, let alone a prosocial, orientation *in principle*. Their reasoning and acting are limited to egoistic (even egotistic), opportunistic, and competitive calculus and behaviour, and they are neither able nor willing to demonstrate a social orientation or behaviour. Their orientation and behaviour are fundamentally *a*-social, and in many respects and instances *anti*-social.

In contrast, democratic organisations are able and willing to empathetically take other actors' genuine interests into account and to demonstrate cooperative and mutually beneficial behaviour.[3] Democratic organisations have a *very* strong social orientation (if not to say a *pro*-social orientation) and show predominantly social behaviour *in principle* – they genuinely care about those they are engaged with and others beyond them (either within or outside the organisation). Many democratic organisations (e.g. community-based organisations, not-for-profit organisations, non-governmental organisations (NGOs), cooperatives, and social enterprises) are even set up to pursue *pro*-social goals and activities, and to change or improve the individual situations of people or the social conditions in which they live.

The following sub-sections focus on the question of how and why democratic organisations (can) display (pro)social orientations and behaviour. The inquiry focuses on (1) the collaborative minds and cooperative behaviour of members of democratic organisations, (2) community orientation and local embeddedness, and (3) the decent business practices and the responsible and ethical behaviour demonstrated by democratic organisations.

Collaborative Minds and Cooperative Behaviour

Democratic organisations can be created for various purposes, but what they all have in common is that one of their main purposes is to be mutually beneficial for their members (and/or clients, customers, or other stakeholders) (Lewis & Swinney 2008, p. 31). The purpose of creating mutual or collective benefits is enshrined in the organisation's partnership agreement and reflected in how the organisation is designed and works on a daily basis.

In pursuit of this purpose, members of democratic organisations have particularly collaborative minds and regularly cooperate with other members of the organisation. There is a 'culture of cooperation and generalized reciprocity among diverse individuals and groups' (Meurs 1996, p. 110). Against the backcloth of such a collaborative mindset and routinely practised cooperation as the usual way of (inter)acting and operating *inside* the organisation, members of the democratic organisation also seek mutually beneficial cooperation with actors *outside* the organisation and demonstrate corresponding cooperative and reciprocal behaviour (Meurs 1996, pp. 110–111, Novkovic & Holm 2011, p. 1). As a consequence, democratic organisations show high levels of cooperative and reciprocal behaviour in their communications, economic exchanges and transactions, and social relations with other actors. Moreover, they are more interested in establishing and maintaining long-term relationships, will sustain and develop relationships with various stakeholders, and may even form alliances or become members of formal or informal networks, interest groups, associations, or cooperatives (Smith & Rothbaum 2014).

It is important to note that a collaborative mindset and cooperative behaviour should not be equated or confused with altruistic or unselfish behaviour. There may well be such motives. But people and democratic organisations cooperate (also) because this mindset and behaviour correspond with *their* sense of purpose, values, and preferences, it is in *their* interest and to *their* advantage to do so. Moreover, the empirical evidence clearly shows that democratic organisations' cooperative behaviour works:

- In their research into cooperation within cooperative networks seen 'from the small firm's perspective', Mazzarol et al. (2013, p. 28) found that:

  Small firms gain benefits from alliances and networks by securing access to resources and capabilities such as access to markets, technologies and knowledge, as well as a degree of protection from competitive threats. … Small producers who join cooperatives secure benefits such as greater market access, better pricing and lower input costs. … The pooling of resources and sharing of knowledge that occurs within co-operatives is also a major benefit to such small firms contributing to the building up of social and economic capacity within their community.[4]

- When Reed (2015, pp. 105–106) investigated the opportunities and limitations of fairtrade practices and certified Fairtrade networks' primary ways of operating, he found that:

  The solidarity between small producers and other SSE trading partners expresses itself in a number of ways:

  - Partnership and shared decision-making over the terms of trade, rather than a [*sic*] imposition of terms based on market power;
  - Transparency and knowledge-sharing, leading to shared autonomy;
  - Commitment to fairer distribution along the value chain, which includes ensuring that the full costs of production of small producers are covered by the price that they receive;
  - Trade based on long-term relations, rather than contracts with a one-year horizon;
  - Commitment to supporting capacity-building and local development …;
  - Long-term relationships with consumers, involving loyalty, more direct trade relations that cut out intermediaries, a commitment to quality products, as well as openness and transparency.

All in all, it can be said that (members of) democratic organisations have a more collaborative mindset; engage in more voluntary, mutually beneficial cooperation and reciprocal behaviour; are more willing to share resources, knowledge, and power; share and distribute benefits, burdens, costs, and profits more fairly; and are more likely to develop and maintain long-term relations with other actors, particularly when they have similar values and ways of operating (e.g. Wright 2010, p. 235). All of this evidences a much stronger social and prosocial orientation and behaviour than is found in orthodox organisations.

Community Orientation and Local Embeddedness

A social, even prosocial orientation can especially be seen in respect to people that are 'close to oneself'. Traditionally, besides family ties, this closeness has been understood and practised in a spatial or geographical sense: the neighbourhood, community, or larger cultural area. Many democratic organisations originate as small, local organisations embedded in the neighbourhood and their communities and establish community-based businesses (in particular many types of cooperative, such as farmer, producer, housing, banking, or consumer cooperatives; community-based organisations; some types of civil society organisation; and non-profits, NGOs, and social enterprises). For example, Nembhard (2008, p. 212) stated:

> Community-based businesses are local enterprises that are owned, run, managed, and/or shared by members of the same community – either a geographic community (locational affiliation), or a community of interest (based on cultural, ethic or economic affiliation). They are elements of the solidarity economy because they exemplify local control, democratic participation, and economic organizing at the grassroots.[5]

Groeneveld (2011, p. 533) explained in regard to cooperative banks:

> Cooperative banks are literally and figuratively closer to their customers and know those customers well through participation in numerous social networks. This is because the cooperative banking model centres above all on 'relationship banking' via local presence. Proximity to their customers is reinforced by actively supporting local communities.

In this sense, many democratic organisations have a strong community orientation and a feeling of local embeddedness, and are concerned about local people's and communities' well-being (e.g. Gibson-Graham et al. 2013). They care about the people 'close to them' and treat them well in their interactions, exchanges, and activities. Rothschild-Whitt and Lindenfeld (1982, p. 7) explain this in more detail:

> The main purpose of each firm is not the maximization of profit, but the maximization of community well-being. This includes fair income for those who work in the enterprise and workers' control of their own

work, with jobs as personally rewarding as possible. Community well-being also includes providing goods or services that are socially useful, of high quality, and ecologically sound. Priority would be given to the conservation of energy and natural resources and to the growth of the organization to an appropriate, medium size. In times of trouble, workers are not laid off, but rather share reduced hours or lower incomes.

Community orientation and 'localism' do make sense. Even in the most developed countries there is a very strong trend towards and appreciation of local businesses; locally produced, provided, and consumed products and services; and the spirit of neighbourhood and community life – and many democratic organisations fit into such a local context with their values and the way(s) they operate. Nonetheless, there are also problems, or misunderstandings, with such an idea of democratic organisations' community orientation.

One aspect is size. Sometimes, people are be inclined to think that alternative, participative organisations can be, or even should be, only small 'corner shop' organisations, and that they should stay small in order to, for example, preserve the founders' spirit; the creative, relatively unstructured, unbureaucratic, and informal ways of communication, direct participation, and decision-making; and their direct relationships with customers and neighbours. This is definitely true for some democratic organisations, as some do legitimately want to continue conducting their business on a small scale and in a manner that is deeply embedded in a specific ('their') neighbourhood. However, democratic organisations can also grow and become regional or even national, nation-wide institutions *without* losing their local connections and identity (as the Mondragón cooperative network and the German Raiffeisen banks have shown so compellingly). Of course, there are always problems and changes when organisations grow, especially in respect to their identity, structures, and processes of governance and management, and their organisational culture. But these challenges can be managed and do not mean that democratic organisations *have* to be, or stay, small in order to demonstrate and keep their community orientation and local embeddedness.

The second aspect is space. Usually, 'local' community is understood as the (immediate) *physical* or *spatial* neighbourhood – which makes sense in many respects when an issue under consideration relates to things or issues where people live. Individuals' work, life, and quality of life as well as community development have a lot to do with the built environment, physical infrastructure, availability and accessibility of facilities and (public) services, and the social fabric of the neighbourhood. Nevertheless, with the emergence of the internet, online applications, and activities (especially social media), many people's work and lives have become increasingly virtual. 'Space' now transcends physical and geographical boundaries, even exists *without* any physical valence or dimension ('virtual reality'). Private, social, and economic activities increasingly take place 'on the internet', for instance in *online* communities. Many people not only spend a large amount of their time online but also have parts of their personal and social identities, work, and lives happening and shaped online, by online activities and online communities (e.g. Swigger 2013).

Additionally, the physical or geographical space has changed. Whereas traditionally most social and economic interactions and exchanges happened locally, they nowadays take place on a global scale. Globalisation describes this worldwide process of increasing social, cultural, and economic interaction and integration among people, organisations, and institutions of and from different local, regional, national, and ethnic backgrounds. Globalisation happens in both the physical and the virtual worlds and creates communities and social context that transcend any local context. For example, (via the internet and virtual applications as well as real-world operations and logistics) many international NGOs and small fairtrade organisations have successfully established close links between donors/sponsors and sponsored persons or projects or between consumers and producers who are thousands of miles away from each other but are part of a 'community' not only in a metaphorical and virtual sense but also in a social and economic sense. This is (pro)social orientation and behaviour in action spanning the globe. In this sense, 'people close to oneself' does *not* mean only local, spatial, or geographical closeness but also globally, virtually, and metaphorical closeness – and democratic organisations' community orientation and local embeddedness should be seen and understood in *that* way too.

Decent Business Practices, and Responsible and Ethical Behaviour

Democratic organisations simply do not behave like capitalist firms (Schweickart 2011, pp. 87–89). Whether they operate in the Social and Solidarity Economy or even in (highly) competitive market environments, they simply do not put as much pressure on themselves – and others! – as profit-maximising organisations or corporations do. This is because they are set up for purposes, and pursue goals, that are per se more decent, fair, and just; their prime purpose(s) are not short-term profit maximisation (for a very few by exploiting or at the expense of many others and the natural environment) but serving key stakeholders (members, clients, customers, community, and humankind); addressing fundamental social, economic, or environmental needs or concerns; or pursuing other decent and ethical purposes.

As a consequence of their more decent and ethical purposes, they also develop and demonstrate more decent and ethical business strategies and practices. Democratic organisations usually do not pursue ambitious profit-maximising or growth strategies (growth in revenues, profits, markets, or market shares to get ahead of or against others) because this is not why they were set up in the first place or how they operate. They follow much more cooperative, balanced, long-term-oriented, and sustainable business strategies and practices (e.g. Carnoy & Shearer 1980, pp. 172–174, Groeneveld 2011, p. 533, Groeneveld 2013, p. 24) – and behave accordingly. Democratic organisations produce and offer products and services that are useful, affordable, sustainable, healthy, and good for people – and perhaps also for the environment. They do not engage in deceptive marketing strategies and practices (or any others that are unethical or annoying). Their 'value chains', operations, and collaborations with partners correspond and comply with standards of ethical conduct and sustainability, and they care about their members and customers or clients, their community, and their neighbourhood routinely, i.e. as part of their daily conduct of business (Kelly 2012). Democratic organisations demonstrate more conservative behaviour in the sense of acknowledging and protecting the *fundamental* (intrinsic) value and integrity of individuals, legitimate social systems, and the natural environment (see next section). Democratic organisations show *prudent* management – and there is quite some empirical evidence for this. For instance, based on his analysis of the business models and conduct of business of 15 European cooperative banking groups, Groeneveld (2011, p. 515) concluded:

> Cooperative enterprises are based on the values of self-help, self-responsibility, democracy, equality, equity and solidarity. In the tradition of their founders, cooperative members believe in the ethical values of honesty, openness, social responsibility and caring for others. With reference to these historical and universal cooperative values, cooperative banks have repeatedly and publicly stated that they have always acted primarily in the interests of their members and customers. They also state that this approach has led to a dominant focus on relationship banking with a moderate risk profile and attention to several different stakeholders. The financial crisis offers a good opportunity to verify many of the longstanding assertions of cooperative banks. ... This specific form of enterprise has proven rather successful in the recent turbulent financial times. Corporate governance with member ownership and influence has ensured the application of relatively high moral and ethical standards in their daily business and contacts with members, who are both the customers and the owners of cooperative banks at one and the same time.

That democratic organisations by and large show (much more) decent business practices and responsible and ethical behaviour than orthodox organisations is *not* because their members are 'better' people per se (some might be) but for *systemic* reasons; members of democratic organisations act and behave more decently within and on behalf of the democratic organisation because this is what these organisations *are*. Decency is part of the organisations' fundamental principles, values, structures, and processes – it is in their fabric and simply the way they operate and 'how to do things'.

Planet: Pro-environmental Behaviour

Pro-environmental Orientation and Behaviour

Besides their social orientation, the question is how the democratic organisation and its members relate to the *natural environment*. The human–nature relationship is a fundamental (even existential) and complex, difficult, and troublesome relationship – *for both*. The discussion here will focus mostly on the question of whether or not democratic organisations (are able and willing to) demonstrate a *pro-environmental orientation* and *pro-environmental behaviour* towards nature and the natural environment or parts of it.

A *pro-environmental orientation* means convictions that (e.g. Purser et al. 1995, p. 1077, Smith 2003, pp. 8–9, 12, Connelly et al. 2012, p. 32):

- humans (should) ascribe, and acknowledge, an *intrinsic value* to the natural environment or parts of it (i.e. nature in general, natural phenomena, ecosystems, species, plants, trees, animals, and other living organisms) *independent* of humans or a possible instrumental, economic, or market value (i.e. these things are considered to be valuable or of value simply for what they are);
- the natural environment – or parts of it – (should) be protected and preserved for its own sake because of its intrinsic value; and
- humans and organisations (should) act environmentally responsibly by acknowledging nature's intrinsic value.

Pro-environmental behaviour means that within their natural environments, humans (individuals and groups of people), organisations, and other social systems act towards nature according to a pro-environmental orientation. In particular, they (Kollmuss & Agyeman 2002, pp. 240, 251, Parry 2012, p. 220, Raymond et al. 2013, pp. 537–538):

- include the relevant natural environment (or parts of it) consciously and explicitly in their reasoning and decision-making processes;
- use, manage, maintain, restore, preserve, and/or enhance the natural environment or parts of it in balanced and sustainable ways, according to the principles of balance and sustainability respectively;
- overall seek to minimise the negative impacts and to maximise the positive impacts of human action and conduct of business on the natural environment in every possible respect.

Orthodox, profit-maximising organisations do not have a pro-environmental orientation and do not demonstrate pro-environmental behaviour – *in principle*. Profit-maximising organisations are set up for the *sole* purpose of generating as much profit and income as possible for some human beings, their owners. Their indisputable paradigm of increasing returns and profits and reducing costs as much as possible suggests the imperative of avoiding all 'unnecessary' costs and externalising internal costs – i.e. by not paying (enough) for any harm or damage done to the natural environment while conducting their business (e.g. when they use and exploit the natural environment, or procure and utilise natural resources and materials in their production processes, operations, logistics, or the types of services or products they offer). Orthodox, profit-maximising organisations are, and behave, *anti*-environmentally (and anti-socially) *by necessity*.

Orthodox organisations can and do show pro-environmental *behaviour* (only) if they are forced to do so (e.g. by law, regulations, or policies) and/or if they deem it to be advantageous in a calculative, monetary sense – i.e. (solely) for opportunistic reasons. For example, there are many orthodox for-profit companies in 'green business' or 'green jobs', i.e. they develop, manufacture, and offer environmentally friendly products or services; make energy from renewable sources such as wind, solar, geothermal, or hydropower; and/or minimise their total environmental impact and achieve environmental sustainability in their conduct of business (e.g. Parry 2012, p. 220, Park 2013, p. 67). They are 'being green' *if*, and as long as, there is 'a market' for it. Alternatively, even if they are not in the 'green business' and operate in fairly conservative industries and markets, some businesses still demonstrate pro-environmental behaviour if this reduces their costs (e.g. to minimise the consumption of resources, materials, or energy, a company might reduce its waste or pollution, or use ecologically sustainable resources or non-toxic substances) and/or provides them with a 'competitive advantage' (Kollmuss & Agyeman 2002, p. 240, Sandhu 2010, p. 294, Parry 2012, p. 220).[6]

Compared to orthodox and/or profit-maximising organisations, democratic organisations are not required to maximise profit and, therefore, are free to decide on their orientation (purpose(s), values, and principles) and corresponding behaviour (conduct of business). One, therefore, might immediately be inclined to think that democratic organisations, since they are fundamentally different from orthodox organisations, might show pro-environmental orientation and behaviour (e.g. Harrison 2013, p. 14) as much as and as easily as they show (pro)social orientation and behaviour. However, the case is not that straightforward. It is not so necessary or automatic for democratic organisations to have a pro-environmental orientation or behaviour as it is for them to have a social or even prosocial orientation and behaviour – but there is a good chance that they will do so – at least a better chance than for orthodox organisations. Thus, the question is why and when would democratic organisations demonstrate a pro-environmental orientation and operate in a more environmentally conscious and friendly manner?

This question will be interrogated in the following sub-sections by focusing on (1) owner-managers' senses of and valuing of nature, (2) people's (pro-) environmental orientation, and (3) the goals and actions of democratic organisations.

Owner-Managers' Senses of and Valuing of Nature

In business research (in particular about small and family businesses and about entrepreneurs' and managers' perceptions and decision-making) it is well established that psychological and social characteristics as well as personal values and convictions have a crucial influence on people's worldviews, attitudes, behaviour, decision-making, and acting (e.g. Parry 2012, p. 221). The question is which factors *exactly* may trigger and shape owner-managers' pro-environmental orientation and behaviour.

The factors influencing human reasoning and behaviour are extremely diverse and complex (Kollmuss & Agyeman 2002, p. 254, Gifford & Nilsson 2014, p. 151) and there can be many different reasons why democratic organisations' members demonstrate a pro-environmental orientation and corresponding behaviour (e.g. McDonald 2014, p. 292, Gifford & Nilsson 2014, p. 141):[7] *external factors* (historical, cultural, societal, institutional or organisational context, situation, and conditions), *intrapersonal factors* (demographic characteristics, personality traits, socialisation, education, knowledge, skills and competencies, values, convictions, political and world views, perceived self-efficacy, motivation, habits, attitudes, behaviour, and social, cultural and ethnic background), and/or *interpersonal factors* (social identity, social norms, prevailing values and ideologies, peer and group pressure, and social processes and interaction).

But whatever factors might trigger or contribute to the emergence of a pro-environmental orientation, one of the key indicators that people or members of democratic organisations have such an orientation is that they *feel connected to* or have a *sense of connectivity with nature* (or oneness, unity, or wholeness), i.e. some kind of emotional involvement with the natural environment or parts of it (e.g. Kollmuss & Agyeman 2002, Dutcher et al. 2007). According to Dutcher et al. (2007, p. 474), 'Connectivity describes a perception of sameness between the self, others, and the natural world. The experience of connectivity involves dissolution of boundaries and a sense of a shared or common essence between the self, nature, and others.' Kollmuss and Agyeman (2002, p. 254) argue that 'an emotional connection seems to be very important in shaping our beliefs, values, and attitudes towards the environment' and, thus, hypothesise that 'the stronger a person's emotional reaction, the more likely that person will engage in pro-environmental behavior'. Dutcher et al. (2007, p. 478) assume that 'people who sense a fundamental sameness between themselves and the natural world (as well as to other people) will feel more empathetic and compassionate toward nature'.

Besides a more general sense of connectivity with nature or emotional involvement with the natural environment, owners and members of democratic organisations may also have more specific values and ethical principles that motivate them to show pro-environmental behaviour and conduct their business accordingly (Parry 2012, pp. 221–222). Such values – which might be called 'biospheric' or 'biophilic' (e.g. Lumber et al. 2017, p. 19) – stress the appeal or worth of nature and imply that the natural environment or parts of it should be cared about, preserved, and nurtured. For example, in their meta-analysis of a comprehensive set of empirical studies about pro-environmental orientations and behaviour, Gifford and Nilsson (2014, p. 144) found that 'persons who hold more self-transcendent and biospheric values report being more environmentally concerned, and the opposite is true for those who hold self-enhancement and egocentric values. The same relations apply for environmental behaviour.'

Whether a person has a more general sense of connectivity with nature or specific biophilic values, both prepare and enable people to be, or to become, *more perceptive about environmental issues.* There is substantial empirical evidence that individuals who feel more connected to and appreciative of nature also show a strong(er) pro-environmental orientation and willingness to demonstrate pro-environmental behaviour (e.g. Gifford & Nilsson 2014, Geng et al. 2015, Lumber et al. 2017).

For this, they need *factual knowledge* – knowledge of issues and knowledge of action strategies (Gifford & Nilsson 2014, p. 151). Via their local embeddedness, owners and members of the democratic organisation are in a good position to gain and develop such knowledge and understanding of (local) environmental issues. And via their democratic organisation, they are also in the position to do something about it.

Having the necessary knowledge (about the issue as well as what can be done about it) instils a *sense of responsibility* that provides the crucial link and step towards action(s). Owners of (democratic) organisations usually have a strong sense of responsibility – it may have been one of the reasons and motivating forces that prompted them to set up the business in the first place, or it may have emerged and developed via their founding and then looking after the business respectively. In the case of owners and members of democratic organisations, their sense of responsibility – and their actions – may also stretch to include environmental issues. Furthermore, owner-managers and members of democratic organisations may also have this higher sense of connectivity to nature because they are *locals*. Locals may feel closer and more connected to their natural environment because it is where they live and because they must bear the consequences of any changes to that environment. In fact, many democratic organisations are established by local people in order to address local issues (e.g. agricultural or housing cooperatives, community-based organisations, local retail businesses, professional partnerships, and social enterprises). They feel a strong sense of responsibility about environmental issues – *and* they have, or can acquire, the knowledge and resources to do something about it.

Overall, it might be said that there is a sequence that may lead people towards having a pro-environmental orientation and behaviour (Stern & Dietz

1994, p. 65, Schultz et al. 2005, p. 460): *if* people have a general sense of connectivity with nature and/or more specific biophilic values and ethical principles, *then* they are likely to be more perceptive about environmental issues and have a strong(er) pro-environmental orientation and willingness to demonstrate pro-environmental behaviour; *if* they then have, or can gain, necessary factual knowledge about environmental issues and ways of doing something about them and have a sense of responsibility, *then* they will take pro-environmental actions.

Localism and Local People's (Pro-)environmental Orientation

Besides people *within* the democratic organisation it is also people from *outside* that shape its pro-environmental orientation and behaviour. Democratic organisations may behave in a more environmentally friendly manner because of *localism*, i.e. the notion that local people and actors embedded in local settings see and treat the local environment and local issues in more concerned and caring ways because they are exposed to, and have to live with, the possible consequences.

Localism does *not* – or should not – claim that *all* local people or organisations operating in a local context (always) demonstrate a more caring mindset and behaviour concerning the local environment or local issues. There are abundant historical and contemporary examples of *local* people over-exploiting nearby natural resources (sometimes to the extent that the area becomes uninhabitable), polluting and littering the neighbourhood, and intentionally or unintentionally damaging or destroying the natural foundations of their livelihood. Local people (can) do a lot of bad things. An undifferentiated localism that claims otherwise is nothing but naive romanticism.

But what localism *can* claim is that many local people have a great(er) sense, awareness, and knowledge of the local natural environment per se because they live with and within it. On average, they also have greater (layman's) knowledge of the causes and consequences of environmental phenomena. Many local people possess traditional ecological knowledge that is 'embodied in life experiences and reproduced in everyday behavior and speech' ('Ethnoecology' 2018). Greater awareness and knowledge of the natural environment, then, *may* lead to greater concern about it, such that, *on average and compared to absent actors*, local people may care more about the conditions of their environment and may show a higher degree of pro-environmental orientation and behaviour. For instance, Caspary (2004, p. 240) argued that 'because worker-owners live in the communities where their factories are, they will be concerned not to pollute their environment'.

In her book *Owning Our Future: The Emerging Ownership Revolution*, about a generative economy, Marjorie Kelly (2012, p. 105) describes this caring mindset and attitude towards nature as 'rooted membership':

This is Rooted Membership at work – operating hand in hand with Living Purpose. The forest is not seen as an object whose sole purpose is permitting owners to extract maximum amounts of financial wealth. It's a living forest, a community of trees and humans. The purpose is to live well together, maintaining the living forest and supporting the human community. Because governance rights are in the hands of humans rooted to that place, they have a natural incentive to be good stewards. And they are able to carry out their mission because they govern the forest; it's Mission-Controlled Governance.

She continued (p. 106):

When ownership rights are in the hands of those whose self-interest depends on the health of the forests, the fish, and the land, they have a natural tendency toward stewardship. Self-interest and the interests of the whole become one and the same. Rooted Membership, Living Purpose, and Mission-Controlled Governance are among the ownership patterns that make this possible.

Traditional ecological knowledge and rooted membership are strong factors that can contribute to people demonstrating a pro-environmental orientation and behaviour. Local people influence how local organisations operate and function (Parry 2012, p. 222). As argued on pp. 132–137, democratic organisations' prime purpose(s) are not profit maximisation (for a very few by exploiting, or at the expense of, many others and the natural environment) but serving key stakeholders (members, clients, customers, community, and humankind). And, since some of their key stakeholders are local people and the community, democratic organisations are also keen to conduct their business according to *their* expectations and concerns. They therefore operate in a more environmentally friendly manner within and on the basis of their local embeddedness and their paradigms of community orientation and member orientation. For example, Hoover (2008, p. 253) noted:

Because co-ops are rooted in their communities, they tend to have more sustainable practices, civic connections, and investment in doing right by community. Worker cooperatives were among the first 'green' businesses, long before green was a trendy marketing term, because they actually cared about the safety and health of their workers and community (which were often one and the same).

Or, to put it more generally, if local people or a local community by and large appreciate the natural environment – or parts of it – then there is a high(er) likelihood that local democratic organisations will act in an environmentally (more) friendly manner because of their community orientation and local embeddedness.

Environmentally Friendly Goals and Actions

Because of their owner-members' personal values and/or because of their community orientation and local embeddedness, democratic organisations may have explicit pro-environmental goals and purposes. Democratic organisations, thus, may have an explicit triple bottom line approach where social, environmental, and economic goals are pursued *equally* and their business model is based on comprehensive and robust concepts of sustainability and sustainable development (World Commission on Environment and Development 1987, Rees 2014, 'Sustainability' 2016) and corporate social responsibility (e.g. Norton 2007, p. 389, Bondy & Matten 2012, p. 519, Bocken et al. 2014, p. 46).[8] One might even say that the democratic organisation and its conduct of business represent a *sustainable business model* (Bocken et al. 2014, p. 42).

With an explicit pro-environmental orientation, democratic organisations also demonstrate pro-environmental behaviour as a fundamental and integral part of their conduct of business. For instance, in keeping with the type and nature of their business and activities, democratic organisations use and offer local, small-scale, decentralised, and more environmentally friendly technologies, products, and services ('appropriate technology', e.g. 'Appropriate Technology' 2014, Pearce 2014), such as:

- *agriculture*: small farms, family businesses, community-based farming, organic farming, protection of biodiversity, fairtrade, and little or no use of pesticides, chemicals, or genetically modified crops;
- *energy generation and usage*: renewable energies, and local and decentralised energy production, storage, and distribution;
- *water and sanitation*: community-scale and household-scale point-of-use designs, local water refill stations, water filtration, wells and pumps, ecological sanitation, and little or no waste water and water pollution;
- *buildings and construction*: ecologically friendly buildings, green building materials, housing cooperatives, and public housing;
- *logistics*: environmentally friendly operations and transport;
- *consumer products*: slow fashion, slow food (i.e. long-lasting consumer products of high quality), environmentally friendly household goods, and ethical goods and consumerism;
- *information and communication technologies*: open-source software, low-cost access to information and the internet, and simple, cheap, and long-lasting computers and mobile phones;
- *finance*: microfinance, and use of savings and credit associations.

All such technologies, products, and services are not only much more ethical and environmentally friendly but also more *attractive and competitive* (especially when national policies, regulations, subsidies, and incentives as well as the markets provide a level playing field and do not unfairly advantage 'big business' and old, outdated industries). It is often the case that markets and industries change to use more appropriate technologies and ethical goods and services because the demand is there (often this change is exponential, as the fairtrade movement has shown so compellingly).

Profit: Economic and Other Performance

The Performance of Organisations

Organisations must *perform*. They need to deliver the intended outcomes linked to the purposes stated explicitly or implicitly by their founders, owners, and members. In that sense, democratic organisations are not different from other types of organisation; whether they operate in highly competitive market environments, in the (non- or partly competitive) public sector, or in the cooperative Social and Solidarity Economy, (also) democratic organisations must perform (well). Although 'performance' can be understood, defined, and measured in various dimensions and in respect to very different things, the focus here is on *economic performance*. Economic performance can be understood as any (positive or negative) change of things (assets) or events (processes or activities) that have an economic value (i.e. a price can be established for them).

In regard to economic performance, it can confidently be said that, on average and in principle, democratic organisations achieve better efficiency, productivity, and overall organisational performance, and are economically more viable, successful, and sustainable than orthodox organisations. There is half a century of compelling arguments and overwhelming evidence for this assertion (e.g. Blumberg 1968, Kanter 1971, Vanek 1971, Dachler & Wilpert 1978, Carnoy & Shearer 1980, Jones & Svejnar 1982, Rosen 1984, Miller & Monge 1986, Bowles & Gintis 1993, Schweickart 1993, Weisskopf 1993, Christman 1994, Doucouliagos 1995, Isham et al. 1995, Nienhaus & Brauksiepe 1997, Strauss 1998, Poole et al. 2001, Fenton 2002, Gill 2003, Bowman & Stone 2004, Clegg & Walsh 2004, de Jong & van Witteloostuijin 2004, Brown et al. 2005, Greasley et al. 2005, Heywood et al. 2005, Fischer 2006, Foley & Polanyi 2006, Greenwood et al. 2007, Carson 2008, Sauser 2009, Erdal 2011, Schweickart 2011, Davidson 2012, Maynard et al. 2012, Schwartz 2012, Malleson 2013, 2014, Altmann 2014, Smith & Rothbaum 2014, Millstone 2015).

But how can democratic organisations' superior economic performance be explained? Using the insights and empirical evidence from the sources quoted above, it is possible to draft a cause-and-effect model that explains the better economic performance and greater economic success of democratic organisations, and *why* and *how* democratic organisations are economically better and more successful than orthodox organisations. To this end, the following subsections particularly look at (1) the relevance of ownership and owner-managers' mindset and behaviour, (2) the effects of democratic management and full participation on performance, and (3) how the institutions and people of the democratic organisation together achieve better economic performance.

Ownership: Owner-Managers Care

As indicated earlier (see the section 'Private Ownership and Property Rights' in Chapter 2), when it is about (the handling of) *assets* it all starts with ownership – *private* ownership. There is nothing more motivating than private property and ownership in *that* respect.[9] When people have ownership *of* something, they care *about* it and *for* it (Erdal 2011, pp. 87, 177, 179). People who own property think and act like owners – and owners *care*. They look after the property – *their* property – and they manage and nurture it. Even people who own something collectively (common good) do so provided they have a feeling of ownership and responsibility for it. They care because their interests are directly linked to the asset, its existence, its use, and what comes out of its use (performance, utility, products, services, revenues, or profit). Owners look after *their* property because it *is* their interest and because it is *in* their interest (Greenwood et al. 2007, p. 224).

What is true in regard to property rights in material things is also true in regard to work and organisations – and perhaps even more so. People who own their work, the product of their work, and the organisation they work for care – much more than any employment contract, supervision, coercion, or 'psychological contract' drivel can ever achieve. As Erdal (2011, p. 19) argued: 'This is where employee ownership makes its most important difference to performance – when you and your colleagues own the company most of you tend to feel pretty committed to making it work well.' People who at the same time own and manage their work and organisation have an *inherent* sense of ownership and responsibility. They *feel* and *act* like owners because they *are* owners. They are committed and put in effort because they are the ones who make things happen and work – the ones who cause and bear the consequences of their work and the organisation's economic success or failure.

The democratic organisation taps into this powerful link between owning and managing things (assets) in the most fundamental and widest possible form; *each and every person* who works for the democratic organisation is at the same time an owner, a manager, and an employee. The democratic organisation is a jointly owned and controlled enterprise based on the concepts of self-ownership (and related inalienable rights) and private ownership (and related property rights), and a comprehensive and detailed partnership agreement (see Chapter 2). Whether the owners of the democratic organisation care about it for ideological, idealistic, and altruistic reasons or for very pragmatic and self-oriented reasons (Nienhaus & Brauksiepe 1997, pp. 1424–1425), it is *their* organisation, *they* are its owners, and *they* are responsible for it – and they will feel, act, and behave like owners

(Fenton 2002, p. 35). *Nothing is more motivating than working for oneself and being one's own boss* (Malleson 2014, p. xxi). Owner-managers make sure that the organisation runs successfully and that its structures, processes, products, and services are good and improve in quality and efficiency (Erdal 2011, p. 189). In so doing, they preserve, maintain, and increase the economic value of the things they own and are responsible for (i.e. the organisation and its assets) and drive the economic performance of the democratic organisation.

This is (another) consequentialist reason and argument for why *everyone* should be the owner of the business (not just a few people who refuse others the status and exclude them from the rights, responsibilities, and advantages they enjoy). The great and fundamental advantage of the democratic organisation compared to orthodox for-profit organisations is that in the former *everyone* is an owner, whereas in the latter only a few people are owners (even *absent* owners like shareholders) and the large majority are employees, who have to be motivated with 'stick-and-carrot' policies. Whether at an individual or a collective level, with its legal and psychological implications, private ownership is one of the great enablers and motivators in the private, economic, and social realm. Private ownership is the founding principle of any economic success – and the democratic organisation is based on that principle, and practises it, like no other organisation.

Effects of Democratic Management and Full Participation on Performance

(Individual and collective) private ownership provides the legal, psychological, and social foundations for 'being in charge', i.e. the legitimate authority and responsibility to manage things. Owners see themselves as being, and want to be, in charge – and ownership provides the owners of an organisation with equal legal and formal status, and especially with far-reaching rights and responsibilities to make decisions and to govern and manage the organisation. This is where the democratic organisation is cutting edge; it puts the owners, *all* owners, in charge. According to its fundamental notion of *democratic management*, it first and foremost provides for, even requires, *self-management* from every one of its members. Following the principles of self-ownership and subsidiarity, *all* members of the democratic organisation are entitled, encouraged, and enabled to organise and manage their work, work-related issues, and organisational affairs as much and as far as possible. As a consequence, in the democratic organisation it is those who *do* the work – and *know* their work – who make the decisions about their work and implement them. It makes considerable sense to make use of people's motivation and knowledge for planning, organising, leading, and controlling organisational affairs and conduct of business (according to democratic principles and standards) in such a way; the closer knowledge, management, and operations are related, the more appropriate and better are analyses of and solutions to problems. In the democratic organisation, the ones who know, who manage, and who operate are the same people. This personal union is a tried and tested recipe for operational efficiency and economic success.

Moreover, all members of the democratic organisation have equal rights and opportunities, if not to say the responsibility, to participate in the governance and management of organisational affairs and the organisation as a whole and in formal decision-making processes at all levels of the organisation (i.e. constitutional, strategic, and operational). Participation in management – or *participative management* – ensures that all members' commitment, knowledge, and ideas can feed into organisational decision-making, governance, and conduct of business. Full participation in the governance and management of the democratic organisation ensures that more relevant information is available for managerial decision-making, that problems are looked at from different angles, that issues are debated, that diverse opinions are voiced, and that various options are considered until a final decision has been achieved collectively. More relevant information, diverse views, and possible options considerably increase the probability that the *quality* and *appropriateness* of solutions will be higher. In addition, full participation in decision-making ensures that solutions are decided democratically and implemented with the support and backing of the majority of members. And it is especially the *implementation* of decisions that accounts for most organisational efficiency and success. Hence, although making decisions can take longer under democratic management and full participation, the actual quality and implementation of decisions – and, thus, overall organisational and economic efficiency and performance – are (much) higher and better than in orthodox, hierarchical, and autocratic organisations.

Besides its organisational implications, full participation in the governance and management of the democratic organisation and organisational affairs has a whole range of positive effects on the people who work for and contribute to the success of the democratic organisation (Blumberg 1968, p. 123, Kanter 1971, p. 66, Dachler & Wilpert 1978, pp. 8–9, Bowles & Gintis 1993, pp. 92–93, Strauss 1998, p. 8, Gill 2003, p. 316, Brown et al. 2005, p. 586, Greasley et al. 2005, p. 358, Erdal 2011, pp. 19, 22, Malleson 2014, p. 56): people who (can and do) participate are much more committed and engaged. They identify more with their work and specific tasks as well as with the organisation and its overall purposes, strategy, and direction. They are keener to contribute, to come up with ideas and solutions, and to implement them. And they are overall more satisfied, motivated, and productive. People who participate feel better and do better – and they produce better results.[10]

But participation does not only create positive (psychological) effects at an individual or *intra*-personal level – it also produces positive effects at an *inter*-personal level. People who can participate (fully) in the governance and management of the social system they are part of and in daily (organisational) affairs also show more commitment and engagement in social interactions.

They communicate more and demonstrate more *collaborative* behaviour simply because participative management and joint decision-making require them to communicate and to cooperate (Bowman & Stone 2004, p. 280, Sauser 2009, p. 151). Cooperation creates trust and reciprocity. Cooperation between free and equal partners, especially, leads to (more) trust (Heywood et al. 2005, p. 557) since their contributions and reciprocal behaviour are entirely voluntarily and can be withheld or withdrawn at any time.[11] Altmann (2014, p. 182) has therefore even talked about a *culture* of trust and reciprocity that typifies the democratic organisation (and differentiates it from orthodox, hierarchical organisations). Cooperation based on trust and reciprocity creates an atmosphere where people are more willing to share their knowledge and other resources, thoughts, and insights; to come up with ideas and make suggestions; and to initiate improvements and innovations (Carson 2008, p. 524, Smith & Rothbaum 2014, p. 222). Cooperation, especially voluntary cooperation, considerably increases efficiency, productivity, and overall organisational performance.

Better Economic Performance Understood in a Broad Sense

So, coming back to the question raised at the beginning of this section – how can democratic organisations' higher efficiency, productivity, and sustainable organisational performance (altogether their superior economic performance) be explained? – the answer to how and why democratic organisations are economically more successful than orthodox, profit-maximising organisations depends on how one defines and understands 'economic performance'. Following the ideologies of neo-classical economists ('perfect market' and 'rational actors') and conservative organisation studies and management scholars ('theory of the firm' and 'shareholder value orientation'), the economic performance of organisations is merely seen and measured in terms of how much *profit* they generate over a short period.[12] Seen in this way, democratic organisations are *not* as economically successful as profit-maximising companies. They may be profitable, but they do not generate as much profit as possible – not because they cannot but because they do not want to.

But even some orthodox economists and organisation studies scholars admit that the goal of profit maximisation is inconsistent with some other orthodox economic measures – such as (increasing the) productivity, efficiency, or competitiveness of an organisation. And from an even more objective position, it is clear that it is simply wrong to equate 'economic performance' with a single financial aggregate that only serves the egoistic interests of a few people (profit only for the single owner or few owners of the capitalist firm). (The uncompromising strive for) 'profit' is actually a profoundly irrelevant or even a threatening and damaging measure for people other than those beneficiaries (e.g. for employees because they are exploited and may lose their jobs for profit-related reasons) and the environment (e.g. damage to or destruction of the natural environment via externalisation of internal costs in order to reduce costs and, thus, increase profits).

Hence, 'economic performance' should be understood in a more general sense as the change (creation or termination, preservation, or increase or decrease) of the *economic value* of things (i.e. tangible or intangible assets), processes (i.e. exchange, transformation, or decision-making processes), or money (i.e. financial assets). Economic performance or economic value can be measured using various dimensions (e.g. financial, technical, natural, or social science) and via various indicators (e.g. profitability, productivity, efficiency, effectiveness, or sustainability).[13]

In this sense, *on average and in the long run*, democratic organisations achieve a *higher* level of economic performance, i.e. they create, preserve, or even increase the economic value of things, processes, and money *more* than orthodox or profit-maximising organisations because of various factors (and their interactions):

1. Earlier in this chapter it was argued that *ownership* matters. People who own property look after it, protect it, and nurture it. *All* members of the democratic organisation are its owners, its managers, and its owner-managers. Owner-managers usually (try to) do things more efficiently and decently (than hired managers or employees) because it is *their* money, time, and effort that goes into (doing) things and *they* carry the costs and burdens if things go wrong or are done inefficiently. People who at the same time own and manage their work and organisation put in effort and make sure that organisational structures and processes are efficient, and that products and services are of good quality and improve over time. It is *their* organisation, and '*their* name' stands for how the organisation conducts its business. Thus, owner-managers have personal, legal, formal, and organisational motivation and reasons to preserve, sustain and grow the economic value of their organisation and its assets.

2. The notion of ownership shows itself in the *governance and management* of the democratic organisation. *All* members govern and manage the organisation as a whole, organisational affairs, their work, and themselves via the concepts of democratic governance (especially the principle of subsidiarity) and democratic management (self-management, participative management, and representative management). This is likely to mean that the structures and processes of governance and management are more complex, more time-consuming, and hence relatively *in*-efficient *in the short term*. However, because more information and knowledge goes into governance and management, and due to the notions of sharing (information and knowledge) and collaborating, the structures and processes of governance and management are more robust and productive, and produce better policies over time. As a consequence, the democratic organisation operates and functions better, and the quality, efficiency, and productivity of its internal operations are higher.

3. According to the principles of self-management and subsidiarity and the notions of (equalising) empowerment and full participation in decision-making, in the democratic organisation *people* are fully empowered to make decisions about their work (and the organisation they work for) and to implement them. Usually, the more people who organise and manage their own work and organisation, collaborate voluntarily, and feel responsible for their work and the products of their work, the more (intrinsically) motivated, committed, and productive they are. Individual commitment and cooperation considerably increase the quality and efficiency of operations and, thus, organisational performance.

4. Ownership, democratic governance and management, equalising empowerment, and full participation work together towards better outcomes; in general and on average, members of the democratic organisation are more motivated and committed, more collaborative, and more productive. Internal operations are more efficient, economical, and sustainable. Democratic organisations employ decent and considerate business practices; have a long-term orientation in their business and investment policies; are more conservative and risk-averse in their decision-making; maintain the economic viability of their business; use surpluses to accumulate reserves, maintain and grow equipment, and invest in efficient technologies; and are more resilient in economically challenging times. The result is higher organisational and economic performance over long periods of time.

Notes

1 The focus in this chapter is mainly on the democratic organisation *as such* – i.e. its *internal* conditions and workings. The chapter is largely abstracted from external conditions or aspects (e.g. political frameworks, legal rules and regulations, market type and market environment, macro-economic conditions, specific markets or industries, competition and competitors' behaviour, consumer behaviour, and images or the public's perceptions of certain types of organisation and the like).

2 In contrast, *other orientation* also means concern for others and their welfare, but less, or not in accordance with, one's self-interest and rationality (Korsgaard et al. 1996, Meglino & Korsgaard 2004, Lester et al. 2008). That is, other orientation can be psychologically problematic, and it can be or become chronically unhealthy since it can lead to obedience, submissiveness, self-denial, and/or leader–follower syndrome.

3 This fundamental difference between orthodox (profit-maximising) and democratic organisations' social orientations is encapsulated to some degree in the two concepts of Friedman's (1962/1982) *shareholder* orientation and Freeman's (1983) *stakeholder* orientation.

4 Mazzarol et al. (2013, p. 36) also provide a whole list of benefits that (small) individual organisations get by being part of a cooperative or cooperative network, such as access to resources, access to services not provided by private industry or government, investment in local communities and creation of social capital, member business development through education, aggregate member bargaining power to gain competitive advantage and a stronger market position, direct

financial (dividend or patronage reward) and indirect benefit (lower transaction cost) for member businesses through cooperative core operations and/or diversified investments, ability to stay small but act and benefit big, marketing and other service benefits, (unlimited) support for sales and profitability growth, added value to products and services, lower transaction costs and environmental risks managed by the cooperative, educational benefits, being part of the cooperative community, creating value for and protecting future generations, and a sense of achievement and pride.

5 For some concepts, ideas, and practical examples relating to such a 'people's economy', i.e. local or community economies that focus on sustainable development, community work, self-help, participation, and cooperation, see Bauhaus Dessau Foundation & European Network for Economic Self-Help and Local Development (1996).

6 For orthodox organisations it is sufficient to *appear* to be 'green' and environmentally responsible while continuing their unsustainable conduct of business (called 'greening of corporations', 'greenwash', or 'hijacking of environmentalism'; Eisner 2004, p. 148, Sandhu 2010, p. 295).

7 Kollmuss and Agyeman (2002), Gifford and Nilsson (2014), and McDonald (2014) provide quite comprehensive and systematic overviews of psychological, socio-psychological, and sociological theories and factors that are relevant to describing and explaining individual (pro-environmental) concerns and behaviour.

8 Some democratic organisations employ even stronger concepts and versions of (ecological) sustainability, such as 'sustaincentrism', 'ecocentrism', or ecocentric environmental ethics and paradigms (Purser et al. 1995, Bondy & Matten 2012).

9 That is, with regard to *assets*, i.e. things that have an *economic* value (value of use or exchange value). Earlier in this chapter, in respect to nature and the natural environment, we saw that people can also be motivated to care about things that have an *intrinsic value*, i.e. things that are *not* assets in an economic sense.

10 The individual-psychological and social advantages of working in a democratic organisation will be addressed and discussed in more detail in the section 'Why People Start or Join Democratic Organisations' in Chapter 8.

11 In contrast, cooperation between superiors and subordinates, or between subordinates (i.e. coordination in hierarchical social systems), is *not* voluntarily but unstable and unequal in almost every respect. Cooperation on such a basis, thus, does not create trust and reciprocity but is built on mistrust (the famous principal–agent problem!), tactical behaviour, and advantage-seeking.

12 There may be additional indicators, mostly from financial accounting and perhaps from strategic management or marketing, that can also be subsumed under the narrow neo-classical understanding of 'economic performance'. Nevertheless, they are all of instrumental, secondary importance; 'profit' is the first and foremost measure (and the only reason why traditional, profit-maximising firms are established and operate).

13 For instance, efficiency can be defined as 'the (often measurable) ability to avoid wasting materials, energy, efforts, money, and time in doing something or in producing a desired result. In a more general sense, it is the ability to do things well, successfully, and without waste. In more mathematical or scientific terms, it is a measure of the extent to which input is well used for an intended task or function (output)' ('Efficiency' 2019). Besides or in addition to such wider economic performance indicators, democratic organisations, obviously, may be evaluated against a whole range of different, 'non-economic' performance criteria and indicators (Kanter 1972, p. 128, Rothschild & Whitt 1986, p. 145), such as doing 'good' things; level of practising their democratic ideals; achieving (various forms of) equality; level of well-being, satisfaction, or happiness of their members or other stakeholders; and contributions to society, societal changes, and developments. But since this sub-section is (only) about 'profit' and economic performance, such non-economic performance measures are not discussed in more detail here.

7

GENERAL MODEL OF THE DEMOCRATIC ORGANISATION

The General Model of the Democratic Organisation

So far, Part I has described the main features of the democratic organisation: (1) the libertarian constitution, (2) democratic governance, (3) democratic management, (4) equalising empowerment, and (5) considerate conduct of business. Each of those elements is essential for the design and functioning of the democratic organisation – and all are typical of the democratic organisation. Together, they constitute the *general model of the democratic organisation.*[1]

Moreover, these are not only crucial elements in their own right but complement and feed into each other; with its focus on establishing and protecting free individuals, their self-ownership and inalienable human, civil, and democratic rights, private ownership and property rights in a legally binding partnership agreement, the libertarian constitution shapes the design and workings of the democratic organisation and all of its parts. All members of the democratic organisation are legally and formally enabled and empowered to govern and to manage themselves, the organisation and organisational affairs via institutions of democratic governance and democratic management. And all members are equally empowered – formally, psychologically, and socially – via the organisational institutions of democratic governance and democratic management (self-, representative, and participative management). A democratic organisation designed and maintained in such ways shows *considerate* conduct of business and performs well in social, environmental, *and* economic terms. Figure 7.1 shows the general model, its elements, and their relationships.

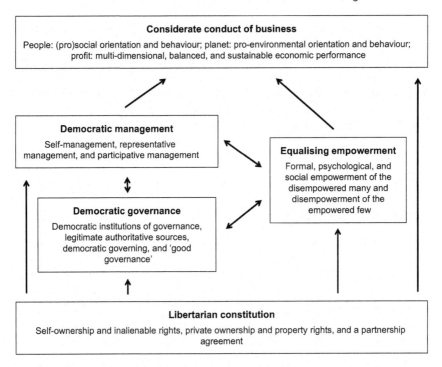

FIGURE 7.1 General model of the democratic organisation

Libertarian Constitution

The democratic organisation is based on libertarian values of individual and collective ownership, in particular self-ownership, private ownership, and freedom of contract. Respect for individuals and their inalienable rights in themselves, as well as property rights and equal rights, is the formal, legal, and substantive foundation of the democratic organisation – and these rights are linked to one consistent framework:

- The notion of *self-ownership* makes very clear that individuals' personalities, minds, individuality, mental competencies, and capabilities are *inalienable* rights *that cannot be transferred* and that any form of 'dependent employment' (i.e. employment based on an employment contract) is therefore illegitimate and invalid.
- The right of *private ownership*, and all the property rights related to it, specifies that every member is an owner and as such has the equal status and rights of an owner of the property. In this sense, the libertarian constitution of the democratic organisation takes individual rights of and to private ownership even more seriously than conservative, right-libertarian approaches.

- As a logical consequence of this appreciation of individuals' rights, the democratic organisation is based on a *partnership agreement* that specifies and guarantees the *equal* legal and formal status, rights, and responsibilities of all people, who *collectively and democratically* own, manage, and control the organisation and its properties, activities, and results. The partnership agreement is *the only legitimate form of legal contract of cooperation between free individuals* that appreciates and protects their inalienable rights and property rights – and the democratic organisation is the *only* type of organisation that enables, guarantees, accommodates, protects, and promotes the status, inalienable rights, and responsibilities of free individuals.

Democratic Governance

The democratic organisation is an *institutionalised organisational democracy*. As a democratic social system, the democratic organisation *must* have *democratic* governance in place, i.e. formal institutions that outline how the organisation is designed and functions according to democratic principles. Key elements of democratic governance (in the democratic organisation) are democratic institutions of governance, legitimate authoritative sources, democratic governing, and 'good governance'. In order to be legitimate, all key elements of democratic governance themselves must be democratic – and they must be intertwined and consistent with each other.

Democratic Institutions of Governance

Within the democratic organisation, formal bodies – 'institutions of governance' – are formally established, maintained, and allocated with the task of governing the organisation (e.g. boards, committees, councils, or assemblies).

In order to be legitimate, institutions of governance must be designed and function according to the very same principles they are designed to realise and protect. This means that the democratic organisation's institutions of governance and control must themselves be *democratic* institutions – i.e. they must be established and maintained democratically, and their structures, their composition, and the way(s) they operate and function must be democratic. Especially in order to avoid an undemocratic concentration of power, there must be strong and robust checks and balances in place relating to the democratic organisation's institutions of governance – horizontally between different organisational institutions (*separation of powers*) and vertically by locating decision-making and control at the lowest possible levels (*principle of subsidiarity*).

Legitimate Authoritative Sources

Governance is based on *authoritative sources*. Authoritative sources provide explicit principles, norms and values, rules and regulations, policies, guidelines, and advice about how a system and its key parts should be designed, maintained, and function; what is more and less preferable (or even 'good' and 'bad'); and how people should behave – even how they should think and feel, and what they should do and not do.

Some authoritative sources exist even before a formal social system (such as an organisation) is established (e.g. a constitution, business and contract laws, rules and regulations, and templates for contracts, governance bodies, and organisational policies). Other authoritative sources are set up by the members of the democratic organisation (e.g. partnership agreement, mission and vision statements, strategy and operational plans, codes of conduct, and ethics and compliance statements).

Together, these authoritative sources provide the foundations for the governance and functioning of the democratic organisation. In order to be *legitimate*, these authoritative sources must have been produced, deliberated, and decided *democratically* – in transparent and participative ways – and their content, implications, and applications must reflect the very ideas and values of a fully fledged democratic system. The authoritative sources must be open to debate, capable of being contested, and – within the regulatory framework – capable of being changed.

Democratic Governing

Members of the democratic organisation govern the organisation and organisational affairs on the basis of authoritative sources either directly or via organisational institutions of governance. Decisions – whether about constitutional, strategic, or operational issues – are made democratically, i.e. by all members of the organisation or its relevant parts (*direct or participative democracy, self-management*), or by elected representatives or office-holders (*representative democracy, representative management*). Office-holders are controlled regularly, are held accountable, and are removable from office by democratic means (*accountability*). Members have free and equal access to all relevant non-confidential information about the democratic organisation's formal policies, rules, and regulations as well as all information relevant to a particular case (*transparency*).

'Good Governance'

Finally, democratic social systems must be governed according to 'good governance'. Democratic governance *is* 'good governance' – and 'good governance' is in its crucial parts democratic governance. In the case of the democratic organisation: 'good governance'

- Makes sure that the basic functions of governance are delivered according to democratic standards, and it especially provides the means to contain and to control institutions and positions of power.

- Ensures that the organisational institutions of governance and management (boards, councils, committees, and/or assemblies) are designed and work on the basis of the rule of law and according to democratic standards. It also ensures that the members of these bodies are elected, controlled, and held accountable by those they represent and that their decision-making processes are democratic and transparent.
- Protects and promotes civil and human rights; the fundamental values of freedom, democracy, equality, and justice; and the equal rights of all owners and members to govern and manage the organisation and organisational affairs collectively and democratically.

Democratic Management

Since *every* member of the democratic organisation has equal rights and responsibilities because of their equal legal and formal status as owners and partners, the democratic organisation can only be a *heterarchical* organisation, i.e. a formalised structure of horizontally arranged social positions of equal power and authority. In the democratic organisation there are no superior–subordinate relationships (either legally or formally), and there is no minority of superiors or majority of subordinates. There are only owner-managers with equal rights and responsibilities.

Equal rights (and equal power and authority) especially means equal rights and responsibilities to make decisions and to manage, and to conduct the *whole* range of management functions (planning, organising, leading, and controlling). Equal rights to manage mean *democratic management*. Democratic management consists of three parts: self-management, representative management, and participative management.

Self-Management

In the democratic organisation, self-management comes first. Acknowledging and following the principles of self-ownership and subsidiarity, individuals and groups of people are entitled, encouraged, and enabled to organise and manage their own work, work-related issues, and organisational affairs as much and as far as possible. Individuals who do the work also manage (their) work – either individually or collectively in self-managed groups that are organised and function according to democratic principles and standards. *All* members of the democratic organisation (are entitled and required to) conduct *all* management functions (planning, organising, leading, and controlling), including regularly making decisions about constitutional, strategic, and operational issues and problems.

Representative Management

Organisational affairs that go beyond individuals' or groups of people's wills and capacities to self-manage are managed by formally established organisational institutions or individual management positions. Especially in larger organisations, there may be organisational institutions of governance and management or individual positions that are charged with the task of providing certain management functions. These positions are designed, staffed, and function according to democratic principles; all office-holders are elected or appointed democratically. They are obliged to execute the will of those whom they represent, carry out their responsibilities within clearly defined boundaries, and have no line management responsibilities whatsoever – on the contrary, they are supervised, controlled, held accountable, reconfirmed, or replaced by those whom they represent.

Participative Management

Finally, participative management links self-management and representative management. It provides fundamental principles and robust mechanisms that enable and guarantee equal opportunities for everyone to participate in decision-making as well as effective democratic containment of formal organisational institutions and positions of management. Participative management means that *all* members of the democratic organisation have equal rights and opportunities to participate in all formal decision-making processes at all levels of the organisation.

Equalising Empowerment

From a legal, formal, and functional perspective, all members of the democratic organisation are equal and have *equal rights* (according to their status as owners or owner-managers) – and equal rights mean *equal power* (to make use of those rights). *All* members of the democratic organisation *must* have equal power since otherwise the idea of *demos kratos* – government or power 'of the people, by the people, for the people' – would be threatened. However, having equal *rights* does not automatically translate into having equal *power*, i.e. being as able as others ('empowered') to exist and to act within a social context. Actions and processes within the social system can lead to a situation where people are formally, psychologically, or socially unequally empowered. The challenge for the democratic organisation, therefore, is to make sure that *all* members are *equally* empowered, and to find ways to empower the disempowered and to disempower the (overtly) empowered until both have (ideally or as a tendency) equal formal, psychological, and social power (*equalising empowerment*). There are various measures the democratic organisation can apply to equalise empowerment: equalising formal power, equalising psychological power, and equalising social power.

Equalising Formal Power

Formal power can be equalised by configuring all organisational institutions of governance and management as well as formal roles and positions according to the fundamental ideas and principles of *democratic governance* and *democratic management.*

On the one hand, this is about *confining* formal power – especially of formal institutions and office-holders, for example via limiting institutions of governance to clearly defined responsibilities regulated by robust laws and regulations, separation of powers and checks and balances, and the principle of subsidiarity; directly limiting office-holders' formal responsibilities and authority of office via representative management, democratic decision-making, transparency, and accountability; limiting the number of memberships, formal positions, and functions office-holders can have; limiting office-holders' terms in office; and tightly controlling office-holders' conduct of office.

On the other hand, it is about *increasing* formal power – especially of those who are *not* formal office-holders, for example via practising self-management and participative management as much as possible; guaranteeing *full* participation, *democratic* decision-making, and comprehensive transparency and accountability in regard to all organisational affairs and matters of public concern; and providing all members of the democratic organisation not only with equal rights but also with *equal opportunities* to participate in the governance and management of the organisation and organisational affairs.

Obviously, the formal institutions of democratic governance and democratic management provide the democratic organisation with a wealth of tools and measures to considerably limit the formal power of the empowered and to considerably increase the formal power of the disempowered.

Equalising Psychological Power

The psychological empowerment or disempowerment of members of the democratic organisation needs to be seen, and done, in more differentiated terms. As a matter of principle, the democratic organisation – like any non-totalitarian social system that appreciates and protects individuals and their inalienable rights of and to themselves (self-ownership) as well as human and civil rights – does not interfere *directly* with the personality or psyche of any of its members. But the democratic organisation provides excellent conditions for the psychological (dis-)empowerment of its members.

With regard to the empowerment of the psychologically disempowered the democratic organisation has formal and social settings (e.g. individuals' legal and actual status as owners, the concepts of democratic governance, self-management, and participative management) that enable and support the disempowered to empower themselves, increase their self-esteem, move the locus of control within themselves, and improve their goal attainment considerably.

In respect to the (necessary) disempowerment of psychologically overtly empowered people (people lacking emotional, social, or cultural intelligence; 'aggrandisers'; aspirational careerists; wannabe managers; micro-managing managers; bullies; and organisational psychopaths) it is, of course, not helpful that the democratic organisation does not attempt to change people's personalities directly. However, the democratic organisation can engage with members who show questionable personality traits, anti-social behaviour, or inappropriate personal management styles (such as an autocratic or authoritarian management style) via formal or social means (see the point in the previous sub-section about 'confining formal power' or the point in the next sub-section about an 'organisational culture of contestation and equal-(ising) power').

Equalising Social Power

The case is different in regard to social empowerment and disempowerment of people because the democratic organisation is explicitly a *social* system, and far more so than the bureaucratic or orthodox profit-oriented organisation. The democratic organisation and its governance and management structures and processes are built on the idea of members being socially active and engaged. And they are comprehensively and systematically encouraged and empowered to be so; self-management, self-managed groups, and full participation especially help and encourage socially disempowered members on a daily basis to pursue their interests within a social context; to manage and maintain social relationships and interactions; to develop a strong social identity and orientation; to feel confident and comfortable among others in their social statuses, positions, roles, and functions; and to enhance their competencies and capabilities.

Socially empowered members of a social system also can – and will – make sure that overtly (self-)empowered members (e.g. 'careerists', 'leaders', and 'aggrandisers') and their social dominance are challenged. For instance, their claims of privileged and exclusive (i.e. privileging and excluding) knowledge, skills, status, or positions can be challenged by demystification, social control (especially upward control), and social actions (e.g. criticising and challenging them openly).

Together, the social empowerment of the disempowered and the disempowerment of the empowered create an open *organisational culture of contestation and equal(ising) power* that corresponds favourably with the mechanisms of democratic governance and democratic management. That the measures to empower the disempowered and disempower the empowered are consistent with the principles and means of democratic governance and democratic management shows that these measures are *an integral part of the democratic organisation*, that they form and represent some of its *social institutions* – they *have* to; even when all the principles and policies of democratic governance and democratic management in place, the empowerment of the few and disempowerment of the many represent *constant threats* to the democratic organisation. Equalising empowerment, therefore, is not a special project but a daily task and duty.

Considerate Conduct of Business

In their purpose(s) and conduct of business, democratic organisations are not confined to a particular narrow orientation (like profit-maximising, shareholder-oriented firms) but are established, and maintained, for very different, multi-dimensional purposes – and demonstrate accordingly appropriate behaviour. Very generally, one might identify at least three orientations and dimensions: social, environmental, and economic ('people, planet, profit').

(Pro)social Orientation and Behaviour

Most democratic organisations are set up primarily for social or even prosocial purposes, i.e. to increase the welfare of their members, clients, community, or other stakeholders. They have this (pro)social orientation, and demonstrate corresponding social behaviour, mainly because most of their owner-managers or members:

- have a more collaborative mindset; employ more voluntary, mutually beneficial cooperation and reciprocal behaviour; are more willing to share resources, knowledge, and power; are more keen to distribute benefits, burdens, costs, and profits fairly; and are more focused on developing and maintaining long-term relations;
- have a stronger community orientation, have a feeling of local embeddedness and belongingness, and are more concerned about individuals' and community well-being;
- overall show more decent and honest, fair and just, and responsible and ethical behaviour.

Pro-environmental Orientation and Behaviour

Democratic organisations are also more inclined to show a pro-environmental orientation and behaviour because:

- local people and the local community – as key stakeholders of the democratic organisation – are likely to appreciate and be concerned about the (local) natural environment, and the democratic organisation has a strong degree of local embeddedness and is founded on paradigms of community orientation and member orientation.

- the owner-members of the democratic organisation are likely to have feelings of connectedness or a sense of connectivity with nature and personal (biophilic) values, the relevant and necessary knowledge to act in pro-environmental ways, and a (strong) sense of responsibility to take action.
- the democratic organisation may even have explicitly pro-environmental goals and purposes in its business model (as part of its triple bottom line approach), and it may use and offer 'appropriate technology' (i.e. local, small-scale, decentralised, and more environmentally friendly technologies, products, and services) as fundamental and integral parts of its conduct of business.

Economic Orientation and Performance

Finally, if 'economic performance' is seen and understood not only as mere 'profit' (or similar financial or market-oriented measures) but also as any kind of long-term creation or protection of economic value, then it is easy to see that democratic organisations are relatively profitable and economically successful, mainly because:

- *Each and every person* who works for the democratic organisation is at the same time an owner and a manager – and owner-managers have an *inherent* sense of ownership and responsibility, are committed and put in effort, try to make things work (and work as well as possible), and try to preserve or even increase the value of the things (*their* property) they own, use, and produce.
- In the democratic organisation it is those who *do* the work – and *know* their work – who make the decisions about their work and implement them (self-management); moreover, via full participation in decision-making (participative management), they ensure that the quality and appropriateness of solutions are better and that solutions are decided upon and implemented collectively and cooperatively.
- People who participate are much more committed and engaged; are keener to contribute, to come up with ideas and solutions, and to implement them (*intra*-personal level); show more commitment and engagement in social interactions; demonstrate more *collaborative* behaviour; and are more willing to share their knowledge and to cooperate (*inter*-personal level). This increases the quality and efficiency of internal organisational processes considerably.
- Organisational performance and, as a consequence, economic performance – measured in multi-dimensional ways and seen in the long term – overall is higher, more robust, and more sustainable than in profit-oriented organisations.

Democratic organisations can be set up for various purposes. They can be established and maintained for specific social, economic, and/or environmental purposes. But, as diverse as democratic organisations may be in their purposes and orientations, in their activities they *all* show behaviour that can be described best as *considerate conduct of business*; on average, democratic organisations and their members show much more considerate governance and management; are more responsible, long-term oriented, and risk-averse in how they operate; and overall demonstrate more ethical, decent, socially oriented, inclusive, and cooperative behaviour in their internal and external activities, with regard to people, planet, and profit.

Democratic Organisations *Are* Better, *Do* Better, and *Perform* Better

The democratic organisation is a *good* organisation. It is *inherently* good because of its libertarian constitution, democratic governance, democratic management, equalising empowerment, and considerate conduct of business. All of these elements are built on, are consistent with, and work according to the universal principles of freedom, democracy, equality, and justice, which are perceived as good in every legitimate culture and society. Democratic organisations are designed and function according to libertarian and democratic principles and provide the broadest possible range of equal (legal, civil, and human) rights and opportunities to all their members. They are based on and committed to the values of freedom (self-ownership), democracy (democratic governance and democratic management), equality (equal rights and responsibilities of all members), and justice (good governance and profit-sharing).

These principles, values, and institutions influence how the organisation is designed and maintained, how it is governed and managed, how it functions and operates – and how the people involved reason and act. Democratic organisations not only *are* better but also *do* better and *perform* better. Why? Because their libertarian constitution, democratic governance, democratic management, equalising empowerment, and considerate conduct of business not only are good in themselves and produce good, desired outcomes on their own but also interconnect and interplay with each other. *These attributes interact with and mutually reinforce each other.* The democratic organisation's (and its members') orientations, activities, and outcomes are a consequence – a *logical* consequence – of the interplay between its *libertarian* and *democratic* institutions and *free* people with *equal* rights and responsibilities.

Ownership is crucial – ownership of *all*, not a few. Ownership – and in the case of the democratic organisation ownership in the form of private ownership/property *and* self-ownership *of everyone*, put together in a partnership agreement – means not only equal status, rights and responsibilities, and power and control but also equal *commitment*; owners are more interested in, considerate, concerned, and caring about what they own (including themselves), their work, and the outcomes and consequences of their property and work. Owner-managers care about things they are responsible for and show a high degree of commitment to keeping them, nurturing them, and making them work as well as possible. Hence, if *all* members of a social system are owners or owner-managers they will appreciate their equal rights and responsibilities as well as the social system (which provides them with those rights and responsibilities and enables them to enact them), how it works, and what it does (to them and others) because this is the – voluntary! – foundation of their existence.

The concerns and commitment of the owners of an organisation are seen in how the social system is designed and maintained, i.e. in its governance and management. If the members of a social system have equal rights and responsibilities, its governance and management can only be democratic – i.e. *democratic* governance (especially in the form of 'good governance') and *democratic* management (especially in the form of self-management and full participation). Because democratic organisations are owned, governed, managed, and controlled democratically and collectively by all of their members, decision-making will also be democratic. By and large, decisions that are made democratically tend to take more aspects into account, and they tend to be more comprehensive and more moderate because more people (with diverse views) are involved[2] – which means that democratic organisations have multiple dimensions and aspects in their orientation (such as social, environmental, *and* economic concerns and issues). The more people are legitimately and regularly involved in free, fair, open, and transparent democratic decision-making, the more they tend towards the middle ground, acknowledge and appreciate multiple dimensions and aspects in their reasoning, and reach more differentiated, comprehensive, and moderate decisions.

The conditions within the democratic organisation do not only lead to more commitment, engagement, participation, and democratic decision-making *as such* but also to more collaborative behaviour, (a culture of) trust and reciprocity, and *considerate* collaboration and decision-making. It is simply different types and qualities of participation and cooperative behaviour that happen within democratic organisations – *voluntary* participation and *considerate* cooperation – and these create mutual trust and even more collaboration. This type of interpersonal behaviour does not happen because members of democratic organisations are 'better people' or altruists (they might be, but not necessarily) but because of the specific organisational conditions and incentives offered by the environment of the democratic organisation (Benkler & Nissenbaum 2006, p. 410, Altmann 2014, p. 190); self-management, participative management, collective decision-making, and considerate collaboration are simply the modi operandi of democratic organisations – and people simply act and behave accordingly. Vanek (1971, p. 17) called this 'genuine motivation', i.e. people behave and operate in these ways not because they are somehow artificially extrinsically motivated by rewards or punishment but because it just seems and feels right and natural for them to do so.

The democratic organisation's and its members' conduct of business, and how they behave towards and interact with others *outside* the organisation and the natural environment, is influenced to quite some extent by the very way the organisation is designed and functions internally (Steen-Johnsen et al. 2011, p. 556). Members' cooperative attitude and behaviour and their considerate and responsible way(s) of doing business guide their market-related behaviour and their actions and interactions with third parties (Fisher 2013, p. 148). Iuviene et al. (2010, p. 6) argued that 'because cooperatives are owned and democratic-ally-controlled by their members, business decisions balance the need for profitability with the needs of their members and the wider interests of the community'. Its internal principles – 'good governance' and participative management, (democratic) structures and processes, and cooperative attitudes and behaviour of members – determine that the democratic organisation acts in way(s) that are good for everyone (social orientation towards internal and external stakeholders and society as a whole), the economy (decent, productive, and sustainable business, products, and services), *and* the natural environment (pro-environmental behaviour and appropriate technologies).

One might say that democratic organisations pursue a business model based on lower-intensity and less material values, and higher-quality and more ethical values. They show (much) more decent and honest, fair and just, and responsible and ethical behaviour (than orthodox, profit-maximising organisations). Democratic organisations demonstrate more decent and more ethical behaviour because they have purposes and goals, governance and management, structures and processes, and operations and policies for conducting business in place that prompt and enable their members to act and behave more decently and ethically – and for individuals it is much easier to be, and to act, (more) decently and ethically when one's day-to-day conditions and operations suggest, support, and appreciate such attitudes and behaviour. These attitudes and behaviour are simply 'in the fabric' of such organisations. Democratic organisations conduct their business *in humane ways*. They offer organisational performance and success with a human face (Bowles & Gintis 1993, p. 94, Malleson 2013, pp. 100–103). In this sense, the democratic organisation's and its members' behaviour and way(s) of doing business are not only fundamentally different from but also (much) better than orthodox for-profit or hierarchical organisations' practices – whether in competitive market environments or a more collaborative Social and Solidarity Economy.

Altogether, it thus can be proposed that if an organisation is owned by all of its members, who have equal rights and responsibilities (*libertarian constitution*); if the organisation has fully fledged and fully functioning systems of *democratic governance* and *democratic management* in place; and if all of the organisation's members are equally empowered to manage their work and organisational affairs by themselves (self-management) or collectively (representative or participative management) and to make all major decisions democratically, then the organisation's and its members' orientations, behaviour, and performance both within the organisation and towards others and the environment will largely be considerate, moderate, balanced, sustainable, decent, ethical, fair, and just (*considerate conduct of business*).

The democratic organisation ticks all of the boxes.

Notes

1 The general model, obviously, describes all features of the democratic organisation comprehensively and in detail, i.e. it suggests a fully-fledged, fairly structured and relatively developed democratic organisation of some size and longer existence. Nevertheless, a democratic organisation can be also a new business established by two or a few partners or a small enterprise. The functions of democratic governance and management, equalising empowerment and considerate conduct are then present and performed more implicitly, ad hoc and as an integral part of daily routines and activities without much policies and paperwork.

2 It is important to stress that this statement about decisions being 'more moderate' should be qualified with 'by and large' or 'as a tendency'. Democratic decision-making can, and does, (sometimes) also produce radical, extremist, irrational, completely inadequate, or inappropriate decisions. Unfortunately, there are many examples of people in free and democratic elections voting for radical, anti-democratic parties, or examples of groups of people or committees making utterly irrational decisions despite having engaged in open debates and decision-making processes. Democracy only provides (some of) the necessary conditions and opportunities – but no guarantees! – for achieving sensible decisions.

PART II

Attractiveness, Legitimacy, and Vulnerabilities of Democratic Organisations

8

THE CASE FOR DEMOCRATIC ORGANISATIONS

(Alleged) Disadvantages and Weaknesses of Democratic Organisations

Why Are There Not More Democratic Organisations?

Organisations that resemble the democratic organisation as described and defined in Part I can be found in every society and economic system. However, for socio-cultural, political, legal, and economic reasons, their scope and range vary from country to country. For example, there are many more (fully fledged or hybrid/imperfect) democratic organisations in social market economies and welfare state countries (e.g. the Scandinavian countries, Germany, Italy, France, Spain, and some South American countries) than in neo-liberal market economies (e.g. the U.S. or Singapore) and in Asian 'third way' socialist market economies (such as China, Taiwan, or Vietnam) (e.g. Curtis et al. 2001, Schwartz 2012, pp. 238–239). But despite these differences, as a crude generalisation one might say that in any given country and epoch the percentage of organisations that are democratic has been very low, somewhere in the single digits (from around as little as 0.1% up to a maximum of 7–8%; e.g. Wright 2010, pp. 238–239, Schwartz 2012, pp. 236–237, Malleson 2014, p. 83). This is unsatisfactory and the opposite of what one would hope for if one believed in values such as freedom, democracy, equality, and justice and also believed that organisations should be built on and function according to these principles.[1]

The question is simple: why? Why are there not more democratic organisations (e.g. Carnoy & Shearer 1980, p. 143, Bowles & Gintis 1993, pp. 75, 95, Carson 2008, p. 517, Schwartz 2012, pp. 220–221, 240, 267, Zamagni 2014, p. 196)? Why have democratic organisations not outcompeted and replaced orthodox organisations – especially since they are seemingly so much better and, allegedly, superior? Or are democratic organisations perhaps not as good and attractive as is claimed? The following sub-sections interrogate and discuss these questions with regard to various arguments and reproaches that are made against democratic organisations, in particular that they:

- are comparatively less attractive than other types of organisation (such as profit-maximising or other orthodox organisations);
- do not fit into, and are not sufficiently supported by, the institutions and institutional framework that regulated market economies provide for organisations;
- do not have, or cannot gain, sufficient financial resources;
- lack qualified personnel and competencies that would enable them to conduct business professionally;
- have somewhat inefficient internal processes (of decision-making);
- achieve insufficient external performance and outcomes.

The (Un)attractiveness of Organisations: People's Choices

In a market economy people basically have *choice* – and they are free to choose. (Within legal and socio-cultural boundaries and actual limitations) people are relatively free to decide what kinds of economic or social activities they (want to) conduct and how to organise them. Usually, there are various (legal) types of organisation available from which people can choose. Whether it is about establishing new organisations or joining or working for existing ones, one of the main arguments against democratic organisations is that people simply do not choose them but find other types of organisation, in particular profit-maximising or at least profit-oriented organisations, (much) more attractive.

It is certainly true that the corporation has become quite a dominant institution – but the argument needs to be more differentiated and nuanced than a universal claim that 'people prefer orthodox over democratic organisations'. For instance, it is only *some*, *certain* people who find orthodox organisations attractive and democratic organisations unattractive:

- According to definitions of the profit-maximising organisation, *only* greedy, egoistic, anti-social, and/or opportunistic investors or entrepreneurs establish these enterprises because they are *only*, or *primarily*, interested in high returns and making as much profit for themselves as possible. Obviously, with their multiple purposes, the principle of profit-sharing, long-term orientation, and sustainable business model, democratic organisations do not cater for people with such motives or orientations.

- Power-oriented and/or opportunistic managers, professionals, and career-ists are particularly likely to work for hierarchical corporations because this is where and how they can gain power and influence and enjoy the privileges, prerogatives, high salaries, bonuses, and other perks that come with higher positions within a hierarchical order. With their heterarchical structures and processes, democratic governance and management, partici-pative and collective decision-making, and notions of equal rights and equal empowerment of everyone, democratic organisations are not attract-ive for people with such motivations or personality traits.

- Most people working for orthodox organisations do not do so as a 'rational choice' (maximising their utility) but because they (think they) have *no* choice. They work 'for the money', to have 'a' job that pays for the bills, and they silently accept all the downsides that come with work-ing in a large, hierarchical, and oppressive machine.[2] They have *not* con-sciously and freely chosen the orthodox organisation and instead work there out of habit and because there (seemingly) are no alternatives. If they knew more about democratic organisations, *and* there were more democratic organisations around as potential employers, many managers, employees, and workers would choose them.

Altogether, people choose profit-oriented organisations such as the corpor-ation because they provide the legal basis and actual means for personal enrich-ment and the systematic control and exploitation of others, or because they provide (fairly) well-paid, (seemingly) secure jobs that require unreflective, unresponsive, and obedient functioning. Many people opt to work for profit-maximising or other types of orthodox organisations because of egoism, greed, opportunism, power orientation, limited choice, years of conditioning, or silent surrender – but not because it is a 'natural law' or a 'rational choice', as neo-classical microeconomics and managerial ideologies want us to believe (e.g. Coase 1937, Jensen & Meckling 1976).

That many people actually find profit-maximising or orthodox organisations highly *un*-attractive is evidenced by the fact that in every market economy there are countless people and market participants that consciously decide *against* setting up or working for (large, hierarchical) orthodox organisations and instead opt for *alternative* types of organisation. The absolute majority of organisations are *not* (large) profit-maximising corporations but small- and medium-sized businesses (most of them are family businesses), civil society organisations, or self-employed (sole proprietors, freelancers, or contract work-ers). It is true that many of these organisations are (also) profit oriented, as family businesses and civil society organisations can be fairly orthodox, auto-cratic, and hierarchical, and freelancers and contract workers can be greedy and opportunistic. But all of these organisational and (self-)employment options still show some features of the democratic organisation – and people prefer them over orthodox organisations for good reasons. For example, most owners of family businesses and self-employed freelancers have very different motives and motivation for establishing and running their businesses than 'maximising profit' or 'managing and controlling others'; they want to continue a (family) tradition, earn a living (but not enrich themselves at the expense of others), support their family, 'live the dream' (i.e. do what they like to do and even get paid for it), produce products or provide services they believe in, serve the community, and/or do something good for the environment. And first and foremost they want to be autonomous, independent, their own master, and do something meaningful. But whatever the exact reasons, motives, and motivation of the owners, founders, managers, and employees who make these innumerable alternative organisations work and be successful under challenging conditions, they are evidence that the profit-maximising enterprise is *not* a must in a competitive environment and that all sorts of organisations and businesses can be attractive for market participants and can strive and survive in market economies and social economies – including democratic organisations.

Institutional Framework and Organisations' (Mis)fit

That many people, indeed, decide in favour of orthodox organisations and against democratic organisations is not only due to individual motives but also to the *institutional context* – perhaps particularly so because institutions shape individual behaviour considerably. Democratic organisations do not fit, so it is said, into the larger (macro- and micro-)environments of market economies or into the institutions of a market economy (e.g. commercial laws and regulations, business laws, industry policies, functioning of markets, competition, and behaviour of market participants and stakeholders).

It is true that there is an *institutional misfit* between democratic organisations and the prevailing institutions of most current market economies – but that misfit is manifested in a very different sense from what the anti-democratic rhetoric suggests:

- *Legal and regulatory institutions*: The legal and regulatory frameworks of countries – whether they have capitalist/neo-liberal, social-democratic, or socialist market economies – *massively* support types of organisation that resemble orthodox organisations. Corporate laws, labour laws, and other national laws and regulations are *specifically* designed to enable, support, and strengthen (large) corporations, traditional industries, profit-seeking business activities, and hierarchical organisations (e.g. Hansmann 1996, Carson 2008, p. 518). Corporate and personal tax laws even actively encourage the establishment and maintenance of profit-maximising enterprises (and associations, non-governmental organisations, and charities) solely for the purpose of maximising revenues for certain individuals (and to protect their wealth and assets). The laws and regulations of most market economies are designed largely, if not entirely, to support a capitalist/neo-liberal agenda and interests.

- *Individual and institutional actors*: Politicians, business associations, analysts, consultants, and the media (including the news media) fall over themselves on a daily basis to celebrate capitalism and its institutions. They also show great concern (followed by calls for swift action) about anything that is (allegedly) relevant to 'the economy' (largely understood as large corporations and traditional industries) and that could positively or negatively impact on 'the economy', traditional institutions, or their key performance indicators. Most of the reasoning and rhetoric of these individual and institutional actors orbits around extremely traditional, one-dimensional, and narrow aspects of the economy and (business) organisations, such as quantitative growth, inflation, productivity, profits, and share prices. Business-related institutions – such as business associations, business consultancies, banks, institutional and private investors, government agencies, and conservative non-governmental organisations – are biased towards profit-oriented organisations and against not-for-profit and democratic organisations.

- *Educational institutions*: Schools and universities (especially their business schools or colleges of business) disseminate primarily, if not solely, traditional, orthodox business knowledge and implant in students the belief that there are no other organisations than corporations, that business is about making money (as much as possible), and that personal development and success are about fitting as closely as possible the stereotypical images of the 'professional' manager, leader, and doer and the organisational corsets of managerial hierarchies.

Over time, the proponents of capitalism and orthodox, profit-maximising, and hierarchical organisations have been very successful at institutionalising their interests and ideologies – in the constitutional and legal frameworks of societies; corporate, business, and private law; tax rules and regulations; economic and fiscal policies; news networks; the curricula of economics and business studies; and practice-oriented consultancy. In contrast, democratic organisations are hardly mentioned and supported by these institutions, even they are systematically, institutionally, and actively neglected, disadvantaged, and fought.

In this sense, there is no institutional *misfit* but rather institutional *bias*, or *biased institutions*. In contemporary societies and market economies there is a profound *ideological* and *institutional bias* towards corporations and other orthodox organisations and against democratic organisations and other alternative types of organisation or social movement. It is *not* democratic organisations' 'fault' that they do not fit many of the currently prevailing institutions; instead, the latter have deviated from the fundamental ideas and principles of freedom, democracy, equality, and justice.

(In)sufficient Financial Resources: (Under)capitalisation

Another set of arguments against democratic organisations concerns their resources – that they do not have, or cannot get, sufficient resources to conduct their business as necessary or even successfully. It is a long-established argument that democratic organisations, and other alternative types of organisation, have difficulty gaining capital and raising funds for investment (e.g. Podivinsky & Stewart 2007). There are internal and external reasons for democratic organisations' (alleged) lack of sufficient financial resources and under-capitalisation, respectively.

Internal reasons mainly include the fact that democratic organisations are owned by their members and, according to their cooperative spirit and fundamental principles, (want to) finance themselves largely internally (in order to stay independent and self-financed). But many members of democratic organisations are common employees or workers who either do not have much capital to invest or are fairly risk-averse (Bowles & Gintis 1993, pp. 78, 95–96, Burczak 2006, p. 123). Besides having limited internal ability to raise capital, democratic organisations also struggle to access external capital (Mayfield et al. 2012). It is argued that institutional and private investors (such as banks and venture capitalists) prefer to do business with orthodox organisations because they have only a few, identifiable owners and the perception is that such business owners are more competent in handling capital. Hence, because of their sub-optimal levels of capitalisation and investment, democratic organisations are at a competitive disadvantage (Burczak 2006, p. 12, Podivinsky & Stewart 2007).

The 'under-capitalisation thesis' as just described has *some* merits – but it should not be understood as a decisive argument against democratic organisations. Many businesses and economic activities do not need *massive*, exceptionally high levels of investment but can be started and developed with relatively little capital. For instance, many start-ups, businesses in the service sector or knowledge economy, and online businesses can be started and run 'from home' or a small office or shop. And even if organisations do need a larger amount of (venture) capital, democratic organisations nowadays are in a much better position to acquire external funding. Usually, they have fairly developed business plans, strategies, and professional management in place. And they are also able and willing to approach external investors. Likewise, there are external investors (venture capitalists, cooperatives, and other alternative banks) that are quite open to promising business ideas, value propositions, and professionally managed organisations – even if these are collectively owned and managed. On both sides, there is barely any ideological prejudice or ballast any more. So, in regard to capitalisation (i.e. the internal or external financing of investments), democratic organisations face more or less the same problems and challenges as other types of organisation – and they have more or less the same portfolio of means and measures to acquire and to handle capital.

Lack of Qualified Personnel and Competencies: (Un)professionalism

Besides capital, democratic organisations are said to lack qualified personnel and, therefore, key competencies required to conduct their business profession-ally. The crucial argument is that it is some of the very fundamental features or characteristics of the democratic organisation that make it less attractive, espe-cially to professional managers, highly qualified experts, and other professionals who might work for the organisation; because of the collective decision-making procedures and egalitarian redistribution of returns within the organisation (i.e. relatively low pay differentials between levels of staff, and redistribution from more to less productive members), highly qualified personnel will not join or will leave the democratic organisation (Kremer 1997, pp. 2, 12, 20, Levin & Tadelis 2005, pp. 157–158). According to this line of reasoning, with fewer highly qualified personnel being attracted to and working for the democratic organisation, the organisation and its affairs are and managed less efficiently, if not in rather unprofessional ways. Carnoy and Shearer (1980, pp. 92–93) pro-vide quite a disturbing, but not atypical, example of the unprofessionalism pre-vailing at a cooperative bank:

> The management of the workers' banks also contributed to their decline. Some union locals insisted that the bank provide jobs for union officials who were ignorant of banking practices. At the same time, many profes-sional banking employees refused to take jobs with workers' banks for ideological reasons, and the workers' bank movement failed to establish its own school to train a cadre of managers who were both technically proficient and pro-working class. Personnel problems and inefficient operations in turn soured working-class depositors on their own banks.

There are definitely democratic organisations that lack qualified personnel, have scarce professional and managerial competencies, and are run and man-aged badly – but these examples are *not* evidence of a *systemic* failure or insuffi-ciency of the democratic organisation. It is assuredly true that *certain* highly qualified, skilled, and capable professionals ('high fliers') are not keen to join or work for democratic organisations: people who can command – and are primarily interested in – a high market price (salary) for themselves, or people who seek formal positions of power and influence. So, there is definitely some loss of talent (though probably some rather questionable talent). At the same time, democratic organisations *attract* highly capable, talented, and professional people – people who want to do more than just making money, want to do meaningful work, are passionate about what they do, know their work, use their creativity, get involved, and put a lot of effort and energy into what they do. Very often, such people are highly skilled, experienced, and knowledge-able. They are experts in their respective fields and highly professional – and they are more than happy to work for democratic organisations *because* of their skills and competencies, because they want to make use of their skills and competencies in the best and most suitable way possible. In this sense, the 'lack of talent and/or competencies and thus professionalism' argument is not really valid.

(In)efficient Internal Processes (of Decision-Making)

Even with sufficient, competent, and willing personnel, democratic organisations are said to operate in rather protracted, inefficient ways. They are purportedly less efficient mostly because of how their institutions of governance and manage-ment operate and function, i.e. their democratic management and collective decision-making (e.g. Hansmann 1996, pp. 44, 79, 91–103): their decision-making processes are slow and lengthy, complicated and impractical. Moreover, the decisions resulting from such processes are said to be more controversial and contested, and represent rather indecisive compromises. Together, the inefficient process of decision-making and the sub-optimal quality of decisions supposedly put the democratic organisation in a disadvantageous position – particularly in competitive, fast-changing market environments. Consequently, Hansmann (1996, p. 119) concluded: 'Paradoxically, the aspect of employee ownership often extolled as its principal virtue – active participation in governance of the firm through democratic institutions – appears in fact to be its greatest liability.'

This portrait of participative or democratic decision-making in democratic organisations is largely correct; democratic, participative decision-making pro-cesses are more complex and comprehensive, (can be) conflictual, and take (much) longer than authoritarian decision-making. In this sense, democratic decision-making, obviously, is *less* efficient than simply giving orders. Neverthe-less, it would be wrong to see the greater comprehensiveness and time demo-cratic decision-making takes solely or primarily as a disadvantage and in a negative way. The 'weaknesses' of participative or democratic decision-making are at the same time actually some of its greatest *strengths* and advantages; a more comprehensive and inclusive decision-making process provides opportunities to get more people involved; to take in more relevant information, (diverse) views, and opinions; to look at problems from different perspectives; to debate and to consider various options; and to produce more, potentially better, and more appropriate solutions. Moreover, it creates much more engagement and commit-ment; decisions have the support and backing of the majority of members (because they were involved in making these decisions) and (therefore) will be implemented in much more cooperative and efficient ways. Hence, *overall* and *on balance* – i.e. if one looks at the *whole* process and all the facets of making decisions in democratic organisations, implementing them, and the related outcomes – participative or democratic decision-making outperforms autocratic or oligarchic decision-making by far. Democratic organisations, *all* social systems, are much better off with than without democratic and participative decision-making.

(In)sufficient External Performance and Outcomes

In addition to – or because of – their (alleged) internal insufficiencies, democratic organisations are also said to underperform in their external activities and the outcomes they achieve. In regard to any organisation, there are certain expectations about how it should be, how it should conduct its business, and what it ought to achieve. And there are performance criteria and indicators against which organisations and their performance are assessed and judged. Usually, organisations are expected to meet the prevailing performance indicators and to act accordingly. Especially in an economic or 'business' context, there are often fairly one-dimensional, hard, and short-term performance measures and indicators against which organisations and their performance are judged, such as financial success (revenues, profit, share price), market share, number of customers or clients, quantitative growth, profitability, productivity, efficiency, and effectiveness. According to such an orthodox, neo-classical, or neo-liberal understanding of 'performance' and 'success', even organisations acting in the social economy should be judged against such or similar (financial, technical, and/or other quantitative) performance criteria. Organisations that do not meet the prevailing performance criteria and indicators are labelled as 'unprofessional', 'underperforming', and 'unsuccessful'; it is said that they are not efficient, productive, competitive, innovative, risk-taking, fast, flexible, agile, or decisive enough, and are doomed to fail.

Democratic organisations may not fare well concerning some of these orthodox performance indicators (e.g. profit, market share, quantitative growth) for various reasons: many democratic organisations *deliberately* are not (primarily or at all) profit oriented; they want to serve only certain members, customers, or clients in particular ways, and they want to stay small and to only grow in qualitative ways. As the discussion of interest- and ownership-oriented democratic organisations and Social and Solidarity Economy organisations in Chapter 1 showed, such democratic organisations are to some extent simply different from orthodox organisations in terms of their primary purposes, how they conduct their business, and the outcomes they (want to) achieve. It is not that democratic organisations *cannot* achieve the benchmarks set by orthodox performance indicators (on the contrary, many democratic organisations *are* economically successful, even measured in orthodox terms) – but that they want to replace the orthodox, capitalist logic of economic and business activities.

And it works. It is sufficiently clear that nowadays even in competitive environments actors can have very different business models and be successful, and that even the notions of 'competitiveness' and (economic) 'success' can be – or even must be – understood quite differently from what economic orthodoxy suggests. For example, contemporary organisations are expected to have multi-dimensional, sustainable, and responsible business goals and business models (*triple bottom line*) and to conduct business accordingly (*considerate conduct of business*; see Chapter 6). Performance and success of organisations, whether they are active in the economic or the social realm, is now increasingly understood and measured rather differently from the narrow-minded and outdated orthodox concepts, i.e. in multiple and balanced ways (e.g. Roelants 2013, p. 50, Millstone 2015, p. 90).[3] And many organisations are increasingly willing and able to be successful according to the new performance and measurement rationales. With its multi-dimensional purposes and business activities, the democratic organisation clearly is in a strong position to demonstrate adequate, if not above-average, performance.

Democratic Organisations Are (Potentially) Attractive, Capable, and Successful

All in all, concerning the questions of why there are not more democratic organisations and why democratic organisations have not outcompeted and replaced orthodox organisations, there is a rather mixed picture – or, better to say, there needs to be a much more differentiated answer than a mere 'democratic organisations are simply not attractive, capable, and competitive (enough)':

1. *(Un)attractiveness*: For many people, the democratic organisation is *not* their first choice when they set up or join an organisation. But it is only *certain* people that do *not* opt for democratic but for profit-maximising or other orthodox organisations. And they are not even the majority because many people opt for alternative types of organisation that are primarily *not* profit oriented, bureaucratic, or hierarchical. The democratic organisation is not 'unattractive' per se but instead is unattractive to *some* or *certain* people because of very specific personal preferences.

2. *Institutional misfit, institutional bias*: It is true that democratic organisations are not a good fit with the institutional context of current market economies, i.e. with legal and regulatory institutions (e.g. commercial laws and regulations, business laws, and industry policies), individual and institutional actors (politicians, business associations, analysts, consultants, and the media, including the news media), and educational institutions (schools and universities). But it is not an institutional *misfit* but a profound institutional *bias* towards corporations and other orthodox organisations and against democratic organisations (and other alternative types of organisation and

social movement) that is responsible for democratic organisations being disadvantaged.

3. *(Under)capitalisation*: Democratic organisations can have problems in raising enough capital internally or externally. Internal capitalisation may not be sufficient because these organisations' owners may have comparatively little capital available to them or that they are willing to invest. And external acquisition of capital may be limited because of the unwillingness of institutional or private investors to invest in the organisation. But such difficulties in acquiring capital are (some of) the usual problems *any* organisation or business owner faces. And contemporary democratic organisations (and their owners and management) are much more knowledgeable and professional concerning capital management than such organisations of the past.

4. *Lack of qualified personnel and competencies, unprofessionalism:* In regard to acquiring, keeping, and developing qualified personnel, democratic organisations are not really disadvantaged. True, *some* professional managers, highly qualified experts, and other professionals may not want to work for democratic organisations, especially those who are primarily interested in high salaries or positions of (autocratic) power and influence. But democratic organisations are (very) attractive to highly qualified, experienced, and knowledgeable people who want to, and will, work professionally for good causes and within a decent working environment.

5. *(In)efficient internal processes:* Internal decision-making processes of democratic organisations are more complex and time consuming and more (openly) debated and challenged than decision-making processes within orthodox organisations. In that sense they are inefficient. However, if one also takes into account the qualitative and quantitative opportunities and advantages (full) participation creates as well as the other stages of organisational decision-making processes (implementation and execution of decisions) then democratic decision-making outperforms any autocratic or oligarchic decision-making style by far.

6. *(In)sufficient external performance and outcomes*: Some democratic organisations are not very successful in meeting orthodox, neo-classical, or neo-liberal performance measures and indicators that are fairly one-dimensional, hard, and short-term oriented – but they usually have quite successful business models, conduct their business activities in rather professional and successful ways, and achieve multi-dimensional, sustainable, and balanced goals.

It is a fact that there are (many) more corporations than cooperatives and more orthodox organisations than democratic organisations – for now. But the fact that the corporation has become *the* prevailing 'standard' model for organising economic, financial, business, social, and even charitable activities, and the fact that there have been comparatively few democratic organisations, has nothing to do with 'natural laws', 'perfect markets', or 'rational choice' – nor with the spurious argument that the orthodox organisation is the most efficient type of organisation and the democratic organisation has 'innate' flaws. Certainly, the democratic organisation – like any other organisation or social system – has its weaknesses and faces internal and external challenges. But even in competitive (market) environments there are absolutely *no principle-based reasons* why democratic organisations cannot be attractive, capable, or successful – on the contrary; potentially, they are (much) *more* attractive, capable, and successful than any orthodox organisation – as the next section will show in some detail.

Why People Start or Join Democratic Organisations

The previous section(s) proved that there are no principle-based or good reasons *against* the democratic organisation. This still leaves the question of whether there are principle-based and good reasons *for* the democratic organisation; why would – or perhaps even *should* – people opt for (a particular type of) democratic organisation when they consider starting an enterprise or working for an organisation?

People do things for a reason (or reasons). And even if people usually are not fully aware of all the intervening factors and motives behind why they consciously or unconsciously do the things they do, there usually are reasons or interests in play, especially when people make such fundamental decisions as setting up or joining an organisation. The following sub-sections discuss how features of the democratic organisation might constitute reasons for people to establish or join a democratic organisation.

Doing Something Meaningful and Decent: Purposes and Conduct of Business[4]

Democratic organisations are set up and maintained for multi-dimensional, (more) ethical, fair, and just purposes. Their primary purpose(s) are serving the needs and interests of various stakeholders (owners, members, clients, customers, communities, and society) and addressing fundamental social, economic, and/or environmental issues, needs, or problems. To pursue their goals, democratic organisations have more conservative, long-term-oriented, and risk-averse goals and strategies than orthodox organisations. Democratic organisations provide products and services that are necessary, useful, value for money, and appropriate. Since democratic organisations are often locally embedded and community oriented, their owners, members, and managers have a stronger feeling of belongingness and community orientation, and are more concerned about community well-being. They show more considerate and prudent management, and they demonstrate more ethical, responsible, decent, honest, fair, just, socially oriented, inclusive, cooperative, and sustainable business practices and behaviour in their internal and external activities. Usually, democratic organisations conduct their business in socially, environmentally, and economically (more) balanced and sustainable ways ('people, planet, profit'). In particular, they:

- engage in a high(er) degree of social orientation and social behaviour, i.e. they have a stronger stakeholder orientation; have a more collaborative mindset; show more voluntary, mutually beneficial cooperation and reciprocal behaviour; are more interested in developing and maintaining long-term relationships; show higher degrees of social responsibility and care for others; are more willing to share resources, knowledge, power, and decision-making responsibilities; and distribute benefits, burdens, costs, and profits more fairly among all parties involved.

- have a strong(er) pro-environmental orientation, i.e. they have explicit pro-environmental goals and purposes in their business model (as part of its triple bottom line approach), are more sensitive to sustainability issues, more concerned about the local environment, and use and/or offer appropriate technology, i.e. local, small-scale, decentralised, and more environmentally friendly technologies, products, and services.

- achieve higher efficiency and productivity, innovativeness and organisational performance, are economically much more viable, stable and sustainable than orthodox organisations; their earnings are more robust and fluctuate less, they are more resilient in the face of economic challenges, they contract or default much less in challenging times, and do not lay off workers as quickly as capitalist firms do.

Because of the purposes democratic organisations pursue and the values they stand for and practise in their conduct of business, democratic organisations are very attractive to people who believe in those purposes and values. It may be political convictions; ethical, moral, or religious beliefs; psychological orientations; personal opinions; or specific interests or concerns that (might) attract individuals to democratic organisations (e.g. Verba et al. 2004, pp. 646–647, Cater et al. 2017, p. 194). For example, Bekkers (2005, p. 447) found that 'political values and attitudes showed clear relationships with civic engagement. ... Citizens with a greater interest in politics and postmaterialistic value orientations were more likely to be members of voluntary associations and were more likely to volunteer for an association.'

Besides more specific political interests and values, a more general *concern for others* or *empathy* is especially likely to lead to *prosocial behaviours*, such as political activism, volunteering, civic engagement, civic participation, and setting up or joining campaigns, social enterprises, or other democratic organisations. Most social entrepreneurs are driven by a desire to address social problems and needs; to take action that will benefit individuals in need, the community, and society; to improve the well-being of a specific group or society at large; to create social value; and to bring about social improvements and change (Bekkers 2005, pp. 447–448, Baggetta 2009, p. 195, Omoto et al. 2010, p. 1718, Yitshaki & Kropp 2016, pp. 546–548, Cater et al. 2017, pp. 185, 188). When Cater et al. (2017, p. 185) studied and analysed the motivations of 35 small fairtrade business entrepreneurs in the U.S. they found 'that shared values (ethical, religious, or business) and the desire to help others (altruism), often triggered by a critical incident, lead social entrepreneurs to found and sustain fair trade businesses'. As Yitshaki and Kropp (2016, p. 547) explained:

> [Social entrepreneurs] are compassionate toward suffering in the community. … This compassion may be rooted in a general sense of empathy toward others based on one's own similar life experiences, or a sense of sympathy that is not based on similar experiences. Both empathy and sympathy can be considered as motivations for prosocial activities.

But it would be quite a misunderstanding to think that only, or primarily, 'left-wing activists', altruists or idealists believe in the values and way(s) of acting of democratic organisations and start or join such organisations. Hansmann (1996, pp. 87–88, 167, 295) rightly pointed out that small (family) businesses, cooperatives, partnerships, worker-owned enterprises, employee-owned firms, associations, charities, and social enterprises are especially likely to be started by farmers, shop owners, small entrepreneurs, lawyers, accountants, investment bankers, or management consultants 'who are conspicuous for their individualism and political conservatism' (p. 295); are an 'intensely commercial, individualistic, and politically conservative class of individuals' (p. 167); and are 'largely unaffected by conspicuous legal, ideological, or historical biases' (p. 167). Many democratic organisations are set up and run by fairly conservative, down-to-earth people.

So, whatever the specific convictions, beliefs, interests, or concerns that people hold, if they want to do something meaningful and in decent, considerate ways – whether it is business or activism, pursuing social, economic, and/or environmental goals – then the democratic organisation is the organisation of choice.

Doing It Via Rewarding Practices: Organisational and Interpersonal Aspects

Democratic organisations are organised, function, and work very differently (compared to orthodox organisations) internally. As argued in Chapter 2, the democratic organisation is based on the idea of individual and collective private ownership, i.e. all members of the organisation are owners with equal legal and managerial rights and responsibilities. Owners do not work *for* others but *with* others. Accordingly, work is organised, managed, and conducted collectively and cooperatively. This means that the organisational structures and processes of governance and management need to be democratic, transparent, and inclusive; there is comprehensive and full participation in decision-making, and control over the organisation is shared.[5] Such design, governance, management, and workings of an organisation have manifold advantages for all of its individual members, including:

- power and control of members over their work and working lives (Erdal 2011, p. 189);
- more collaboration and participation, which provide voice to the disadvantaged and reduce power differences (Mulder 1971, p. 32, Strauss 1998, p. 8, Fung & Wright 2001, pp. 27–28);
- more trust, sociability, collegiality, cooperation, and reciprocity between members, and members show more commitment and engagement in social interactions, demonstrate more collaborative behaviour, and are more willing to share their knowledge and to cooperate (Bowman & Stone 2004, p. 280, Heywood et al. 2005, pp. 557, 559, Carson 2008, p. 524, Altmann 2014, p. 182);
- more innovative ideas contributed by members, and quicker implementation of change (Erdal 2011, p. 22);
- higher quality and appropriateness of decisions and solutions (Strauss 1998, p.8);
- higher level of responsibility and accountability since decisions are made by those who implement them (Anderson 1999, p. 328, Collier & Esteban 1999, p. 177);
- more respectful treatment of people (Vredenburgh & Brender 1993, p. 102, Wolff 1998, p. 107, Brown 2005, pp. 28–29, O'Neill 2009, p. 384);
- more attractive work and workplaces, and better workplace conditions (Nembhard 2008, p. 214, Macdonald 2013, p. 18);
- fairer remuneration, and greater equality of wages and profit-sharing (Malleson 2014, p. 56);
- greater job stability and security (Nembhard 2008, p. 214, Malleson 2014, p. 56);
- lower rates of absenteeism and turnover (Brown et al. 2005, p. 586, Carson 2008, p. 524, Maynard et al. 2012, pp. 1247–1249);
- higher levels of job performance, organisational efficiency, and overall performance (Strauss 1998, p. 8, Brown et al. 2005, p. 586, Maynard et al. 2012, pp. 1247–1249).

The list of advantages for individuals working in a self-governed, collaborative, and democratic working environment – and, as a consequence, advantages for the organisation – is impressive. Of course, it is not easy, or easier, to work for a democratic organisation. In some respects it can even be more challenging than working for an orthodox organisation. Participation, although voluntary, requires personal skills and competencies but also personal strength, motivation, and even personality traits not everyone has readily at hand.[6] People have to cope with more social interaction, communication, and responsibilities. And, like any other organisation, democratic organisations are contested terrains and political arenas, i.e. people may disagree, need to convince others, and need to come to agreements, even more so than in orthodox organisations. Therefore, in democratic organisations, the social aspects of work are more demanding for people.

But these greater challenges are more than compensated by the obvious advantages work in and for democratic organisations offers. The conditions of work, the actual work, and workplaces in the democratic organisation are just so much more rewarding (concerning extrinsic as well as intrinsic aspects) that they make working for the democratic organisation highly attractive for almost everyone – at least for everyone who knows that economic activities are not only about maximising profit and that work is not only about seeking personal advantages at the expense of others.

Doing It in Self-Enhancing Ways: Psychological, Intrapersonal, and Attitudinal Aspects

The advantages of working for a democratic organisation mentioned in the previous sub-section are mostly of a social, interpersonal nature. But democratic organisations provide a whole range of advantages and incentives that are *directly relevant to individuals themselves*, i.e. that are of psychological or intrapersonal kinds.

As already indicated, people who work for the democratic organisation *own* it (in legal, practical, *and* metaphorical senses). They are *owners*. Owners – or owner-managers – care (more) about the things or the business they own; they have a higher, *inherent* sense of ownership and responsibility, are committed and put in effort, and try to make things work (and work as well as possible) because it is *their* interest – and *in* their interest (Erdal 2011, pp. 87, 179). Moreover, ownership creates a sense of personal competence (self-efficacy), increased levels of personal control and control of one's environment (locus of control), and psychological empowerment. Owner-managers and empowered members also have a greater sense of dignity and personal worth, and greater self-respect (Kanter 1971, p. 66, Bowles et al. 1993, p. 141, Christman 1994, p. 236, Strauss 1998, p. 8, Anderson 1999, p. 328, Brown 2005, pp. 28–29, Fischer 2006, p. 22, Greenwood et al. 2007, p. 224, O'Neill 2009, p. 384, Maynard et al. 2012, p. 1243).

People's sense of ownership – and of being an owner – also shows in their attitudes and feelings; they *feel* empowered and they *are* empowered. Empowered members show greater motivation and engagement; work harder; have increased motivation to come up with ideas, find solutions to problems, and improve the performance of the organisation; have a stronger commitment to the organisation, a greater sense of organisational loyalty, and a stronger identification with the organisation; and have more (job) satisfaction. (Therefore) they show higher individual productivity.[7] The democratic organisation provides *the best* conditions for people to develop their skills and competencies as well as themselves as people, i.e. for personal growth, self-realisation, and self-actualisation (Mulder 1971, p. 31, Dachler & Wilpert 1978, p. 7, Strauss 1998, p. 8). Thus, also at an individual level and in a psychological sense, there are plenty of reasons and motivations for people to work for an organisation they own – for a democratic organisation.

Strengths and Advantages of the Democratic Organisation

People can have very different motivations for starting or joining an organisation – often based on a combination of various personal, psychological, social, political, and economic factors (Bekkers 2005, Jussila et al. 2012).[8] But, as the discussion in the sub-sections above has shown, there are reasons for (almost) everyone to opt for democratic organisations – *many* good reasons:

- Democratic organisations' purposes, the way they conduct their business, what they aim to achieve, and how they do it resonate with people's desire to do something meaningful and decent (*purposes and conduct of business*).
- The organisational structures and processes of democratic organisations, how they function and work, how decisions are made, and how people cooperate within the organisation meet people's desire for rewarding work and appropriate working conditions (*formal, organisational, and social/ interpersonal aspects*).
- The fact that each and every member of the democratic organisation has the status of owner (as well as all the corresponding rights and responsibilities) puts people in control of themselves, their work, and their lives and enables them to develop their skills and competencies as well as themselves with the aim of achieving self-realisation and self-actualisation (*psychological/intrapersonal and attitudinal aspects*).

Table 8.1 summarises the democratic organisation's main strengths and advantages as they were addressed in the three sub-sections above.

TABLE 8.1 Strengths and advantages of the democratic organisation

Purposes and conduct of business
- They are set up and maintained for multi-dimensional, (more) ethical, fair, and just purposes; prime purpose(s) are serving the needs and interests of various stakeholders (owners, members, clients, customers, communities, and society) and addressing fundamental social, economic, and/or environmental issues, needs, or problems.
- They are more conservative, long-term oriented, and risk-averse goals and strategies.
- They have a locally embedded and community oriented; owner-managers have a stronger feeling of belongingness and community orientation, and they are more concerned about community well-being.
- They provide products and services that are necessary, useful, value for money, and appropriate.
- They employ considerate and prudent management, demonstrating more ethical, responsible, decent, honest, fair, just, socially oriented, inclusive, cooperative, and sustainable business practices and behaviour in internal and external activities.
- They conduct business in (more) socially, environmentally, and economically balanced and sustainable ways ('people, planet, and profit').
- They have a high(er) degree of social orientation and social behaviour, i.e. they have a stronger stakeholder orientation; have a more collaborative mindset; show more voluntary, mutually beneficial cooperation and reciprocal behaviour; are more interested in developing and maintaining long-term relationships; show higher degrees of social responsibility and care for others; are more willing to share resources, knowledge, power, and decision-making responsibilities; and distribute benefits, burdens, costs, and profits more fairly among all parties involved.
- They have a strong(er) pro-environmental orientation, i.e. they have explicit pro-environmental goals and purposes in their business model (as part of the triple bottom line approach), are more sensitive to sustainability issues, are more concerned about the local environment, and use and/or offer appropriate technology (i.e. local, small-scale, decentralised, and more environmentally friendly technologies, products, and services).
- They have higher efficiency, productivity, innovativeness, and organisational performance; they are much more economically viable, stable, and sustainable than orthodox organisations; their earnings are more robust and fluctuate less; they are more resilient in the face of economic challenges; they contract or default much less in challenging times; and they do not lay off workers as quickly as capitalist firms.
- They have genuine authenticity, value, and trustworthiness because of their purposes, values, behaviour, and conduct of business.

Formal, organisational, and social/interpersonal aspects
- They have individual and collective private ownership, i.e. all members of the organisation are owners with equal rights as well as equal legal and managerial responsibilities.

(Continued)

TABLE 8.1 (Cont).

- They are based on and committed to the values of freedom (self-ownership and private ownership), democracy (democratic governance, management, and decision-making), equality (equal rights and responsibilities of all members), and justice (good governance and profit-sharing).
- Their organisational structures and processes of governance and management are democratic, transparent, participative, and inclusive; key features include shared control of the organisation, democratic governance, self-management, representative management, participative management, and comprehensive and full participation in decision-making.
- Work is organised, managed, and conducted collectively and cooperatively.
- Members have actual power and control over their work and their working lives.
- Collaboration and participation provide voice to the disadvantaged and reduce power differences.
- There is more trust, sociability, collegiality, cooperation, and reciprocity between members, and members show more commitment and engagement in social interactions, demonstrate more collaborative behaviour, and are more willing to share their knowledge and to cooperate.
- Members contribute more innovative ideas and implement change more quickly.
- The quality and appropriateness of decisions and solutions are higher.
- There is more responsibility and accountability since decisions are made by those who implement them.
- They offer more attractive work and workplaces, and better workplace conditions.
- There is fairer remuneration, and greater equality of wages and profit-sharing.
- There is greater job stability and security.
- There are lower rates of absenteeism and turnover.
- There are higher levels of job performance, organisational efficiency, and overall performance.

Psychological/intrapersonal and attitudinal aspects
- Owner-managers care more about the things or the business they own; have a higher, *inherent* sense of ownership and responsibility; are committed and put in effort; and try to make things work (and work as well as possible) because it is *their* interest – and *in* their interest.
- Ownership creates a sense of personal competence (self-efficacy), increased levels of personal control and control of one's environment (locus of control), and psychological empowerment.
- Owner-managers and empowered members have a greater sense of dignity and personal worth, and greater self-respect.
- Ownership, self-management, and participation develop and foster the individual, social, and political capacities of each individual.
- Empowered members show greater motivation and engagement; work harder; have increased motivation to come up with ideas, find solutions to problems, and improve the performance of the organisation; have a higher commitment to the organisation; have a greater sense of organisational loyalty; and have a strong(er) identification with the organisation,

(Continued)

TABLE 8.1 (Cont).

- Empowered members show higher individual productivity.
- Empowered members have higher (job) satisfaction.
- Empowered members experience more personal growth, and a stronger sense of self-realisation and self-actualisation.
- Empowered members have a higher quality of work life and a greater feeling of well-being.

The sheer length of the list as well as the huge variety of the strengths and advantages of the democratic organisation are simply mind-blowing. Of course, no real democratic organisation – or *any* organisation – has all of these strengths or provides all of these advantages. Moreover, many real democratic organisations deviate quite considerably from their original blueprint, intended purposes, and functioning, and from the basic ideas of the democratic organisation. That is, they can be, or can become, fairly hierarchical, autocratic, oligarchic, unequal, unfair, and/or unjust[9] – i.e. nothing but a nightmarish version of the orthodox organisation (which may be even worse considering all the hypocrisy and disappointed hopes that would prevail in such fallen democratic organisations). But what this chapter's discussion of the democratic organisation has shown is that the democratic organisation *as such* is a very worthy type of organisation. It has a whole range of strengths and advantages that makes it (very) attractive, capable, and successful. There is a strong – a *very* strong – case for the democratic organisation.

Notes

1 The great British social philosopher and economist John Stuart Mill (1848/1936, p. 764) anticipated, even expected, that 'the relation of masters and workpeople will be gradually superseded by partnership in one of two forms: in some cases, association of the labourers with the capitalist; in others, and perhaps finally in all, association of labourers among themselves'.
2 Benello (1971, p. 212) called the incentive(s) to work for orthodox organisations 'the carrot which motivates men to enslave themselves'.
3 Roelants (2013, p. 50) made the valid point that 'the cooperative movement no longer needs to be on the defensive nor to remain trapped within the old paradigm, as it now finds itself in front of a golden opportunity to avail itself of updated innovative policy and theory …, to start having a much stronger transformational role …, and to tackle the sustainability challenge (with its environmental, components) in redefining and measuring components [and] in redefining and measuring growth in a multidimensional fashion'.
4 The arguments provided here are mainly based on the concept of 'considerate conduct of business' developed in Chapter 6. For references see the material there.
5 See Chapter 3 ('Democratic Governance') and Chapter 4 ('Democratic Management') for more details on the democratic institutions of governance, self-management, representative management, and participative management.

6 Psychological issues and specific personality traits, social skills, and competencies probably influence to quite some extent people's decision to start or join a particular type of organisation, to stay or to leave, and their social behaviour and actions within the organisation. For example, open, extraverted, and conscientious people are more inclined toward social interaction; engaging with others; demonstrating political behaviour, participation, and civic engagement; and establishing or joining democratic organisations (e.g. Gerber et al. 2010, Mondak et al. 2010, Omoto et al. 2010).

7 There is plenty of empirical evidence and there are many arguments to support these claims; for example, Kanter (1971, p. 66), Vanek (1971, p. 17), Dachler & Wilpert (1978, pp. 8–9), Bowles & Gintis (1993, pp. 92–93, 141), Nienhaus & Brauksiepe (1997, pp. 1424–1425), Rothschild and Ollilainen (1999, p. 588), Gill (2003, p. 316), Clegg & Walsh (2004, p. 227), Greasley et al. (2005, p. 358), Carson (2008, p. 522), Erdal (2011, p. 19), Maynard et al. (2012, pp. 1247–1249), Schwartz (2012, footnote 38, p. 230), and Altmann (2014, p. 182).

8 Several researchers have created complex models that take into account various factors influencing people's political, social, and pro-environmental values, attitudes, and behaviour. For example, Omoto et al. (2010) developed a *volunteer process model*, Gifford and Nilsson (2014) identified and grouped 18 personal and social factors, and Cater et al. (2017) created a comprehensive *model of fair trade social entrepreneurship* that can explain such behaviour.

9 Chapter 9 ('Legitimate and Illegitimate Organisations') and Chapter 10 ('The Iron Threat(s) of Disproportional Empowerment') interrogate and discuss such troubling aspects, and what can be done about them, comprehensively and in detail.

9

LEGITIMATE AND ILLEGITIMATE ORGANISATIONS

Freedom of Contract and the Legitimacy of Organisations

Clearly, people often want to organise themselves, want to collaborate with others in formally organised ways, want to establish or join organisations in order to conduct business, economic, social or environmental activities. The question is what types of organisations would be not only appropriate but legitimate to do so. For any kind of formal social relationship to be established legitimately, the free will of the parties involved and freedom of contract are paramount. Freedom of contract allows for organisations to be set up for very different purposes and for them to be designed and run in very different ways. For a long time right-wing libertarians, radical conservatives, extremist neo-liberals, capitalists, and anarchists have argued that *any* form of contract, and *any* type of organisation, should be possible. According to them, 'freedom of contract' so to speak supersedes all (other) principles and values of a free and democratic society. Mayer (2001), a typical proponent of this position, claimed that organisations do not need to be democratic (in order to be legitimate and legal) as long as they are established, run, and joined by people under the 'freedom of contract' doctrine. As he argued (Mayer 2001, p. 240):

> Clubs [organisations] do not have to be democratic, even in a democratic society. Founders are free to craft the governance structure they deem best, and new members have no moral right to require political equality where it does not exist as long as they have been accorded a subjection option. Once members are admitted they may press for democratic rights, but no fundamental injustice is done to them if equal voice is not granted.

Of course, the right of freedom of contract also – and especially – counts for private organisations. Founders and/or members of organisations *in principle* are entitled to design and maintain organisations and their constitution, governance, management, and conduct of business as *they* deem right. *However,* the free constitution and maintenance of institutions and organisations have their limits. In order to be legitimate and legal, institutions and organisations *must* be in line with the fundamental principles, rules, and regulations of their legitimate legal, political, economic, and socio-cultural environments. Even if the founders, owners, or members of private organisations want to shape the internal design and workings of their organisation as *they* deem appropriate, they *still* need to comply with the principles and laws of the wider social system(s) they belong to and operate in, since otherwise the organisation's internal agreements and arrangements would be illegitimate or even illegal. *Setting up an organisation does not happen in, does not mean, and does not create a lawless and value-free vacuum where everything is possible.*

Not everything that *is* possible *should* be possible. For example, there are certain types of contracts that are illegitimate, null and void, and even deemed illegal and outlawed because they go against fundamental principles, norms, or values of the social system in which they exist. Hence, like any freedom, freedom of contract in regard to organisations raises the question of limits and limitations; *not all organisations are – or should be – legitimate or legal.*

The problem is *on which grounds* organisations should be assessed and judged as to whether or not they are legitimate. By and large, *the minimal formal criterion of legitimacy is that any social system (e.g. an organisation) must be consistent with the fundamental principles of the larger system it belongs to (e.g. a society or nation-state).*

For a free and fully fledged democratic society, *human, civil, and democratic rights* are founding elements and principles – and they are inalienable and non-negotiable; no institution, organisation, or individual can or should disrespect those fundamental rights of every person. On the contrary, organisations *have to* appreciate, comply with, actively defend, and promote these fundamental rights and principles. Organisations, therefore, *cannot* – and *must not* – be structured, organised, or managed in ways that would go against these fundamental rights and principles.

Beside adhering to individuals' fundamental human, civil, and democratic rights, organisations have to meet another criterion in order to be legitimate market participants; they need to comply with, and apply *democratic standards* (i.e. a libertarian constitution, democratic governance and democratic management). For example, Held (1987, p. 259) argued that 'For self-determination to be achieved, democratic rights need to be extended from the state to the economic enterprise and the other central institutions of society.' This is the so-called 'parallel argument': an organisation that exists and operates in a democratic society must be democratic. Or, to put it differently: in a free and democratic society any formally established organisation *must* be a democratic organisation since this is the only *form* that is consistent with the fundamental principles and values of a free and democratic society, the *only* form that accommodates, protects and enables free and autonomous individuals, their fundamental human, civil and democratic rights and democratic standards of governance and management (Bowles & Gintis 1993, p. 98, Harrison & Freeman 2004, p. 52, Malleson 2014, p. xii). Democracy and the market, democratic institutions and market participants are not antithetical but two sides of the same coin (Restakis 2010, p. 19).Thus, it can be declared:

> Within a free and democratic society, no institution or organisation can be anti-libertarian or anti-democratic.

Or, to formulate the proviso positively:

> Within a free and democratic society, any institution or organisation must adhere to libertarian and democratic principles, standards, and practices.

Hence, in order to be, and to remain, legitimate in a free and democratic society, *any* organisation (i.e. not only civil rights organisations or political parties but also business organisations, associations, clubs, and special purpose organisations) *must* appreciate in their constitution, governance, management, and internal workings the fundamental human, civil, and democratic rights of each and every individual, in particular the principles of freedom, democracy, equality, and justice of and for all of their members. This is not a choice but a constitutional condition for any institution or organisation.

In this sense, it can be said that *within a free and democratic society the decisive criteria for the legitimacy of an organisation are whether or not it adheres to the fundamental principles of freedom, democracy, equality, and justice, and whether or not it appreciates, enables, and protects the fundamental and inalienable human, civic, and democratic rights of its members and others in its purpose(s) and (formal and legal) constitution, governance, and management as well as in its (internal and external) conduct of business.*

The question, therefore, is how libertarian, democratic, equal, and just an organisation *should* – or *must* – be in order to be considered a *legitimate* organisation – and when it *cannot* be regarded as legitimate anymore and perhaps should even be outlawed. The following section interrogates five types of organisation – radical, profit-maximising, conservative, alternative, and democratic organisations – in terms of how well they appreciate, meet, and put into practice people's inalienable rights and democratic standards.

The Legitimacy of Various Types of Organisations

Radical Organisations

Organisations can be set up for purposes that constitute a legal wrong (or that are *very* close to doing so), for example criminal organisations or networks pursuing illegal activities (e.g. the Mafia, drug cartels, human trafficking rings, pyramid schemes, and white-collar crime); terrorist organisations (e.g. the Ku Klux Kahn and ISIS); extremist political organisations, parties, or movements (e.g. violent far-left or far-right parties); or totalitarian regimes (certain political or faith-based communes) (e.g. Powell 2007, pp. 6–7, Wright 2010, p. 146, Kohn 2011, p. 238, Nicholls 2011, p. 88, Lewis 2014, pp. 71–72).

Together, such organisations might be called 'radical organisations'. Their prime purpose(s) are to pursue extremist values and agendas that are 'above' or outside the law; go *directly* against (certain) other people's human, civil, or democratic rights; and inflict *deliberately* physical, psychological, emotional, and/or financial harm on people. Usually, such organisations are organised in extremist or totalitarian ways; they have very authoritarian organisational structures and processes, are extremely hierarchical and centralised, and require total commitment and obedience from their members and followers. In this sense they also harm (most of) their own people, although this may not be portrayed or perceived as so (on the contrary, very often, their members and followers see it as a privilege and deem themselves lucky to belong to the radical organisation and to serve its purposes – and its leaders!). In order to pursue and achieve their goals and purposes, radical organisations encourage, and often force, their members and followers to use methods and conduct activities that may be legitimate but are mostly illegitimate or even illegal.

It is often not easy to determine whether or not an organisation is radical (Held 1992/2006, p. 692, Bob 2011, p. 215). Some organisations and movements have extreme, and extremely contested, agendas (e.g. the eugenics movement), may even use unlawful actions in order to highlight certain issues or causes (e.g. activist organisations), or may be portrayed as 'radical' by their opponents (e.g. political groups striving for change in government or even systemic change) – but they *still* may be regarded as legitimate, may pursue (from *their* perspective and according to their beliefs) 'higher' causes, and may even be necessary to highlight pressing plights and address certain problems that otherwise would not be tackled sufficiently. Or there may be organisations that are truly radical (and bad in both their purposes and their deeds) but quite successful in conveying images of decency and correctness (all of the examples of organisations mentioned at the beginning of this sub-section) and manage to exist and operate for quite a long time while avoiding prosecution.

Nonetheless, despite the 'technical' difficulties in precisely pinning down whether a particular organisation is or is not radical, there definitely is a type or category containing organisations that are radical in the senses that their purpose, orientation, and activities harm, limit, or threaten (certain) people and/or their fundamental human, civil, or democratic rights *deliberately*; that their design and functioning and authoritarian and anti-democratic *in principle*; and that they use unlawful means and force *regularly* in order to achieve their goals. In most countries, especially in free and fully fledged democratic societies, such organisations are not only perceived as illegitimate but also – sooner or later – deemed illegal, outlawed, and prosecuted.

Profit-Maximising Organisations

Then there are organisations that also pursue extremist values and agendas – but they do not do so 'above' or outside the law (at least not officially). On the contrary, they exemplify, practise, and deliver the prevailing ideology of a particular epoch or society – and are celebrated for doing exactly that.

The best example of such a type of organisation is the *profit-maximising organisation* – the (neo-classical) ideal-typical model of the *capitalist firm*.[1] As its name indicates, it has the single, one-dimensional purpose of maximising profits (for its owners). The profit-maximising organisation is overwhelmingly seen as entirely legitimate (from a conservative, capitalist, or right-libertarian perspective), even 'necessary' (from the perspective of the neo-classical 'perfect market' model and 'theory of the firm'), and legal on the basis of corporate and business law – largely against the backcloth that maximising profits and/or utility, unhindered (quantitative) growth, the celebration of greed, and the pursuit of happiness via monetary means have become the prevailing values and ideologies of our age.

As history has shown – and still demonstrates in many respect and corners of the world – even when its purpose has been legalised, the profit-maximising organisation can, and often does, pursue its purpose very aggressively and violently and can operate in semi-legal or even illegal manners. But even if it operates within legal boundaries it still deviates fundamentally and in principle from libertarian and democratic standards in various ways.

The main reason for this is that the for-profit or profit-maximising organisation is set up for the sole purpose of generating as much profit as possible for a few people, its owners. To do this, it must maximise income and minimise costs by any means. Therefore, the profit-maximising organisation *must* be exploitative *by necessity*, i.e. it must ask for the maximum possible prices and it must pay all factors of production the absolute minimum. Concerning the latter this, for example, means that employees *cannot* be remunerated for their actual contributions to the generation of value-added and cannot be given their fair share of the profits but only their minimum salary. The profit-maximising organisation *must* take advantage of its employees systematically and in principle and *must* exploit them (just as it must also exploit social and natural resources in a similar vein).

For this, the profit-maximising organisation is *deliberately* – and *by necessity* – based on an illegitimate standard employment contract (or similar exploitative contractual arrangements) that enables it to exploit people legally. The purpose of enriching a few *by using, and at the expense of others* (workers, employees) can – and *must* – be achieved via exploitative agreements, exchanges, and activities; anti-libertarian and strictly hierarchical organisational structures and processes of governance and management; opportunistic behaviour; and exploitation of natural, human, and social resources. And it *must* ignore people's human, civil, and democratic rights because these rights either mean costs or may threaten the exploitative character of the relationship between employer and employees (or it only acknowledges such rights if they 'pay off', i.e. to comply with labour laws or with social or environmental rules and regulations in order to avoid penalties or punishment, or to have a corporate social responsibility agenda in order to increase the organisation's competitiveness and attractiveness).

The exploitative character and nature of the profit-maximising organisation is also reflected in its organisational structures and processes. In order to have employees functioning smoothly, behaving subserviently, and fulfilling their duties diligently, the for-profit organisation is structured in a strictly hierarchical and authoritarian manner and is based on highly unequal superior–subordinate or master–servant relationships in which the former is in complete control of the latter.

With its strict legal (standard employment contract) and organisational (hierarchy) basis, the profit-maximising organisation not only establishes highly asymmetrical relationships between owners and workers and between employer and employees but also goes against the spirit of freedom, democracy, equal rights, and equal opportunities – *deliberately and in principle*: the absolute majority of its members (the employees) do not have equal rights and equal status, freedom of thought, freedom of opinion and expression, or the rights to participate in collective decision-making, democratic governance, self-management, participative or representative management, or democratic control and accountability. The organisation is not only 'not democratic' but also *anti*-democratic and *authoritarian* in the very meaning of the word; it gives *all* power to make decisions, govern, manage, and control only to some (the owner(s), employer, and superiors), and it leaves no power for the many (employees and subordinates). The absolute majority of its members are systematically excluded from basic human, civil, and democratic rights, from their fundamental and actually inalienable rights. Such an organisation is inconsistent with the Universal Declaration of Human Rights, the constitutions and founding principles of democratic nation-states, and the principles and standards of democratic governance.

Radical and profit-maximising organisations are different in the sense that the former harms people (others as well as their members and followers) and ignores, even attacks, their fundamental human, civil, and democratic rights *deliberately* and *directly* whereas the latter harms people (employees but also external stakeholders) more indirectly by using and exploiting them and accepts such harm and human suffering as an (irrelevant) side-effect of economic efficiency and productivity. Because of its principle-based exploitative and oppressive character and its anti-libertarian and anti-democratic design and workings, the for-profit or profit-maximising organisation is illegitimate and alien to any society and economy that upholds the principles of freedom, democracy, equality, and justice. It should be rendered illegal.

Conservative Organisations

In contrast to radical and profit-maximising organisations, which have single and one-dimensional purposes that they pursue uncompromisingly, there are many organisations that have multiple, and multi-dimensional, purposes and are more moderate in their orientations, design, and workings. For instance, the absolute majority of organisations operating in market economies and society are *not* profit-maximising (large) corporations but small and medium-sized enterprises and local businesses, family businesses, cooperatives, or civil society organisations (CSOs). The founders, owners, members, and even employees of these organisations, whether they are business organisations or CSOs, have fairly traditional and conservative values and orientations. And they set up, run, and maintain their organisations accordingly. Such organisations might be called 'conservative organisations'.

The owners and members of profit-oriented conservative organisations want to generate *some* income and want to make *some* profit, but they do not want to maximise it. Profit is seen as a means, not as an end. The main purposes of these organisations are, for example, to generate a steady flow of income, to continue a tradition and traditional businesses, to create and offer certain products or services as part of one's identity or creativity as a lifestyle, to be independent, and/or to serve members, customers, the local community, or society in general. And if such organisations operate as not-for-profit CSOs in the social realm (the so-called third sector besides the market and the state), their purposes are even more multiple and social, for example improving the conditions of individuals, supporting groups and certain ways of life, or promoting traditions and traditional social institutions, social stability, and continuity.

Conservative organisations often develop and demonstrate relatively prudent, decent, cooperative, balanced, and sustainable business models and business practices. Conservative values and purposes provide the basis for, and are reflected in, how these organisations conduct their business; they do business based on traditional values, a strong sense of duty and responsibility, community orientation, and a feeling of local embeddedness, and are primarily concerned about and work for the well-being of their members, supporters, community, neighbourhood, clients, and customers (e.g. Nembhard 2008, p. 212, Groeneveld 2011, p. 533, Gibson-Graham et al. 2013; see also Chapter 6: 'Considerate Conduct of Business').

Such conservatism is also reflected in the governance and management structures and processes of these organisations; conservative organisations are fairly rule based, thoroughly structured, and hierarchical, with clear roles and responsibilities, and (respect for) authority, law, and order, established institutions, and procedural routines. Even partnerships and professional service firms (such as law firms) can be fairly exclusive (only some of their members are actually partners, while many others are common employees), hierarchical, and managerial. Schwartz (2012, p. 237, footnote 66) pointed out that:

While smaller law and other professional service firms organized as partnerships may approximate producer labor management and ownership, there is significant variation. The larger firms are, unlike standard labor-managed enterprises, extremely 'hierarchical'. ... Moreover, larger professional partnerships rarely embody the democratic structures characteristic of producer cooperatives.[2]

In this sense, conservatism – and conservative organisations – is not actively against or opposed to the human, civil, and democratic rights of individuals. These rights are just seen and interpreted differently from a conservative perspective (compared to, say, a progressive perspective), i.e. they are understood and interpreted in rather narrow and limited ways: human rights are reduced to the absolute minimum of *negative freedom rights* (but not equal rights of positive freedom for all), civil rights are reduced to those of a *well-functioning and obedient citizen* (but not the rights of free and independent citizens), and democratic rights are mostly understood as the basic rights in and needed for a *representative democracy* (but not for democratic self-governance or participative governance).

So, with their multi-dimensional social and economic purposes and traditional values, their strong sense of duty and responsibility, and their mostly decent and moderate conduct of business, conservative organisations in many ways *positively* contribute to societies and individuals' well-being. The flip side, however, lies in their relative strictness and rigidness, rule orientation, strong hierarchical order, authoritarianism, and oppressive culture. Conservative organisations are both a blessing and a curse – for individuals who need order and stability more of the former, and for individuals who strive for independence and their own development more of the latter. In this sense, conservative organisations are legitimate and can be tolerated, but at the same time they should be encouraged to change their strict and rigid policies, cultures, structures, and processes.

Alternative Organisations

The different types of organisation discussed so far have in common that they are fairly narrow in their orientations (radical, profit-maximising, or conservative) and fairly hierarchical and authoritarian in their organisational design and functioning. They therefore might be understood as variants (of different degrees and intensities) of the same orthodox or hierarchical 'standard model' of organisation (Diefenbach 2013a).

Obviously, in both theoretical and practical terms, fundamentally different models of organisation can be imagined and are possible. Such types can be called 'alternative organisations'. Alternative organisations have, and pursue, multiple and multi-dimensional social values and purposes, in particular freedom, democracy, equality, and justice – all understood in a broad and comprehensive sense. These values are reflected in their libertarian constitutions and the fundamental goals they aim (or claim) to pursue. For example, in contrast to *conservative* (civil society) organisations, many *alternative* CSOs (e.g. *progressive* cooperatives, not-for-profit organisations, social enterprises, non-governmental organisations, and activist organisations) as well as alternative business or for-profit organisations not only want to 'do good' but also want to change the conditions of individuals in particular and society in general. And they want to do so and achieve this in alternative ways. For this purpose, their internal formal structures and processes are fairly non-hierarchical (e.g. learning organisation, 'flat' organisation, or network organisation), and democratic governance and participative management, especially participative decision-making, are formally institutionalised throughout the organisation.

In reality, however, alternative organisations might not live up to (their own) expectations. They may not be structured or governed sufficiently democratically and their internal democratic processes may function poorly. Such organisations do not provide for democratic participation, do not give their members any meaningful roles or say in governance, and (therefore) have a largely passive membership (e.g. Anheier & Themudo 2002, pp. 210–211, Fung 2003, p. 524, Halpin 2006, pp. 920–922, Greenwood 2007, p. 348, Rodekamp 2010, pp. 1, 5, Wright 2010, p. 213, Bob 2011, pp. 212–213, Rosenblum & Lesch 2011, p. 290, Connelly et al. 2012, p. 102, Kokkinidis 2012, p. 249, Smith & Teasdale 2012, p. 165, Lewis 2014, pp. 74, 221–223). In this sense, alternative organisations may not be as democratic, participative, and egalitarian as they claim to be, could be, or should be.

Moreover, there is compelling evidence that in alternative organisations *informal* hierarchies and oligarchies are quite common phenomena: there can be (abuse of) power; conflict; internal politics; political game-playing; mutual monitoring, peer review, criticism, and/or control of employees professionally, socially, and psychologically; authoritarian tendencies; paternalism; a tendency towards oligarchisation; and/or social dominance of informal groups and elites.[3] Despite (or because of) the absence of *formal* hierarchy and hierarchical control systems, informal, individualised, and subjectivised forms of power and control can emerge that make the alternative organisation even *more* controlling and oppressive than orthodox types of organisation.

Although alternative organisations officially have, and uphold, fundamental values of comprehensive freedom, democracy, equality, and justice, and although they pursue good causes and conduct their business largely in considerate and decent ways, they *can* be fairly hierarchical, oligarchic, exclusive, and oppressive, and may be ruled by the few – either because of insufficient *formal* organisational structures and processes of (democratic) governance and management or because of (the emergence of) *informal* hierarchies and social dominance (probably both because formal and informal phenomena are related and often work together). Even (allegedly) 'alternative' or 'progressive' organisations can be fairly orthodox and nightmarish places to be. In this case they must be changed.

Democratic Organisations

The democratic organisation is actually a type of alternative organisation (just as the profit-maximising organisation is a form of radical organisation) – but a very distinct and much better one because of its uniquely comprehensive design and features, which are based on a libertarian constitution; its all-embracing democratic governance and democratic management; its equalising empowerment; and its considerate conduct of business. In this sense, it is qualitatively different from all other alternative organisations and is listed here as a separate type.

The democratic organisation has its *constitutional foundations* (i.e. its legal, formal, and substantive foundations) in libertarian values and concepts of self-ownership, individual and collective private ownership, and a partnership agreement that specifies and guarantees the equal legal and formal status, rights, and responsibilities of all people who collectively and democratically own, manage, and control the organisation, its properties and assets, and its activities and results (*libertarian constitution*).

Based on its libertarian constitution, this type of organisation is a fully fledged democratic system. The democratic organisation is based on and governed by the principles of *democratic governance*, i.e.:

- Its *democratic institutions of governance* (boards, committees, councils, or assemblies) are designed and function according to democratic standards and the principles of separation of power or 'checks and balances', and subsidiarity.
- Its *legitimate authoritative sources* (partnership agreement, mission and vision statements, strategy and operational plans, codes of conduct, and ethics and compliance statements) are drafted and applied democratically and provide the basis for the functioning of the institutions of governance, governance, and management according to democratic standards.
- The *governing* of the organisation and organisational affairs happens *democratically*, i.e. on the basis of democratic decision-making, transparency, and accountability;.
- Democratic governance is *'good governance'*, i.e. the organisational institutions of governance and management are designed and work according to democratic standards and apply democratic rules according to the rule of law in formal and substantive terms.

Moreover, the democratic organisation has *democratic management* in place that provides for heterarchical structures and processes and consists of three parts:

- *Self-management*: individuals and groups of people are entitled, encouraged, and enabled to organise and manage their own work, work-related issues, and organisational affairs as much and as far as possible.

- *Representative management*: organisational affairs that go beyond individuals' or groups of people's wills and capacities to self-manage are managed by formally established organisational institutions or individual management positions that are designed, staffed, and function according to democratic principles.
- *Participative management*: *all* members of the democratic organisation have equal rights and opportunities to participate in all formal decision-making processes at all levels of the organisation.

Together, self-management, representative management, and participative management establish *democratic management* as *one comprehensive and consistent concept*. In the democratic organisation, management is done by the people – all people. They manage their work and organisational affairs either directly (self-management) or, if this is not possible or efficient, via representatives who execute the people's will and act in their name (representative management). *Full* (voluntary) participation of all members of the organisation in management and decision-making makes sure that individuals are (still) in charge (participative management).

Besides its democratic *institutions* (libertarian constitution, democratic governance, and democratic management), it is the *people* that make the democratic organisation truly democratic. The democratic organisation is built on the notion that all of its members are not only equal and have equal rights but also (should) have *equal power*, i.e. that they are *formally, psychologically, and socially equally empowered* (*equalising empowerment*) so that they can fully participate in the governance and management of the organisation:

- *formally* by configuring all formal roles, positions, and organisational institutions of governance and management according to the fundamental ideas and principles of democratic governance and democratic management (i.e. to confine the formal power of office-holders and increase the formal power of those who are not formal office-holders);
- *psychologically* by increasing individual members' self-esteem, sense of an internal locus of control, and sense of goal attainment via self-management and participative management;
- *socially* by promoting the ideas of self-management, self-managed groups, and full participation, which help members to develop a strong social identity and orientation, confidence, the ability to manage and maintain social relationships and interactions, and the ability to pursue their interests within a social context and by challenging overtly (self-)empowered members (e.g. 'leaders', 'aggrandisers') and confining their social dominance through demystification, social control, and social actions.

Finally, the democratic organisation is designed and maintained in order to pursue and achieve multi-dimensional social, environmental, and economic goals and purposes (the 'triple bottom line' concept of 'people, planet, profit') in balanced ways and to act in accordance with their fundamental values (considerate conduct of business). In particular, the democratic organisation demonstrates more socially oriented, community-based, community-oriented, cooperative, and considerate conduct of business and practises more decent and prudent management; shows more pro-environmental behaviour in its internal and external activities, products, and services; and achieves higher efficiency, productivity, and organisational performance and is economically more successful and sustainable than orthodox organisations.

Different Types of Organisation – and What to Do about Them

This chapter has briefly addressed five different types of organisation (radical, profit-maximising, conservative, alternative, and democratic), in particular by focusing on the legitimacy of their primary values and purposes, formal structures, and processes of governance and management as well as their internal workings and conduct of business. Table 9.1 summarises the main findings in regard to each type of organisation.

TABLE 9.1 Levels of legitimacy of organisations

Level	Type of organisation	Description
5	Democratic	Values and purposes of freedom, democracy, equality, and justice; libertarian and democratic constitution; democratic governance; democratic (self-, representative, and participative) management; equalising empowerment; considerate conduct of business.
4	Alternative	Values and purposes of freedom, democracy, equality, and justice; libertarian and democratic constitution, but the possibility of insufficient formal structures and processes of democratic governance and management; emergence of informal hierarchy or oligarchisation; largely considerate conduct of business.
3	Conservative	Conservative values and multi-dimensional purposes; relatively authoritarian constitution, governance, and management; strong and comprehensive formal hierarchy, autocracy, and/or oligarchy; conservative, rule-based conduct of business.
2	Profit-maximising	One-dimensional purpose of maximising profits to be achieved via exploitative agreements, exchanges, and activities; anti-libertarian and hierarchical organisational structures and processes of governance and management; opportunistic behaviour; exploitation of natural, human, and social resources.
1	Radical	Values and purposes that constitute a legal wrong (criminal, terrorist, or extremist political agendas and activities); authoritarian structures and processes of governance and management; anti-human conduct of business.

The table represents a *continuum*, or better to say (overlapping) *levels*, of how organisations do in regard to appreciating and putting into practice the fundamental values and principles of freedom, democracy, equality, and justice as well as people's human, civil, and democratic rights in their purposes, design, and functioning (with level 1 the lowest and level 5 the highest). The more an organisation appreciates and puts into practice those principles, rights, and values, the more it meets democratic standards and the more legitimate it is – and the higher it ranks.

Ideally, organisations should develop and converge towards the highest level of legitimacy. That is, in a free and democratic society, organisations are deemed (the most) legitimate if they resemble as closely as possible the model of the democratic organisation, i.e. if they have a libertarian constitution, embody multi-dimensional and moderate purposes and values, have comprehensive and robust structures and processes of democratic governance and democratic management, demonstrate considerate conduct of business (both internally and externally), and overall appreciate, enable, and protect the fundamental values and principles of freedom, democracy, equality, and justice for *all* of their members as well as external stakeholders.

The question is what to do about organisations that do or do *not* meet democratic standards. Not *every* form and type of organisation that *is* possible *should* be possible. Organisations should be judged and treated according to, and consistent with, their level of legitimacy. This means in particular:

1. *Radical organisations* are not only illegitimate but also illegal because of their criminal, terrorist, and/or totalitarian purposes, design, and activities. They therefore should be outlawed, terminated, and prosecuted.
2. *Profit-maximising organisations* are illegitimate because of their primary purpose of maximising income and profit for a few (the owners) by taking advantage of, and at the expense of, others (workers and employees) via exploitative social and legal relationships with most of its members and authoritarian, anti-libertarian, and anti-democratic organisational structures and processes of governance and management. They therefore should be deemed illegal, outlawed, and terminated.
3. *Conservative organisations* are legitimate because of their multi-dimensional social purposes and their value-based considerate conduct of business. However, their often autocratic, oligarchic, or otherwise anti-democratic governance and management cause serious harm to many people, especially to their members and followers but also to people outside the organisation. They can be tolerated but must be challenged and changed.
4. *Alternative organisations* are legitimate because of their values and purposes of freedom, democracy, equality, and justice, and their libertarian and democratic constitution. Nonetheless, they can have relatively insufficient formal structures and processes of democratic governance and management and can degenerate into informal hierarchies and oligarchisation. They therefore should be propagated, but also protected and repaired.

5. *Democratic organisations* are legitimate because of their values and purposes of freedom, democracy, equality, and justice; their libertarian and democratic constitution; their democratic governance and management; their equalising empowerment; and their considerate conduct of business. However, they can come under threat of disproportional empowerment and oligarchisation and need protection and support. They should be pursued and propagated so that they become the prevailing standard model of organisation.

Thus, the framework developed in this chapter provides clear guidelines concerning what to do about organisations according to their level of legitimacy: (1) outlaw, terminate, and prosecute radical organisations; (2) deem illegal and terminate profit-maximising organisations; (3) tolerate but challenge and change conservative organisations; (4) promote but protect and repair alternative organisations; and (5) pursue, propagate, and support democratic organisations.

Only organisations from level 3 upwards – i.e. conservative, alternative, and democratic organisations – are sufficiently legitimate to exist and to operate in free and democratic societies and their economies, because only these types of organisation provide the blueprint and conditions for adhering to the fundamental principles of freedom, democracy, equality, and justice and for protecting and promoting people's inalienable fundamental human, civil, and democratic rights.[4]

Free and democratic societies based on the formal and substantive rule of law have the means, even the responsibility, to provide the appropriate constitutional, legal, and regulatory framework for organisations (such as corporate laws, labour laws, and other national laws relating to professional partnerships, cooperatives, associations, not-for-profit organisations, special purpose organisations, clubs, and charities) (e.g. Hirst 1994, p. 56). Via such laws and regulations, the purposes, design, and workings of organisations can be specified, and certain types of organisation can be legalised or outlawed relatively easily.[5] The basic and leading principle should be that in free and democratic societies organisations that do not grant *all* of their members *all* fundamental rights and freedoms, and (therefore) do not meet democratic standards, are illegitimate and – if they are either not willing or not able to change – should be deemed illegal and outlawed.

Notes

1 The capitalist firm might be defined as a formally constituted enterprise where one actor (a natural or legal person) or a group of people ('owners') provide capital and employ other people ('employees') in order to make a profit out of, and via, some economic activity.
2 For some further description and analysis of traditional professional partnerships and professional service firms and how they resemble corporations, see, for example, Lancaster and Uzzi (2004) or Empson and Chapman (2006).

3 For example, Kanter (1972, p. 203), Rothschild-Whitt (1976, p. 82), Cornforth et al. (1988, p. 141), Barker (1993), Rohrschneider (1994), Cheney (1995, p. 175), Cornforth (1995, p. 508), Jacques (1996), Jermier (1998), Courpasson (2000), Nelson (2001), Akella (2003, p. 52), Kärreman and Alvesson (2004), Varman and Chakrabarti (2004, p. 183), Anderson and Henehan (2005), Ekbia and Kling (2005), Leach (2005, pp. 312–314, 330–331), Ravlin and Thomas (2005, p. 969), Bogason and Musso (2006, p. 14), Courpasson and Clegg (2006), Guimerà et al. (2006), Hernandez (2006), Osterman (2006, pp. 623–625), Ackroyd and Muzio (2007), Atzeni and Ghigliani (2007, pp. 11–13), Singh et al. (2007, p. 286), Oberg and Walgenbach (2008), Rank (2008), Sauser (2009, p. 155), Tolbert and Hiatt (2009), Kienle (2011, p. 153), Rosenblum and Lesch (2011, p. 290), Crowley (2012), and Martin (2015, p. 60).

4 Nonetheless, as indicated earlier in this chapter, conservative and alternative organisations do have their flaws and would need to change in order to be fully legitimate (e.g. they would need to get rid of illegitimate employment contracts and replace them with legitimate partnership or membership contracts, change their hierarchical structures and processes into more democratic and participative ones, and so on).

5 As Hirst (1994, p. 202) argued: 'The public power has the right to set limits to the conduct of associations and ... the foundation of that right is the liberty of citizens and of future citizens.' In a similar vein, Rosenblum and Lesch (2011, p. 287) asked: 'What constraints should government impose on the formation, internal life, and activities of groups and associations, and what limits should it set to the authority that groups exercise over their own members and outsiders?'

10

THE IRON THREAT(S) OF DISPROPORTIONAL EMPOWERMENT

The Phenomenon of Disproportional Empowerment

As indicated so far in this book, the democratic organisation is the most advanced and fitting organisation one can imagine for free and democratic societies and market economies. It promotes and practises the fundamental values and principles of freedom, democracy, equality, and justice in the most comprehensive and robust form, and it pursues good causes and conducts business in considerate and decent ways. It does so because its libertarian and democratic constitution, governance, and management reflect, are built on, and function according to the very same principles and values it pursues.

However, like any other organisation, the democratic organisation can come under serious threats: challenges can come *from outside* or emerge *within* the democratic organisation and threaten its very nature and existence. Here in this chapter the focus is on internal threats and challenges that mainly emanate from individual behaviour, social processes, and dynamics that are detrimental to the spirit and nature of the democratic organisation and its fundamental principles, structures, and processes, such as *organisational misbehaviour* (i.e. behaviour that goes against fundamental human or civil rights, ethical norms, and values, and negatively impacts on other people), *social dominance* (i.e. some people have greater social power and influence and dominate others), *social inequalities* (i.e. some people have better access to resources, more material goods, more social privileges and advantages, and/or generally better opportunities to pursue their interests), *stratification* (i.e. people have qualitatively different social statuses and positions within a social system because of socially defined and valued characteristics), *hierarchisation* (i.e. positions and people are put into a horizontal order of command and control), and/or *autocratisation* or *oligarchisation* (i.e. the emergence of a single autocratic leader or a group of people – a power elite – that rules a social system without being sufficiently controlled).

These phenomena and (emerging) patterns within social systems have one thing in common: they systematically privilege and empower *some* individuals or groups and disadvantage and disempower *many* others. They, hence, can be subsumed under the term *disproportional empowerment* – the empowerment of the few and disempowerment of the many (Diefenbach 2016).[1] Disproportional empowerment means the formal, psychological, and/or social empowerment of some (a few) members of a social system and the formal, psychological, and/or social disempowerment of many other members of the social system (see the section 'Meaning(s) and a Three-Dimensional Concept of Empowerment and Disempowerment' in Chapter 5). Disproportional empowerment means that (opportunities for) empowerment and (threats of) disempowerment are distributed *systematically unequally* among the members of a social system; *certain* people are empowered or empower themselves, and certain others are *dis*-empowered or *dis*-empower themselves. There are processes and patterns of empowerment and disempowerment at work that privilege *some* individuals and groups and disadvantage others *systematically* and *routinely*. Moreover, the empowerment of the few triggers, contributes to, and magnifies the disempowerment of the many – which empowers the former even more.

Disproportional empowerment is not only disadvantageous for a majority of people, unfair, and unjust but can also turn an alternative or democratic organisation into a rather managerial, orthodox, hierarchical, autocratic and/or oligarchic, exclusive, and oppressive social system that is ruled and exploited by a few at the expense of the many. There is a (constant) danger that disproportional empowerment might happen in the democratic organisation. Thus, the question is why and how disproportional empowerment can emerge in the democratic organisation (or in any organisation or social system) – and what (pre-emptively) can be done about it.

The following section presents some empirical examples of disproportional empowerment happening in alternative organisations in order to give an idea of how counterproductive such social processes and dynamics are to the democratic organisation. Next, a model is developed that shows the causes and a (possible) sequence of how disproportional empowerment can emerge within (democratic) organisations. The model reveals that *people* – *certain*, *particular*, and *identifiable* people – are responsible for these patterns and processes happening and unfolding. The second half of this chapter, therefore, focuses especially on people's part in the emergence of disproportional empowerment – *who* exactly and in what particular ways people may intentionally or unintentionally *cause* disproportional empowerment to happen. The chapter also provides some ideas about which specific formal, psychological, and social measures democratic organisations can apply in order to prevent disproportional empowerment happening.

Social Processes and Dynamics Detrimental to the Democratic Organisation

Organisations, seen as *social* systems, draw attention to social processes and dynamics that are the result of people's (intertwined) decisions, actions, attitudes, behaviour, communication, and interactions. Social actions and processes happen on the basis of, and within the framework of, formal principles, structures, and processes – in the case of the democratic organisation, the principles, structures, and processes of democratic governance and democratic management. Evidently, there are countless social actions and processes happening every single moment that make the organisation function. And there are also, of course, social actions and processes that are 'counterproductive', i.e. that go against the (official and/ or agreed) principles, norms, values, rules, and regulations of the organisation and its members. In the case of the *democratic* organisation, this would be social actions and processes that are not consistent or compatible with its democratic principles, governance, and management. They might be so detrimental to the ideas and values of the democratic organisation that they seriously threaten its functioning – if not to say its essence. To give some examples.

Referring to Cornforth et al.'s (1988) research into decision-making at Suma, a food wholesale cooperative in the UK, in the 1970s and 1980s, Cornforth (1995, p. 508) stated that:

> A more difficult issue was the feeling among many members of the co-operative that meetings were not very effective and the co-operative was being run by an informal elite. ... In these circumstances, many felt Suma was run by a group consisted of long serving ... members of the co-operative. Their dominance was built upon the expertise and knowledge that they had built up over time and their close association with each other. Clearly knowledge and expertise is likely to be an important power base in any organisation; however, this was exacerbated by the lack of structure and formal procedures in the co-operative. ... There was a shortage of management information in the co-operative, and much of what was produced was held in people's heads rather than written down and circulated. As a result many members lacked the information necessary to make decisions. In addition the informality of meetings meant that it was easier for those with greater knowledge or stronger personalities to dominate.

In her investigation of 'family rhetoric' at a large 'participative' U.S. company, Casey (1999, p. 172) found that:

> Favoritism and political maneuvering were present in the older style bureaucracies, but the more formalized structure in which one expected to

progress encouraged impersonality and some protection from advancement by nepotist practices. But now, the flatter, closer team-family structure covertly revives interpersonal suspicion, sibling-like rivalry and nepotism at the same time as it overtly, officially, promotes egalitarian teammate cooperation, familial warmth, and overriding commitment to the product.

When Varman and Chakrabarti (2004) researched the problems encountered by a workers' cooperative in India (SAMITI) in attempting to institutionalise democracy, they (p. 183) uncovered a

persistent tendency toward oligarchization within SAMITI, whether in the beginning it was the MCAs [middle-class associates] and the 'activists' or later when it incorporated some of the workers as well, or at present when all the office-holders are workers. The problem is that the lack of participation and tendency toward oligarchization feed into each other. Thus at best some kind of a paternalistic system develops, but at times distinctly authoritarian tendencies emerge. Worse, some of the informal members of the oligarchy, such as the MCAs, are very difficult to hold accountable, since they are not part of any formal structure.

When Leach (2005, p. 314) developed a model of 'legitimate and illegitimate forms of formal and informal power' based on a comprehensive analysis of the literature on oligarchies and oligarchisation, she warned that:

There is no reason to assume that simply by virtue of a lack of formal authority, such [non-bureaucratically structured] groups are immune to being pushed around by a domineering minority. On the contrary, they probably suffer at least as much from the malady of oligarchization as do bureaucratic organizations. … Oligarchy is *more* difficult to prevent in informal organizations due to the lack of bureaucratic constraints on informal authority.

Bogason and Musso (2006, p. 14) summarised their research into democratic network governance among non-governmental organisations in Ghent and Los Angeles as follows:

The dangers confronting network governance are the age-old issues of accountability and abuse of power that come into play in any system of government. There is a danger that interest groups and political insiders will manipulate the system for their own gains and to the disadvantages of those who do not have the resources to organize. … And in any democratic system, there is a tendency for more powerful factions to overwhelm the weak and to perpetuate their advantage through institutional means.

Hernandez (2006, p. 128) gave a vivid account of how 'lively' organisational decision-making can be:

> In the decision-making process through representative democracy we see that forces pushing toward oligarchy include the development of charismatic and professional leadership; the individual search for power; corruption; amiguismo [cronyism]; shop-floor politics; and the varying degrees to which each leader allows participation within and between boards and committees. Forces pushing for democracy include scepticism toward, and willingness to challenge, authority; readiness to recall representatives; expectations that the representatives maintain contact with rank-and-file, honesty and effectiveness; expectation to participate fully in board and committee meetings; and a participatory culture (belief in workers' right to self-determination and commitment to defend this right) developed through the labor struggle.

Finally, when Oberg and Walgenbach (2008, p. 183) investigated and analysed the internal email communications of an explicitly anti-hierarchical network company, they discovered

> a split between the symbolic activities for creating a non-hierarchical network organization and the actual intranet communication behaviour of the organization members. In their daily communication on the intranet, they persistently reproduced hierarchical structures and official channels – elements typically associated with bureaucratic organizations. Further, we find many signals in the content of the intranet messages, reflecting a social hierarchy that has evolved within the organization.

Organisations, obviously, are anything but homogeneous and tranquil social entities – and democratic organisations are no different. They may have legally, constitutionally, and formally overcome the antagonism between owners, managers, and employees but they are not conflict free (and never will be) – on the contrary, the reality of democratic organisations is more complex and differentiated than idealistic or naive images of them may suggest.

A Sequence of Disproportional Empowerment

As the empirical examples above show, in the democratic organisation there may be social actions and processes occurring that are detrimental to its very idea, values, principles, and functioning. Moreover, these social actions and processes can represent not just single, individual incidents but *patterns* that happen repeatedly and are part of a *sequence* that leads to the emergence and institutionalisation of *disproportional empowerment* – the empowerment of the few and disempowerment of the many. Such social actions and processes leading to disproportional empowerment can unfold in a sequence, as follows.

First, as in any other social system or organisation, within democratic organisations individuals and groups of people have, and pursue, their individual or group *interests* (e.g. Rutledge & Karim 1999, Darke & Chaiken 2005, O'Brien & Crandall 2005). Some members of the organisation may primarily or entirely pursue what might be called *anti-social interests*. These can be selfish, egoistic interests, for instance gaining or increasing one's individual power and influence, relevance, roles and responsibilities, salary and other material benefits, privileges and prerogatives, and status and prestige, or pursuing one's career and career prospects at the expense of and/or by using others (e.g. Waller et al. 1995, Willmott 1996, Osterman 2006, p. 623, Diefenbach 2013b). Alternatively, anti-social interests can be interests that put abstract rules, regulations, operations, systems, or 'the system' first even where these go against the fundamental rights of individuals or go against the fundamental principles and values of a free and democratic social system. Hence, people pursuing anti-social interests are either egoists or apparatchiks (i.e. bureaucrats in a negative sense), and sometimes both.

Second, usually, individuals or groups with anti-social interests are constantly active to pursue their (anti-social) interests, to get *their* interests through, and to steer and influence decision-making processes accordingly. They see, and interpret, things and people solely or largely from their own narrow anti-social perspective and are keen to shape structures and processes, how things are done, and others' actions according to their views. By and large, they may do so in two different ways. If they have more *extroverted* personalities and feel stronger about themselves, they will pursue their anti-social interests more openly and will be keener and more confident to use the public space provided and/or create opportunities for themselves to put forward their agenda (e.g. at meetings, in forums, or via online and social media). They will turn themselves into 'change agents' and 'leaders'. People with more *introverted* personalities will pursue their anti-social interests more silently – will pull the levers from behind their desks. They will be 'desk perpetrators' focusing more on drafting documents, number crunching, and formulating policies, rules, and regulations. Egoists tend to be more extroverted 'leaders', whereas apparatchiks tend to be more introverted 'desk perpetrators'. Either way, both are 'doers'. They focus on getting things done (their way), work constantly, participate and engage more in formal and informal decision-making processes, and use their (more developed) skills of communication, rational argumentation, and persuasion openly or in more tacit ways (Mansbridge 1980, p. 187, Cheney 1995, pp. 175, 183, Morand 1996, pp. 544–545, Malleson 2013, p. 99). They pursue their anti-social interests for the best part of their working day – this is their job! – and are quite flexible, opportunistic, and (over time) successful in doing so. Little by little, they empower themselves, gaining power and influence.

Third, because the doers pursue their anti-social interests constantly and unflinchingly, the organisation becomes contested terrain (Mintzberg 1985). *Organisational politics* starts to prevail and influence how issues are seen and addressed, and how social interactions and decision-making unfold. This (can) happen in *any* organisation (e.g. Burns 1961, Coopey & Burgoyne 2000). Whether it is direct participation in the workplace to decide more operational issues or indirect participation via and within organisational institutions of democratic governance and management, if some people pursue their anti-social interests, decision-making processes will become fairly political, individuals will navigate the organisation in a calculative way, and the organisational culture will become rather pathetic and toxic (Cotton et al. 1988, Boehm 1993, Cheney 1995, Stohl & Cheney 2001, Varman & Chakrabarti 2004, Ekbia & Kling 2005, Palgi 2006a, 2006b).

Fourth, those people who pursue their (anti-social) interests openly or 'behind closed doors' more vigorously, engaging and contributing more actively to formal and informal decision-making processes (the doers), gradually become more influential and powerful (Rothschild-Whitt 1979, p. 524). They strive in a climate of organisational politics (and *particularly* in such a climate). Sooner or later, those ambitious and psychologically and socially more empowered people will gain – or create for themselves – formal or informal positions of elevated status and responsibility and will show the corresponding behaviour – which will empower them even further. For example, Panayotakis (2011, p. 133) noticed that:

> Individuals with political talent and/or empowering jobs that gave them an advantage in the democratic game would not just be more likely to be elected to the democratic institutions within the workplace. In fulfilling the duties attached to their elected positions, they would also cultivate their political and organizational skills even further, thus further increasing the gap between their skills and those of their fellow workers.

In other words, *social dominance* (Sidanius & Pratto, 1999) – i.e. unequal power relations, asymmetries in the social distribution of power and resources, or structural and social inequalities – becomes institutionalised as the prevailing social structure and process (Nielsen 1990, p. 84, Knight & Johnson 1997, p. 294, Young 2008).

Fifth, the structures and behavioural patterns of social dominance become increasingly evident in *all* people's communication styles and behaviour. The more active members of the organisation progressively dominate communication, discussions, and decision-making processes whereas the more passive members become even more quiet. The former become psychologically and socially even more empowered, increasingly demonstrating leadership behaviour and manipulating, dominating, and ruling the latter, who become more and more disempowered and demonstrate follower behaviour. Members show the classical traits and behaviour of superiors, subordinates, domination, and obedience – and they are perceived, judged, and ranked by others according to their social roles and status (differentials), demonstrated behaviour, assumed influence, and 'importance'. Forms of power, control, dominance, and obedience become the prevailing modes of social structures and processes. People find themselves increasingly in vertical social relationships via official rule systems and formal order (*formal hierarchy*) *and* via unofficial, personal, and informal order (*informal hierarchy*) – and behave accordingly.[2] Disproportional empowerment is thereby institutionalised not only in the organisation's structures and processes but also in people's hearts and minds.

Sixth, people who have succeeded in gaining formal or informal positions of extended responsibility, power, and influence increasingly demonstrate the same set of values, preferences, attitudes, and behaviour. In other words, they become, and constitute, a *power elite* (Mills 1956). According to Scott (2003, p. 157), 'an elite in the fullest sense is a social grouping whose members occupy similarly advantaged command situations in the social distribution of authority and who are linked to one another through demographic processes of circulation and interaction'. Elster (1997, p. 14) even went so far as to say that participatory systems, especially, 'create a self-elected elite whose members spend time on politics because they want power, not out of concern for the issues'. As a minority, the power elite is keen to make sure – and will do almost everything to this end – that its members not only stay empowered but also become more empowered, whereas 'the rest', i.e. the *majority* of the members of the social system, remain disempowered. The members of the power elite gradually establish and widen their power and influence; institutionalise their values, worldviews, policies, and positions; and increasingly steer (large parts of) the organisation such that it becomes less and less democratically controlled, i.e. they institutionalise their rule, their power, and themselves, and – in doing so – turn the organisation into a *de facto oligarchy* – i.e. the 'concentration of illegitimate power in the hands of an entrenched minority' (Leach 2005, p. 312). Osterman (2006, pp. 633, 625) defined oligarchy as 'a self-perpetuating leadership group that dominates decision making via its control over knowledge, resources, and communication' and that 'use[s] the organizational levers to maintain internal power for personal gain'.

Altogether, a possible sequence leading to disproportional empowerment might look as shown in Table 10.1.

TABLE 10.1 A sequence of disproportional empowerment

1. *Anti-social interests*: Within a social system, there may be individuals or groups of people that have, and pursue, primarily *anti-social interests*, i.e. interests that serve only them at the expense of others, that go against the fundamental rights or legitimate interests of others, that are otherwise to others' direct or indirect disadvantage, or that go against the common good (egoists or apparatchiks).

2. *'Doers'*: People who feel more confident about themselves, their (anti-social) interests, and common issues on which a decision needs to be made will be more active, flexible, and opportunistic; will participate more in formal and informal decision-making processes; and, in so doing, will empower themselves (leaders or desk perpetrators).

3. *Organisational politics*: Because the doers pursue their anti-social interests actively, constantly, and unflinchingly, the organisation, its governance, and its management become contested terrain. Organisational politics starts to prevail and influence how issues are addressed, how people reason and behave, and how decision-making unfolds (in rather calculative and opportunistic ways).

4. *Social dominance*: Those people who engage in and contribute more actively to formal and informal decision-making processes and who more vigorously pursue their anti-social interests (either openly or 'behind closed doors') – the 'doers' – gradually become more influential and powerful, gain formal or informal power and positions, and increasingly demonstrate formal or informal leadership behaviour.

5. *Hierarchisation*: The more active members of the organisation progressively dominate communication and decision-making processes and demonstrate leadership behaviour whereas the more passive members show more and more follower behaviour. Members increasingly display the classical traits and behaviour of superiors and subordinates: domination and obedience. Structures and processes gradually become formal and informal hierarchies.

6. *Power elite*: People who have succeeded in gaining formal or informal positions of power and influence (increasingly) demonstrate the same set of values, preferences, attitudes, and behaviour. They constitute a *power elite*. As a minority, the power elite makes sure that its members stay empowered – and are more empowered. The members of the power elite continue to institutionalise their rule, power, and themselves, and they design, shape, and maintain institutions, policies, structures, and processes according to *their* worldviews and anti-social interests.

The sequence put forward here is only *one* possible process leading to disproportional empowerment or oligarchisation (i.e. the emergence of oligarchy)[3]. Such processes can be described from functional, organisational, socio-psychological, social, or political perspectives. Various sequences, models, and theories comprising different elements, steps, or phases have been developed in order to identify, describe, and analyse such processes (e.g. Michels 1915/2001, Mills 1956, Cornforth et al. 1988, Varman & Chakrabarti 2004, p. 185, Sauser 2009, p. 154, Diefenbach 2019).

Processes leading to disproportional empowerment and oligarchisation like the one described above – or the threat of such processes – are well known and have been at least since the German sociologist Robert Michels published his impressive and highly influential research and analysis *Political Parties: A Sociological Study of the Oligarchical Tendencies of Modern Democracy* at the beginning of the 20th century. According to Michels (1915/2001, p. 26), 'organization implies the tendency to oligarchy' and 'who says organization, says oligarchy' (p. 241). He added (p. 27, italics added), 'it is indisputable that the oligarchical and bureaucratic tendency of party organization is a matter of technical and practical *necessity*. It is the *inevitable* product of the very principle of organization'. The main, and crucial, point Michels made was that, despite good intentions, oligarchy will *always* emerge. His theorem is even called the 'iron law of oligarchy' in the sense of a *natural law* (Michels himself called it the 'law of the historic *necessity* of oligarchy' (p. 240, italics added)). In my paper on Michels' iron law of oligarchy (Diefenbach 2019), though, I argued that oligarchisation *can* happen (and that, regrettably, it *does* happen much too often), but that it does *not* need to happen *by necessity* ('always', i.e. like a natural law) and that we can find measures to prevent oligarchisation. Accordingly, the sequence or model put forward here does not claim *necessity* but only the *possibility* of the emergence of disproportional empowerment or an oligarchy – and later in this chapter I will show what can be done to prevent them from happening.

But Michels was more than right to draw attention to such unwelcome phenomena as oligarchisation. Unfortunately, his theorem has been confirmed by many researchers and there is compelling evidence for the contention that negative social processes leading to lasting patterns of disproportional empowerment and oligarchy *can* happen not only in orthodox or hierarchical but also in alternative or democratic organisations (e.g. Cornforth et al. 1988, p. 141, Rohrschneider 1994, Varman & Chakrabarti, 2004, p. 183, Leach 2005, pp. 314, 330–331, Ravlin & Thomas 2005, p. 969, Bogason & Musso 2006, p. 14, Hernandez 2006, Osterman 2006, pp. 623–624, Atzeni & Ghigliani, 2007, pp. 11–13, Sauser 2009, p. 155, Tolbert & Hiatt, 2009, Martin 2015, p. 60). Although it is too much to say that oligarchy is 'inevitable', there definitely is a *serious* and *constant* threat that democratic and other alternative organisations will be usurped by power elites and turned into oligarchies and fairly orthodox organisations.

Consequentialist and Non-consequentialist Arguments against Disproportional Empowerment

There might not be an *iron law* but there is definitely *a constant threat* that democratic organisations and societies will end up as oligarchies ruled by the few at the expense of the many. But, if disproportional empowerment is such a common thing that seemingly can happen to *any* organisation, even to democratic organisations, then why should we bother to prevent it at all? There are various good reasons – consequentialist as well as non-consequentialist arguments – that we should be very concerned about the possible emergence of disproportional empowerment in social systems.

Consequentialist Arguments against Disproportional Empowerment

Consequentialist arguments against disproportional empowerment focus on the (positive and negative) consequences it has for systems and people. Disproportional empowerment causes *a lot* of *actual damage* to the democratic organisation and/or to those involved in it. Some of the main forms of damage that disproportional empowerment can cause for people are briefly highlighted in the following three sub-sections.

Abuse of Power

A first (potential) threat and damage related to autocratic or oligarchic systems or other forms of disproportional empowerment is the well-known *abuse of power*. As soon as (formal or informal) positions of power or power differentials exist between people, abuse of power becomes a possibility (e.g. Erdal 2011, p. 196). As Dahl (1998, p. 74) explained:

> However wise and worthy the members of a ruling elite entrusted with the power to govern a state may be when they first take power, in a few years or a few generations they are likely to abuse it. If human history provides any lessons, one surely is that through corruption, nepotism, the advancement of individual and group interests, and abuse of their monopoly over the state's coercive power to suppress criticism, extract wealth from their subjects, and insure their obedience by coercion, the Guardians of a state are likely to turn into despots.

Abuse of power is bad in various ways:

*   It means that a person, or a group of people, governs, rules, and manages at whim, i.e. that they may make decisions that are not in line with formal institutions, the law, official rules and regulations, policies, or accepted practices, *but are arbitrary and illegitimate, if not illegal.*
*   These decisions are either in favour or to the personal advantage *only* of *particular* people (e.g. the power-holder or people close to that person, such as family members, friends, political allies, or influential people), i.e. the abuse of power constitutes *egoism, nepotism, cronyism, corruption*, and/or *criminal conduct*. Alternatively, the decisions may be to the personal *dis*-advantage of *particular* people (e.g. political opponents, competitors, or enemies, or people with certain actual or perceived characteristics), i.e. the abuse of power constitutes *discrimination* and *despotic rule*.
*   When favours are granted or done for oneself or others, and when punishment is inflicted on others, it is *without (their) merit*, i.e. the people receiving the favour or the punishment *do not deserve it*.

- The favours and punishment, as well as the allocation of resources related to them, are *inefficient*, i.e. they inappropriately increase or reduce individual welfare and utility functions (material assets, opportunities and life chances, dignity, personal well-being, or development) and reduce public welfare (e.g. misallocation of funds supposed to be for the general public or particular purposes).
- The favours and punishment are not only *unfair* and *unjust* for those who receive them but also for everyone else.

The more unequally a social system is structured, i.e. the greater the disproportional empowerment, the greater is the possibility of misbehaviour such as abuse of power.[4] Even in strongly stratified and hierarchical social systems, abuse of power is usually frowned on, at least officially. For democratic systems, abuse of power not only causes too much damage but is simply not acceptable.

Exclusive Privileges and Prerogatives

However, even if disproportional empowerment has been made legitimate and legalised (e.g. by creating new or modifying existing laws, rules, regulations, formal positions, organisational structures, and processes) and even if disproportionately empowered individuals' conduct of office is in line with existing frameworks, disproportional empowerment nonetheless can establish some rather worrying cases. Disproportional empowerment creates a system of *exclusive, unequally allocated* privileges and prerogatives, of *unequally privileged* individuals and groups (Wrong 1971, pp. 132–133, Mousnier 1973, p. 10, Lukes 1974, p. 16, Ravlin & Thomas 2005, p. 976). Those who benefit are placed in (formal or informal) positions that better enable them to pursue, promote, and defend their vested interests, and to gain, secure, and enjoy their privileges and prerogatives. Differences between the privileges and prerogatives enjoyed by specific individuals and groups can be of various kinds (e.g. Thompson 1961, p. 486, Rueschemeyer 1986, p. 31, Beetham 1991, p. 50, Jacques 1996, p. 120, Jost & Elsbach 2001, p. 182, Braynion 2004, p. 449, Magee & Galinsky 2008, p. 11):

- formal and informal positions, social roles, status, power, and influence;
- material and immaterial resources and advantages (more, better access to, and/or usage of land, property, capital, institutions, infrastructure, information, knowledge, education, personal development, health and health care, lifestyle, life chances, and opportunities);
- responsibilities, tasks, and functions related to roles and positions (official, symbolic, and sense-giving actions; identifying and defining problems; setting agendas, goals, and objectives; making decisions; influencing decision-making processes; communicating; evaluating and appraising performance; and promoting, rewarding, and sanctioning others);

- opportunities to pursue one's interests, develop one's personality, and live one's life;
- satisfaction and personal well-being (e.g. sense of gratification, higher self-esteem, feelings of agency, personal and social identity, and happiness).

These are some of the most common, and typical, privileges and prerogatives that elevated people (rulers, members of the power elite, high society, and superiors) enjoy in stratified, hierarchical, autocratic, oligarchic, or otherwise non-egalitarian social systems. Nevertheless, for a democratic system based on the fundamental principles of freedom, democracy, equality, and justice, such an unequal allocation of privileges among its members raises serious questions about its legitimacy as well as alienating the majority of its members (who are excluded from these privileges and prerogatives).

Discrimination, Oppression, Exploitation, and Infantilisation

It is the nature – if not to say the main purpose and reason for, and justification of its existence – of disproportional empowerment to empower the few and to disempower the many. Those who are empowered enjoy their privileges and prerogatives as outlined in the previous sub-section. And those who have *no* or *less* privileges and prerogatives are *discriminated against*, *oppressed*, *exploited*, and *infantilised* because of, and via, disproportional empowerment:

- Disproportional empowerment *discriminates* against those who are either not able or not willing to acquire positions of status and power, i.e. the poor, the weak, the introverted, the decent, and those who belong to certain social categories that are stigmatised (e.g. certain races, ages, genders, nationalities, religions, family or social backgrounds, languages, professions, norms and values, attitudes, and behaviour – the list is endless and depends on the epoch and social context).
- Moreover, disproportional empowerment means systematic, and systemic, formal, psychological, and social *oppression* for those who are not among the privileged and powerful (Tajfel & Turner 1979, Ashforth & Mael 1989, Sidanius & Pratto 1999, Sidanius et al. 2004, Elstak & Van Riel 2005, Jost & Hunyady 2005, Musson & Duberley 2007). Oppression can take the form of crude physical or spatial oppression or more 'sublime' ideological, cultural, economic, social, or psychological oppression.
- Discriminated against and oppressed people are *exploited* – illegally and legally. Whereas illegal exploitation can only happen unofficially and in secret, legal forms of exploitation happen officially in broad daylight and are legalised, even celebrated. For example, organisational constructs like hierarchy and legal constructs like the standard employment contract are

specifically designed and maintained instruments for social dominance and exploitation (e.g. Scott 1990, p. 21, Beetham 1991, p. 58). Hierarchical social systems and disproportional empowerment are nothing more than the most common institutionalised and systemised forms of exploitation.

- Discriminated against, oppressed, and exploited people will have, and *shall* have in the opinion of the powerful, deeply internalised feelings of inferiority and 'learned helplessness' as well as moral ideas of obedience and serfdom, and will show the typical character and behaviour traits of 'the good subordinate' (e.g. Scott 1990, p. 58, Beetham 1991, p. 3, Bassman & London 1993, p. 22, Ashforth 1994, p. 759, Jacques 1996, p. 81, Alvesson & Willmott 2002, p. 619, Courpasson & Dany 2003, p. 1232, Diamond & Allcorn 2004, p. 26, Van Vugt 2006, p. 361).[5] This *infantilisation* of subordinates, the disadvantaged, and the vulnerable makes sure that they do not only function well because they *have to* but because they *want to* – that they accept how they are treated and cannot think of alternatives.

Altogether, it can be concluded that disproportional empowerment is not right, fair, or just. It is wrong, unfair, and unjust fundamentally and in principle because it represents comprehensively and thoroughly *institutionalised* forms of (potential) abuse of power, undeserved exclusive privileges, and prerogatives for the few, and discrimination, oppression, exploitation, and infantilisation of the many for the sake of the well-being of the few (e.g. Burnham 1941, p. 123, Mills 1956, p. 246, Gouldner 1960, p. 165, Levy et al. 2001, p. 2, Sidanius et al. 2004, p. 847).

Non-consequentialist Arguments against Disproportional Empowerment

One non-consequentialist argument against disproportional empowerment concerns legitimacy. *Legitimacy* means that an entity or phenomenon corresponds in key characteristics with a point of reference that is seen as the right and relevant standard. The right and relevant standards of social systems are their fundamental principles, norms, and values, which define the system as well as people's behaviour. One of the fundamental principles of the democratic organisation is that all of its members have *equal rights* and *equal power*, just as *all members of a democratic social system have equal power* – especially, and at least, equal rights and opportunities relating to political power and influence in and via governance, management, and decision-making. Equal rights and equal power are the points of reference for the legitimacy of a democratic system. Democratic organisations, and all their rules and regulations, structures, and processes as well as people's actions or inactions within and for the organisations, are legitimate as long as they are consistent with and comply with this, and other, fundamental democratic principle of equal rights and equal power.[6]

For *orthodox* organisations, disproportional empowerment is *not* a problem at all; on the contrary, it is a systemic, structural, and procedural part of all non-egalitarian and non-democratic social systems and social relationships (e.g. hierarchical organisations, stratified societies, and autocratic or oligarchic regimes). It is not only *not* a problem but a *necessary* constitutional and defining element of such systems. *In contrast,* (the possible emergence of) disproportional empowerment is a theoretical as well as practical problem, and a serious and constant challenge, for all social systems – such as the democratic organisation – that were built for and aim at providing all of their members with fundamental human, civil, and democratic rights as well as equal power and equal opportunities. It would be a *very* serious problem if a democratic organisation were hierarchical, autocratic, oligarchic, and oppressive and also privileged some of its members while treating others unfairly and unjustly. First, it would be a *serious inconsistency* because disproportional empowerment goes against the very purposes, values, and beliefs on which a democratic organisations is founded and run in the first place. And second, it would damage, if not to say destroy, its legitimacy because a hierarchised and oligarchised democratic organisation would be perceived as a betrayal of the ideals and promises of democratic organisations.[7]

Disproportional empowerment of the few and disempowerment of the many – i.e. social dominance, formal and informal hierarchies, elites, autocratisation, oligarchisation, autocracy, oligarchy, or similar regimes – do *not* correspond with the fundamental principles of the democratic organisation and the fundamental and inalienable rights of free individuals. In a social system that is based on democratic principles, it is neither legitimate nor acceptable for people's pursuit of their interests and social actions to create, contribute to, maintain, or increase inequalities in the fundamental rights, power, or opportunities of others – and, thus, advantage and empower some, and disadvantage and disempower others (Boehm 1993, p. 228, Helliwell 1995, p. 359). *No individual or group of people should be allowed to dominate other members of a social system or directly or indirectly cause their discrimination or disempowerment.*

Disproportional empowerment is detrimental to the idea and values of a democratic system. The idea that in a democratic system some are, or should be, more empowered than others (and probably even rule the system or parts of it), i.e. that rights and power should be allocated unequally among people, is inconsistent with a democratic system and, therefore, has no legitimacy. In fact, there is no merit to the idea that in *any* social system, constellation, or relationship a person or a group of people should be more powerful than others (except when a person or group has *legitimate* authority). If some are disproportionately empowered (while many others are disempowered), or if some disproportionately empower themselves without being formally entitled to do so, it is *illegitimate*. The emergence or existence of disproportional empowerment – of *any* form of social relationships reflecting systemic unequal power distributions and relationships that are not based on legal and legitimate authority – is *fundamentally* wrong. It is neither acceptable for, nor compatible with, a democratic system.

People's Part in the Emergence of Disproportional Empowerment

All in all, there are good and valid (consequentialist and non-consequentialist) arguments against disproportional empowerment – especially if it happened in a democratic system like the democratic organisation; disproportional empowerment goes against its fundamental and constitutional principles, and it threatens the original idea and the very purpose(s) and values for which the democratic organisation was built and exists. Once initiated, disproportional empowerment becomes a vicious circle from which democratic organisations struggle to escape. It is therefore paramount to know the possible *causes* and early beginnings of the process and what can, or should, be done to prevent disproportional empowerment happening.

The causes are *people* – or, to give a slightly more comprehensive and differentiated answer: in the social realm, things are not the result of abstract 'forces of nature' and do not just happen 'out of the blue'. In social systems there are *always* individuals behind abstract processes. Causes of events and phenomena can be found in people's ways of reasoning, feeling, behaving, and acting. Social and organisational processes are the direct or indirect result, or the intended or unintended consequence, of particular, identifiable individuals' behaviour, actions, or inactions. In trying to identify possible causes of phenomena in the social realm, it therefore makes sense to focus (also) on *concrete* individuals and how they and their actions relate to the emergence and continuation of the phenomenon in question.[8]

In this sense, there are people-related reasons for (the emergence of) hierarchies, autocracies, and oligarchies – the iron threat(s) of disproportional empowerment. If equal empowerment 'goes wrong', the causes can be traced back to (unintentional and intentional) actions or inactions, attitudes, and behaviours of specific, identifiable individuals – *certain* people with certain characteristics who strive for, cause, and maintain non-democratic social systems.

The following sub-sections examine several aspects of human behaviour that presumably are highly relevant to, if not to say responsible for, the emergence of disproportional empowerment, in particular:

- People contribute *deliberately* and *intentionally* to the emergence of disproportional empowerment ('anti-social perpetrators' such as organisational psychopaths, careerists, and aggrandisers).
- People contribute *accidentally* and *unintentionally* to the emergence of disproportional empowerment ('unreflective doers' such as extroverts and well-intentioned activists).

- People let the emergence of disproportional empowerment simply happen ('the disengaged', such as non-participating members and 'the silent majority').

People Who Consciously Strive for Power and Empowerment: 'Anti-social Perpetrators'

Mindsets, Personality Traits, and Patterns of Behaviour of Anti-social Perpetrators

In the section 'A Sequence of Disproportional Empowerment' earlier in this chapter, it was established that the vicious circle of disproportional empowerment, hierarchisation, and oligarchisation starts with people pursuing *anti-social interests*. 'Anti-social interests' can be defined as interests in gaining things (e.g. material resources, personal gains, privileges, prerogatives, status, roles, positions, power, influence, or other intangible assets) for oneself or for people close to oneself at the expense, and to the disadvantage, of others or the whole and without taking others' legitimate rights and interests into account and consideration.

Only certain types of people have, and pursue, predominantly anti-social interests – egoists, opportunists, careerists, (organisational) psychopaths, sociopaths, petty tyrants, egomaniacs, aggrandisers, and autocratic leaders (Bassman & London 1993, Ashforth 1994, Rayburn & Rayburn 1996, Vredenburgh & Brender 1998, Vickers & Kouzmin 2001, Maibom 2005, Boddy 2006, Restakis 2010).[9] Altogether, people with such mindsets, personality traits, and patterns of behaviour might be called *anti-social perpetrators*.

From a *psychological* perspective, it is relatively clear that anti-social perpetrators have a rather damaged, distorted, asocial, or anti-social personality. According to the 'Big Five' personality traits ('Big Five personality traits' 2018) scale their scores would be:

- mixed score in *openness to experience* (although probably appreciating unusual ideas, adventure, and the idea of engaging in risky behaviour and seeking out euphoric experiences (high openness), they actually demonstrate strong perseverance as well as dogmatic and closed-minded behaviour (low openness));
- high score in *conscientiousness* (strong tendency to be organised, dutiful, dependable, and self-disciplined, with planned behaviour, stubbornness, and obsession);
- high score in *extraversion* (high energy, strong emotions, attention-seeking, and strong tendency towards dominance);
- low score in *agreeableness* (despite portraying an *image* of themselves as compassionate, cooperative, trustworthy, and helpful, they are actually

fundamentally antagonistic, competitive, suspicious, and challenging towards others);

- high score in *neuroticism* (emotional instability and low impulse control, and a strong tendency to easily experience unpleasant emotions, such as anger, anxiety, depression, and vulnerability).

In a word, anti-social perpetrators predominantly demonstrate dogmatic and closed-minded behaviour (low openness to experience); show stubbornness and obsession (high score in conscientiousness); have a strong tendency towards dominance (high score in extraversion); are antagonistic, competitive, suspicious, and challenging towards others (low score in agreeableness); and can easily show negative emotions, such as anger or anxiety (high score in neuroticism).

Anti-social perpetrators have fairly narrow minds. The way they see the world, *what* they *can* see (and what they *can't* see), and *how* they see things and people is rather limited; they see things and people simplistically and pragmatically only through, and in regard to, their anti-social interests, and have a dualistic framework through which they make sense of things and people, judge, and act (e.g. order or disorder, domination or obedience, incentives or punishment, 'them' or 'us', win or lose, good or bad, right or wrong). They are only capable of thinking within their dualistic framework and pursuing anti-social interests.

In order to pursue their anti-social interests, they constantly seek opportunities and little powers for themselves. Anti-social perpetrators are rather power oriented and actively attempt to become (even more) powerful: formally by taking on positions and responsibilities, psychologically by acting within (their) dualistic frameworks, and socially by constantly manoeuvring within the social context, acting politically and tactically, and taking sides opportunistically. Despite of – or better to say *because of* – their dualistic framework, anti-social perpetrators are very flexible, capable, and willing to navigate the shallows of political or politicised social systems and to engage with organisational politics.[10] Mansbridge (1980, pp. 211, 214) called them 'the power-hungry' and talked about their 'lust for power'. Elster (1997, p. 14) even went so far as to say that participatory systems, especially, 'create a self-elected elite whose members spend time on politics because they want power, not out of concern for the issues'. It is *particularly* anti-social perpetrators who are keen to engage with, and use, politics to influence or even to dominate communication, discussions, and decision-making processes, so as to shape agendas, policies, rules, and regulations (according to their dualistic frameworks and anti-social interests). They use a range of tactics and a combination of formal and informal means in order to pursue their individual or group interests and, since they do so continuously and endlessly, will finally succeed (in getting their agendas and interests through and/or creating and obtaining formal positions and responsibilities for themselves). This, by the way, explains why most senior managers, politicians, and leaders are anti-social perpetrators. It is (predominantly) anti-social perpetrators, and *not* prosocial individuals, who have careers in prominent fields.

With their narrow minds, anti-social interests, and power orientation, anti-social perpetrators show predominantly, if not entirely, egoistic, egocentric, opportunistic, and anti-social behaviour.[11] Within the context of the democratic organisation, such behaviour might be subsumed under the term 'organisational misbehaviour' (Bassman & London 1993, Ashforth 1994, Rayburn & Rayburn 1996, Vredenburgh & Brender 1998, Vardi & Weitz 2004, Maccoby 2005, Maibom 2005). Within the democratic organisation, *organisational misbehaviour* means attitudes, behaviour, actions, or inactions that harm other people's human, civil, or democratic rights and their integrity or personal well-being, and that go against the democratic organisation's fundamental principles of freedom, democracy, equality, or justice or against the structures and processes of democratic governance and democratic management.

Anti-social perpetrators' organisational misbehaviour is *not* a direct result of their incompetence (or only to some extent), but (mostly) conducted *consciously* and *deliberately*, i.e. anti-social perpetrators show low levels of both moral reasoning and development, and ethical and decent conduct.[12] Their mindset, moral development, and corresponding behaviour are largely, if not entirely, at *pre-conventional levels of moral development*, i.e. stages 1 (self-interest) and 2 (obedience and punishment orientation) of moral development.[13]

To sum it up: very often, disproportional empowerment is triggered by *anti-social perpetrators*. Such people (can) only pursue interests that fit, and make sense within, their narrow minds, i.e. *anti-social interests*. In order to get their interests through, anti-social perpetrators seek, and need, *power* for themselves, i.e. they are rather *power oriented* and willing to engage in (organisational) politics. To achieve their goals they act opportunistically and commit *organisational misbehaviour*. Anti-social perpetrators misbehave *consciously* and *deliberately*, i.e. they show *low levels of moral development*. In so doing, they empower themselves but disempower everyone else. Anti-social perpetrators may not be psychopaths or even sociopaths in a clinical sense, but they definitely are in a common sense. With their anti-social interests, dualistic framework for making sense of things and people, authoritarian personality traits, power orientation, and organisational misbehaviour, they simply do not fit into a collegial social context or a fully fledged democratic system of equal rights – even worse, with their constant (successful) anti-social actions and manoeuvring, over time they can severely damage or even destroy such systems (i.e. by triggering the vicious circle of disproportional empowerment and thereby turning the democratic organisation into an autocracy or oligarchy).

The possibility – or threat – of the disproportional empowerment of the few (at the expense of the many), corrupt behaviour, concentration of power, and abuse of power is *always* present (Bogason & Musso 2006, p. 14, Hernandez 2006, p. 115, Erdal 2011, p. 196). As I have warned elsewhere (Diefenbach 2019, p. 559):

> There is *always* the danger that aggrandizers and organisational psychopaths, powerful leaders or power elites will emerge, pursue their own

interests, gain illegitimate influence and power, institutionalise their social dominance (as an autocracy or oligarchy), rule relatively uncontrolled (and undisturbed) and enjoy more or less undeserved privileges and prerogatives.

In this sense, anti-social perpetrators and their organisational misbehaviour represent a constant threat and quite a problem for the democratic organisation. The question is what the democratic organisation can do to stop anti-social perpetrators taking over and to keep them at bay.[14]

Keeping Anti-social Perpetrators at Bay

As outlined in Part I, the democratic organisation's formal principles, policies, regulations, structures, and processes of democratic governance and democratic management are the most comprehensive and robust one can imagine as means for organisations to considerably confine, check, and balance power; these means include the principles of 'good governance' and legitimate authoritative sources, democratic institutions of governance (especially separation of powers or 'checks and balances', and the principle of subsidiarity), democratic governing (especially democratic decision-making, transparency, and accountability), and democratic self-management, and representative and participative management. These formal arrangements of the democratic organisation can limit the conduct and personal manoeuvrings of anti-social perpetrators to *some* extent, but they cannot stop them completely (see the section on the formal disempowerment of the empowered few in Chapter 5). This is mainly so because anti-social perpetrators gain, or create for themselves, formal (administrative and/or managerial) positions of power and influence; conduct office in *their* way (i.e. in opportunistic ways); demonstrate a rather authoritarian management style; and simply use (or even abuse) formal policies, structures, and processes to their advantage, as tools to pursue their interests and to empower themselves *whatever the formal institutions, rules, regulations, policies, and settings.* And they are pretty good at doing it.

Additionally, psychological and ethical concepts (such as the idea of balance, a prosocial orientation or decent behaviour, and high levels of moral development) simply don't work for anti-social perpetrators; they are neither willing nor able to comprehend and apply such concepts. Anti-social perpetrators are cognitively and psychologically *unable* to understand prosocial or ethical concepts, just like colour-blind people can't see colours.

But if *they* cannot do it, perhaps *others* can. Since social dominance and disproportional empowerment are *relational* constructs – it takes superior *and* subordinate, oppressor *and* oppressed, and so on to establish the parties as well as their relationship – perhaps others might have the *social* means to handle and to confine anti-social perpetrators. In the section on the social disempowerment of the empowered few in Chapter 5, some social means were mentioned that can probably be applied to anti-social perpetrators, especially:

- *Demystification*: Knowledge and positions can, as I formulated in Part I, create social inequalities and power differentials when used and applied in certain ways and provide the possessor of that knowledge with the possibility of enlarging their status, to dominate others, rule over them, (mis) lead them, and exploit them (e.g. via management functions, leadership roles, and orthodox images of 'the manager' or 'the leader'). People can challenge such privileged and privileging knowledge and positions, and they can 'demystify' anti-social perpetrators' pretence of 'being important' and 'doing important things' (that common people cannot do).
- *Social control*: Democratic governance and democratic management mean that especially the holders of elevated formal positions, formal or informal leaders, and doers can not only be *formally* but also *socially* controlled. Hence, within a democratic system it is perfectly normal, and perfectly legitimate, to put social pressure on (powerful) members of the social system so that they 'behave decently', i.e. so that they abide by the democratic system's prevailing norms and values. It is possible to imagine that within a fully fledged democratic system members will disapprove of anti-social perpetrators' actions and provide appropriate reactions and sanctions (rewards or punishment).
- *Social actions*: Such reactions and sanctions can be provided via social actions, i.e. where the members of a social system sanction, oppose, and confine anti-social perpetrators and their behaviour directly or indirectly. There is a whole range of measures available for social actions, for example critical public opinion or voicing concerns; holding people accountable; discontent; open criticism and ridicule; disobedience; symbolic or concrete actions (political activism); and limitation, reduction, or even termination of people's elevated roles.
- *Organisational culture of equal(ising) power*: Together, demystification, social control, and social actions create and maintain an open and vibrant 'culture of contestation'. Such an (organisational) culture challenges, confines, and reduces the status, power, and influence of the powerful considerably and on a regular basis. It does not change anti-social perpetrators but it keeps them at bay.

Comprehensive and robust institutions (of democratic governance and democratic management) *and* actively engaged people (participating in the governance and management of the social system, decision-making, the conduct of business, and the social control of other members) provide – especially when combined with and mutually reinforcing each other – effective democratic control of the powerful and measures against (the emergence of) autocratic leaders and other

aggrandisers. There is compelling empirical evidence that people's full participation, social control, and social actions, enabled and supported by formal
institutions of democratic governance, can be quite effective in controlling
anti-democratic behaviour and holding anti-social perpetrators at bay (e.g.
Lipset 1952/2010, Ostergaard & Halsey 1965).

People Who Cause Disproportional Empowerment Accidentally: 'Unreflective Doers'

The Unintentional Empowerment of Unreflective Doers

Besides deliberate attempts to initiate and maintain the (vicious) circle of disproportional empowerment, people can also cause it *accidentally*. When Sutherland et al. (2014, p. 774) explored radical, participative democratic
alternatives to leadership in four social movement organisations (SMOs) from
2002 to 2009, they found some 'unintentional disproportional empowerment'. I provide a longer excerpt from their study because it offers quite
a vivid example of this phenomenon:

> In EG2 [Environmental Group 2] it was apparent that some members,
> especially the highly educated, were more 'competent' than others, and
> their cultural capital could create inequalities that disempowered other
> members. For example, one member had influence over the group
> because he took the lead on writing funding proposals. Educated to
> post-graduate level and with grant writing experience, this member was
> able to articulate the group's concerns in a framework that was compat-
> ible with the interests of funding bodies. During the process, EG2's con-
> cerns were subtlety altered to frame them in terms that the funding
> bodies would recognize. For some members, this steered the projects in
> directions that they were not comfortable with, even leading some mem-
> bers to leave, feeling that the focus and concerns of the group had drifted
> too far. In liaising on details with outside bodies some members of the
> organization unintentionally leveraged their cultural capital in order to
> advance projects, effectively occupying a position of leadership. This cre-
> ated difficulties for total participatory equality, as there was a danger that
> the most competent would determine what the organization did and
> how it did it, thereby marginalizing the less competent. ... The congru-
> ity of means and ends was essential for these organizations, so this kind
> of inequality was more than a minor detail. It was understood as symp-
> tomatic of an emergent inequality and hierarchical form of leadership.
>   Elsewhere, the informality of inter-personal relationships in ASG
> [Anarchist Student Group] led to the formation of cliques of the most
> enthusiastic members, who also shared accommodation. These groups

wielded considerable meaning-making power and instead of every member being invited to participate and having the potential to become a leadership actor, only a select few were in the 'in-crowd' who held exclusive discussions. These people had greater decision-making weight and gradually came to assume more permanent leadership positions.

Democratic and other alternative organisations offer more active, flexible, and opportunistic individuals more opportunities to act. Since empowerment in such organisations is predominantly a result of social processes, psychologically empowered people ('doers', 'change agents', 'initiators', extroverts, and more eloquent people) initially do not need much formal empowerment to empower themselves but use their social, interactional, and communication skills. They attend and speak at meetings more often (Mansbridge 1980, p. 187, Fenton 2002, p. 72, Burrows 2008), use their (more developed) skills of communication and persuasion and of rational argumentation, and demonstrate their emotions in tactical ways to influence others (Cheney 1995, pp. 175, 183, Morand 1996, pp. 544–545, Panayotakis 2011, p. 133, Malleson 2013, p. 99). They participate widely in all sorts of formal and informal decision-making in order to gain social power and influence. Rothschild-Whitt (1979, p. 524) concluded: 'Not surprisingly, members who are more articulate, responsible, energetic, glamorous, fair, or committed carry more weight in the group.' Malleson (2013, p. 99) called it the 'tyranny of the eloquent' and argued that:

> Democracy tends to be biased towards the powerful talkers (that is, the articulate and charismatic); the knowledgeable (that is, those who are educated, have been around for a long time, and have all the relevant information); the extrovert (that is, those who are loud, have more energy, emotionally thick skin, are sociable, and participate …); and the authoritative (that is, those who are seen as possessing authority by virtue of their identity).

Individuals who are more active in informal political processes, who are more present in committees, and who voice their concerns publicly or more vigorously 'behind closed doors' will increasingly dominate decision-making processes (Lake 2009). Over time, people's individual differences in style and intensity of communication and behaviour become more obvious; more active members progressively influence communication and discussions within a particular social system, whereas more passive members apply a 'wait-and-see' strategy. The former become psychologically and socially even more empowered and increasingly manipulate, dominate, and rule the latter, who become more and more disempowered. Members increasingly show the classic traits and behaviour of superiority and subordination, and dominance and obedience.

There can be a whole range of possible (psychological and sociological) factors that let people become more dominant, let them gain (informal and formal, unofficial and official) influence and power, and make them (unwillingly and unknowingly) contribute to the (unintended) emergence of social dominance and (informal) hierarchies, disproportional empowerment, and oppressive regimes:

- *Being more active, extroverted, impressive, and/or outspoken*: Personality traits, physical characteristics, 'natural' skills and talent (cognitive, emotional, social, and cultural), intelligence, abilities, self-image, motives, interests, experience, knowledge, likeability, attractiveness, and social skills that 'impress' others and have an impact on others.
- *Doing more*: Higher engagement, being more present, putting in more time and effort, attending meetings, and speaking at meetings.
- *Doing things of more relevance*: Conducting tasks, filling positions and roles, and taking on responsibilities that have relevance to the social system and (some of) its members.
- *Doing things differently*: Personal attitudes and behaviour (e.g. differences in way(s) of communicating, frequency and intensity of communication, showing emotions, reasoning and persuasion, social interaction, and style).

The important thing is that those who are empowered in such ways (by and large) neither intend for it to happen nor realise it is happening (Mansbridge 1980, p. 213); (in that respect) they are just *'unreflective doers'*. This differentiates them from the anti-social perpetrators described in the previous sub-section, i.e. the causes of, or motivational factors behind, their empowerment are different; anti-social perpetrators *consciously and intentionally* attempt to empower themselves, whereas unreflective doers become influential and powerful *accidentally and unintentionally*.

Turning Unreflective Doers into Reflective Practitioners

It is difficult to stop unreflective doers. And, in fact, the democratic organisation should *not* (attempt to) stop them. Unreflective doers actively contribute to and participate in democratic governance and democratic management – which members are supposed to do. It is the very idea of the democratic organisation to have *active* members, to have its members be *active* (in ways that are consistent with its fundamental principles and values). The formal principles, structures, and processes of democratic governance and management in the democratic organisation are deliberately designed and maintained to turn members into active participants, decision-makers, and doers. They are there in order to encourage, enable, and empower members, not to *dis*-empower them. Formal policies and measures of democratic governance and management (e.g. policies of collective decision-making, transparency and accountability, and participative and representative management) are only meant to confine the power of office-holders and possible misconduct – they cannot, and are not meant to, stop or limit (unreflective) doers per se.

But there is another way to tackle this problem than formal policies and measures. Unreflective doers are especially keen to play an active role in the democratic organisation because of their social, if not to say prosocial, orientation (see the sub-section '(Pro)social Orientation and Behaviour' in Chapter 6). People with a (pro)social orientation are psychologically and cognitively able and willing to see the social dimensions and implications of their reasoning and acting, i.e. to *reflect* on the social dimension of their behaviour. They are aware of that their thoughts, behaviour, and actions are influenced by and impact on others, they care about others and social systems, and they are concerned about their part within a social context, how they are seen and treated by others, and how they see and treat others. In this sense, if it were pointed out to them, unreflective doers would be able and willing to understand the negative consequences that their overtly active and engaging behaviour might have for the systems and processes of democratic governance and management, collaboration, and decision-making as well as for other members of the democratic organisation. They would be able and willing to problematise it and reflect on it – and to change their behaviour accordingly.[15]

In this sense, unreflective doers' different mindsets and motivation mean that the social measures a democratic organisation and its members can, or should, apply to stop them empowering themselves disproportionately (and disempowering others) are different (compared to the range of measures that can be employed for the social disempowerment of the empowered few). These social actions can take place in less challenging and more friendly, supportive, and cooperative ways than in regard to anti-social perpetrators because unreflective doers as such (or their personality or personal attitudes) are *not* 'the problem' – only the indirect and unintended consequences of their behaviour – and it can realistically be assumed that they would be concerned about the unintended consequences.

People Who Let Disproportional Empowerment Happen: 'The Disengaged'

Reasons for the Non-participation of the Disengaged

Disproportional empowerment can not only happen by people consciously or unconsciously triggering or even pursuing it but also by people *not* doing something about it. Any kind of organisation or social system depends on the active contributions and participation of its members – and alternative organisations like the democratic organisation even more so. The democratic organisation's structures and processes of governance and management are democratic, inclusive, and participative. Moreover, concerning the *social disempowerment of the empowered few*, measures such as *challenging privileging knowledge and privileging positions, social control, especially upward control*, using *social actions to confine leaders (and other aggrandisers) and their social dominance*, and an *organisational culture of equal(ising) power* (see the relevant sections in Chapter 5) indicate and underline the importance of *participation*. They *depend* on participation.

Insufficient participation, or even the absence of participation, can lead to the vicious circle of disproportional empowerment. This sub-section therefore looks at the possible causes of, and reasons for, a lack of participation (by the majority of people). The focus is on the *individual and psychological* dimensions of participation within an organisational context.[16]

As early as the beginning of the 20th century, the aforementioned German sociologist Robert Michels (1915/2001, pp. 36, 38) observed that:

> It is only a minority which participates in party [organisational] decisions, and sometimes that minority is ludicrously small. The most important resolutions taken by the most democratic of all parties, the socialist party, always emanate from a handful of the members. ... A small minority only will continue to avail itself of the right which the majority voluntarily renounces, and that the minority will always dictate laws for the indifferent and apathetic mass.

Very often, it is only a (small) minority of (very) active members that participates (fully and regularly) in organisational decision-making, whereas the majority does not participate regularly or at all (Ostergaard & Halsey 1965, p. 83, Heeks 1999, p. 3). Michels (1915/2001, p. 127) even called the passivity of members the 'apathy of the masses'. In a similar vein, Rothschild and Whitt (1986, p. 79) identified 'the age-old problem of member apathy' as one of the main reasons for the deterioration of democratic or participative organisations into fairly orthodox, hierarchical, or even oligarchic organisations.

Some reasons for a lack of participation are of a mere 'technical' nature. For instance, there is a negative relationship between the size of a social system (such as a group or an organisation) and the individual participation of its members; the larger the social system, the smaller the absolute and relative sizes of an individual's share of opportunities to participate and both shape and influence policies and collective decision-making (Dahl 1970, p. 99, Chickering 1971, pp. 216, 219, Ostrom 1971/1987, pp. 96–97, Abrahamsson 1985, pp. 46–47). Moreover, there can be severe time restraints; especially organisational members with operational tasks (e.g. frontline staff, professionals, and employees without line-management responsibilities), i.e. the ones who do the real work, usually have full workloads and little or no time for events or processes requiring participation (such as meetings and serving on committees or in formal or informal steering groups).

Then there is the broad scope and intensity of participation, especially in many alternative and participative organisations. As outlined in Part I, the democratic organisation has very comprehensive and robust formal institutions, principles, policies, regulations, structures, and processes of democratic governance and democratic management, such as rights and responsibilities stemming from co-ownership, the principles of 'good governance' and legitimate authoritative sources, democratic institutions of governance (especially separation of powers or 'checks and balances', and the principle of subsidiarity), non-hierarchical organisational structures, democratic governing (especially democratic decision-making, transparency, and accountability), and democratic self-management as well as representative and participative management. Via its institutions, the democratic organisation not only provides all means for *full* participation but also suggests to its members that they should fully govern and manage themselves, and fully participate in their self-governance, self-management, and participative and representative management.

However, what is definitely one of the main characteristics and strengths of the democratic organisation is probably also one of its greatest challenges for its members: self-governance, democratic management, participation, and engagement are required at a scope and to an extent that is, or can be, rather overwhelming and wearying. Participation can be quite challenging and demanding for people. For example, when Jane Mansbridge investigated social processes at a town governance meeting in a small town in Vermont, U.S., in the late 1960s and early 1970s, she found that 'in this town meeting, as in many face-to-face democracies, the fears of making a fool of oneself, of losing control, of criticism, and of making enemies all contribute to the tension that arises in the settlement of disputes' (Mansbridge 1980, p. 70). She concluded (p. 71): 'Participation in face-to-face democracies is not automatically therapeutic: it can make participants feel humiliated, frightened, and even more powerless than before.'

The challenges and 'psychological costs' of participation are greater for certain people, especially people who feel more comfortable in hierarchical or bureaucratic social systems, who are of lower social status, who have lower self-esteem and feel less confident in social contexts, who are shy or introverted, who lack the social skills to engage in communication and discussions with others, or who have philosophical, ethical, or cultural values (e.g. principles of seniority, goodness, decency, or harmony, or a fear of losing face) that do not encourage them 'to argue' or to disagree with others. 'Participatory democracy is hard work. It does not allow you to sit back and let others do your thinking, talking, and deciding for you' (Brookfield 2005, p. 177). Some people may find participation too much hard work and too challenging (Dahl 1970, p. 134, Mulder 1971, p. 32, Cleaver 2001, p. 51, Taylor 2001, p. 136, Greasley et al. 2005, p. 358, Hernandez 2006, p. 126, Burrows 2008, p. 295, Malleson 2014, p. 47). Quite understandably, people may find it easier, more beneficial for themselves, and better for their (psychological) health and well-being *not* to participate, or to participate at a minimal scale. Seen in that way, *non*-participation seems to be a rather rational choice. The psychological challenges und unpleasant experiences participation can represent for certain people therefore already explain to some extent why they pull out and, in so doing, leave the field open for the more active and robust members of the organisation.

Finally, there may be a rather sinister side to participation – even *full* participation at the highest level on the participation ladder – as 'joint decision-making' or 'codetermination' may not be as 'full' and 'equal' as the labels suggest. For example, concepts of empowerment and participation can be propagated and maintained in rather formalistic ways. Heeks (1999, p. 6) called this 'token participation', i.e. when all of the focus is on the formal institutions and processes, and not on the actual content and outcomes of participation. Participation then meets all formal requirements but lacks substance (Varman & Chakrabarti 2004, p. 199). In such cases, participation is often rather instrumentalised; it is introduced and managed *top down* and transformed into a tool to protect *existing* social arrangements, to pursue individual or group interests, and to secure the status, positions, privileges, and prerogatives of power elites (Diefenbach 2013a, pp. 217–218). For the majority of members, there remains little other option than to fit in and contribute as required while they are given the *feeling* of being empowered (Jacques 1996, p. 141, Jermier 1998).

It therefore may be appropriate to talk about *false* or even *fake* empowerment and participation; via converting potentially power-challenging concepts into managed and controlled techniques, empowerment and participation may be turned into institutionalised and non-perilous parts of the established abstract organisational order. The results of such *managed* and *controlled* empowerment and participation are that superiors keep, gain, and/or even increase their power and control and that power differentials are created, enlarged, and cemented. In this sense, empowerment and participation even contribute to the re-establishment of existing relationships of dominance and obedience and of superiority and subordination. (Almost) paradoxically, an increase in participation actually *increases* the power differences between members of the organisation: empowerment measures actually *dis*-empower (Mulder 1971, pp. 33–34, Shaw 2011, p. 129). The many are systematically excluded from any meaningful participation *via* participation. As Mulder (1971, p. 34) explained:

> The greater expert power of managers and specialists … refers to potential power. Those with expertise must communicate with the less powerful to influence them effectively and to become powerful. Thus, when there are large differences in expert power, the introduction of greater participation provides the more powerful with an opportunity to exercise their influence over the less powerful, and thereby make their greater power a reality.

In such cases, empowerment and participation are just empty rhetoric and yet another management concept for superiors to use to gain more influence over the actions of their subordinates, to gain more managerial and administrative control over potential opposition, and to suppress and exploit employees (Alutto & Belasco 1972, p. 117, Cheney 1995, p. 181, Greasley et al. 2005, p. 359). Empowerment and participation are then nothing more than mere buzzwords and window-dressing exercises to cover up authoritarian and oligarchic leadership, individuals' attempts to gain power, greater control and surveillance of employees, and oppressive work regimes (Cheney 1995, p. 180, Cornwall & Brock 2005). And the majority let all of this happen by participating in formally participative but actually non-participative governance schemes.

To conclude: it might well be that even in alternative organisations or the democratic organisation only a minority participates (fully and regularly), whereas some members, or even the majority, do *not* participate as expected and become 'the disengaged' for various reasons:

- *Technical reasons*: (Large) size of the organisation and time restraints on members participating routinely and effectively.
- *Institutional settings*: Self-governance, democratic management, participation, and engagement are required at a scope and to an extent that is, or can be, rather overwhelming.
- *Psychological challenges*: (Perceived) emotional, cognitive, and social challenges relating to participation, debates, discussions, negotiations, decision-making, and conflict resolution; individual psychological problems (e.g. anxiety), unwillingness to participate, and other motivational factors.
- *Fake participation*: Participation is just a formal window-dressing exercise; it consists of controlled empowerment and mendacious, empty rhetoric while increasing managerial and administrative control.

Measures to Enable Full Participation

The democratic organisation can do various things to overcome the obstacles outlined above and to achieve full participation. First, it should be noted that participation, *democratic* participation, is not *compulsory* but is, and always has to be, *voluntary*. 'Freedom from politics' (i.e. the freedom *not* to participate in collective action) is one of the fundamental rights and negative liberties of individuals and citizens (Held 1987, p. 291). Dahl (1971, p. 5) even talked about 'the right to oppose the right to "participate"'. Understood in this way, an obligation to participate would impose unwarranted paternalistic interference on members of democratic systems (Elster 1997, p. 13). Participation does not mean that everyone *must* participate but that everyone must be given equal *opportunities* and the means to participate in meaningful ways.

In this sense, the main challenge, even *obligation*, for the democratic organisation is to enable all of its members to participate *if they want to*, and to remove all obstacles that might prevent them from participating. To do this, it must make participation *attractive for individuals*. Participation must make sense *from the individual's perspective*, i.e. it must be of immediate relevance and advantage to the individual (Cleaver 2001, p. 48).[17] This is the case when governance, management, decision-making, and participation are about matters and affairs that are relevant and important to people's daily work and life context (e.g. Mulder 1971, pp. 35–36). Participation needs to start *there*. As explained in Chapters 3 and 4, in the democratic organisation participation happens from the bottom up.[18]

- Participation starts with the *individual*. Via self-managing their work as well as organisational issues related to their work, each individual member of the democratic organisation has complete control over their area of work and responsibilities.
- The individual then participates routinely and intensively in *self-managing groups*. Self-managing groups are organised and function according to democratic principles and standards. Within the democratic organisation they probably reflect the notion of *direct democracy* the most. Collective formal decision-making within these groups is open, transparent, inclusive, and deliberative.
- Self-managing individuals and groups may also create temporary or permanent self-managing institutions (e.g. project teams, steering groups, or committees). These self-managing institutions are at operational level, close to, and embedded in the individuals' and groups' work.
- Besides self-managing groups and institutions, members of the democratic organisation may also work with individual formal office-holders ('representatives' or 'managers'). Managers are elected or appointed, controlled, held accountable, and removable from office by those whom they represent. Against this backcloth there clearly is much scope for direct participation in the sense of collaboration and joint decision-making between individual members and managers.
- Finally, within a (larger) democratic organisation there are institutions of democratic governance and representative management at constitutional, strategic, and operational levels, such as boards, committees, councils, and/or assemblies. Participation here is fairly formalised and less direct. Participation of individual members mostly takes the form of receiving and providing information, debate and deliberation, giving opinions, and voting.

Such a bottom-up, individual-oriented mode of participation helps with the many psychological and motivational challenges participation might represent for certain people or members of a social system; with its focus on self-management, participation is not some sort of artificial, formal, and political process disconnected from individuals' daily work and routines. Participation is systematically embedded in all organisational structures and processes and part and parcel of people's individual work. It therefore comes more naturally and the level of reluctance is probably relatively low in democratic organisations. Moreover, practising (small-scale) participation on a daily basis psychologically empowers those who, for whatever reason, are not the most proactive, engagement-focused, and participative people. It enables and helps such people to develop personally and, thus, to be or to become more amenable to, capable of, and committed to participating in more collective institutions and matters (Pateman 1970, pp. 45–46, Kanter 1972, pp. 65–67).

Participation also empowers individuals *socially*. Individual-oriented participation provides equal opportunities in regard to the governance and management of the social system, or parts of it (Dworkin 1981a, b, Arneson 1989, p. 88, Helliwell 1995, pp. 360–361, Roemer 1998, Phillips 2006, pp. 18–19). All members of the democratic organisation have equal legal, managerial, and social status; have equal access to its institutions; enjoy the same rights; have equal opportunities to appropriate, access, and develop resources within the organisation; and are equally enabled to pursue their goals, to carry out activities they personally intend to do, to participate, and to shape the governance and social affairs of the organisation as they deem appropriate and necessary. Or, as Jussila et al. (2012, p. 18) concluded: 'It is through the participation, debate, learning, and mutual understanding that the members are empowered and true (i.e. well-functioning) democracy is realized.'

Preventing the Threat(s) of Disproportional Empowerment

Democratic organisations empower their members – but even in democratic organisations it may be the case that some people are not as formally, socially, or psychologically as empowered as others. Very often, empowering people does *not* empower people – or not all people equally. Even worse, empowering people may empower only *some* while *dis*-empowering *many* – the problematic phenomenon of *disproportional empowerment*.

Disproportional empowerment is caused by *people* – whether by contributing *intentionally or deliberately* to the emergence of disproportional empowerment ('anti-social perpetrators'), by contributing *unintentionally or accidentally* ('unreflective doers'), or by letting the emergence of disproportional empowerment simply happen ('the disengaged'). No social system and no comprehensive governance or control system is immune to the anti-social behaviour, ignorance, or apathy of its members.

The threat of the emergence of disproportional empowerment is very real for the democratic organisation (Diefenbach 2019). It is a *serious, profound,* and *fundamental* problem *especially* for fully fledged democratic systems like the democratic organisation, because they have everything to lose; if disproportional empowerment takes over, the democratic organisation continues to exist only on paper – actually, it has ceased to exist. Therefore, measures need to be in place that can prevent, or at least reduce, the potential for the emergence and existence of disproportional empowerment within the democratic organisation. And the democratic organisation *is* equipped with a whole range of means and measures that can (help to) prevent it from descending into oligarchy.

First, the democratic organisation has formal structures and processes of governance and management that empower all of its members – the highly active ones as well as the disengaged. As outlined in Part I (see the section 'How Equalising Empowerment Works' in Chapter 5), the democratic organisation's institutions are specifically designed and maintained to *empower and enable individuals* – especially those who are *not* empowered. Via the principles, concepts, and mechanisms of self-ownership, subsidiarity, self-management, and representative and participative management (*full* participation), *all* members of the democratic organisation are entitled, encouraged, and enabled to individually and/or collectively organise and manage their work, work-related issues, organisational affairs, and the organisation as a whole. Self-management and participation are attractive for all members because they are part and parcel of members' daily life and work and are of immediate relevance and advantage to them. Practising management and participation – and being one's own boss and manager – on a daily basis psychologically empowers and motivates more than anything else.

Second, at the same time the democratic organisation's formal structures and processes of governance and management are designed to *confine and control power*, anti-social perpetrators, their anti-social behaviour, and their conduct of business considerably. To this end, the democratic organisation's formal institutions of governance and management are fundamentally democratic, comprehensive and robust, and have features such as separation of powers or 'checks and balances', the principle of subsidiarity, democratic governing, democratic self-management, representative and participative management, full transparency, and accountability and upward control of all formal roles and positions, managers, managerial decision-making, behaviour, and conduct of business. Such formal institutions of fully fledged democratic systems such as the democratic organisation can limit (the abuse of) power and the organisational misbehaviour of power-oriented actors such as anti-social perpetrators – perhaps not completely, but to quite some extent (see the section on the formal disempowerment of the empowered few in Chapter 5).

Third, besides its *formal* structures and processes, the democratic organisation has *social* means and mechanisms that can handle and confine anti-social perpetrators and particularly empower, engage, and encourage the disengaged (see the relevant section on the social disempowerment of the empowered few in Chapter 5). Disempowerment of the powerful and empowerment of the powerless can especially be achieved through demystification of exclusive and privileging knowledge and positions (e.g. management positions and functions, leadership roles, and orthodox images of 'the manager' or 'the leader'); social control and upward control of office-holders, formal and informal managers, leaders, and overtly ambitious doers; direct or indirect social actions against anti-social perpetrators (i.e. open criticism and ridicule, disapproving reactions and sanctions, discontent and disobedience, and rewards and punishment), and an organisational culture of contestation and equal(ising) power. Such social measures work very well against anti-social perpetrators but also (can) turn unreflective doers into reflective practitioners because of their prosocial orientation.

All in all, one can conclude that the democratic organisation, like *any* social system imaginable, is *not* immune to fundamental threats (from within or outside). Disproportional empowerment *can* also happen in, or to, the democratic organisation. People can turn it, willingly or unintentionally, into an autocracy or oligarchy – which means its downfall. Nonetheless, of all organisations imaginable, the democratic organisation has the broadest range of legitimate institutions and measures in place to cope with anti-democratic or otherwise illegitimate deeds or processes in the most comprehensive, effective, and compelling ways. It may not always be enough, and it may not always succeed, but there is a very high probability that most democratic organisations – *if* their institutions remain strong *and* their members remain engaged – will withstand any direct usurpation or indirect erosion and will remain intact for a very long time.

Notes

1 'Empowerment of the few and disempowerment of the many' does not mean a dichotomy or a two-class system (ruling elite and 'the people'; the powerful and the powerless). Disproportional empowerment is more meant as a *relational* construct indicating that in any given non-egalitarian, complex, and diversified social system there are people who are systematically more empowered or less empowered relative to others.

2 In my book *Hierarchy and Organisation: Toward a General Theory of Hierarchical Social Systems* (2013a), I developed a general theory of hierarchical social systems that describes and explains in more detail how formal and informal hierarchies emerge and work.

3 For example, instead of, or in addition to people actively pursuing their anti-social interests it could also be that 'unreflective doers' and well-intentioned activists contribute unintentionally to the emergence of disproportional empowerment or that inactive members of the organisation let the emergence of disproportional empowerment simply happen by keeping silent and disengaged (see the section 'People's Part in the Emergence of Disproportional Empowerment' further down).

4 In its strongest form, this theorem converges with Lord Acton's famous aphorism, 'Power corrupts, and absolute power corrupts absolutely!'

5 See also the sections on the psychological and social disempowerment of the many in Chapter 5.

6 This corresponds with the argument made about the legitimacy of organisations, i.e. that it is only alternative and especially democratic organisations that appreciate

and enable the fundamental human, civil, and democratic rights of all their members and, thus, fully or at least partly meet democratic standards.

7 Sometimes it is argued that because alternative organisations are established and run 'for a good cause' (e.g. organisations of faith, activist organisations, charities, social enterprises, and political parties or movements), they can be absolved from the obligation to meet democratic standards and to grant all human, civil, and democratic rights to all their members and followers. It is argued that they might be more 'efficient' and 'effective' if they are structured and operate, for example, in hierarchical ways, uncontrolled, with little or no transparency. Nonetheless, such a 'pragmatic' argument does not hold sway. The end does *not* justify the means. Alternative organisations' integrity depends *especially* on their living up to their own principles, values, objectives, and claims. And it is *especially* alternative organisations that *should* demonstrate their commitment to the principles of freedom, democracy, equality, and justice in their own constitutional foundations, purposes, values, and governance and management structures and processes as well as in the way(s) they act (internally and externally) and conduct their business.

8 Such an approach is called 'methodological individualism' (e.g. Weber 1921/1980, p. 13, Hodgson 2007). However, from the model of the democratic organisation and its analysis it should be clear that the approach followed here does not deny the relevance and importance of institutions, the systemic and structural characteristics of social systems, or micro and macro phenomena. The model of the democratic organisation is based on methodological individualism *and* methodological holism / institutionalism (it is people *and* institutions that make a social system).

9 Particularly in neoclassical economics, anti-social perpetrators have been immortalised and celebrated as the epitome of rationality, as the 'rational actor', 'utility maximiser', or 'homo economicus'.

10 Vickers and Kouzmin (2001, p. 105) provided a fitting description of the modern careerist: they 'epitomize the "damaged" organizational actor, who appears to say and to act as is required through a process of adaptation which is beneficial for career advancement but disastrous for emotional health. This is evidenced by the apparent promulgation of "automatons" ... – colourless, dull and unimaginative individuals characterizing the quintessential "organization man" ... – an essentially calculating animal pursuing the necessities of organizational life.' Boddy (2006) called people with such mindsets 'organisational psychopaths'. According to him (p. 1462), organisational psychopaths 'are employees with no conscience ... who are willing to lie and are able to present an extrovert ..., charming façade in order to gain managerial promotion via a ruthlessly opportunistic and manipulative approach to career advancement.'

11 See the section on the social empowerment of the few in Chapter 5.

12 For example, Rayburn and Rayburn's (1996) study on organisational misbehaviour found a close relationship between personality traits and ethical orientation and called the behaviour and acting of people with low levels of moral development 'Machiavellianism'. In their words, this term describes 'an individual that has an immoral reputation for dealing with others to accomplish his/her own objectives, and for manipulating others for his/her own purpose' (p. 1209). According to them, a 'modern-day Machiavellian employs aggressive, manipulative, exploiting, and devious moves to achieve personal or organization objectives' (p. 1210). Moreover, and more worryingly, they also found evidence that Machiavellians are more likely to be ambitious individuals and that individuals of higher intelligence tend to indicate that they would behave less ethically.

13 For Kohlberg's taxonomy of the stages of moral development see Kohlberg (1973, 1976), Kohlberg and Hersh (1977), Kohlberg and Wasserman (1980), Crain (1985, pp.

118–136), Trevino (1986), Rahim et al. (1999), or Krebs and Denton (2005). For criticisms of Kohlberg's model see e.g. Barraquier (2011) or De Cremer et al. (2011).

14 This is a problem *only* for fully fledged democratic systems because for *non-democratic* systems (such as hierarchical organisations, autocracies, or oligarchies) confining anti-social perpetrators – or, more generally, disempowering the powerful (see Chapter 5) – is a non-issue and anathema.

15 One of the key criteria that differentiate *anti-social perpetrators* and *prosocial unreflective doers* is that the former *deliberately* whereas the latter *accidently* empower themselves and, in so doing, cause or contribute to the emergence of disproportional empowerment. Clearly, in real life the psychological and motivational aspects of a person are difficult to detect and it is hard to tell whether someone is doing something deliberately/knowingly or accidently/unknowingly, or whether someone has the personality traits of an anti-social perpetrator or those of a prosocial unreflective doer. But the litmus test would be their reactions if the consequences of their behaviour were brought to their attention; anti-social perpetrators would *not* be able to see such negative consequences and would reject such claims or would justify their actions, behaviour, and related consequences as inevitable (and would *not* do anything that could change this process in the future). In contrast, prosocial doers would be genuinely surprised and upset about such consequences (and their involvement, if not to say responsibility), would reflect on those events and their behaviour, and would be highly likely to change their behaviour. This is another criterion of distinction between unreflective, prosocial doers and anti-social perpetrators/psychopaths; the former are psychologically, cognitively, morally, and socially able to see, understand, and reflect on social phenomena, their behaviour, and its relevance to or impact on others, and are willing and able to make appropriate changes, whereas the latter are not.

16 *Participation* is understood here as defined in the section 'Participative Management' in Chapter 4, i.e. as *full* participation of *all* members on the basis of equal and democratic principles, or as 'complete control' and 'joint decision-making and codetermination' on the participation ladder.

17 For a list of some of the main advantages and disadvantages of democratic processes and participation in organisations, see, for example, Harrison and Freeman (2004, p. 50).

18 The five points correspond with the *levels of participation in self-management and representative management* presented in Table 4.1.

FINAL REMARKS

This book has made the case for a different type of organisation, the *democratic organisation* (Chapter 1). It has developed a comprehensive and detailed model of this type of organisation and shown how it works and functions (Part I), and it has discussed some key issues and concerns relating to it (Part II).

It has been argued, even demonstrated, that the democratic organisation has a whole range of strengths and advantages that make it (far) superior to any other type of organisation, especially to orthodox, profit-maximising or profit-oriented, hierarchical, and managerial organisations. In particular, the democratic organisation is based on, committed to, and functions according to the universal values and principles of *freedom* (self-ownership), *democracy* (democratic governance and democratic management), *equality* (equal rights and responsibilities of all members), and *justice* ('good governance' and the considerate conduct of business). The democratic organisation upholds, maintains, and defends these principles and values. It is the *only* type of organisation that upholds, maintains, and defends these principles and values comprehensively and robustly.

This book has shown in detail how *democratic organisations* can look; what their main features, characteristics, strengths, and advantages are; and *how* and *that* they can work. With their principles, structures, processes, democratic governance, and democratic management, democratic organisations are crucial, *indispensable* tools for establishing and guaranteeing fundamental and inalienable equal rights and opportunities for all members of a social system. People *deserve* to work in and for good organisations (and not to be oppressed, exploited, or belittled like they are in the absolute majority of current organisations). *We need to have institutions and organisations where everyone's freedom is appreciated and protected as much as possible; where people have equal rights and responsibilities; where people are entitled, encouraged, and enabled to manage their work, common affairs, and their lives by democratic means and according to democratic standards; and where every-one is equally empowered and treated fairly and justly.* The democratic organisation is the type of organisation that provides these conditions.

In my paper on Michels' iron law of oligarchy (Diefenbach 2019, p. 559), I argued that it is important

> not to pessimistically give in to the antisocial and anti-democratic pursuit of individual or group interests by individual psychopaths or a small power elite but to actively pursue and protect democratic institutions, including democratic organisations, against the enemies of an open society (I refer here to a book of the social philosopher Karl Popper, 1945/1980). More-over, we *can*, even *must*, do everything we can to set up and maintain democratic institutions and organisations – including, and particularly, in the economic sphere.

The democratic organisation is the best organisation possible – and it is pos-sible to establish and to maintain organisations like the democratic organisation. In every possible respect it is worth doing so.

BIBLIOGRAPHY

Abercrombie, N., Hill, S., & Turner, B. S. (1980). *The dominant ideology thesis*. London: Allen and Unwin.

Abrahamsson, B. (1985). On form and function in organization theory. *Organization Studies*, *6*(1), 39–53.

Ackoff, R. (1994). *The democratic corporation: A radical prescription for recreating corporate America and rediscovering success*. Oxford: Oxford University Press.

Ackroyd, S., & Munzio, D. (2007). The reconstructed professional firm: Explaining change in English legal practices. *Organization Studies*, *28*(5), 729–747.

Adler, P. S., Kwon, S., & Hecksher, C. (2008). Professional work: The emergence of collaborative community. *Organization Science*, *19*(2), 359–376.

Agirre, I., Reinares, P., & Agirre, A. (2014). Antecedents to market orientation in the worker cooperative organization: The Mondragón group. *Annals of Public and Cooperative Economics*, *85*(3), 387–408.

Akella, D. (2003). A question of power: How does management retain it? *Vikalpa*, *28*(3), 45–56.

Allard, J., & Matthaei, J. (2008). Introduction. In J. Allard, C. Davidson, & J. Matthaei (Eds.), *Solidarity economy: Building alternatives for people and planet – Papers and reports from the US Social Forum 2007*. Chicago: ChangeMaker Publications, 1–16.

Allard, J., Davidson, C., & Matthaei, J. (Eds.). (2008). *Solidarity economy: Building alternatives for people and planet – Papers and reports from the US Social Forum 2007*. Chicago: ChangeMaker Publications.

Altmann, M. (2014). Are co-operatives a viable business form? Lessons from behavioural economics. In S. Novkovic & T. Webb (Eds.), *Co-operatives in a post-growth era: Creating co-operative economics*. London: Zed Books, 176–193.

Alutto, J. A., & Belasco, J. A. (1972). A typology for participation in organizational decision-making. *Administrative Science Quarterly*, *17*, 117–125.

Alvesson, M., & Willmott, H. (2002). Identity regulation as organizational control: Producing the appropriate individual. *Journal of Management Studies*, *39*(5), 619–644.

Anderson, B. L., & Henehan, B. M. (2005). What gives agricultural co-operatives a bad name? *International Journal of Co-operative Management*, *2*(2), 9–15.

Anderson, E. (1999). What is the point of equality? *Ethics*, *109*(2), 287–337.

Anheier, H., & Themudo, N. (2002). Organisational forms of global civil society: Implications of going global. In M. Glasius, M. Kaldor, & H. Anheier (Eds.), *Global civil society*. Oxford: Oxford University Press, 191–216.

Appropriate technology. (2014). Retrieved 5 November 2014 from http://en.wikipedia.org/wiki/Appropriate_technology

Archer, R. (1995). *Economic democracy: The politics of feasible socialism*. Oxford: Clarendon Press.

Arneson, R. (1989). Equality and equality of opportunity for welfare. *Philosophical Studies*, *56*(1), 77–93.

Arneson, R. J. (2010). Self-ownership and world ownership: Against left-liberalism. In E. F. Paul, F. D. Jr. Miller, & J. Paul (Eds.), *Ownership and justice*. Cambridge: Cambridge University Press, 168–194.

Arnold, N. S. (1994). *The philosophy and economics of market socialism: A critical study*. Oxford: Oxford University Press.

Arnstein, S. R. (1969). A ladder of citizen participation. *Journal of the American Planning Association*, *35*(4), 216–224.

Aronson, E. (2001). Integrating leadership styles and ethical perspectives. *Canadian Journal of Administrative Sciences*, *18*(4), 244–256.

Ashforth, B. E. (1994). Petty tyranny in organizations. *Human Relations*, *47*, 755–778.

Ashforth, B. E., & Mael, F. (1989). Social identity theory and the organization. *Academy of Management Review*, *14*(1), 20–39.

Atzeni, M., & Ghigliani, P. (2007). Labour process and decision-making in factories under workers' self-management: Empirical evidence from Argentina. *Work, Employment and Society*, *21*(4), 653–671.

Azevedo, A. B., & Gitahy, L. (2013). Innovation, the cooperative movement, and self-management: From the technical school to the centers of research and development and the university in the trajectory of the Mondragón experience. In J. Shantz & J. B. MacDonald (Eds.), *Beyond capitalism: Building democratic alternatives for today and the future*. New York: Bloomsbury Academic, 95–126.

Bachrach, P., & Baratz, M. S. (1970). *Power and poverty: Theory and practice*. Oxford: Oxford University Press.

Bachrach, P., & Botwinick, A. (1992). *Power and empowerment: A radical theory of participatory democracy*. Philadelphia: Temple University Press.

Baggetta, M. (2009). Civic opportunities in associations: Interpersonal interaction, governance experience and institutional relationships. *Social Forces*, *88*(1), 175–199.

Barker, J. R. (1993). Tightening the iron cage: Concertive control in self-managing teams. *Administrative Science Quarterly*, *38*, 408–437.

Barley, S. R., & Kunda, G. (2006). Contracting: A new form of professional practice. *Academy of Management Perspectives*, *20*(1), 45–66.

Barraquier, A. (2011). Ethical behaviour in practice: Decision outcomes and strategic implications. *British Journal of Management*, *22*, S28–S46.

Bass, B. M., Waldman, D. A., & Avolio, B. J. (1987). Transformational leadership and the falling domino effect. *Group and Organization Studies*, *12*, 73–87.

Bassman, E., & London, M. (1993). Abusive managerial behaviour. *Leadership & Organization Development Journal*, *14*(2), 18–24.

Bauhaus Dessau Foundation & European Network for Economic Self-Help and Local Development (1996). *People's economy – Wirtschaft von Unten: Approaches towards a new social economy in Europe*. Dessau: Bauhaus Dessau Foundation.

Beetham, D. (1991). *The legitimation of power*. Basingstoke: Macmillan Education.

Bekkers, R. (2005). Participation in voluntary associations: Relations with resources, personality, and political values. *Political Psychology, 26*(3), 439–454.

Benello, C. G. (1971). Organization, conflict, and free association. In C. G. Benello & D. Roussopoulos (Eds.), *The case for participatory democracy: Prospects for democratizing democracy*. New York: Grossman, 195–212.

Benkler, Y., & Nissenbaum, H. (2006). Commons-based peer production and virtue. *Journal of Political Philosophy, 14*, 394–419.

Berger, P. L., & Neuhaus, R. J. (2000). To empower people: From state to civil society. In D. E. Eberly (Ed.), *The essential civil society reader: The classic essays*. Oxford: Rowman & Littlefield, 143–181.

Bevir, M. (2006). Democratic governance: Systems and radical perspectives. *Public Administration Review, 66*(3), 426–436.

Bevir, M. (2013). Governance as theory, practice, and dilemma. In M. Bevir (Ed.), *The SAGE handbook of governance*. London: SAGE, 1–16.

Big Five personality traits. (2018). Retrieved 6 January 2018 from https://en.wikipedia.org/wiki/Big_Five_personality_traits

Birchall, J. (2014). *The governance of large co-operative businesses: A research study for Co-operatives UK*. Manchester: Co-operatives UK.

Blumberg, P. (1968). *Industrial democracy: The sociology of participation*. London: Constable.

Boaz, D. (Ed.). (1998). *The libertarian reader* (1st paperback ed.). New York: Free Press.

Bob, C. (2011). Civil and uncivil society. In M. Edwards (Ed.), *The Oxford handbook of civil society*. New York: Oxford University Press, 209–219.

Bocken, N. M. P., Short, S. W., Rana, P., & Evans, S. (2014). A literature and practice review to develop sustainable business model archetypes. *Journal of Cleaner Production, 65*, 42–56.

Boddy, C. R. (2006). The dark side of management decisions: Organisational psychopaths. *Management Decision, 44*(10), 1461–1475.

Boehm, C. (1993). Egalitarian behaviour and reverse dominance hierarchy (and comments and reply, comments by Barclay, H. B., Dentan, R. K., Dupre, M.-C., Hill, J. D., Kent, S., Knauft, B. M., Otterbein, K. F., & Rayner, S.). *Current Anthropology, 34*(3), 227–254.

Bogason, P., & Musso, J. A. (2006). The democratic prospects of network governance. *American Review of Public Administration, 36*(1), 3–18.

Bondy, K., & Matten, D. (2012). The relevance of the natural environment for corporate social responsibility research. In P. Bansal & A. J. Hoffman (Eds.), *The Oxford handbook of business and the natural environment*. Oxford: Oxford University Press, 519–536.

Bovaird, T., & Löffler, E. (2009). Understanding public management and governance. In T. Bovaird & E. Löffler (Eds.), *Public management and governance*. Abingdon: Routledge, 3–13.

Bovens, M. (2006). Analysing and assessing public accountability: A conceptual framework. *European Governance Papers* (EUROGOV), No. C-06-01.

Bowles, S., & Gintis, H. (1993). A political and economic case for the democratic enterprise. *Economics and Philosophy, 9*, 75–100.

Bowles, S., Gintis, H., & Gustafsson, B. (Eds.). (1993). *Markets and democracy: Participation, accountability and efficiency.* Cambridge: Cambridge University Press.

Bowman, B., & Stone, B. (2004). Cooperativization on the Mondragon model: Alternative to globalizing capitalism. *Humanity & Society, 28*(3), 272–297.

Boyte, H. C. (2005). Reframing democracy: Governance, civic agency, and politics. *Public Administration Review, 65*(5), 536–546.

Braynion, P. (2004). Power and leadership. *Journal of Health Organization and Management, 18*(6), 447–463.

Breindl, Y. (2010). Critique of the democratic potentialities of the internet: A review of current theory and practice. *tripleC: Cognition, Communication, Co-operation, 8*(1), 43–59.

Brock, D. M. (2006). The changing professional organization: A review of competing archetypes. *International Journal of Management Reviews, 8*(3), 157–174.

Brookfield, S. D. (2005). *The power of critical theory for adult learning and teaching.* Maidenhead: Open University Press.

Brown, A. (2005). If we value individual responsibility, which policies should we favour? *Journal of Applied Philosophy, 22*(1), 23–44.

Brown, G., Lawrence, T. B., & Robinson, S. L. (2005). Territoriality in organizations. *Academy of Management Review, 30*(3), 577–594.

Brown, M. B. (2006). Survey article: Citizen panels and the concept of representation. *Journal of Political Philosophy, 14*(2), 203–225.

Bryant, M., & Cox, J. W. (2003). The telling of violence: Organizational change and atrocity tales. *Journal of Organizational Change Management, 16*(5), 567–583.

Burczak, T. A. (2006). *Socialism after Hayek.* Ann Arbor: University of Michigan Press.

Burnham, J. (1941). *The managerial revolution.* New York: John Day Company.

Burns, J. M. (1978). *Leadership.* New York: Harper & Row.

Burns, T. (1961). Micropolitics: Mechanisms of institutional change. *Administrative Science Quarterly, 6*(3), 257–281.

Burrows, P. (2008). Parecon and workers' self-management: Reflections on Winnipeg's Mondragon Bookstore & Coffee House Collective. In C. Spannos (Ed.), *Real utopia: Participatory society for the 21st century,* Oakland: AK Press, 275–305.

Canovan, M. (2008). The people. In J. S. Dryzek, B. Honig, & A. Phillips (Eds), *The Oxford handbook of political theory.* Oxford: Oxford University Press, 349–362.

Carlyle, T. (1841/1888). *On heroes, hero-worship and the heroic in history.* New York: Fredrick A. Stokes & Brother.

Carnoy, M., & Shearer, D. (1980). *Economic democracy: The challenge of the 1980s.* Armonk: M. E. Sharpe.

Carson, K. A. (2008). *Organization theory: A libertarian perspective.* Charleston: BookSurge.

Carter, I., Kramer, M. H., & Steiner, H. (Eds.). (2007). *Freedom: A philosophical anthology.* Oxford: Blackwell.

Casella, A., & Frey, B. (1992). Federalism and clubs: Towards an economic theory of overlapping political jurisdictions. *European Economic Review, 36,* 639–646.

Casey, C. (1999). 'Come, join our family': Discipline and integration in corporate organizational Culture. *Human Relations, 52*(1), 155–176.

Caspary, W. R. (2004). Prospects and limits of a democratic economy. *Humanity & Society, 28*(3), 235–253.

Cater, J. J., Collins, L. A., & Beal, B. D. (2017). Ethics, faith, and profit: Exploring the motives of the U.S. Fair Trade social entrepreneurs. *Journal of Business Ethics, 146*(1), 185–201.

Chandler, A. D. (1962). *Strategy and structure: Chapters in the history of the industrial enterprise.* Cambridge, MA: MIT Press.

Chartier, G., & Johnson, C. W. (Eds.). (2012). *Markets not capitalism: Individualist anarchism against bosses, inequality, corporate power, and structural poverty.* London: Minor Compositions.

Chekroun, P. (2008). Social control behavior: The effects of social situations and personal implication on informal social sanctions. *Social and Personality Psychology Compass, 2*(6), 2141–2158.

Chen, C. C., Zhang, A. Y., & Wang, H. (2014). Enhancing the effects of power sharing on psychological empowerment: The roles of management control and power distance orientation. *Management and Organization Review, 10*(1), 135–156.

Cheney, G. (1995). Democracy in the workplace: Theory and practice from the perspective of communication. *Journal of Applied Communication Research, 23*(3), 167–200.

Cheney, G. (2002). *Values at work: Employee participation meets market pressure at Mondragón* (updated ed.). Ithaca: Cornell University Press.

Chickering, A. W. (1971). How many make too many? In C. G. Benello & D. Roussopoulos (Eds.), *The case for participatory democracy: Prospects for democratizing democracy.* New York: Grossman, 213–227.

Chisolm, L. B. (1995). Accountability of nonprofit organizations and those who control them: The legal framework. *Nonprofit Management & Leadership, 6*(2), 141–156.

Christman, J. (1994). *The myth of property: Towards an egalitarian theory of ownership.* Oxford: Oxford University Press.

CICOPA. (2004). *World declaration on worker cooperatives.* Brussels: International Organisation of Industrial, Artisanal and Service Producers' Cooperatives.

Cleaver, F. (2001). Institutions, agency and the limitations of participatory approaches to development. In B. Cooke & U. Kothari (Eds.), *Participation: The new tyranny?* London: Zed Books, 36–55.

Clegg, C., & Walsh, S. (2004). Change management: Time for a change! *European Journal of Work and Organizational Psychology, 13*(2), 217–239.

Coase, R. H. (1937). The nature of the firm. *Economica, 4*(16), 386–405.

Cohen, J. (1998). Democracy and liberty. In J. Elster (Ed.), *Deliberative democracy.* Cambridge: Cambridge University Press, 185–231.

Cohen, J., & Rogers, J. (Eds.). (1995). *Associations and democracy.* London: Verso.

Collier, J., & Esteban, R. (1999). Governance in the participative organisation: Freedom, creativity and ethics. *Journal of Business Ethics, 21*, 173–188.

Conger, J. A., & Kanungo, R. N. (1988). The empowerment process: Integrating theory and practice. *Academy of Management Review, 13*(3), 471–482.

Connelly, J., Smith, G., Benson, D., & Saunders, C. (2012). *Politics and the environment: From theory to practice* (3rd ed.). London: Routledge.

Considine, M., & Afzal, K. A. (2013). Legitimacy. In M. Bevir (Ed.), *The SAGE handbook of governance.* London: SAGE, 369–385.

Coopey, J., & Burgoyne, J. (2000). Politics and organisational learning. *Journal of Management Studies, 37*(6), 869–885.

Cornforth, C. (1995). Patterns of cooperative management: Beyond the degeneration thesis. *Economic and Industrial Democracy, 16*, 487–523.

Cornforth, C., Thomas, A., Spear, R., & Lewis, J. (1988). *Developing successful cooperatives.* London: SAGE.

Cornwall, A. (2008). Unpacking 'participation': Models, meanings and practices. *Community Development Journal*, *43*(3), 269–283.

Cornwall, A., & Brock, K. (2005). What do buzzwords do for development policy? A critical look at 'participation', 'empowerment' and 'poverty reduction'. *Third World Quarterly*, *26*(7), 1043–1060.

Coser, L. (1956). *The functions of social conflict*. New York: Free Press.

Cotton, J. L., Vollrath, D. A., Froggatt, K. L., Lengnick-Hall, M. L., & Jennings, K. R. (1988). Employee participation: Diverse forms and different outcomes. *Academy of Management Review*, *13*(1), 8–22.

Courpasson, D. (2000). Managerial strategies of domination: Power in soft bureaucracies. *Organization Studies*, *21*(1), 141–161.

Courpasson, D., & Clegg, S. R. (2006). Dissolving the iron cages? Tocqueville, Michels, bureaucracy and the perpetuation of elite power. *Organization*, *13*(3), 319–343.

Courpasson, D., & Dany, F. (2003). Indifference or obedience? Business firms as democratic hybrids. *Organization Studies*, *24*(8), 1231–1260.

Coutu, D. L. (2005). Putting leaders on the couch: A conversation with Manfred F. R. Kets de Vries. In *Harvard Business Review on the mind of the leader*. Boston: Harvard Business School, 53–71.

Crain, W. C. (1985). *Theories of development: Concepts and applications*. Englewood Cliffs: Prentice-Hall.

Crowe, D. (2013). Between the market and the state. In R. Harrison (Ed.), *People over capital: The co-operative alternative to capitalism*. Oxford: New Internationalist Publications, 76–84.

Crowley, M. (2012). Control and dignity in professional, manual and service-sector employment. *Organization Studies*, *33*(10), 1383–1406.

Curtis, J. E., Baer, D. E., & Grabb, E. G. (2001). Nations of joiners: Explaining voluntary association membership in democratic societies. *American Sociological Review*, *66*(6), 783–805.

Dachler, P. H., & Wilpert, B. (1978). Conceptual dimensions and boundaries of participation in organizations: A critical evaluation. *Administrative Science Quarterly*, *23*(1), 1–39.

Dafermos, G. (2012). Authority in peer production: The emergence of governance in the FreeBSD project. *Journal of Peer Production*, *1*. Retrieved 11 August 2013 from http://peerproduction.net/issues/issue-1/peer-reviewed-papers/authority-in-peer-production

Dahl, R. A. (1970). *After the revolution? Authority in a good society*. New Haven: Yale University Press.

Dahl, R. A. (1971). *Polyarchy: Participation and opposition*. New Haven: Yale University Press.

Dahl, R. A. (1979/2006). Procedural democracy. In R. E. Goodin & P. Pettit (Eds.), *Contemporary political philosophy* (2nd ed.). Oxford: Blackwell, 107–125.

Dahl, R. A. (1985). *A preface to economic democracy*. Berkeley: University of California Press.

Dahl, R. A. (1998). *On democracy*. New Haven: Yale University Press.

Darke, P. R., & Chaiken, S. (2005). The pursuit of self-interest: Self-interest bias in attitude judgment and persuasion. *Journal of Personality and Social Psychology*, *89*(6), 864–883.

Davidson, C. (2012). The Mondragon cooperatives and 21st century socialism: A review of five books with radical critiques and new ideas. *Perspectives on Global Development and Technology*, *11*, 229–243.

Davis, P. (2001). The governance of co-operatives under competitive condition: Issues, processes and culture. *Corporate Governance, 1*(1), 28–39.

De Cremer, D., van Dick, R., Tenbrunsel, A., Pillutla, M., & Murnighan, J. K. (2011). Understanding ethical behavior and decision making in management: A behavioural business ethics approach. *British Journal of Management, 22*, S1–S4.

de Jong, G., & van Witteloostuijin, A. (2004). Successful corporate democracy: Sustainable cooperation of capital and labor in the Dutch Breman Group. *Academy of Management Executive, 18*(3), 54–66.

Deem, R., & Brehony, K. J. (2005). Management as ideology: The case of 'new managerialism' in higher education. *Oxford Review of Education, 31*(2), 217–235.

Defourny, J., & Develtere, P. (1999). The social economy: The worldwide making of a third sector. In J. Defourny, P. Develtere, & B. Fonteneau (Eds.), *Social economy north and south.* Leuven/Liège: Katholieke Universiteit Leuven, Hoger Instituut voor de Arbeid, Université de Liège, and Centre d'Économie Sociale, 17–47.

Deutsch, M. (1985). *Distributive justice.* New Haven: Yale University Press.

Deutsch, M. (1986). Cooperation, conflict, and justice. In H. W. Bierhoff, R. L. Cohen, & J. Greenberg (Eds.), *Justice in social relations.* New York: Plenum Press, 3–18.

Deutscher Bundestag. (2018). *Basic Law for the Federal Republic of Germany, 23 May 1949, last amended on 13 July 2017.* Berlin: German Bundestag Public Relations Division.

Diamond, M. A., & Allcorn, S. (2004). Moral violence in organizations: Hierarchic dominance and the absence of potential space. *Organisational & Social Dynamics, 4*(1), 22–45.

Diefenbach, T. (2009a). *Management and the dominance of managers.* London: Routledge.

Diefenbach, T. (2009b). New public management in public sector organizations: The dark sides of managerialistic 'enlightenment'. *Public Administration, 87*(4), 892–909.

Diefenbach, T. (2013a). *Hierarchy and organisation: Toward a general theory of hierarchical social systems.* London: Routledge.

Diefenbach, T. (2013b). Interests behind managers' decisions: Why and when do managers decide for managerial or alternative concepts? *International Journal of Management and Decision Making, 12*(4), 413–432.

Diefenbach, T. (2016). Empowerment of the few and disempowerment of the many: Disempowerment in Thai 'One Tambon One Product' organisations (OTOPs). *South East Asian Journal of Management, 10*(1), 30–53.

Diefenbach, T. (2019). Why Michels' iron law of oligarchy is not an iron law – and how democratic organisations can stay 'oligarchy-free'. *Organization Studies, 40*(4), 545–562.

Diefenbach, T., & Sillince, J. A. A. (2011). Formal and informal hierarchy in different types of organisations. *Organization Studies, 32*(11), 1515–1537.

Doran, J. (2013). Working towards economic democracy. In R. Harrison (Ed.), *People over capital: The co-operative alternative to capitalism.* Oxford: New Internationalist Publications, 85–102.

Doucouliagos, C. (1995). Worker participation and productivity in labor-managed and participatory capitalist firms: A meta-analysis. *Industrial and Labor Relations Review, 49*(1), 58–77.

Drucker, P. F. (1954). *The practice of management.* New York: Harper and Row.

Dutcher, D. D., Finley, J. C., Luloff, A. E., & Johnson, J. B. (2007). Connectivity with nature as a measure of environmental values. *Environment and Behavior, 39*(4), 474–493.

Dworkin, R. (1981a). What is equality? Part 1: Equality of welfare. *Philosophy & Public Affairs*, *10*(3), 185–246.

Dworkin, R. (1981b). What is equality? Part 2: Equality of resources. *Philosophy & Public Affairs*, *10*(4), 283–345.

Eberly, D. E. (2000). The meaning, origins, and applications of civil society. In D. E. Eberly (Ed.), *The essential civil society reader: The classic essays*. Oxford: Rowman & Littlefield, 3–29.

Ebrahim, A. (2003). Accountability in practice: Mechanisms for NGOs. *World Development*, *31*(5), 813–829.

Efficiency. (2019). Retrieved 18 February 2019 from https://en.wikipedia.org/wiki/Efficiency

Eisner, M. A. (2004). Corporate environmentalism, regulatory reform, and industry self-regulation: Toward genuine regulatory reinvention in the United States. *Governance: An International Journal of Policy, Administration, and Institutions*, *17*(2), 145–167.

Ekbia, H., & Kling, R. (2005). Network organizations: Symmetric cooperation or multivalent negotiation? *Information Society*, *21*(3), 155–168.

Eliasoph, N. (2011). Civil society and civility. In M. Edwards (Ed.), *The Oxford handbook of civil society*. New York: Oxford University Press, 220–231.

Ellerman, D. (1992). *Property and contract in economics: The case for economic democracy*. Cambridge, MA: Basil Blackwell.

Ellwood, W. (2013). Can co-ops crowd out capitalism? In R. Harrison (Ed.), *People over capital: The co-operative alternative to capitalism*. Oxford: New Internationalist Publications, 31–39.

Elstak, M. N., & Van Riel, C. B. M. (2005). Organizational identity change: An alliance between organizational identity and identification. *Academy of Management Best Conference Paper 2005 MOC*: E1–E6.

Elster, J. (1997). The market and the forum: Three varieties of political theory. In J. Bohman & W. Rehg (Eds.), *Deliberative democracy: Essays on reason and politics*. Cambridge, MA: MIT Press, 3–33.

Employment Rights Act 1996. (2019). Retrieved 30 March 2019 from https://www.legislation.gov.uk/ukpga/1996/18/contents

Empson, L., & Chapman, C. (2006). Partnership versus corporation: Implications of alternative forms of governance. In R. Suddaby & R. Greenwood (Eds.), *Professional service firms: Research in the sociology of organizations* (Vol. 24). London: Elsevier, 139–170.

Empson, L., Muzio, D., Broschak, J. P., & Hinings, B. (2015). Researching professional service firms: An introduction and overview. In L. Empson, D. Muzio, J. P. Broschak, & B. Hinings (Eds.), *Oxford handbook of professional service firms*. Oxford: Oxford University Press, 1–24.

Epstein, R. (1987/1998). Self-interest and the constitution. In D. Boaz (Ed.), *The libertarian reader* (1st paperback ed.). New York: Free Press, 42–48.

Erdal, D. (2011). *Beyond the corporation: Humanity working*. London: Bodley Head.

Esmark, A. (2008). Democratic accountability and network governance: Problems and potentials. In E. Sørensen & J. Torfing (Eds.), *Theories of democratic network governance*. London: Palgrave Macmillan, 274–296.

Ethnoecology. (2018). Retrieved 5 August 2018 from https://en.wikipedia.org/wiki/Ethnoecology

Fairtlough, G. (2005). *The three ways of getting things done: Hierarchy, heterarchy and responsible autonomy in organizations*. Greenways: Triarchy.

Fayol, H. (1949). *General and industrial management.* London: Pitman.

Fenton, T. L. (2002). *The democratic company.* Washington: World Dynamics.

Fernandez, S., & Moldogaziev, T. (2013). Employee empowerment, employee attitudes, and performance: Testing a causal model. *Public Administration Review, 73*(3), 490–506.

Fischer, F. (2006). Participatory governance as deliberate empowerment: The cultural politics of discursive space. *American Review of Public Administration, 36*(1), 19–40.

Fisher, A. (2013). Is there a co-operative solution to sustainable development? In R. Harrison (Ed.), *People over capital: The co-operative alternative to capitalism.* Oxford: New Internationalist Publications, 139–153.

Foley, J. R., & Polanyi, M. (2006). Workplace democracy: Why bother? *Economic and Industrial Democracy, 27*(1), 173–195.

Fournier, V. (2002). Utopianism and the cultivation of possibilities: Grassroots movements of hope. In M. Parker (Ed.), *Utopia and organization.* Oxford: Blackwell, 189–216.

Francescato, D., & Aber, M. S. (2015). Learning from organizational theory to build organizational empowerment. *Journal of Community Psychology, 43*(6), 717–738.

Freeman, R. E. (1983). Strategic management: A stakeholder approach. *Advances in Strategic Management, 1,* 31–60.

Fried, B. (2004). Left-libertarianism: A review essay. *Philosophy and Public Affairs, 32*(1), 66–92.

Friedman, M. (1962/1982). *Capitalism and freedom.* Chicago: University of Chicago Press.

Fromm, E. (1956/1971). *The sane society.* London: Routledge.

Fung, A. (2003). Associations and democracy: Between theories, hopes, and realities. *Annual Review of Sociology, 29,* 515–539.

Fung, A., & Wright, E. O. (2001). Deepening democracy: Innovations in empowered local governance. *Politics and Society, 29*(1), 5–41.

Gand, S. (2010). Analyzing and comparing professional service firms over services, time and space: Proposition of a foundation framework. EGOS, July 2010, Lisbon, Portugal, hal-00708241.

Gandz, J., & Bird, F. G. (1996). The ethics of empowerment. *Journal of Business Ethics, 15*(4), 383–392.

Geng, L., Xu, J., Ye, L., Zhou, W., & Zhou, K. (2015). Connections with nature and environmental behaviors. *PLOS ONE, 10*(5), 1–11.

Gerber, A. S., Huber, G., Doherty, D., Dowling, C. M., & Ha, S. E. (2010). Personality and political attitudes: Relationships across issue domains and political contexts. *American Political Science Review, 104*(1), 111–133.

Gibson-Graham, J. K., Cameron, J., & Healy, S. (2013). *Take back the economy: An ethical guide for transforming our communities.* Minneapolis: University of Minnesota Press.

Gifford, R., & Nilsson, A. (2014). Personal and social factors that influence pro-environmental concern and behaviour: A review. *International Journal of Psychology, 49*(3), 141–157.

Gill, R. (2003). Change management – or change leadership? *Journal of Change Management, 3*(4), 307–318.

Girard, M., & Stark, D. (2002). Distributing intelligence and organising diversity in new-media projects. *Environment and Planning A, 34*(11), 1927–1949.

Gouldner, A. W. (1960). The norm of reciprocity: A preliminary statement. *American Sociological Review, 25*(2), 161–178.

Grant, A. M., & Berg, J. M. (2010). Prosocial motivation at work: How making a difference makes a difference. In K. Cameron & G. Spreitzer (Eds.), *Handbook of positive organizational scholarship*. Oxford: Oxford University Press, 28–44.

Greasley, K., Bryman, A., Dainty, A., King, N., & Price, A. (2005). Perceptions of empowerment in construction projects. *Employee Relations, 27*(4/5), 354–368.

Greenwood, J. (2007). Organized civil society and democratic legitimacy in the European Union. *British Journal of Political Science, 37*(2), 333–357.

Greenwood, R., Deephouse, D. L., & Li, S. (2007). Ownership and performance of professional service firms. *Organization Studies, 28*(2), 219–238.

Gregory, D. (2013). Towards a new economy based on co-operation. In R. Harrison (Ed.), *People over capital: The co-operative alternative to capitalism*. Oxford: New Internationalist Publications, 58–75.

Grey, C. (1999). 'We are all managers now'; 'We always were'; on the development and demise of management. *Journal of Management Studies, 36*(5), 561–585.

Grimond, J. (1971). Participation in politics. In British Humanist Association (Eds.), *Towards an open society: Ends and means in British politics*. London: Pemberton Books, 93–103.

Grint, K. (2010). The sacred in leadership: Separation, sacrifice and silence. *Organization Studies, 31*(1), 89–107.

Groeneveld, H. (2013). Cooperative banks and the real economy: A long-standing and close connection. In B. Roelants (Ed.), *Cooperative growth for the 21st century*. Brussels: International Cooperative Alliance, 23–29.

Groeneveld, J. M. (2011). Morality and integrity in cooperative banking. *Ethical Perspectives, 18*(4), 515–540.

Guérin, D. (1980/2005). *No gods, no masters*. Oakland: AK Press.

Guimerà, R., Danon, L., Díaz-Guilera, A., Giralt, F., & Arenas, A. (2006). The real communication network behind the formal chart: Community structure in organizations. *Journal of Economic Behavior and Organization, 61*(4), 653–667.

Hales, C. (2002). Bureaucracy-lite and continuities in managerial work. *British Journal of Management, 13*(1), 51–66.

Halpin, D. R. (2006). The participatory and democratic potential and practice of interest groups: Between solidarity and representation. *Public Administration, 84*(4), 919–940.

Hansmann, H. (1996). *The ownership of enterprise*. Cambridge, MA: Harvard University Press.

Haque, M. S. (2013). Non-governmental organizations. In M. Bevir (Ed.), *The SAGE handbook of governance*. London: SAGE, 330–341.

Harlacher, D., & Reihlen, M. (2014). Governance of professional service firms: A configurational approach. *Business Research, 7*, 125–160.

Harrison, J., & Freeman, E. R. (2004). Is organizational democracy worth the effort? *Academy of Management Executive, 18*(3), 49–53.

Harrison, R. (2013). Introduction. In R. Harrison (Ed.), *People over capital: The co-operative alternative to capitalism*. Oxford: New Internationalist Publications, 10–18.

Heeks, R. (1999). *The tyranny of participation in information systems: Learning from development projects*, Working Paper No. 4, Institute for Development Policy and Management, University of Manchester.

Held, D. (1987). *Models of democracy*. Cambridge: Polity Press.

Held, D. (1992/2006). Democracy: From city-states to a cosmopolitan order? In R. E. Goodin & P. Pettit (Eds.), *Contemporary political philosophy* (2nd ed.). Oxford: Blackwell, 674–696.

Heller, F. A., Drenth, P. J. D., Koopman, P., & Rus, V. (1977). A longitudinal study in participative decision making. *Human Relations*, *30*, 567–587.

Heller, F., Pusic, E., Strauss, G., & Wilpert, B. (1998). *Organizational participation: Myth and reality*. Oxford: Oxford University Press.

Helliwell, C. (1995). Autonomy as natural equality: Inequality in 'egalitarian' societies. *Journal of the Royal Anthropological Institute*, *1*(2), 359–375.

Hernandez, S. (2006). Striving for control: Democracy and oligarchy at a Mexican cooperative. *Economic and Industrial Democracy*, *27*(1), 105–135.

Heywood, J. S., Jirjahn, U., & Tsertsvadze, G. (2005). Getting along with colleagues: Does profit sharing help or hurt? *Kyklos*, *58*(4), 557–573.

Hirst, P. (1994). *Associative democracy: New forms of economic and social governance*. Cambridge: Polity Press.

Hodgson, G. (1984). *The democratic economy*. Harmondsworth: Penguin Books.

Hodgson, G. M. (2007). Meanings of methodological individualism. *Journal of Economic Methodology*, *14*(2), 211–226.

Hogg, M. A., Terry, D. J., & White, K. M. (1995). A tale of two theories: A critical comparison of identity theory with social identity theory. *Social Psychology Quarterly*, *58*(4), 255–269.

Hohfeld, W. (1913). Some fundamental legal conceptions as applied in judicial reasoning. *Yale Law Journal*, *23*(1), 16.

Hohfeld, W. (1917). Fundamental legal conceptions as applied in judicial reasoning. *Yale Law Journal*, *26*(10), 710.

Honoré, A. M. (1961). Ownership. In A. G. Guest (Ed.), *Oxford essays in jurisprudence*. Oxford: Oxford University Press, 107–147.

Hoover, M. (2008). Another workplace is possible: Co-ops and workplace democracy. In J. Allard, C. Davidson, & J. Matthaei (Eds.), *Solidarity economy: Building alternatives for people and planet – Papers and reports from the US Social Forum 2007*. Chicago: ChangeMaker Publications, 239–254.

Howard, M. W. (2003). Libertarianism, worker ownership, and wage slavery: A critique of Ellerman's labor theory of property. *Journal of Social Philosophy*, *34*(2), 169–187.

Hunnius, G. (1971). The Yugoslav system of decentralization and self-management. In C. G. Benello & D. Roussopoulos (Eds.), *The case for participatory democracy: Prospects for democratizing democracy*. New York: Grossman, 140–177.

Hutter, B. M., & O'Mahony, J. (2004). *The role of civil society organisations in regulating business*, Discussion Paper No. 26, ESRC Centre for Analysis of Risk and Regulation, London School of Economics and Political Science.

Ilies, R., Judge, T., & Wagner, D. (2006). Making sense of motivational leadership: The trail from transformational leaders to motivated followers. *Journal of Leadership and Organizational Studies*, *13*(1), 1–22.

Ingram, A. (1994). *A political theory of rights*. Oxford: Clarendon Press.

International Co-operative Alliance. (2010). *Global300 report 2010: The world's major co-operatives and mutual businesses*. Geneva: International Co-operative.

International Co-operative Alliance. (2013). *Blueprint for a co-operative decade*, Planning Work Group of the International Co-operative Alliance, Cliff Mills and Will Davies, Centre for Mutual and Employee-owned Business, University of Oxford.

Isham, J., Narayan, D., & Pritchett, L. (1995). Does participation improve performance? Establishing causality with subjective data. *World Bank Economic Review*, *9*(2), 175–200.

Iuviene, N., Stitely, A., & Hoyt, L. (2010). *Sustainable economic democracy: Worker cooperatives for the 21st century*, MIT CoLab Community Innovators Lab.

Jacques, R. (1996). *Manufacturing the employee: Management knowledge from the 19th to 21st centuries*. London: SAGE.

Jaques, E. (1990). In praise of hierarchy. *Harvard Business Review, 68*(1), 127–133.

Jaumier, S. (2016). Preventing chiefs from being chiefs: An ethnography of a co-operative sheet-metal factory. *Organization, 24*(2), 218–239.

Jegers, M. (2009). 'Corporate' governance in nonprofit organizations. *Nonprofit Management and Leadership, 20*(2), 143–164.

Jensen, M. C., & Meckling, W. H. (1976). Theory of the firm: Managerial behavior, agency costs and ownership structure. *Journal of Financial Economics, 3*(4), 305–360.

Jermier, J. M. (1998). Introduction: Critical perspectives on organizational control. *Administration Science Quarterly, 43*(2), 235–256.

Jessop, B. (2013). Metagovernance. In M. Bevir (Ed.), *The SAGE handbook of governance*. London: SAGE, 106–123.

Jones, D. C., & Svejnar, J. (Eds.). (1982). *Participatory and self-managed firms*. Toronto: Lexington.

Jost, J. T., & Elsbach, K. D. (2001). How status and power differences erode personal and social identities at work: A system justification critique of organizational applications of social identity theory. In M. Hogg & D. Terry (Eds.), *Social identity processes in organizational contexts*. Philadelphia: Psychology Press, 181–196.

Jost, J. T., & Hunyady, O. (2005). Antecedents and consequences of system-justifying ideologies. *Current Directions in Psychological Science, 14*(5), 260–265.

Jussila, I., Goel, S., & Tuominen, P. (2012). Governance of co-operative organizations: A social exchange perspective. *Business and Management Research, 1*(2), 14–25.

Kanter, R. M. (1971). Some social issues in the community development corporation. In C. G. Benello & D. Roussopoulos (Eds.), *The case for participatory democracy: Prospects for democratizing democracy*. New York: Grossman, 64–71.

Kanter, R. M. (1972). *Commitment and community*. Cambridge, MA: Harvard University Press.

Kark, R., & Van Dijk, D. (2007). Motivation to lead, motivation to follow: The role of the self-regulatory focus in leadership processes. *Academy of Management Review, 32*(2), 500–528.

Kärreman, D., & Alvesson, M. (2004). Cages in tandem: Management control, social identity, and identification in a knowledge-intensive firm. *Organization, 11*(1), 149–175.

Kekes, J. (2010). The right to private property: A justification. In E. F. Paul, D. F. Miller Jr., & J. Paul (Eds.), *Ownership and justice*. Cambridge: Cambridge University Press, 1–20.

Kellerman, B. (2005). How bad leadership happens. *Leader to Leader, 35*, 41–46.

Kelly, M. (2012). *Owning our future: The emerging ownership revolution*. San Francisco: Berrett-Koehler.

Keohane, R. O. (2003/2006). Global governance and democratic accountability. In R. E. Goodin & P. Pettit (Eds.), *Contemporary political philosophy* (2nd ed.). Oxford: Blackwell, 697–709.

Kerlin, J. A., & Gagnaire, K. (2009). United States. In J. A. Kerlin (Ed.), *Social enterprise: A global comparison*. London: Tufts University Press, 87–113.

Kerr, S. & Jermier, J. M. (1978). Substitutes for leadership: Their meaning and measurement. *Organizational Behavior and Human Performance, 22*(3), 375–403.

Kienle, E. (2011). Civil society in the Middle East. In M. Edwards (Ed.), *The Oxford handbook of civil society*. New York: Oxford University Press, 146–158.

Kneuer, M. (2012). Who is greener? Climate action and political regimes: Trade-offs for national and international actors. *Democratization, 19*(5), 865–888.

Knight, J., & Johnson, J. (1997). What sort of equality does deliberative democracy require? In J. Bohman & W. Rehg (Eds.), *Deliberative democracy: Essays on reason and politics*. Cambridge, MA: MIT Press, 279–319.

Knights, D., & O'Leary, M. (2006). Leadership, ethics and responsibility to the other. *Journal of Business Ethics, 67*(2), 125–137.

Kohlberg, L. (1973). The claim to moral adequacy of a highest stage of moral judgment. *Journal of Philosophy, 70*(18), 630–646.

Kohlberg, L. (1976). Moral stages and moralization. In T. Lickona (Ed.), *Moral development and behavior: Theory, research, and social issues*. New York: Longman, 31–53.

Kohlberg, L., & Hersh, R. H. (1977). Moral development: A review of the theory. *Theory into Practice, 16*(2), 53–59.

Kohlberg, L., & Wasserman, E. R. (1980). The cognitive-developmental approach and the practicing counselor: An opportunity for counselors to rethink their roles. *Personnel and Guidance Journal, 58*(9), 559–567.

Kohn, S. (2011). Civil society and equality. In M. Edwards (Ed.), *The Oxford handbook of civil society*. New York: Oxford University Press, 232–244.

Kokkinidis, G. (2012). In search of workplace democracy. *International Journal of Sociology and Social Policy, 32*(3/4), 233–256.

Kollmuss, A., & Agyeman, J. (2002). Mind the gap: Why do people act environmentally and what are the barriers to pro-environmental behavior? *Environmental Education Research, 8*(3), 239–260.

Korsgaard, M. A., Meglino, B. M., & Lester, S. W. (1996). The effect of other-oriented values on decision making: A test of propositions of a theory of concern for others in organizations. *Organizational Behavior and Human Decision Processes, 68*, 234–245.

Kramnick, I. (Ed.). (1995). *The portable enlightenment reader*. New York: Penguin Books.

Krebs, D. L., & Denton, K. (2005). Toward a more pragmatic approach to morality: A critical evaluation of Kohlberg's model. *Psychological Review, 112*(3), 629–649.

Kremer, M. (1997). *Why are worker cooperatives so rare?* NBER Working Paper Series, Working Paper 6118, National Bureau of Economic Research.

Krishna, G. J. (2014). Community economic development lawyers and the new democratic economy. *Community Economic Development Committee Newsletter*, ABA Business Law Section, July 2014. Retrieved 5 March 2020 from https://institute.coop/sites/default/files/resources/new-democratic-economy-201407.pdf

Lake, D. A. (2009). Hobbesian hierarchy: The political economy of political organization. *Annual Review of Political Science, 12*, 263–283.

Lancaster, R., & Uzzi, B. (2004). From colleague to employee: Determinants of changing career governance structures in elite law firms. In A. Grandori (Ed.), *Corporate governance and firm organization*. Oxford: Oxford University Press, 349–372.

Langmead, K. (2016). Challenging the degeneration thesis: The role of democracy in worker cooperatives? *Journal of Entrepreneurial and Organizational Diversity, 5*(1), 79–98.

Lans, C. (2013). Co-operatives and their place in a global social economy. In R. Harrison (Ed.), *People over capital: The co-operative alternative to capitalism*. Oxford: New Internationalist Publications, 164–179.

Laumann, E. O., Siegel, P. M., & Hodge, R. W. (Eds.). (1971). *The logic of social hierarchies*. Chicago: Markham Publishing Company.

Laville, J.-L. (2015). Social and solidarity economy in historical perspective. In P. Utting (Ed.), *Social and solidarity economy: Beyond the fringe?* London: Zed Books, 41–56.

Leach, D. K. (2005). The iron law of what again? Conceptualizing oligarchy across organizational forms. *Sociological Theory, 23*(3), 312–337.

Leach, D. K. (2013). The structure of tyrannylessness: Assessing resistance to oligarchy in the German nonviolence and autonomous movements. In *Conference Papers – American Sociological Association*, 1–41.

Leblebici, H., & Sherer, H. D. (2015). Governance in professional service firms: From structural and cultural to legal normative views. In L. Empson, D. Muzio, J. P. Broschak, & B. Hinings (Eds.), *The Oxford handbook of professional service firms*. Oxford: Oxford University Press, 189–212.

Lee, M. Y., & Edmondson, A. C. (2017). Self-managing organizations: Exploring the limits of less-hierarchical organizing. *Research in Organizational Behavior, 37*, 35–58.

Lester, S. W., Meglino, B. M., & Korsgaard, M. A. (2008). The role of other orientation in organizational citizenship behaviour. *Journal of Organizational Behavior, 29*, 829–841.

Levi-Faur, D. (2014). From 'big government' to 'big governance'? In D. Levi-Faur (Ed.), *The Oxford handbook of governance*. Oxford: Oxford University Press, 3–18.

Levin, J., & Tadelis, S. (2005). Profit sharing and the role of professional partnerships. *Quarterly Journal of Economics, 120*(1), 131–172.

Levy, D. L., Alvesson, M., & Willmott, H. (2001). Critical approaches to strategic management, paper presented at the Critical Management Studies Conference 2001, conference stream: Strategy.

Lewis, D. (2014). *Non-governmental organizations, management and development* (3rd ed.). London: Routledge.

Lewis, M., & Swinney, D. (2008). Social economy & solidarity economy: Transformative concepts for unprecedented times? In J. Allard, C. Davidson, & J. Matthaei (Eds.), *Solidarity economy: Building alternatives for people and planet – Papers and reports from the US Social Forum 2007*. Chicago: ChangeMaker Publications, 28–41.

Lipset, S. M. (1952/2010). Democracy in private government: A case study of the International Typographical Union. *British Journal of Sociology 61*(Suppl. S1), 9–27.

Lipset, S. M., Trow, M., & Coleman, J. S. (1956). *Union democracy: The internal politics of the International Typographical Union*. New York: Free Press.

Locke, J. (1689/1998). Of property and government (from *Second treatise of government*, included in *Two treatises of government*). In D. Boaz (Ed.), *The libertarian reader* (1st paperback ed). New York: Free Press, 123.

Lukes, S. (1974). *Power: A radical view*. London: Macmillan.

Lumber, R., Richardson, M., & Sheffield, D. (2017). Beyond knowing nature: Contact, emotion, compassion, meaning, and beauty are pathways to nature connection. *PLOS ONE, 12*(5), 1–24.

Lynn, L. E., Jr. (2014). Public management. In B. G. Peters & J. Pierre (Eds.), *The SAGE handbook of public administration* (2nd ed.). London: SAGE, 17–31.

Maccoby, M. (2005). Narcissistic leaders: The incredible pros, the inevitable cons. In *Harvard Business Review on the mind of the leader*. Cambridge, MA: Harvard Business School Publishing, 123–148.

Macdonald, J. B. (2013). The challenge of a democratic economy. In J. Shantz & J. B. MacDonald (Eds.), *Beyond capitalism: Building democratic alternatives for today and the future*. New York: Bloomsbury Academic, 1–23.

Mack, E. (2010). The natural right of property. In E. F. Paul, D. F. Miller Jr., & J. Paul (Eds.), *Ownership and justice*. Cambridge: Cambridge University Press, 53–78.

Magee, J. C., & Galinsky, A. D. (2008). The self-reinforcing nature of social hierarchy: Origins and consequences of power and status, paper presented at the IACM 21st Annual Conference. Retrieved 24 January 2011 from http://ssrn.com/abstract=1298493

Maibom, H. L. (2005). Moral unreason: The case of psychopathy. *Mind and Language, 20* (2), 237–257.

Malhotra, N., Morris, T., & Hinings, C. R. (2006). Variation in organizational form among professional service organizations. In R. Suddaby & R. Greenwood (Eds.), *Professional service firms: Research in the sociology of organizations* (Vol. 24.). London: Elsevier, 171–202.

Malleson, T. (2013). Economic democracy: The left's big idea for the twenty-first century? *New Political Science, 35*(1), 84–108.

Malleson, T. (2014). *After occupy: Economic democracy for the 21st century*. New York: Oxford University Press.

Mansbridge, J. J. (1977). Acceptable inequalities. *British Journal of Political Science, 7*, 321–336.

Mansbridge, J. J. (1980). *Beyond adversary democracy*. New York: Basic Books.

Marshall, P. (1993). *Demanding the impossible: A history of anarchism*. London: Fontana.

Martin, E. J. (2015). Oligarchy, anarchy, and social justice. *Contemporary Justice Review, 18* (1), 55–67.

Masi, R. J., & Cooke, R. A. (2000). Effects of transformational leadership on subordinate motivation, empowering norms, and organizational productivity. *International Journal of Organizational Analysis, 8*(1), 16–47.

Mayer, R. (2001). Robert Dahl and the right to workplace democracy. *Review of Politics, 63*(2), 221–247.

Mayfield, C., Purnell, J., & Davies, W. (2012). Why aren't there more companies like John Lewis? The difficulties of breaking the stranglehold of shareholder capitalism. *Public Policy Research, 18*(4), 216–221.

Maynard, M. T., Gilson, L. L., & Mathieu, J. E. (2012). Empowerment – fad or fab? A multilevel review of the past two decades of research. *Journal of Management, 38*(4), 1231–1281.

Mazzarol, T., Limnios, E. M., & Reboud, S. (2013). Co-operatives as a strategic network of small firms: Case studies from Australian and French co-operatives. *Journal of Co-operative Organization and Management, 1*, 27–40.

McDonald, F. V. (2014). Developing an integrated conceptual framework of pro-environmental behavior in the workplace through synthesis of the current literature. *Administrative Sciences, 4*, 276–303.

Meade, J. (1993). *Liberty, equality and efficiency*. New York: New York University Press.

Meglino, B. M., & Korsgaard, A. (2004). Considering rational self-interest as a disposition: Organizational implications of other orientation. *Journal of Applied Psychology, 89*(6), 946–959.

Melman, S. (2001). *After capitalism: From managerialism to workplace democracy*. New York: Alfred A. Knopf.

Meurs, M. (1996). Market socialism as a culture of cooperation. In J. E. Roemer & E. O. Wright (Eds.), *Equal shares: Making market socialism work.* London: Verso, 110–121.

Michels, R. (1915/2001). *Political parties: A sociological study of the oligarchical tendencies of modern democracy* [*Zur Soziologie des Parteiwesens in der modernen Demokratie; Untersuchungen über die oligarchischen Tendenzen des Gruppenlebens*], translated by Eden Paul and Cedar Paul. Kitchener: Batoche Books.

Miguel, M. C., Ornelas, J. H., & Maroco, J. P. (2015). Defining psychological empowerment construct: Analysis of three empowerment scales. *Journal of Community Psychology, 43*(7), 900–919.

Mill, J. S. (1848/1936). *Principles of political economy with some of their applications to social philosophy,* edited by W. J. Ashley (7th ed.). London: Longmans, Green & Co.

Mill, J. S. (1859/1998), Objections to government interference, from: *On liberty and other essays* (Oxford: Oxford University Press, 1991 (originally 1859)). In D. Boaz (Ed.), *The libertarian reader* (1st paperback ed.). New York: Free Press, 13–14, 121–123.

Miller, D. (1990). *Market, state and community: Theoretical foundations of market socialism.* Oxford: Clarendon Press.

Miller, K. I., & Monge, P. R. (1986). Participation, satisfaction, and productivity: A meta-analytic review. *Academy of Management Journal, 29*(4), 727–753.

Mills, C. (2013). Past, present and future. In R. Harrison (Ed.), *People over capital: The co-operative alternative to capitalism.* Oxford: New Internationalist Publications, 40–56.

Mills, C. W. (1956). *The power elite.* New York: Oxford University Press.

Millstone, C. (2015). Can social and solidarity economy organisations complement or replace publicly traded companies? In P. Utting (Ed.), *Social and Solidarity Economy: Beyond the fringe?* London: Zed Books, 86–99.

Mintzberg, H. (1985). The organization as political arena. *Journal of Management Studies, 22*(2), 133–154.

Mondak, J., Hibbing, M., Canache, D., Seligson, M., & Anderson, M. (2010). Personality and civic engagement: An integrative framework for the study of trait effects on political behavior. *American Political Science Review, 104*(1), 85–110.

Mondragon Corporation. (2019). Retrieved 9 September 2019 from https://en.wikipedia.org/wiki/Mondragon_Corporation

Morand, D. A. (1996). Dominance, deference, and egalitarianism in organizational interaction: A sociolinguistic analysis of power and politeness. *Organization Science, 7*(5), 544–556.

Morlino, L. (2004). What is a 'good' democracy? *Democratization, 11*(5), 10–32.

Morrell, K., & Hartley, J. (2006). A model of political leadership. *Human Relations, 59*(4), 483–504.

Moulaert, F. & Nussbaumer, J. (2005). Defining the social economy and its governance at the neighbourhood level: A methodological reflection. *Urban Studies, 42*(11), 2071–2088.

Mousnier, R. (1973). *Social hierarchies.* New York: Schocken Books.

Mulder, M. (1971). Power equalization through participation? *Administrative Science Quarterly, 16*(1), 31–38.

Murray, R. (2013). The potential for an alternative economy. In R. Harrison (Ed.), *People over capital: The co-operative alternative to capitalism.* Oxford: New Internationalist Publications, 20–30.

Musson, G., & Duberley, J. (2007). Change, change or be exchanged: The discourse of participation and the manufacture of identity. *Journal of Management Studies, 44*(1), 143–164.

Nauclér, E. (2005). Autonomy and multilevel governance: Experiences in Nordic and continental European cooperation. In M. Weller & S. Wolff (Eds.), *Autonomy, self governance and conflict resolution: Innovative approaches to institutional design in divided societies.* Abingdon: Routledge, 98–116.

Neamtan, N. (2005). The social economy: Finding a way between the market and the state. *Policy Options, 26*(6), 71–76.

Nelson, R. E. (2001). On the shape of verbal networks in organizations. *Organization Studies, 22*(5), 797–823.

Nembhard, J. G. (2008). Community-based economic development. In J. Allard, C. Davidson, & J. Matthaei (Eds.), *Solidarity economy: Building alternatives for people and planet – Papers and reports from the US Social Forum 2007.* Chicago: ChangeMaker Publications, 211–220.

Nicholls, A. (2011). Social enterprise and social entrepreneurs. In M. Edwards (Ed.), *The Oxford handbook of civil society.* New York: Oxford University Press, 80–92.

Nielsen, K. (1985). *Equality and liberty: A defense of radical egalitarianism.* Totowa: Rowman and Allanheld.

Nielsen, K. (1990). Liberal and socialist egalitarianism. *Laval théologique et philosophique, 46* (1), 81–96.

Nienhaus, V., & Brauksiepe, R. (1997). Explaining the success of community and informal economies. *International Journal of Social Economics, 24*(12), 1422–1438.

North, P., & Cato, M. S. (2018). Introduction: New economies north and south – Sharing the transition to a just and sustainable future. In P. North & M. S. Cato (Eds.), *Towards just and sustainable economies: The social and solidarity economy north and south.* Bristol: Policy Press, 1–12.

Norton, S. D. (2007). The natural environment as a salient stakeholder: Non-anthropocentrism, ecosystem stability and the financial markets. *Business Ethics: A European Review, 16*(4), 387–402.

Novkovic, S., & Holm, W. (2011). Co-operative networks as a source of organizational innovation, paper presented at the ICA Global Research Conference, Mikkeli, Finland, 25–27 August.

Novkovic, S., & Webb, T. (2014). Conclusion. In S. Novkovic & T. Webb (Eds.), *Co-operatives in a post-growth era: Creating co-operative economics.* London: Zed Books, 285–299.

Nyssens, M. (2009). Western Europe. In J. A. Kerlin (Ed.), *Social enterprise: A global comparison.* London: Tufts University Press, 12–34.

O'Mahony, S., & Ferraro, F. (2007). The emergence of governance in an open source community. *Academy of Management Journal, 50,* 1079–1106.

O'Brien, L. T., & Crandall, C. S. (2005). Perceiving self-interest: Power, ideology, and maintenance of the status quo. *Social Justice Research, 18*(1), 1–24.

O'Neill, M. (2009). Liberty, equality and property-owning democracy. *Journal of Social Philosophy, 40*(3), 379–396.

Ober, J. (2003). Gadfly on trial: Socrates as citizen and social critic. *Dēmos.* Retrieved 12 March 2012 from http://www.stoa.org/projects/demos/home

Oberg, A., & Walgenbach, P. (2008). Hierarchical structures of communication in a network organization. *Scandinavian Journal of Management, 24*(3), 183–198.

Omoto, A. M., Snyder, M., & Hackett, J. D. (2010). Personality and motivational antecedents of activism and civic engagement. *Journal of Personality, 78*(6), 1703–1734.

Ostergaard, G. N., & Halsey, A. H. (1965). *Power in co-operatives: A study of democratic control in British retail societies.* Oxford: Basil Blackwell.

Osterman, P. (2006). Overcoming oligarchy: Culture and agency in social movement organizations. *Administrative Science Quarterly, 51*, 622–649.

Ostrom, V. (1971/1987). *The political theory of a compound republic* (2nd ed.). Lincoln: University of Nebraska Press.

Otsuka, M. (2003). *Libertarianism without inequality.* Oxford: Oxford University Press.

Ould Ahmed, P. (2015). What does 'solidarity economy' mean? Contours and feasibility of a theoretical and political project. *Business Ethics: A European Review, 24*(4), 425–435.

Palgi, M. (2006a). Experiences of self-management and employee participation. *International Review of Sociology, 16*(1), 49–53.

Palgi, M. (2006b). Pitfalls of self-management in the kibbutz. *International Review of Sociology, 16*(1), 63–77.

Panayotakis, C. (2011). *Remaking scarcity: From capitalist economic inefficiency to economic democracy.* London: Pluto Press.

Park, M. (2013). Imagining a just and sustainable society: A critique of alternative economic models in the global justice movement. *Critical Sociology, 39*(1), 65–85.

Parker, M., Cheney, G., Fournier, V., & Land, C. (Eds.). (2014). *The Routledge companion to alternative organization.* Abingdon: Routledge.

Parry, S. (2012). Going green: The evolution of micro-business environmental practices. *Business Ethics: A European Review, 21*(2), 220–237.

Pateman, C. (1970). *Participation and democratic theory.* Cambridge: Cambridge University Press.

Pearce, J. M. (2014). Free and open source appropriate technology. In M. Parker, G. Cheney, V. Fournier, & C. Land (Eds.), *The Routledge companion to alternative organization.* Abingdon: Routledge, 308–328.

Peel, E. (2011). *The law of contract* (13th revised ed.). London: Sweet & Maxwell.

Perkins, D. D., & Zimmerman, M. A. (1995). Empowerment theory, research, and application. *American Journal of Community Psychology, 23*(5), 569–579.

Petit, T. A. (1961). Management ideology: Myth and reality. *California Management Review, 3*(2), 95–103.

Phillips, D. (2006). Relationships are the core value for organisations: A practitioner perspective, *Corporate Communications, 11*(1), 34–42.

Podivinsky, J. M., & Stewart, G. (2007). Why is labour-managed firm entry so rare? An analysis of UK manufacturing data. *Journal of Economic Behavior & Organization, 63*(1), 177–192.

Pollitt, C. (1990). *Managerialism and the public services: The Anglo-Saxon experience.* Oxford: Basil Blackwell.

Poole, M. (1996). *Towards a new industrial democracy.* London: Routledge.

Poole, M., Lansbury, R., & Wailes, N. (2001). A comparative analysis of developments in industrial democracy. *Industrial Relations, 40*(3), 490–525.

Popper, K. R. (1945/1980). *Die offene Gesellschaft und ihre Feinde* (6th ed.) [*The open society and its enemies*]. Muenchen: UTB.

Powell, F. (2007). *The politics of civil society.* Bristol: Policy Press.

Pratto, F. (2016). On power and empowerment. *British Journal of Social Psychology, 55*(1), 1–20.

Pretty, J. (1995). Participatory learning for sustainable agriculture. *World Development, 23*(8), 1247–1263.

Proudhon, P.-J. (1851/2012). General idea of the revolution in the nineteenth century. In G. Chartier & C. W. Johnson (Eds.), *Markets not capitalism: Individualist anarchism against bosses, inequality, corporate power, and structural poverty*. London: Minor Compositions, 37–58.

Purser, R. E., Park, C., & Montuori, A. (1995). Limits to anthropocentrism: Toward an ecocentric organization paradigm? *Academy of Management Review, 20*(4), 1053–1089.

Rahim, M. A., Buntzman, G. F., & White, D. (1999). An empirical study of the stages of moral development and conflict management styles. *International Journal of Conflict Management, 10*(2), 154–171.

Rank, O. N. (2008). Formal structures and informal networks: Structural analysis in organizations. *Scandinavian Journal of Management, 24*(2), 145–161.

Ravlin, E. C., & Thomas, D. C. (2005). Status and stratification processes in organizational life. *Journal of Management, 30*(6), 966–987.

Rayburn, J. M., & Rayburn, L. G. (1996). Relationship between Machiavellianism and type A personality and ethical-orientation. *Journal of Business Ethics, 15*(11), 1209–1219.

Raymond, C. M., Singh, G. G., Benessaiah, K., Bernhardt, J. R., Levine, J., Nelson, H., Turner, N. J., Norton, B., Tam, J., & Chan, K. M. A. (2013). Ecosystem services and beyond: Using multiple metaphors to understand human-environment relationships. *BioScience, 63*(7), 536–546.

Raz, J. (1986/2009). *The morality of freedom*. Oxford: Clarendon Press.

Reed, D. (2015). Scaling the social and solidarity economy: Opportunities and limitations of fairtrade practice. In P. Utting (Ed.), *Social and solidarity economy: Beyond the fringe?* London: Zed Books, 100–115.

Reedy, P. (2002). Keeping the black flag flying: Anarchy, utopia and the politics of nostalgia. In M. Parker (Ed.), *Utopia and organization*. Oxford: Blackwell, 169–188.

Rees, W. E. (2014). Are prosperity and sustainability compatible? In S. Novkovic & T. Webb (Eds.), *Co-operatives in a post-growth era: Creating co-operative economics*. London: Zed Books, 83–100.

Reno, B. J. (2009). Private property and the law of nature in Locke's *Two Treatises*. *American Journal of Economics and Sociology, 68*(3), 639–663.

Restakis, J. (2010). *Humanizing the economy: Co-operatives in the age of capital*. Gabriola Island: New Society Publishers.

Rodekamp, M. (2010). *Representatives or experts? Civil society organizations in the EU's external relations*, TranState Working Papers No. 137, University of Bremen.

Roelants, B. (2013). Conclusions and proposals. In B. Roelants (Ed.), *Cooperative growth for the 21st century*. Brussels, International Cooperative Alliance, 48–54.

Roemer, J. E. (1998). *Equality of opportunity*. Cambridge, MA: Harvard University Press.

Rohrschneider, R. (1994). How iron is the iron law of oligarchy? Robert Michels and national party delegates in eleven West European democracies. *European Journal of Political Research, 25*(2), 207–238.

Romme, A. G. L. (1999). Domination, self-determination and circular organizing. *Organization Studies, 20*(5), 801–832.

Rosen, M. (1984). Myth and reproduction: The contextualization of management theory, method and practice. *Journal of Management Studies, 21*(3), 304–322.

Rosenblum, N. L., & Lesch, C. H. T. (2011). Civil society and government. In M. Edwards (Ed.), *The Oxford handbook of civil society*. New York: Oxford University Press, 285–297.

Rothschild, J. (2009). Workers' cooperatives and social enterprise: A forgotten route to social equity and democracy. *American Behavioral Scientist, 52*, 1023–1041.

Rothschild, J., & Ollilainen, M. (1999). Obscuring but not reducing managerial control: Does TQM measure up to democracy standards? *Economic and Industrial Democracy, 20*, 583–623.

Rothschild, J., & Whitt, J. A. (1986). *The cooperative workplace. Potentials and dilemmas of organizational democracy and participation.* Cambridge: Cambridge University Press.

Rothschild-Whitt, J. (1976). Conditions facilitating participatory-democratic organizations. *Sociological Inquiry, 46*(2), 75–86.

Rothschild-Whitt, J. (1979). The collectivist organization: An alternative to rational-bureaucratic models. *American Sociological Review, 44*(4), 509–527.

Rothschild-Whitt, J., & Lindenfeld, F. (1982). Reshaping work: Prospects and problems of workplace democracy. In F. Lindenfeld & J. Rothschild-Whitt (Eds.), *Workplace democracy and social change.* Boston: Porter Sargent, 1–18.

Rueschemeyer, D. (1986). *Power and the division of labour.* Cambridge: Polity Press.

Russell, D. C. (2010). Embodiment and self-ownership. In E. F. Paul, F. D. Miller Jr., & J. Paul (Eds.), *Ownership and justice.* Cambridge: Cambridge University Press, 135–167.

Rutledge, R. W., & Karim, E. K. (1999). The influence of self-interest and ethical considerations on managers' evaluation judgments. *Accounting, Organizations and Society, 24*, 173–184.

Saguier, M., & Brent, Z. (2017). Social and solidarity economy in South American regional governance. *Global Social Policy, 17*(3), 259–278.

Salamon, L. M., & Anheier, H. K. (1998). Social origins of civil society: Explaining the nonprofit sector cross-nationally. *Voluntas: International Journal of Voluntary and Nonprofit Organizations, 9*(3), 213–248.

Sandhu, S. (2010). Shifting paradigms in corporate environmentalism: From poachers to gamekeepers. *Business and Society Review, 115*(3), 285–310.

Sargent, L. (2008). The making of South End Press and Z. In C. Spannos (Ed.), *Real utopia: Participatory society for the 21st century.* Oakland: AK Press, 264–274.

Sauser, W. I. (2009). Sustaining employee-owned companies: Seven recommendations. *Journal of Business Ethics, 84*, 151–164.

Schillemans, T. (2008). Accountability in the shadow of hierarchy: The horizontal accountability of agencies. *Public Organization Review, 8*, 175–194.

Schneider, V. (2014). Governance and complexity. In D. Levi-Faur (Ed.), *The Oxford handbook of governance.* Oxford: Oxford University Press, 129–142.

Schultz, P. W., Gouveia, V. V., Cameron, L. D., Tankha, G., Schmuck, P., & Franek, M. (2005). Values and their relationship to environmental concern and conservation behaviour. *Journal of Cross-Cultural Psychology, 36*(4), 457–475.

Schwartz, J. (2012). Where did Mill go wrong? Why the capital-managed rather than the labor-managed enterprise is the predominant organizational form in market economies. *Ohio State Law Journal, 73*(2), 219–285.

Schweickart, D. (1993). *Against capitalism.* Cambridge: Cambridge University Press/Paris: Editions de la Maison des Sciences de l'Homme.

Schweickart, D. (2011). *After capitalism* (2nd ed.). Lanham: Rowman & Littlefield.

Scott, C. (2000). Accountability in the regulatory state. *Journal of Law and Society, 27*(1), 38–60.

Scott, J. (2003). Transformations in the British economic elite. In M. Dogan (Ed.), *Elite configurations at the apex of power.* Leiden: Brill, 155–173.

Scott, J. C. (1990). *Domination and the arts of resistance: Hidden transcripts*. New Haven: Yale University Press.

Seibert, S. E., Silver, S. R., & Randolph, W. A. (2004). Taking empowerment to the next level: A multiple-level model of empowerment, performance and satisfaction. *Academy of Management Journal, 47*(3), 332–349.

Shaw, M. (2011). Stuck in the middle? Community development, community engagement and the dangerous business of learning for democracy. *Community Development Journal, 46*(Suppl.2), ii128–ii146.

Sidanius, J., & Pratto, F. (1999). *Social dominance: An intergroup theory of social hierarchy and oppression*. Cambridge: Cambridge University Press.

Sidanius, J., Pratto, F., van Laar, C., & Levin, S. (2004). Social dominance theory: Its agenda and method. *Political Psychology, 25*(6), 845–880.

Siebens, H. (2005). Facilitating leadership. *EBS Review, 20*, 9–29.

Singh, P., Bartkiw, T. J., & Suster, Z. (2007). The Yugoslav experience with workers' councils. *Labor Studies Journal, 32*(3), 280–297.

Smith, G. (2003). *Deliberative democracy and the environment*. London: Routledge.

Smith, G., & Teasdale, S. (2012). Associative democracy and the social economy: Exploring the regulatory challenge. *Economy and Society, 41*(2), 151–176.

Smith, S. C., & Rothbaum, J. (2014). Co-operatives in a global economy: Key issues, recent trends and potential for development. In S. Novkovic & T. Webb (Eds.), *Co-operatives in a post-growth era: Creating co-operative economics*. London: Zed Books, 221–241.

Solidarity Economic Working Group for USSF 2007. (2008). The emerging solidarity economy: Some common themes. In J. Allard, C. Davidson, & J. Matthaei (Eds.), *Solidarity economy: Building alternatives for people and planet, papers and reports from the US Social Forum 2007*. Chicago: ChangeMaker Publications, 392–394.

Srivastva, S., & Cooperrider, D. L. (1986). The emergence of the egalitarian organization. *Human Relations, 39*(8), 683–724.

Steen-Johnsen, K., Eynaud, P., & Wijkström, F. (2011). On civil society governance: An emergent research field. *Voluntas: International Journal of Voluntary and Nonprofit Organizations, 22*(4), 555–565.

Stern, P. C., & Dietz, T. (1994). The value basis of environmental concern. *Journal of Social Issues, 50*(3), 65–84.

Stoddart, M. C. J. (2007). Ideology, hegemony, discourse: A critical review of theories of knowledge and power. *Social Thought and Research, 28*, 191–226.

Stohl, C., & Cheney, G. (2001). Participatory processes, paradoxical practices: Communication and the dilemmas of organizational democracy. *Management Communication Quarterly, 14*(3), 349–407.

Strauss, G. (1998). An overview. In F. Heller, E. Pusic, G. Strauss, & B. Wilpert (Eds.), *Organizational participation: Myth and reality*. Oxford: Oxford University Press, 8–39.

Sud, M., & VanSandt, C. V. (2011). Of fair markets and distributive justice. *Journal of Business Ethics, 99*, 131–142.

Suddaby, R., & Muzio, D. (2015). Theoretical perspectives on the professions. In L. Empson, D. Muzio, J. P. Broschak, & B. Hinings (Eds.), *The Oxford handbook of professional service firms*. Oxford: Oxford University Press, 25–47.

Sustainability. (2016). Retrieved 19 December 2016 from https://en.wikipedia.org/wiki/Sustainability

Sutherland, N., Land, C., & Böhm, S. (2014). Anti-leaders(hip) in social movement organizations: The case of autonomous grassroots groups. *Organization*, *21*(6), 759–781.

Swigger, N. (2013). The online citizen: Is social media changing citizens' beliefs about democratic values? *Political Behaviour*, *35*, 589–603.

Tajfel, H. (1978). Social categorization, social identity, and social comparison. In H. Tajfel (Ed.), *Differentiation between social groups: Studies in the social psychology of intergroup relations*. London: Academic Press, 61–76.

Tajfel, H., & Turner, J. C. (1979). An integrative theory of intergroup conflict. In W. G. Austin & S. Worchel (Eds.), *The social psychology of intergroup relations*. Monterey: Brooks-Cole, 33–47.

Taylor, F. W. (1911/1967). *The principles of scientific management*. New York: Norton & Co.

Taylor, H. (2001). Insights into participation from critical management and labour process perspectives. In B. Cooke & U. Kothari (Eds.), *Participation: The new tyranny?* London: Zed Books, 122–138.

Teegen, H., Doh, J. P., & Vachani, S. (2004). The importance of nongovernmental organizations (NGOs) in global governance and value creation: An international business research agenda. *Journal of International Business Studies*, *35*, 463–483.

Thompson, V. A. (1961). Hierarchy, specialization, and organizational conflict. *Administrative Science Quarterly*, *5*(4), 485–521.

Tocqueville, A. de. (1835–1840/2003). *Democracy in America*. London: Penguin Books.

Tolbert, P. S., & Hiatt, S. R. (2009). On organizations and oligarchies: Michels in the twenty-first century. Retrieved 25 December 2015 from http://digitalcommons.ilr. cornell.edu/articles/1011

Trevino, L. K. (1986). Ethical decision making in organizations: A person-situation interactionist model. *Academy of Management Review*, *11*(3), 601–617.

Turnbull, S. (1997). Corporate governance: It's scope, concerns and theories. *Corporate Governance*, *5*(4), 180–205.

Turner, C. (2013). *Unlocking employment law*. Abingdon: Routledge.

Ulrich, P. (1993). *Transformation der ökonomischen Vernunft: Fortschrittsperspektiven der modernen Industriegesellschaft* [*Transformation of economic reason: Progress perspectives of the modern industrial society*]. Bern: Haupt.

United Nations. (2003). *Handbook on non-profit institutions in the system of national accounts*, Series F., No. 91. New York: Department of Economic and Social Affairs, Statistics Division.

United Nations Economic and Social Commission for Asia and the Pacific. (2009). *What is good governance?* Retrieved 14 June 2015 from http://www.unescap.org/sites/default/files/good-governance.pdf

Upchurch, M., Daguerre, A., & Ozarow, D. (2014) Spectrum, trajectory and the role of the state in workers' self-management. *Labor History*, *55*(1), 47–66.

Utting, P. (2015). Introduction: The challenge of scaling up social and solidarity economy. In P. Utting (Ed.), *Social and solidarity economy: Beyond the fringe?* London: Zed Books, 1–37.

Vakil, A. C. (1997). Confronting the classification problem: Toward a taxonomy of NGOs. *World Development*, *25*(12), 2057–2070.

Van der Meer, T. W. G., & Van Ingen, E. J. (2009). Schools of democracy? Disentangling the relationship between civic participation and political action in 17 European countries. *European Journal of Political Research*, *48*, 281–308.

van Dop, N., Depauw, J., & Driessens, K. (2016). Measuring empowerment: Development and validation of the service user psychological empowerment scale. *Journal of Social Service Research, 42*(5), 651–664.

Van Lange, P. A. M. (2000). Beyond self-interest: A set of propositions relevant to interpersonal orientations. *European Review of Social Psychology, 11*(1), 297–331.

Van Parijs, P. (1995). *Real freedom for all: What (if anything) can justify capitalism?* Oxford: Oxford University Press.

Van Vugt, M. (2006). Evolutionary origins of leadership and followership. *Personality and Social Psychology Review, 10*(4), 354–371.

Vanberg, V. J. (2004). *Market and state: The perspective of constitutional political economy,* Freiburg Discussion Papers on Constitutional Economics 04/10, Walter Eucken Institut.

Vandekerckhove, W., & Commers, R. M. S. (2003). Downward workplace mobbing: A sign of the times? *Journal of Business Ethics, 45*, 41–50.

Vanek, J. (1971). *The participatory economy.* London: Cornell University Press.

Vardi, Y., & Weitz, E. (2004). *Misbehavior in organizations. Theory, research, and management.* London: Lawrence Erlbaum Associates.

Varman, R., & Chakrabarti, M. (2004). Contradictions of democracy in a workers' cooperative. *Organization Studies, 25*(2), 183–208.

Verba, S., Schlozman, K. L., & Brady, H. E. (2004). Political equality: What do we know about it? In K. M. Neckerman (Ed.), *Social inequality.* New York: Russell Sage Foundation 635–666.

Vickers, M. H., & Kouzmin, A. (2001). Resilience in organizational actors and rearticulating voice. *Public Management Review, 3*(1), 95–119.

Victor, P. A. (2014). Living well: Explorations into the end of growth. In S. Novkovic & T. Webb (Eds.), *Co-operatives in a post-growth era: Creating co-operative economics.* London: Zed Books, 101–114.

Vilchez, J. L. (2017). The solution for the behavioural constellation of deprivation: The popular and solidarity economy. *Psychology and Developing Societies, 29*(2), 246–263.

Von Nordenflycht, A. (2007). Is public ownership bad for professional service firms? Ad agency ownership, performance, and creativity. *Academy of Management Journal, 50*(2), 429–445.

Von Nordenflycht, A. (2010). What is a professional service firm? Toward a theory and taxonomy of knowledge-intensive firms. *Academy of Management Review, 35*(1), 155–174.

Vredenburgh, D., & Brender, Y. (1993). The relevance of democracy to organizational management. *Employee Responsibilities and Rights Journal, 6*(2), 99–114.

Vredenburgh, D., & Brender, Y. (1998). The hierarchical abuse of power in work organizations. *Journal of Business Ethics, 17*, 1337–1347.

Waller, M. J., Huber, G. P., & Glick, W. H. (1995). Functional background as a determinant of executives' selective perception. *Academy of Management Journal, 38*, 943–974.

Wallimann, I. (2014). Social and solidarity economy for sustainable development: Its premises – and the social economy Basel example of practice. *International Review of Sociology/Revue Internationale de Sociologie, 24*(1), 48–58.

Ward, C. (1971). The anarchist contribution. In C. G. Benello & D. Roussopoulos (Eds.), *The case for participatory democracy: Prospects for democratizing democracy.* New York: Grossman, 283–294.

Watner, C. (1980). 'Come what, come will!' Richard Overton, libertarian leveller. *Journal of Libertarian Studies, 4*(4), 405–432.

Watson, T. (2006). *Organising and managing work* (2nd ed.). Harlow: Pearson Education.

Webb, T., & Cheney, G. (2014). Worker-owned-and-governed co-operatives and the wider co-operative movement: Challenges and opportunities within and beyond the global economic crisis. In M. Parker, G. Cheney, V. Fournier, & C. Land (Eds.), *The Routledge companion to alternative organization*. Abingdon: Routledge, 64–88.

Webb, T., & Novkovic, S. (2014). Introduction: What is the new economy and why do we need it? In S. Novkovic & T. Webb (Eds.), *Co-operatives in a post-growth era: Creating co-operative economics*. London: Zed Books, 1–11.

Weber, M. (1921/1980). *Wirtschaft und Gesellschaft [Economy and society]* (5th revised ed.). Tübingen: J.C.B. Mohr (Paul Siebeck).

Weir, G. (2003). Self-employment in the UK labour market. *Labour Market Trends*, September, 441–451.

Weiss, T. (2000). Governance, good governance and global governance: Conceptual and actual challenges. *Third World Quarterly, 21*(5), 795–814.

Weisskopf, T. E. (1993). A democratic-enterprise-based market socialism. In P. Bardhan & J. Roemer (Eds.), *Market socialism: The current debate*. Oxford: Oxford University Press, 120–141.

Wiessner, P. (2002). The vines of complexity, egalitarian structures and the institutionalization of inequality among the Enga. *Current Anthropology, 43*(2), 233–269.

Wilkinson, A. (1998). Empowerment: Theory and practice. *Personnel Review, 27*(1), 40–56.

Willetts, P. (2006). What is a non-governmental organization? In *UNESCO encyclopaedia of life support systems*, Article 1.44.3.7. Retrieved 5 March 2020 from http://www.staff.city.ac.uk/p.willetts/CS-NTWKS/NGO-ART.HTM

Willmott, H. C. (1984). Images and ideals of managerial work: A critical examination of conceptual and empirical accounts. *Journal of Management Studies, 21*(3), 349–368.

Willmott, H. C. (1996). A metatheory of management: Omniscience or obfuscation? *British Journal of Management, 7*(4), 323–328.

Wolff, J. (1998). Fairness, respect, and the egalitarian ethos. *Philosophy and Public Affairs, 27*(2), 97–122.

Wolff, S. (2005). Complex autonomy arrangements in Western Europe: A comparative analysis of regional consociationlism in Brussels, Northern Ireland and South Tyrol. In M. Weller & S. Wolff (Eds.), *Autonomy, self governance and conflict resolution: Innovative approaches to institutional design in divided societies*. Abingdon: Routledge, 117–157.

World Commission on Environment and Development. (1987). *Our common future* [Brundtland Report]. Retrieved 8 December 2016 from www.un-documents.net/our-common-future.pdf

Wright, E. O. (2010). *Envisioning real utopias*. London: Verso.

Wrong, D. H. (1971). The functional theory of stratification: Some neglected considerations. In E. O. Laumann, P. M. Siegel, & R. W. Hodge (Eds.), *The logic of social hierarchies*. Chicago: Markham, 132–142.

Yitshaki, R., & Kropp, F. (2016). Motivations and opportunity recognition of social entrepreneurs. *Journal of Small Business Management, 54*(2), 546–565.

Young, I. M. (2008). Structural injustice and the politics of difference. In G. Craig, T. Burchardt, & D. Gordon (Eds.), *Social justice and public policy: Seeking fairness in diverse societies*. Bristol: Policy Press, 77–104.

Yu, M., Vaagaasar, A. L., Müller, R., Wang, L., & Zhu, F. (2018). Empowerment: The key to horizontal leadership in projects. *International Journal of Project Management, 36*(7), 992–1006.

Zamagni, V. N. (2014). The co-operative enterprise: A valid alternative for a balanced society. In S. Novkovic & T. Webb (Eds.), *Co-operatives in a post-growth era: Creating co-operative economics*. London: Zed Books, 194–209.

Zapf, D., & Gross, C. (2001). Conflict escalation and coping with workplace bullying: A replication and extension. *European Journal of Work and Organizational Psychology, 10*(4), 497–522.

Zeitlin, M. (1974). Corporate ownership and control: The large corporation and the capitalist class. *American Journal of Sociology, 79*(5), 1073–1119.

Zimmerman, M. A. (1995). Psychological empowerment: Issues and illustrations. *American Journal of Community Psychology, 23*(5), 581–599.

INDEX

Numbers in **bold** refer to tables.

accountability 13, 62–63, 70, 91, 99, 126, 127, 185; multidimensional 63
activist groups 28
aggrandisers 107, 111, 117, 122, 161, 223
agreeableness 110, 111, 223
agreements: and mutual consent 37; *see also* partnership agreement
alternative organisations 3, 17–18, 199–200, 204
anti-democratic governance 16–17
anti-social behaviour 132, 161, 225
anti-social interests 212–213, 225
anti-social perpetrators 223–228
anti-social personality 223–224
assemblies 53; *see also* general assemblies
associations 3, 19–21, 28, 30
authoritarianism 118
authoritative sources 51, 57–59, 156–157, 201; application 59; emergence 59; internal consistency 58; legal hierarchy 71; legitimacy 58–59, 66, 71, 156–157
authority: challenges to 117–120; limiting through democratic means 108–109; of offices and office-holders 108–110; scepticism about 121
autocracy 56, 57, 108, 239; and decision-making 60
autocratic leaders 111
autocratisation 207

belongingness 97
Berlin, Isaiah 37
biophilic values 142, 143
biospheric values 142
business-related institutions 175

capitalist firms 132, 196
capitalist market economies 27
capitalist/neoliberal agenda 175
careerists 108, 111, 122, 161, 173
chain of command 57
'checks and balances' 55–56, 67, 105
civic engagement 29, 183
civic participation 183
civil rights 199
civil society 65
civil society organisations (CSOs) 173, 198, 200
collaboration 45, 81, 83, 165, 185
collaborative behaviour 150, 163, 165
collaborative mindset 133–135
collectivist organisation 3, 24–26, 90
collegiality 91, 185
community-based businesses 135
community-based organisations 3, 28
community building 29
community development trusts 28
community orientation 135–137
community projects 28

community well-being 25, 135–136
competencies 89, 187; and democratic
  organisations 177–178, 180; social
  102–103
confidence 93, 95, 106
conformity 16, 96
connectivity with nature 141, 143
conscientiousness 110, 111, 223
conservative organisations 198–199, 204
considerate conduct of business 2, 31,
  131–152, 161–163
constitutional foundations: democratic
  organisations 201; social systems 38
contestation, culture of 120–121
contractual relations 37
control 57, 96
cooperation 185; culture of 133; and
  disempowerment 96; and
  empowerment 91; and participation
  163; and reciprocity 150; and trust 150
cooperative banks 135, 138
cooperative behaviour 133–135
cooperatives 3, 21–22, 28, 133; and
  democratic accountability 63; and
  democratic practices 54; and
  empowerment 90; as environmentally
  friendly 144; principles of 21
corporate social responsibility 145
credit unions 28
criminal organisations 194
CSOs *see* civil society organisations
culture: of contestation 120–121; of
  cooperation 133; of participation 54; of
  reciprocity 150, 165; of trust 150, 165

Dahl, Robert 45, 55, 217
decent business practices 137–138, 166
decision-making: bottom-up approach 57;
  in collectivist organisation 25;
  constructional issues 84; democratic 31,
  60–61, 165, 178–179; and democratic
  self-management 76–77; efficiency of
  internal processes 178–179; monopoly
  on 55; operational issues 84; in
  orthodox organisations 13; and
  participative management 99; in
  participatory democracy 27; and
  principle of subsidiarity 57; and social
  system 60; strategic issues 84; and
  transparency 61, **62**; top-down
  approach 57
democracy: and associations 21; and
  collaboration of equals 45; and

decision-making 60–61; developmental
  88; and disproportional empowerment
  220–221; economic 54; parliamentarian
  54; political 54; representative 61, 199;
  workplace 31, 54, 70; *see also*
  participatory democracy
democratic accountability 63
democratic competition 53
democratic control 53
democratic governance 2, 7, 31,
  50–67, 156–158, 165, 201; and
  democratic organisation 66–67; as
  institutionalised organisational
  democracy 156; key elements
  156–158; and participation 81; and
  transparency 61
democratic institutions 52, 202
democratic management 2, 7–8, 69–86,
  158–159, 165, 201–202; key elements
  85–86, 158–159; and participation 81;
  and performance 148–150; and
  self-management 148
democratic organisations: attitudinal
  aspects 186–187; case for 171–190;
  constitutional foundations 201;
  definition 31, 45; detrimental social
  processes and dynamics 209–211;
  feasibility 5–6; features and purposes 18;
  general model of 2, 31, 154–167; as
  inherently good 164–167; intrapersonal
  aspects 186–187; issue of choice
  172–174; key criteria 30–31; legal
  ownership 43, 46; legitimacy of
  201–203; libertarian constitution of
  45–47, 155; necessity of 3–5; novelty of
  3; prevalence of 171–172; psychological
  aspects 186–187; purposes and conduct
  of business 182–184; reasons to opt for
  182–187; strengths and advantages
  187–190; types of **18**
demos kratos 45, 159
Demosthenes 117–118
dictatorship 112, 119
dignity, sense of 91, 186
discrimination 219–220; institutionalised 13
disempowerment **124–125**; definition 93;
  three-dimensional concept of 93–94; *see
  also* formal disempowerment;
  psychological disempowerment; social
  disempowerment
'disengaged, the' 231–237
disproportional empowerment 10,
  207–239; arguments against 216–222;

causes 222–237; and 'the disengaged' 231–237; legitimacy issues 220–222; prevention 237–239; processes leading to 211–216

ecological knowledge 143, 144
economic democracy 3, 54
economic orientation 163–164
economic performance 146–147, 150–152, 163–164
economic value 151
efficacy 96; *see also* self-efficacy
egalitarian behaviour 112
egalitarian spirit 112
egalitarian tribes 107
egocentric values 142
egotistic leaders 108
election 53; of managers 79; of representatives 79, 85
emotional connection 141
empathy 183
employee-owned companies 3, 24, 47
employment status 44
empowerment 2, 31, **123–124**; advantages 91; definition 90; of the disempowered 97–98, 108, 161; equalising 88–128, 159–162; fake 234, 235; and participation 231–237; and principle of subsidiarity 98; and self-management 98; three-dimensional concept of 90–94; and work 106; *see also* disempowerment; disproportional empowerment; formal empowerment; psychological empowerment; social empowerment
empresas recuperadas por sus trabalhadores (ERTs) (worker-recovered enterprises) 26
engagement: civic 29, 183; and empowerment 91, 97; and participation 163
Enlightenment 40
environmental issues 142; *see also* pro-environmental behaviour; pro-environmental orientation
equalising empowerment 88–128, 159–162
equality 185; and associations 19–20; *see also* inequality
equal power 89, 159
equal rights 24, 43–44, 46, 81, 88–89, 128; and democratic management 158
ethical behaviour 137–138, 166
ethical businesses 28
ethical leadership 108

exchange networks 3, 28
exploitation 13, 16, 78, 196–197, 220
external performance 179–180
extraversion 110, 111, 223

fairtrade organisations 3, 28, 134, 137, 184
family businesses 173, 174
financial resources 176–177
formal disempowerment 93–95, 108–110
formal empowerment 8, 91–94, 98–99, 103–105, 123–126, 202
formal positions, accumulation of 104, 105, 109
formal power 160
free individuals 37–39, 111
free will 37–39, 46
freedom 38, 45; of contract 192–194; individual 37, 38, 47; positive 37; and property rights 42–43
freelancers 47, 173–174
Fromm, Erich 106

general assemblies 53, 54, 55, 75
goal attainment 92, 100, 101, 106, 126, 160, 202
goals: economic 145, 202; environmentally friendly 145–146; social 28, 29, 133; *see also* goal attainment
'good governance' 51, 64–66, 157–158
'good subordinates' 96, 220
governance 50–51; anti-democratic 16–17; assessment of quality and conduct 61; authoritative sources 57, 156–157; basic functions of 64; 'checks and balances' 55–56; conduct of 51; definition 51; democratic institutions of 52–57, 66, 156; emergence of 109; institutional hierarchy 71; organisational institutions of 52–56; 'shared' 31; and social system 50–51, 59; *see also* democratic governance; 'good governance'
Guillaume, James 20

heterarchical relationships 31
heterarchy 55, 69–72; and principle of subsidiarity 57
hierarchisation 207, 215, 223
hierarchy 31, 69–72; and chain of command 57; formal 200, 214; informal 200, 214; institutional 71; legal 71; in

orthodox organisation 12–13, 15–16; social 71; *see also* hierarchisation
Hierarchy and Organisation 5–6
homo economicus 132
Honoré, Tony 42
hubris 106, 110
human–nature relationship 139
hybrid organisations 90

income 25, 135; *see also* remuneration; *see also* wages
independent intellect 101
individual differences 89–90
inequality 16; and hierarchy 12–13; structural 95
infantilisation 15, 78, 96, 219–220
inferiority, feelings of 17, 95, 220
information 93, 95, 98–99
institutional bias 175, 180
institutional hierarchy 71
institutionalised discrimination 13
institutional misfit 174–176, 180
interest-oriented organisations 19–24, 30
internal processes 178–180
internet 136–137
interpersonal communication 92, 96
'iron law of oligarchy' 26

job performance 91, 185
job satisfaction 91, 187
job security 185
job stability 185

Kelly, Marjorie 143–144
knowledge 89; accumulation of 105; challenging 112–115; demystification of 112–114; ecological 143, 144; and empowerment 91; factual 142; privileging 112–115; specialised 112–113
Kohlberg, Lawrence 122

labour: division of 77, 112; rights 44
'ladder of participation' 27, 80–81, 234
leaders: autocratic 111; egotistic 108; flawed 14; public image 14; social actions as a way of challenging 117–120; *see also* leadership
leadership: as an archaic notion 114; bottom-up approach 57; distributed 114–115; ethical 108; top-down approach 57; trait theory 106, 114; *see also* leaders
'learned helplessness' 17, 97, 220
left-libertarianism 39
legitimacy: of authoritative sources 58–59, 66, 71, 80, 99, 156–157; of disproportional empowerment 220–222; of institutions of governance 156; of organisations 192–205; of representative management 80; of social systems 37
legitimate authority 80, 99
libertarian constitution 2, 37–47, 155–156, 201
libertarianism 7, 40
liberty 38, 55
Lipset, Seymour Martin 53, 118, 120
local businesses 136
local community 136, 162
local embeddedness 135–137, 144, 145
localism 136, 143–144, 162
Locke, John 39, 40
locus of control 100, 101, 126, 186

'Machiavellians' 108
Malleson, Tom 54, 71, 239
management: bottom-up approach 57; definition 69; and human agency 113; knowledge 103, 105, 113–114; non-hierarchical modes 31; top-down approach 57, 69; *see also* participative management; representative management; self-management
managerialism 105
managers 4, 14–15, 78–79, 113–114; and representative management 77–80; and disempowerment 108–122; and equalising empowerment 159–161; as representatives 99; *see also* office-holders; owner-managers
Mansbridge, Jane 104, 233
marginalisation 93, 96
member apathy 232
membership participation 53
Michels, Robert 216, 232
micro-managing 110
Mill, John Stuart 19–20
mindsets: of anti-social perpetrators 223–226; collaborative 223
Mondragón cooperative 21–22, 53, 112, 136
Montesquieu 55
moral development 15, 17, 122, 225–226
motivation 89, 91, 92; 'genuine' 165–166

nation-state, separation of branches 55
natural environment 139, 143
nature 141–143
negative freedom rights 199
neighbourhood organisations 28
networks: collaboration in 81, 83;
    and empowerment 90; and self-
    management 74
neuroticism 110, 111, 224
NGOs *see* non-governmental organisations
non-governmental organisations (NGOs)
    3, 28, 133, 137
non-profit organisations 3, 28, 47
not-for-profit organisations 3, 28, 47, 133

obedience 17, 220
obedient personality 93, 96
office-holders 103–105
oligarchisation 53, 200, 207–208, 215–216
oligarchy 56, 57, 210, 214; and
    accumulation of formal positions
    104–105; and decision-making 60;
    informal 200; 'iron law' of 216; *see also*
    oligarchisation
'open-source communities' 117
openness to experience 110, 223
opportunities, access to 92, 93
organisational citizenship behaviour 91
organisational commitment 89, 92, 187
organisational culture: and anti-social
    perpetrators 227; of equal(ising) power
    120–122, 161, 227; toxic 213
organisational misbehaviour 107–108,
    207, 225
organisational performance 146, 163, 183
organisational politics 213
organisational psychopaths 14–15, 17, 111,
    122, 160, 225–226
organisations: definition 11; legitimacy of
    192–205; principle of subsidiarity 57;
    types of 192–205; *see also* democratic
    organisations; orthodox organisations
orthodox organisations 4, 11–17; choice of
    172–174; and disempowerment 94, 95;
    features of 16–17; hierarchical system
    12–13, 15–16; management of 78;
    people of 14–16; and pro-
    environmental behaviour 140
Ostrom, Vincent 55
owner-managers 141, 147–148, 151, 163,
    164, 168–169, 186
ownership 147–148, 151–152, 164–165;
    collective 31; individual 31; universal

26; *see also* ownership rights; private
    ownership
ownership rights 24
ownership-oriented organisations
    24–27, 30

parliamentarian democracy 54
participation 80–84, 185; civic 183; and
    collaborative behaviour 163; and
    commitment 163; and cooperation 163;
    culture of 54; and democratic
    governance 81; and empowerment 102,
    231–237; and engagement 163; full
    148–150, 233, 235–237; individual-
    oriented 236–237; lack of 231–235;
    'ladder' of 27, 80, 234; membership 53;
    and organisational performance
    148–150; voluntary 165, 235–236
participative management 31, 80–86, 127,
    159, 201–202; and decision-making 99;
    and performance 149
participative organisations 3
participatory democracy 3, 26–27, 54; and
    decision-making 60
partnership agreement 43–47, 58, 156
partnerships 3, 22–24; hybrid 24;
    managerial 23; organisational structure
    23; 'perfect' 24; *see also* partnership
    agreement
patronising treatment 110
performance 91; and democratic
    management 148–150; economic
    146–147, 150–152, 163–164; external
    179–180; and full participation
    148–150; job 91, 185; measurement of
    179–180; organisational 146–147,
    163, 183; orthodox understanding
    of 179
personal control 100, 186
personal development 92
personal growth 187
personal identity 101
personality 111–112; extrovert 212;
    introvert 212; *see also* personality traits
personality traits 106, 110–111, 223–226;
    see also personality
personal management styles 105, 110
personal values 141
personal worth, sense of 91, 186
'petty tyrants' 108
political activism 119, 183
political committees 53
political democracy 54

political equality 60, 88–89
political movements 3, 28
political rights 60
power: abuse of 55, 112, 217–218;
  concentration of 156; controlling 127;
  dimensions of 102; equal 89, 120–122;
  formal 160; institutionalisation of 54;
  and liberty 55; monopoly on 55, 56;
  psychological 160–161; social 28, 78,
  94, 112, 159, 161–162; see also power
  elites; power distance; separation of
  powers
power distance 93, 95
power elites 111–113, 214
private ownership 38, 40–43, 45, 147–148,
  155–156, 164; and property rights 46,
  155; and self-ownership 43
privileges 218–219
productivity 183, 187
pro-environmental behaviour 31,
  139–146, 162–163
pro-environmental orientation 139–140,
  162–163, 183
professionalism 118, 177–178, 181
professional service firm (PSF) 22, 23; see
  also partnerships
profit maximisation 137, 150, 173
profit-maximising organisations: legitimacy
  of 196–197, 204; pro-environmental
  behaviour 139–140
profit-oriented organisations 173
profits 44, 185; see also profit maximisation
property rights 24, 26, 38, 40–43, 60,
  155–156; distinction between natural
  and artificial 40; and freedom 42–43;
  and private ownership 46
prosocial behaviour 132–133,
  162, 183
prosocial orientation 132–133, 162
Proudhon, Pierre-Joseph 20
PSF see professional service firm
psychological disempowerment 93–96,
  110–111, 125, 126, 160–161
psychological distress 101
psychological empowerment 8, 91–92,
  99–101, 106–107, 110–111, 123–126,
  186, 202; behavioural dimension 100;
  definition 100, 106; illegitimate
  106–107; interactional dimension 100;
  intrapersonal dimension 100
psychological power 160–161; see also
  psychological empowerment
psychological strength 96

qualified personnel 177–178, 180

radical organisations 194–196, 204
reciprocal behaviour 133; see also
  reciprocity
reciprocity 185; and cooperation 150;
  culture of 150, 165; and empowerment
  91; see also reciprocal behaviour
regulatory institutions 174–175
remuneration 44, 185; see also income; see
  also wages
representative management 77–80, 85, 99,
  159, 202; legitimacy of 80; levels of
  participation in 81–84
representatives 78–79, 127; conduct of
  office 79, 85; control of 79, 85; election
  of 79, 85; managers as 99
resources, access to 93, 95
responsibility 185; and accountability 63;
  and disempowerment 93, 95; and
  empowerment 91; equal 43–44;
  sense of 142
right-libertarianism 39
rights: civil 199; fundamental 39, 40;
  inalienable 39–40, 45, 46, 155, 156;
  individual 155; labour 44; legal 60;
  natural 40; negative freedom 199;
  ownership 40; political 60;
  self-ownership 40; see also equal rights;
  property rights
'rituals of subordination' 97
Rothschild, Joyce (also known as
  Rothschild-Whitt) 24–25, 60, 70–71,
  112–113, 118, 135–136, 232
Rousseau, Jean-Jacques 40
rule of law 64, 67, 71, 158

self-actualisation 187
self-concept 101
self-determination 26
self-development 95
self-efficacy 91, 92, 186
self-enhancement 142
self-esteem: and disempowerment 93, 95,
  96; and empowerment 92, 94, 100,
  101, 126
self-help 3, 28, 138
self-image 41, 92, 106, 107, 230
self-managed firms 3
self-management 31, 72–80, 85, 127, 148,
  158, 201; and empowerment 98, 161;
  groups 73–75, 96; individuals 73, 75;

institutions 74–75; levels of participation in 81–84; networks 74, 75; principle of subsidiarity 75–77
self-managing organisations (SMOs) 24, 75–76, 228
self-mastery 101
self-ownership 38–40, 45, 111, 147, 148, 154, 164; and inalienable rights 39–40, 46; and private ownership 43
self-realisation 187
self-regulation 26
self-respect 91, 186; and disempowerment 93, 95
self-responsibility 138
self-selection 14, 16
self-transcendent values 142
self-worth 101
separation of powers (*trias politica*) 54–56, 67, 105, 127, 156
serfdom 220
skills 89, 187; and empowerment 91; social 92, 102–103
sociability 91, 185
social actions 209, 210–211; and anti-social perpetrators 227; and challenge of authority 117–120
social and solidarity economy (SSE) organisations 3, 27–30, 134, 137, 146, 179
social behaviour 132–138, 162, 183
social change 184
social competencies 102–103
social control 28, 115–117, 227
social differences 89
social disempowerment 93–94, 96–97, 111–122, 126–127
social dominance 71, 78, 111, 161, 207, 213–214, 221
social embeddedness 97
social empowerment 8, 92–94, 101–103, 111, 123, 126–127, 202; definition 107; illegitimate 107–108; and participation 102, 237
social enterprises 3, 28, 133, 183
social entrepreneurs 184
social exclusion 96
social goals 28, 133
social hierarchy 71, 211
social identity 92, 93, 102, 107
social improvements 184
social inequalities 71, 113, 207, 213, 227
social interactions 132, 149, 163, 185, 213

social movements 3, 28
social oppression 219–220
social order, hierarchical 96
social orientation 31, 101, 121, 132–138, 162, 183
social power 28, 78, 94, 112, 159, 161–162
social pressure 97
social processes 209–211
social relations 37, 112; *see also* social relationships
social relationships 89; and disempowerment 96; and social empowerment 92, 102; unequal 71, 78; *see also* social relations
social skills 92, 102–103
social status 89, 92, 96, 97, 122
social systems 37, 38, 43–44, 50–51, 59, 60
social value 28, 184
socialisation 14, 16
socialist market economies 172
socio-legal interactions 37
solidarity 29
SSE *see* social and solidarity economy (SSE) organisations
state, and principle of subsidiarity 57
stigmatisation 96
stratification 207
structural injustice 95
subordinates: 'damaged' 17; and disempowerment 94, 96; 'good' 96, 220; ideology of 14; infantilisation of 15, 78, 96, 219–220
subsidiarity: principle of 56–57, 127, 156; and self-management 72–73, 75–77, 98
superiors 12–17, 63, 70, 78, 106
sustainability 145
sustainable business models 145
sustainable business strategies 138

terrorist organisations 195
Tocqueville, Alexis de 19, 21
top-down control 13
totalitarian regimes 195
transparency 54, 61, **62**, 126, 127; and accountability 61, 99; compulsory 109; and information imbalance 98
trias politica see separation of powers
'triple bottom line' 132
trust 185; and cooperation 150; culture of 150, 165; and empowerment 91

under-capitalisation 176–177, 180
Universal Declaration of Human
 Rights 197
unprofessionalism 177, 180
'unreflective doers' 212–213, 222,
 228–231
utopian communities 90

voluntary organisations 28
voluntary participation 165,
 235–236
volunteer groups 28

volunteering 182
voting 61, 84

wages 185; *see also* income; remuneration
well-being: community 25, 135–136; and
 disempowerment 95; improving 183
work, and empowerment 106
worker-managed companies 3, 24, 28, 47
worker-managed economies 3
worker-owned companies 24, 26
worker-recovered enterprises 26
workplace democracy 31, 54, 70

Printed in the United States
by Baker & Taylor Publisher Services